# Integrated Upland Monitoring Protocol for the Southern Colorado Plateau Network

Natural Resource Report NPS/SCPN/NRR—2012/577

# Integrated Upland Monitoring Protocol for the Southern Colorado Plateau Network

Natural Resource Report NPS/SCPN/NRR—2012/577

James K. DeCoster
Chris L. Lauver
Jodi R. Norris
Allison E. C. Snyder
Megan C. Swan
Lisa P. Thomas

National Park Service
Southern Colorado Plateau Network
P.O. Box 5765
Northern Arizona University
Flagstaff, Arizona 86011


Mark E. Miller
Dana L. Witwicki

U.S. Geological Survey
Canyonlands Research Station
2290 SW Resource Blvd.
Moab, UT 84532

September 2012

U.S. Department of the Interior
National Park Service
Natural Resource Stewardship and Science
Fort Collins, Colorado

The National Park Service, Natural Resource Stewardship and Science office in Fort Collins, Colorado publishes a range of reports that address natural resource topics of interest and applicability to a broad audience in the National Park Service and others in natural resource management, including scientists, conservation and environmental constituencies, and the public.

The Natural Resource Report Series is used to disseminate high-priority, current natural resource management information with managerial application. The series targets a general, diverse audience, and may contain NPS policy considerations or address sensitive issues of management applicability.

All manuscripts in the series receive the appropriate level of peer review to ensure that the information is scientifically credible, technically accurate, appropriately written for the intended audience, and designed and published in a professional manner.

This report received formal peer review by subject-matter experts who were not directly involved in the collection, analysis, or reporting of the data, and whose background and expertise put them on par technically and scientifically with the authors of the information.

Views, statements, findings, conclusions, recommendations, and data in this report do not necessarily reflect views and policies of the National Park Service, U.S. Department of the Interior. Mention of trade names or commercial products does not constitute endorsement or recommendation for use by the U.S. Government.

A portion of the funding for this project was provided by the Southern Colorado Plateau and the Northern Colorado Plateau Networks of NPS through Interagency Agreement F2121040003 with U.S. Geological Survey, Canyonlands Research Station.

This report is available from the Southern Colorado Plateau Network, Intermountain Region (http://science.nature.nps.gov/im/units/scpn/products.cfm), and the Natural Resource Publications Management Web site (http://www.nature.nps.gov/publications/nrpm/) on the Internet.

Please cite this publication as:

DeCoster, James K., Chris L. Lauver, Mark E. Miller, Jodi R. Norris, Allison E. C. Snyder, Megan C. Swan, Lisa P. Thomas, and Dana L. Witwicki. 2012. Integrated upland monitoring protocol for the Southern Colorado Plateau Network. Natural Resource Report NPS/SCPN/NRR–2012/577. National Park Service, Fort Collins, Colorado.

# Contents

# Contents (continued)

# Figures

# Tables

# Acronyms

| | | | |
|---|---|---|---|
| AIC | Akaike's Information Criterion | GPS | Global Positioning System |
| ANOSIM | Analysis of Similarities | I&M | Inventory and Monitoring |
| ANOVA | Analysis of Variance | IRMA | Integrated Resource Management Applications |
| BLM | Bureau of Land Management | MVT | Master Version Table |
| CBH | Crown Base Height | NAU | Northern Arizona University |
| CCA | Canonical Correspondence Analysis | NMDS | Non-metric Multi-Dimensional Scaling |
| CV | Coefficient of Variation | NRCS | Natural Resources Conservation Service |
| DBH | Diameter at Breast Height | NPS | National Park Service |
| DCA | Detrended Correspondence Analysis | NRDT | Natural Resources Database Template |
| DDI | Distilled De-Ionized | NVCS | National Vegetation Classification System |
| DRC | Diameter at Root Crown | QA/QC | Quality Assurance/Quality Control |
| GIS | Geographic Information Systems | SCPN | Southern Colorado Plateau Network |
| GRTS | Generalized Random Tesselation Stratified | SIMPER | Analysis of Similarity Percentages |
| | | SOP | Standard Operating Procedure |
| GS | General Schedule | USGS | United States Geological Survey |
| GSA | General Services Administration | VK | Version Key |

# Acronyms for Southern Colorado Plateau Network Park Units

| Park | Abbreviation | State | Hectares[a] |
|---|---|---|---|
| Aztec Ruins National Monument | AZRU | NM | 108 |
| Bandelier National Monument | BAND | NM | 13,287 |
| Canyon De Chelly National Monument | CACH | AZ | 33,930 |
| Chaco Culture National Historical Park | CHCU | NM | 13,290 |
| El Malpais National Monument | ELMA | NM | 44,495 |
| El Morro National Monument | ELMO | NM | 421 |
| Glen Canyon National Recreation Area | GLCA | AZ/UT | 501,263 |
| Grand Canyon National Park | GRCA | AZ | 477,831 |
| Hubbell Trading Post National Historic Site | HUTR | AZ | 65 |
| Mesa Verde National Park | MEVE | CO | 21,147 |
| Navajo National Monument | NAVA | AZ | 146 |
| Petrified Forest National Park | PEFO | AZ | 44,129–89,661[b] |
| Petroglyph National Monument | PETR | NM | 1187 |
| Rainbow Bridge National Monument | RABR | UT | 65 |
| Salinas Pueblo Missions National Monument | SAPU | NM | 397 |
| Sunset Crater Volcano National Monument | SUCR | AZ | 1230 |
| Walnut Canyon National Monument | WACA | AZ | 1316 |
| Wupatki National Monument | WUPA | AZ | 14,327 |
| Yucca House National Monument | YUHO | CO | 14 |

[a]Hectares are derived from the "NPS Fee Acres" column of the NPS Land Resources Division, Listing of Acreage (Summary), available from http://www.nature.nps.gov/stats/acreagemenu.cfm (accessed August 14, 2012).

[b]Recently approved boundary addition to Petrified Forest NP will bring the total area to 89,661 ha pending additional funding.

# Executive Summary

Vegetation composition and structure, upland hydrologic function, and soil stability were identified as core vital signs for long-term monitoring in the Southern Colorado Plateau Network of the National Park Service. Vegetation is a dominant biological feature of ecosystems, providing habitat on which all fauna depends. Measures of soil stability and hydrologic function may provide early warning of degradation in dryland environments. These vital signs are combined together into one protocol, describing the integrated upland monitoring project.

This protocol narrative and 14 Standard Operating Procedures (SOPs) detail the rationale and methods to monitor these vital signs, including (1) background and objectives (2) sampling design (3) field methods (4) data management, analysis and reporting, and (5) personnel and operation requirements. Appendices provide supplemental information describing the sampling frames used for monitoring in the parks, outlining the yearly project list, listing commonly used landforms found in the Colorado Plateau, describing the use of Global Positioning Systems, and detailing use of the database.

Monitoring of these vital signs will occur at Aztec Ruins National Monu-ment, Bandelier National Monument, Chaco Culture National Historical Park, El Malpais National Monument, El Morro National Monument, Glen Canyon National Recreation Area, Grand Canyon National Park, Mesa Verde National Park, Petrified Forest National Park, Petroglyph National Monument, Walnut Canyon National Monument and Wupatki National Monument.

Ecosystems selected for monitoring are based upon Natural Resources Conservation Service ecological sites, which are in turn based on soil surveys. The final sampling frame for each ecological site is the area from which sampling sites are randomly selected, and hence is the area to which statistical inferences can be made. Sites are selected using a Generalized Random Tesselation Stratified design. Permanent 0.5 hectare plots are established at each site, and are visited on a regular schedule based on a revisit design. Vegetation data that are collected include cover and frequency by species for the herbaceous and shrub layers, tree size and species, canopy cover and canopy closure. Soil data that are collected include basal gaps, soil stability and soil surface features.

Data entry, management, and analysis are completed at the end of each field season and project summary reports are produced annually. Trend reports will be developed at longer intervals.

# 1 Introduction

Vegetation composition and structure, soil stability, and upland hydrologic function were selected as core vital signs for long-term monitoring within the Southern Colorado Plateau Network (SCPN) (Thomas et al. 2006).The network will monitor vegetation and soils within predominant upland vegetation types across most SCPN parks.

The integrated upland monitoring protocol consists of a narrative, 14 Standard Operating Procedures and 6 appendices. The narrative portion of the protocol describes the rationale for monitoring upland vegetation and soils, establishes specific monitoring objectives, and provides an overview of the monitoring efforts. The Standard Operating Procedures (SOPs) provide detailed descriptions of all activities related to vegetation and soils monitoring. Monitoring methods outlined in this protocol apply to the full range of targeted upland vegetation types occurring within SCPN parks, from semi-arid grasslands and shrub steppe at lower elevations, through pinyon-juniper woodlands at mid-elevations, to montane forests and meadows at higher elevations.

# 2 Background and objectives

## 2.1 Selecting vegetation and soils as vital signs

Vegetation was identified as a vital sign for SCPN parks because it is the dominant biological feature of terrestrial ecosystems and provides habitat (food, shelter, and substrate) upon which all animals depend. Moreover, in dryland ecosystems, vegetation stabilizes soil and enhances the capture and retention of soil resources. In fire-adapted systems, fuel loading and fuel connectivity are largely controlled by vegetation structure, thus vegetation structure affects fire return intervals and fire severity.

Soil was identified as a vital sign because erosion is a significant threat to many dryland ecosystems. Soil is a thin layer of mineral and organic matter that supports both flora and fauna, and consequently determines ecosystem health. Soil regulates

hydrologic processes and the cycling of mineral nutrients. Soils on the Colorado Plateau exhibit tremendous spatial heterogeneity as a result of the combined effects of geology, topography, and geomorphic processes. They are weakly developed, with physical and chemical characteristics that closely match the shales, sandstones, limestones and igneous materials from which they were derived (Brotherson et al. 1985, Norton et al. 2003).

Vegetation and soils are tightly linked across the Colorado Plateau. While disturbances, such as wildland fire, may be responsible for generating landscape patterns in more mesic environments (Clark 1991), inherent edaphic heterogeneity is a primary cause of landscape patterns in dryland ecosystems of the Colorado Plateau (Miller 2005). There can also be interactions between the dynamics of vegetation and soil. For example, soil erosion may increase when an extended droughts causes plant die-off. Plant litter can be incorporated into the soil as organic matter, increasing the nitrogen content and altering soil texture.

Thus, information on vegetation and soils and their dynamics is directly related to ecosystem preservation, restoration and management, and indirectly relevant to a host of natural resource management issues, including wildlife, exotic species, and fire management. Limited funding necessitates that we focus on selected predominant ecosystems rather than attempting to track vegetation across all ecosystems within SCPN parks. Depending on park size and complexity, the network will monitor one to three upland ecosystems within many of the park units.

## 2.2 Vegetation dynamics

A plant community generally refers to the vegetation occurring in a relatively homogenous area of land, with a relatively uniform composition and structure that is distinct from the surrounding vegetation (van der Maarel 2005). Plant communities are generally quantified by examining the relative abundance of the component species. Abundance can be measured in many ways—most commonly in the form of cover, density, frequency, and biomass (Elzinga et al. 1998).

Plant communities can be described in multiple ways, as systems with dozens of species are inherently complex. A common approach, and the basis of vegetation classification, is to examine the dominant species. Another approach is to identify indicator species that track overall community conditions, or keystone species that have a disproportionate effect on their environment relative to their abundance or biomass (Mills et al. 1993). The presence and/or abundance of non-native species can be used to evaluate the integrity of a community. Multi-variant approaches, such as Non-linear Multi-Dimensional Scaling (NMDS) and other ordination techniques, can collapse vegetation into 2 or more dimensions, making patterns in species composition clearer. Grouping species into life forms (sensu Raunkier 1934) or functional groups can simplify the data, yet still be ecologically meaningful. Community and ecosystem attributes can also provide meaningful metrics. For example, species diversity is a community attribute reflecting the combined effects of processes including immigration, competition, predation, and extinction (Peet 1992), thus providing information on overall ecosystem health.

> *"Vegetation change is based on the fundamental idea that the different capacities of plants to match the prevailing environment determines the nature of the plant assemblages that will exist in a place."* (Pickett and Cadenasso 2005).

Both endogenous and exogenous factors can affect vegetation dynamics, and these are evident at multiple temporal and spatial scales, ranging from short-term, local fluctuations due to environmental conditions, to fine-scale gap or patch dynamics, to secondary succession following a major disturbance, to long-term change in response to climate change (Glenn-Lewin and van der Maarel 1992). Long-term vegetation monitoring will likely capture changes at each of these scales. Finally, trend analyses will assist us in discerning and interpreting the temporal and spatial patterns that underlie observed vegetation dynamics.

## 2.3 Soil stability and upland hydrologic function

Soils regulate hydrologic processes, re-cycle nutrients, and sustain plant and animal populations. Soil quality, the capacity of a specific kind of soil to perform these functions, is determined by both static and dynamic properties. Static properties include soil texture, depth, and mineralogy; dynamic properties include organic matter content, aggregate stability, soil-surface roughness, and structure (Karlen et al. 1997; Herrick et al. 2002; Norfleet et al. 2003). Dynamic soil properties can change as a result of climatic fluctuations, land-use activities, natural disturbances, and management actions. Measures of soil stability and upland hydrologic function may provide early warning of degradational change in dryland environments (Herrick and Whitford 1995; Havstad et al. 2000).

Soil stability is a key dynamic soil property that describes the soil's resistance to disturbance. Soil aggregate stability is a direct measure of the degree to which soil particles bind together through a combination of physical, chemical and biological processes. The ability of the soil to bind together (aggregate development) is an important indicator of the soil's ability to resist wind and water erosion (Herrick et al. 2005a).

Soil cover, another dynamic property, has a strong effect on wind and water erosion (Herrick et al. 2005a). Soil erosion can occur on any area of exposed soil. A strong positive correlation exists between the amount of exposed soil and the erosion rate (Davenport et al. 1998). The amount of vegetative cover is important because plant roots physically hold the soils in place. Plant stems, leaves, and plant litter (particularly thick litter and duff), also provide cover, preventing the underlying soil particles from being removed by raindrop impact and subsequent runoff, or by wind transport. Rocks and gravel can act to stabilize soil in a similar fashion.

Biological soil crusts are highly specialized communities of cyanobacteria, algae, lichen and bryophytes that occupy the soil crust in arid and semi-arid regions. Biological soil crusts function both as soil cover that is resistant to erosion, and as contributors to soil aggregate stability. Lichens and mosses have small anchoring structures which, like plant roots, hold the soil in place. Biological soil crusts also secrete polysaccharides that contribute to soil aggregation. In addition to providing resistance to erosion, they also perform other ecological functions, such as nitrogen fixation, increasing infiltration, and contributing organic matter (Belnap et al. 2003).

## 2.4 Upland ecosystems of the Southern Colorado Plateau

The Southern Colorado Plateau Network is comprised of 19 national park units that encompass a broad range of elevations (from 350 to 3080 m elevation) and precipitation zones (mean annual precipitation ranging from 16 to 54 cm), resulting in a diverse array of vegetation types. Dryland ecosystems (generally found below 2300 meters, and receiving less than 45 cm mean annual precipitation) predominate across the Colorado Plateau and are characterized by pinyon-juniper woodlands, big sagebrush, four-wing saltbush, sand-shrub shrublands, and galleta and blue grama grasslands (West and Young 2000; Miller 2005). Montane and sub-alpine ecosystems occur at higher elevations and include ponderosa pine forest, mixed conifer forest, spruce-fir forest, Gambel oak shrubland, and montane grasslands (Vankat 2006).

Most of the Southern Colorado Plateau Network coincides with the Colorado Plateau physiognomic province, but also extends into the Southern Rocky Mountain and Basin and Range physiognomic province. Table 1 lists the National Vegetation Classification System (NVCS) macrogroups prevalent within SCPN parks (NatureServe 2003) and Figure 1 illustrates macrogroup distribution across the southern Colorado Plateau overlaid with the SCPN park units. Macrogroups are mid-level natural units within the NVCS designed to bridge the gap between formation and alliance (Faber-Langendoen et al. 2009).

## 2.5 Developing dryland and montane conceptual models

A successful monitoring program must provide information that enables interpretation of trends in resource condition against the backdrop of intrinsic variation. Conceptual models are essential for designing credible and effective ecological monitoring programs because ecological systems are highly integrative and complex, and their responses to novel environmental or biotic conditions are often poorly understood.

In using conceptual models for monitoring design, our intent is not to represent the full complexity of a system, but rather to use current knowledge to identify a limited set of integrative elements that provide information on multiple aspects of ecosystem condition (Noon 2003). Moreover, conceptual models motivate hypotheses regarding the consequences of natural and anthropogenic processes on system structure and function.

Early in the vital signs planning process, SCPN funded development of conceptual models for dryland and montane terrestrial ecosystems (Miller 2005; Vankat 2006). These conceptual models initially informed vital signs selection and, as the program matures, will also be useful in interpreting long-term monitoring results. Key ecosystem drivers and anthropogenic stressors incorporated into the models are summarized below, but see Miller (2005) and Vankat (2006) for a more complete discussion.

### 2.5.1 Drivers and natural disturbance processes

Dryland ecosystems. Precipitation is the most important climatic factor defining the characteristics of dryland ecosystems because it regulates key water-limited ecological processes, such as primary production, nutrient cycling, and plant reproduction. Seasonality influences the partitioning of precipitation among evaporation, transpiration, runoff, drainage, and soil-water storage, and determines vegetative dominance. Strong winds are common in dryland ecosystems, affecting evapotranspiration rates, redistributing soil resources, and interacting with topography to influence wildland fire behavior. *continued on page 12...*

Table 1. National Vegetation Classification Standard Macrogroups representing major components of SCPN park uplands. Network staff developed the descriptions for each macrogroup focusing on the primary upland Groups and Associations that occur in SCPN park units.

| Macrogroup | SCPN Location | Description |
|---|---|---|
| *Forest and Woodland Macrogroups* | | |
| Rocky Mountain Subalpine & High Montane Conifer Forest | BAND | This macrogroup is widespread throughout the Southern and Central Rocky Mountains, but occurs throughout much of the western United States and north into Canada. In New Mexico it occurs from 1737 to 3414 m on moist to mesic soils. Tree composition ranges from pure canopies of *Populus tremuloides* to stands of *Picea engelmannii* with *Pseudotsuga menziesii*. The herbaceous layer may be lush and species diverse. Common species include *Festuca thurberi*, *Thalictrum fendleri*, *Acer glabrum*, *and Erigeron eximius*. |
| Southern Rocky Mountain Lower Montane Forest | BAND, ELMA, ELMO, GLCA, GRCA, WACA | This macrogroup is widespread throughout the Rocky Mountains and Great Basin, and occurs in SCPN park units with higher elevations. It is characterized by conifer forests with tree species that include *Abies concolor*, *Pseudotsuga menziesii*, *Picea engelmannii*, *Picea pungens*, *Pinus ponderosa* and *Populus tremuloides*, but also includes savannas of *Pinus ponderosa*. Sites range from mesic to dry. Shrub and herbaceous layers are variable, ranging from sparse to dense cover. Common shrubs include *Robinia neomexicana*, *Juniperus communis*, *Mahonia repens* and *Quercus gambelii*. Herbaceous species include *Fragaria virginiana*, *Carex rossii*, and *Poa fendleri*. |
| Northern Rocky Mountain Lower Montane & Foothill Forest | BAND | This macrogroup occurs primarily in the Northern and Central Rocky mountains but extend into the mountains of northern New Mexico and the Colorado Plateau of northern Arizona. In northern New Mexico it occurs between 1375 and 2595 m. It generally occurs on dry, nutrient-poor sites. The tree canopy consists of a closed canopy of *Pseudotsuga menziesii*, but other species such as *Pinus ponderosa* and *Populus tremuloides* may also be present. The understory is typically sparse due to canopy shading, with *Mahonia repens* being dominant. Other understory species include *Festuca arizonica* and *Thalictrum fendleri*. |
| Rocky Mountain Two-needle Pinyon - Western Juniper Woodland | BAND, CHCU, ELMA, ELMO, GLCA, GRCA, MEVE, PEFO, PETR, WACA | This macrogroup is widespread across the Colorado plateau and extends into the Southern Rocky Mountains and the plains of southeastern Colorado, and occurs in the majority of the SCPN park units at elevations ranging from 1100 to 2440 m. It includes woodlands, savannas and scrub. It is characterized by a dominance of *Juniperus osteosperma* and *Pinus edulis*. *Juniperus monosperma* and *Juniperus deppeana* may also be present. Shrub and herbaceous layers are variable ranging from dense to sparse cover. Common shrub species include *Purshia tridentata*, *Purshia stansburiana*, *Quercus gambelii* and *Cercocarpus montanus*. Common grasses include *Poa fendleriana*, *Pleuraphis jamesii* and *Bouteloua gracilis*. |
| Intermountain Singleleaf Pinyon - Western Juniper Woodland | AZRU, ELMA, GRCA | This macrogroup ranges from southern Idaho, to northwestern New Mexico. On the Colorado Plateau it occupies dry foothills and sandsheets between 1341 and 1860 m. Stands generally occur in relatively small patches within a matrix of other pinyon-juniper / grass understory woodland types. In the parks where this macrogroup occurs, *Juniperus osteosperma* is the dominant tree, although *Juniperus monosperma* and *Pinus edulis* may be present. Common species include *Artemisia tridentata*, *Pleuraphis jamesii*, *Gutierrezia sarothrae*, and *Opuntia whipplei*. |
| Madrean Warm Lowland Evergreen Woodland | BAND | This macrogroup ranges from Mexico, west Texas, southeastern Arizona to southern and central New Mexico, occurring on plains, foothills, plateaus and mountains. In BAND, in the northern part of its range, it is characterized by woodlands composed of *Juniperus deppeana*, and primarily occurs between 2050 and 2440 m. The sites generally occur on southwestern to southeastern aspects of backslopes and mesa shoulders. Tree density is variable. Herbaceous and shrub cover are also variable from sparse to dense grass or shrub layers. In BAND other tree species present include *Juniperus monosperma* and *Pinus edulis*. Common species include *Quercus X pauciloba*, *Bouteloua gracilis*, *Elymus elymoides*, *Cercocarpus montanus*, *Yucca baccata* and *Opuntia* spp. |

**Table 1** (*continued*)

| Macrogroup | SCPN Location | Description |
|---|---|---|
| Madrean Warm Montane Forest & Woodland | BAND | This macrogroup ranges from Mexico, west Texas, and southeastern Arizona to southern and central New Mexico, occurring on plains, foothills, plateaus and mountains. In BAND, in the northern part of its range, it represents a minor component of the vegetation. It is characterized by woodlands, composed of *Pinus ponderosa* and *Quercus grisea*. |

### Grassland and Shrubland Macrogroups

| Macrogroup | SCPN Location | Description |
|---|---|---|
| Great Plains Mixedgrass Prairie & Shrubland | WACA, PETR | This macrogroup is found primarily from the Western Great Plains in the rainshadow of the Rocky Mountains south into Texas and New Mexico, and occurs primarily on flat to rolling uplands with loamy soils. The short grasses that dominate this system are extremely drought- and grazing-tolerant. *Bouteloua gracilis* generally dominates. Associated graminoids are various, including *Aristida purpurea, Hesperostipa comata, Koeleria macrantha, Pleuraphis jamesii, Sporobolus airoides,* and *Sporobolus cryptandrus.* Although mid-height grass species may be present, especially on more mesic land positions and soils, they are secondary in importance to the sod-forming short grasses. Scattered shrub and dwarf-shrub species such as *Artemisia filifolia, Atriplex canescens,* and *Gutierrezia sarothrae* may also be present. Large-scale processes such as climate, fire and grazing influence this system and high variation in amount and timing of annual precipitation impacts the relative cover of cool- and warm-season herbaceous species. |
| Great Plains Sand Grassland & Shrubland | PETR | This macrogroup is found mostly in south-central areas of the Western Great Plains Division, ranging from southwestern Wyoming and southwestern Nebraska up into the Nebraska Sandhill region, south though eastern Colorado, and New Mexico to central Texas. This type is found in semi-arid to arid regions on somewhat excessively well-drained, deep sandy soils often associated with dune systems and ancient floodplains. Typically characterized by a sparse to moderately dense woody layer dominated or co-dominated by *Artemisia filifolia,* with other characteristic species, including *Rhus trilobata,* and *Yucca glauca.* Associated herbaceous species can vary with geography, amount and season of precipitation, disturbance, and soil texture. The herbaceous layer typically has a moderate to dense canopy but may include stands with sparse understory. Several mid- to tallgrass species characteristic of sand substrates are usually present to dominant, such as *Sporobolus cryptandrus, Sporobolus giganteus,* or *Hesperostipa comata.* |
| Southern Rocky Mountain Montane Grassland & Shrubland | BAND, ELMA, GLCA, GRCA, MEVE | This macrogroup comprises grassland and shrublands that occur in the mountains, plateaus and foothills of the Southern Rocky Mountains and Colorado Plateau, 1500 to 3000 m in elevation. Shrublands include those dominated or co-dominated by *Quercus gambelii, Amelanchier alnifolia, Amelanchier utahensis, Artemisia tridentata, Cercocarpus montanus, Prunus virginiana, Purshia stansburiana, Purshia tridentata,* and *Robinia neomexicana.* Grasslands are characterized by an open to dense perennial graminoid layer consisting of a mosaic of 2 or 3 plant associations including the following dominant bunch grasses: *Blepharoneuron tricholepis, Danthonia parryi, Festuca arizonica, Muhlenbergia montana,* or *Pseudoroegneria spicata* at lower elevation/warmer aspects, or *Danthonia intermedia, Festuca idahoensis, Festuca thurberi* at subalpine elevation/cooler aspects. |
| Cool Interior Chaparral | GRCA | This macrogroup represents chaparral that occurs on sideslopes between low-elevation desert landscapes and higher pinyon-juniper woodlands of the western and central Great Basin and throughout the montane zone of most mountain ranges of the western U.S., in very limited, small-patch occurrences. These are typically fairly open-canopy shrublands with open inter-spaces either bare or supporting patchy grasses and forbs. They are dominated by sclerophyllous shrubs that are adapted to freezing temperatures and cold winters. At GRCA this type is dominated by *Purshia stansburiana.* Typical fire regime in this group varies with the amount of organic accumulation, but most examples are post-fire shrublands in areas previously dominated by woodlands. |

**Table 1 (continued)**

| Macrogroup | SCPN Location | Description |
|---|---|---|
| Warm Interior Chaparral | GRCA | This macrogroup occurs prominently across central Arizona (Mogollon Rim) and western New Mexico. Stands are found on foothills, xeric mountain slopes and canyons in hotter and drier habitats and often dominate along the mid-elevation transition zone between desert scrub and montane woodlands (1000–2200 m). Sites are often steep and rocky. The vegetation is characterized by moderate to dense evergreen shrub layer dominated by sclerophyllous shrubs such as *Quercus turbinella*. Other common shrubs include *Garrya wrightii*, *Purshia stansburiana*, and *Rhus trilobata*, with *Arctostaphylos* at higher elevations. Scattered remnant pinyon and juniper trees may be present. Occasional desert scrub species may also be present in drier, rockier, more open transition sites. Most chaparral species are fire-adapted, resprouting vigorously after burning or producing abundant fire-resistant seeds. Stands occurring within montane woodlands are seral and a result of recent fires. |
| Apacherian-Chihuahuan Semi-Desert Grassland & Steppe | BAND, PEFO, PETR, WUPA | This macrogroup represents a broadly defined desert grassland/shrub-steppe that is typical of Arizona, New Mexico and northern Mexico (Apacherian region) but extends west to the Sonoran Desert, north into the Mogollon Rim, and occurs throughout much of the Chihuahuan Desert and includes the driest grasslands in the intermountain western U.S. The vegetation is characterized by an open to dense herbaceous layer typically dominated by a diverse mixture of perennial drought resistant grasses. Common species include desert grasses such as *Bouteloua eriopoda*, and *Muhlenbergia porteri*, as well as widespread species such as *Bouteloua gracilis*, *Achnatherum hymenoides* and *Pleuraphis jamesii*. Scattered shrubs and succulents are usually present, but usually have lower total cover than the herbaceous layer. |
| Chihuahuan Desert Scrub | PETR | This macrogroup represents open desert scrub of vegetated coppice dunes and sandsheets. Stands are usually dominated by *Artemisia filifolia*, or dominated or co-dominated by *Atriplex canescens* and *Ephedra torreyana*, usually with 10–30% total vegetation cover. *Yucca* spp., *Gutierrezia sarothrae*, *Bouteloua eriopoda*, and *Sporobolus flexuosus* are commonly present. At PETR this type is dominated by *Psorothamnus scoparius* and *Sporobolus flexuosus*. |
| Mojave-Sonoran Semi-Desert Scrub | GRCA | This desert vegetation macrogroup represents the extensive desert scrub that forms the vegetation matrix in broad valleys, lower bajadas, plains and low hills in the Mojave, Sonoran and Lower Colorado deserts. It is represented by the inner canyon vegetation at GRCA. Components of this group are quite variable, usually characterized by a sparse to moderately dense layer (2–50% cover) of xeromorphic, microphyllous and broad-leaved shrubs. *Larrea tridentata* and/or *Ambrosia dumosa* may dominate, but varied shrubs, dwarf-shrubs, and cacti may co-dominate or form typically sparse understory layers. Less common are stands with scattered Joshua trees and a saltbush short-shrub layer. The herbaceous layer is typically sparse, but may be seasonally abundant with ephemerals. Stands can often appear as very open sparse vegetation, with the mostly barren ground surface being the predominant feature. |
| Great Basin & Intermountain Dry Shrubland & Grassland | AZRU, BAND, CHCU, ELMA, ELMO, GLCA, GRCA, MEVE, PEFO, PETR, WACA, WUPA | This macrogroup represents widespread semi-arid grasslands and shrublands that occur throughout the Colorado Plateau, intermountain western U.S. and into the Mohave desert at elevation ranges from 560 to 3900 m. Vegetation includes extensive semi-arid shrublands and steppe, typically dominated by *Coleogyne ramosissima* or one of three species of *Ephedra* or other shrubs, such as *Atriplex canescens*, *Eriogonum corymbosum*, *Krascheninnikovia lanata*, *Gutierrezia sarothrae*, *Artemisia filifolia* and *Ericameria nauseosa*, as well as semi-arid to arid grasslands dominated by perennial bunch grasses such as *Achnatherum* spp., *Bouteloua* spp., *Hesperostipa comata*, or *Pleuraphis jamesii* and scattered dwarf shrubs. Disturbance and grazing have impacted many occurrences, and in some cases may be important in maintaining woody components. Eolian processes are often evident, such as pediceled plants, occasional blowouts or small dunes. |

**Table 1 (continued)**

| Macrogroup | SCPN Location | Description |
|---|---|---|
| Great Basin & Intermountain Dwarf Sage Shrubland & Steppe | GRCA, MEVE | This macrogroup represents a broadly defined semi-arid dwarf-shrubland and steppe and occurs throughout much of the intermountain western U.S. on generally xeric sites. Substrates are typically shallow, gravelly or finer-textured alkaline, calcareous soils. Most stands occur from 1000 to 3000 m. The vegetation in this broadly defined shrubland and steppe group includes an open to moderately dense shrub or dwarf-shrub layer with a sparse to dense herbaceous layer. Several different taxa of sagebrush may dominate depending on location and by habitat. *Artemisia nova* is most widespread, occurring throughout most of the region on mid- to low-elevation, gravelly, calcareous soils, and represents this group at MEVE. *Artemisia bigelovii* occurs throughout much of the Colorado Plateau and extends across northern New Mexico and southeastern Colorado on shallow soils on limestone hills and shale outcrops and is an important component of this group at GRCA. Other shrubs, such as *Purshia* spp. or *Ephedra* spp. may also be included. The herbaceous layer, if present, ranges from sparse cushion plants such as *Arenaria hookeri*, and *Phlox hoodii* to moderate to dense cover of typically drought resistant perennial bunch grasses including *Achnatherum hymenoides*, *Bouteloua gracilis*, *Festuca idahoensis*, *Hesperostipa comata*, *Pascopyrum smithii*, *Pleuraphis jamesii*, and *Poa fendleriana*. Some stands have significant biological crust formation on the soil surface. |
| Great Basin & Intermountain Tall Sagebrush Shrubland & Steppe | AZRU, CHCU, ELMA, GLCA, GRCA, MEVE | This shrubland and shrub/herbaceous macrogroup is widely distributed from the Great Basin, Columbia River Basin, Colorado Plateau, northern Rocky Mountains, northeastern Great Plains and as far east as the Dakotas at elevations as low as 500 m in the northwestern Great Plains to 2500 m in the Rocky Mountains and Colorado Plateau. It occurs on flat to steeply sloping upland slopes on alluvial fans and terraces, toeslopes, lower and middle slopes, draws, badlands, and foothills. Sites with little slope tend to have deep soils, while those with steeper slopes have shallow to moderately deep soils. Climate ranges from arid in the western Great Basin to subhumid in the northern plains and Rocky Mountains. Stands are dominated by *Artemisia tridentata* and may be co-dominated by *Amelanchier utahensis*, *Atriplex canescens*, *Ephedra* spp.. *Ericameria nauseosa*, or *Sarcobatus vermiculatus* with other common shrubs. The herbaceous layer may be sparse to dense cover of graminoids including *Achnatherum hymenoides*, *Bouteloua gracilis*, *Elymus elymoides*, *Festuca idahoensis*, *Hesperostipa comata*, *Poa fendleriana* , *Sporobolus airoides*, and *Sporobolus cryptandrus*. A sparse layer of cold-deciduous needle-leaved or scale-leaved evergreen trees may occasionally be emergent over the shrubs. |
| Great Basin Saltbrush Scrub | AZRU, CHCU, ELMA, ELMO, GLCA, GRCA, PEFO, PETR | This extensive group includes open-canopied shrublands of typically saline basins, alluvial slopes and plains across the Intermountain western U.S. and also extends in limited distribution into the southern Great Plains. Substrates are often saline and calcareous, medium- to fine-textured, alkaline soils. Vegetation is characterized by a typically open to moderately dense shrubland composed of one or more *Atriplex* species. Other shrubs present to co-dominant may include *Artemisia tridentata*, *Chrysothamnus viscidiflorus*, *Ericameria nauseosa*, and *Lycium* spp. The herbaceous layer varies from sparse to moderately dense and is dominated by perennial graminoids such as *Achnatherum hymenoides*, *Bouteloua gracilis*, *Pascopyrum smithii*, *Pleuraphis jamesii*, or *Sporobolus airoides*. |

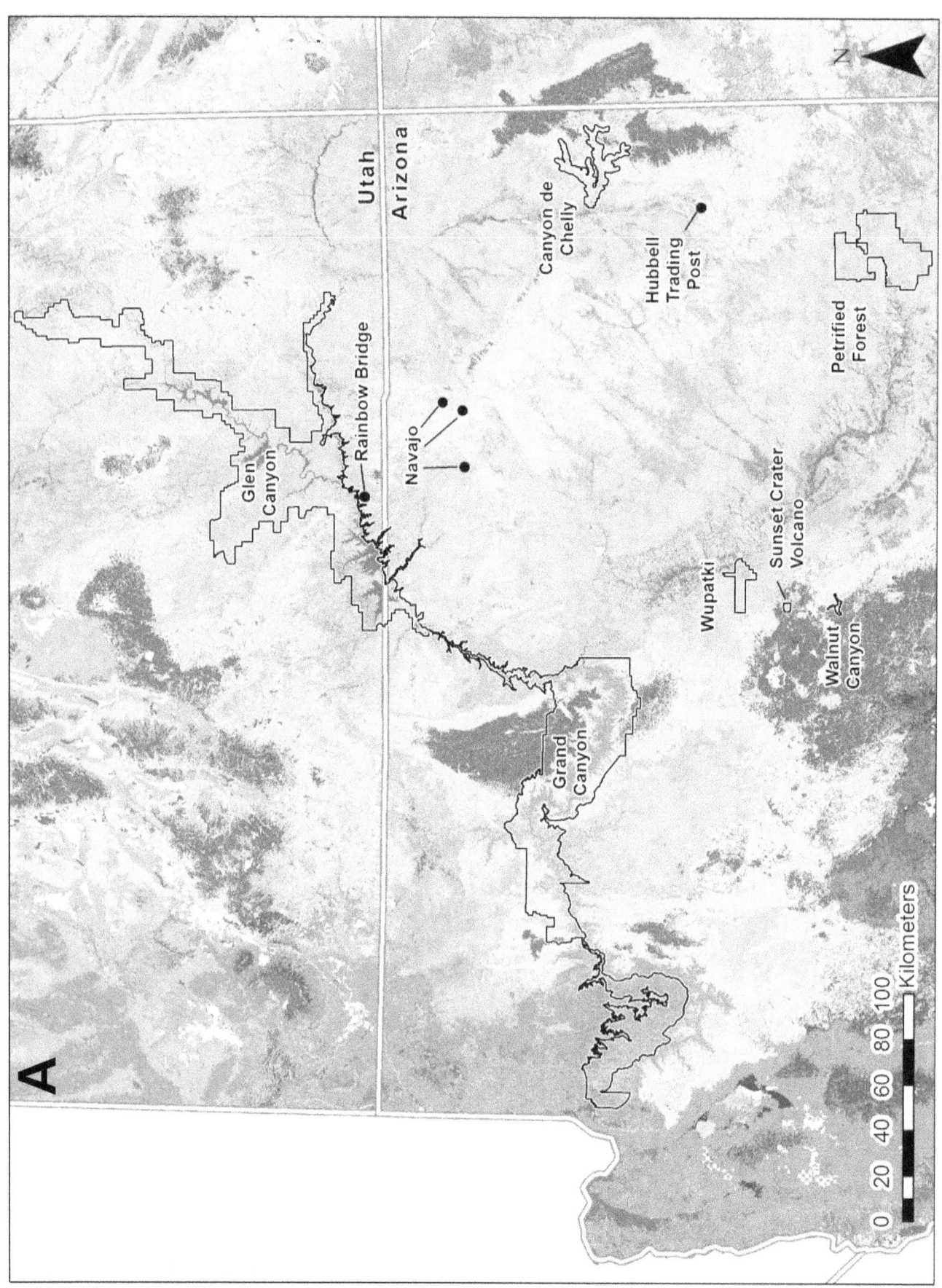

## Legend

- Park boundary
- State boundary
- Open Water

### Semi-Desert

- Chihuahuan Desert Scrub
- Chihuahuan Semi-Desert Grassland
- Cool Semi-Desert Alkali-Saline Wetland
- Cool Semi-Desert Saltbrush Scrub
- Intermountain Dry Shrubland & Grassland
- Warm Alkaline-Saline Semi-Desert Scrub
- Warm Interior Chaparral
- Western North America Dwarf Sage Shrubland & Steppe
- Western North America Tall Sage Shrubland & Steppe

### Shrub and Grassland

- Rocky Mountain-Vancouverian Montane Dry Grassland
- Southern Rocky Mountain Montane Shrubland
- Western North American Wet Meadow & Low Shrub Carr

### Altered Area

- Includes development and burns

### Forest and Woodland

- Intermountain Singleleaf Pinyon-Western Juniper Woodland
- Rocky Mountain Two-needle Pinyon-Juniper Woodland
- Madrean Warm Lowland Evergreen Woodland
- Madrean Warm Montane Forest & Woodland
- Southern Rocky Mountain Lower Montane Forest
- Rocky Mountain Subalpine & High Montane Conifer Forest
- Introduced
- Rocky Mountain and Great Basin Flooded & Swamp Forest
- Warm Desert Freshwater Shrubland, Meadow & Marsh
- Warm Desert Riparian, Flooded & Swamp Forest

### Nonvascular and Sparse Vascular Vegetation

- Inter-Mountain Basin Cliff, Scree & Rock Vegetation
- Mojave-Sonoran Semi-Desert Scrub
- North American Warm Semi-Desert Cliff, Scree & Rock Vegetation
- Rocky Mountain Alpine Cliff, Scree & Rock Vegetation
- Rocky Mountain Cliff, Scree & Rock Vegetation
- Warm Semi-Desert & Mediterranean Alkaline-Saline Wetland

**Figure 1a. Map of the distribution of National Vegetation Classification Standard Macrogroups across the Colorado Plateau and surrounding areas. Map A (top) with legend (bottom) shows the western half of the map (the eastern half is shown in fig. 1b).** *Source: map data from NatureServe Ecology (2012).*

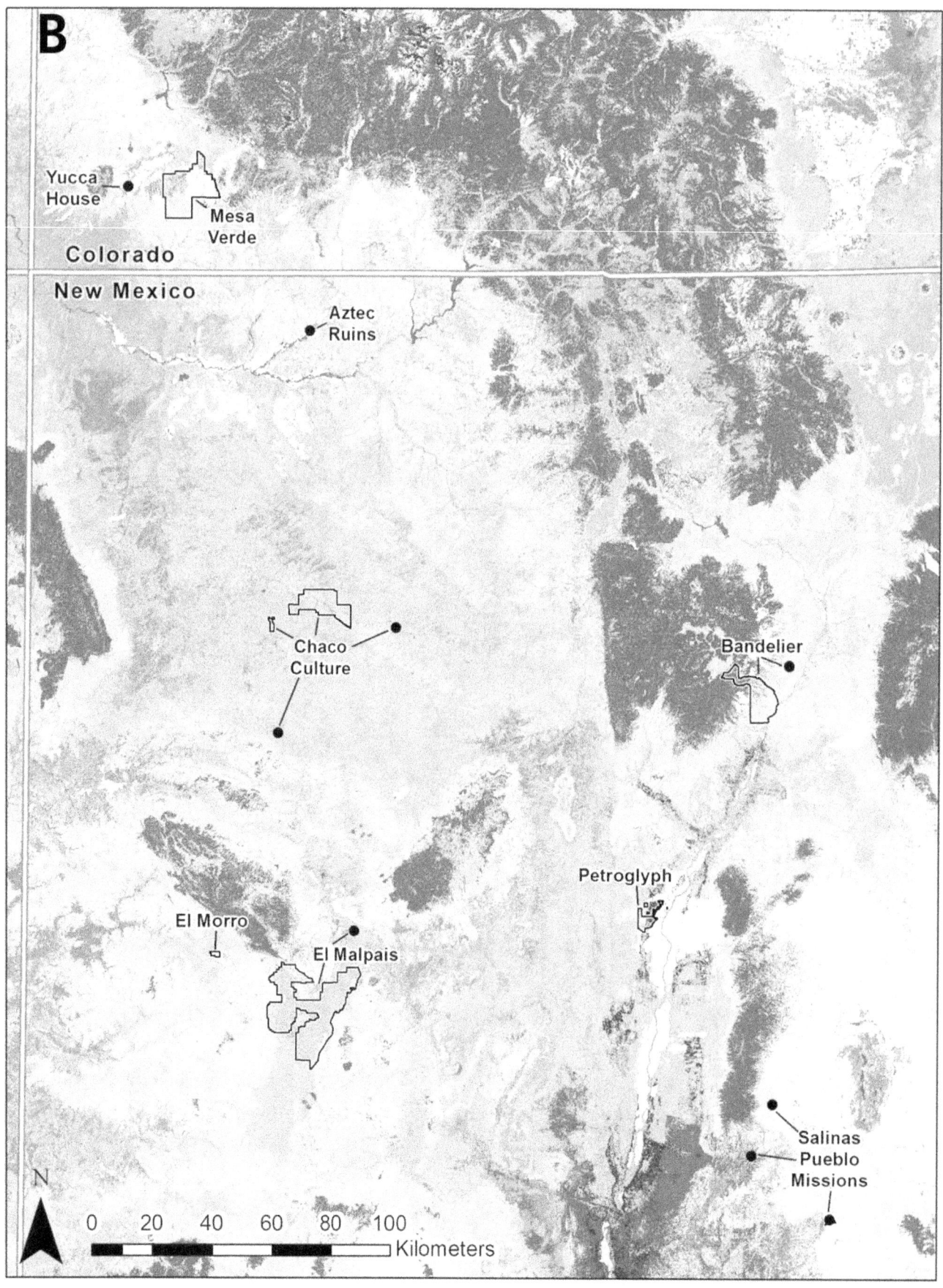

B

Yucca
House

Mesa
Verde

Colorado

New Mexico

Aztec
Ruins

Chaco
Culture

Bandelier

Petroglyph

El Morro

El Malpais

Salinas
Pueblo
Missions

N

0  20  40  60  80  100
Kilometers

# Legend

☐ Park boundary

☐ State boundary

▨ Open Water

## Semi-Desert

▪ Chihuahuan Desert Scrub

▨ Chihuahuan Semi-Desert Grassland

☐ Cool Semi-Desert Alkali-Saline Wetland

☐ Cool Semi-Desert Saltbrush Scrub

☐ Intermountain Dry Shrubland & Grassland

▪ Warm Alkaline-Saline Semi-Desert Scrub

▨ Western North America Dwarf Sage Shrubland & Steppe

☐ Western North America Tall Sage Shrubland & Steppe

## Shrub and Grassland

☐ Great Plains Mixedgrass Prairie & Shrubland

☐ Great Plains Sand Grassland & Shrubland

☐ Great Plains Shortgrass Prairie & Shrubland

☐ Rocky Mountain-Vancouverian Montane Dry Grassland

☐ Southern Rocky Mountain Montane Shrubland

☐ Western North American Wet Meadow & Low Shrub Carr

## Altered Area

☐ Includes development and burns

## Forest and Woodland

▨ Intermountain Singleleaf Pinyon-Western Juniper Woodland

☐ Rocky Mountain Two-needle Pinyon-Juniper Woodland

▨ Madrean Warm Lowland Evergreen Woodland

☐ Madrean Warm Montane Forest & Woodland

▨ Southern Rocky Mountain Lower Montane Forest

▨ Rocky Mountain Subalpine & High Montane Conifer Forest

▨ Introduced

☐ Rocky Mountain and Great Basin Flooded & Swamp Forest

☐ Warm Desert Freshwater Shrubland, Meadow & Marsh

☐ Warm Desert Riparian, Flooded & Swamp Forest

## Nonvascular and Sparse Vascular Vegetation

☐ Great Plains Cliff, Scree & Rock Vegetation

☐ Inter-Mountain Basin Cliff, Scree & Rock Vegetation

▨ Mojave-Sonoran Semi-Desert Scrub

▪ North American Warm Semi-Desert Cliff, Scree & Rock Vegetation

▪ Rocky Mountain Alpine Cliff, Scree & Rock Vegetation

☐ Rocky Mountain Cliff, Scree & Rock Vegetation

☐ Warm Semi-Desert & Mediterranean Alkaline-Saline Wetland

**Figure 1b. Map of the distribution of National Vegetation Classification Standard Macrogroups across the Colorado Plateau and surrounding areas. Map B (left) with legend (right) shows the eastern half of the map (the western half is shown in fig. 1a).** *Source*: **map data from NatureServe Ecology (2012).**

*...continued from page 3*

Extreme climatic events typify dryland ecosystems and contribute to their natural spatio-temporal variability. The role of wildland fire varies among dryland ecosystems, with greater importance in sagebrush shrublands and shrub steppe, productive semi-desert grasslands, and juniper savannas and pinyon-juniper woodlands. Insect and disease outbreaks are linked to climatic conditions that diminish the vigor and insect resistance of host plants. As with fire, insect outbreaks interact with climate to generate long-term changes in vegetation structure.

Montane ecosystems. The occurrence of forested systems on the Colorado Plateau is directly related to mountainous terrain and elevation-mediated precipitation gradients. A winter snowpack is common in mixed conifer and subalpine systems and provides water for plants during the growing season. A critical weather component in these systems is the high frequency of lightning, which acts as a source of forest fire ignitions.

Fire is a major disturbance in montane ecosystems with regimes and effects varying with elevation and vegetation type. High frequency, low intensity surface fires at lower elevations consume surface fuels and small stems, and rarely result in overstory mortality. Low frequency, high intensity, stand-replacing fires occur at higher elevations, creating a patch mosaic of post-fire successional forests.

### 2.5.2 Stressors

A number of anthropogenic stressors threaten the ecological integrity of dryland and montane ecosystems. They include drought, climate change, alteration of fire regimes, visitor impacts, land use change, and the introduction of exotic species.

Increasing soil and air temperatures, reduced winter precipitation, earlier springs, and more extreme droughts are among the climate changes predicted for the Southwest (Seager et al. 2007). All of these can directly affect the structure and functioning of both dryland and montane ecosystems, as well as contribute to altered fire regimes and other types of disturbance regimes. In the recent past, multi-year droughts have been responsible for widespread mortality of pinyon pine (*Pinus edulis*) (Breshears et al. 2005), which, in turn, has caused increased soil erosion. Global climate change will likely cause directional change in vegetation composition within ecosystems, and boundaries between systems to shift.

Historic land uses have had major impacts on the soils and vegetation of the Southern Colorado Plateau. In shrub and grasslands, extensive livestock grazing has altered vegetation through selective removal of palatable grasses and shrubs. Intensive grazing has been responsible for soil erosion and soil compaction. While grazing no longer occurs in many of the SCPN park units and vegetation is recovering, cattle grazing continues in large areas of Glen Canyon Recreation Area.

Natural fire regimes have been altered across the ecosystems of the Colorado Plateau, but most significantly in forested ecosystems. Beginning with European settlement and continuing through the twentieth century, wildfires were suppressed, causing changes in forest structure and composition. The problem was exacerbated by increased fire fighting capabilities and increased landscape fragmentation. While restoration through the use of prescribed fire has slowed and in some places reversed this trend, many forests have been adversely affected by the change in fire regimes. A major effect of this fire regime alteration has been an increase in tree density in ponderosa pine and mixed conifer forests, and a subsequent decrease in herbaceous cover. As a consequence, the severity of wildfires has increased, with fire regimes dominated by crown fires that remove overstory trees and subsequently increase soil erosion.

Invasive nonnative plants also pose a serious risk to the plant communities of the Southern Colorado Plateau. Not only do invasive species alter community structure through competitive exclusion of native species, but they can also have significant impacts on ecosystem function, including alteration of disturbance regimes and nutrient cycling.

Finally, in some parks, visitor use is responsible for damage to the soils and vegetation. Human foot traffic has destroyed biological soil crusts, and off-road vehicle use, though limited in extent, has destroyed vegetation, compacted soils, and increased soil erosion.

## 2.6 Monitoring objectives

The SCPN integrated upland monitoring project has 3 objectives:

1. Determine the status and trends in composition, structure and diversity of plant communities in selected predominant ecological sites.

2. Determine the status and trends in soil stability and upland hydrologic function within selected predominant upland ecological sites.

3. Determine the relationships between vegetation patterns and soil stability/ hydrologic function.

With data collected following this protocol, SCPN will be able to provide park managers with information describing the status and long-term trends of vegetation and soil resources, and to identify associations between vegetation and soils. These data will provide park managers with information which can serve as a guide for evaluating the effectiveness of management actions aimed at protecting, restoring and managing terrestrial ecosystems.

# 3 Integrated upland monitoring design

A long-term monitoring program must be designed to enable effective and efficient sampling of numerous parameters over time and meet the requirements of the monitoring objectives (see *2.6 Monitoring objectives*). Our monitoring design is comprised of 3 components:

- spatial design—the area of statistical inference and how sample sites are located within it
- response design—the layout of the field plot and the methods of data collection
- revisit design—the frequency and pattern of revisits to the field plots

To develop our monitoring design, we looked at monitoring procedures currently in use, and conducted a pilot program to compare different methods of monitoring shrub and herbaceous vegetation. For monitoring upland hydrologic function, we modified methods used at the Jornada Experimental Range (Herrick et al. 2005a). These methods are the most comprehensively tested procedures for monitoring soils in grassland and desert ecosystems. The methods we chose for monitoring trees were modified from the NPS Fire Monitoring Handbook (U.S. Department of Interior 2003). This will allow collaborative monitoring efforts with the parks' fire ecology programs, and facilitate data sharing.

Selecting a monitoring design for shrub and herbaceous vegetation was not as straightforward. Many methods can be used to sample vegetation, and each has its strengths and weaknesses (see Elzinga et al. 1998). Moreover, the effectiveness of monitoring designs varies from community to community, and from ecosystem to ecosystem, based on the spatial variability of the attributes to be measured.

To guide us in selecting the most efficient and effective monitoring methods, we conducted a pilot study to compare 3 methods of estimating herbaceous and shrub cover: 1 m$^2$ quadrats, 10 m$^2$ quadrats, and line-point intercept methods

(Miller et al. 2006). The results of the study were not definitive. While all 3 methods were found to be repeatable among observers, they demonstrated that there were trade-offs between time-intensive sampling and the ability to capture species richness. We chose to use cover estimation in 10 m$^2$ quadrats, as this size was best at capturing species richness, and had the lowest within-plot variability.

The monitoring design selected was deemed appropriate as it meets the following criteria:

- appropriate for long-term monitoring of vegetation in a variety of ecosystems
- appropriate for monitoring soil stability
- can detect changes in species cover or frequency
- can be compared with data collected by different monitoring methods
- easy to learn
- repeatable among data collectors

## 3.1 Spatial design: Site selection and sampling frame

### 3.1.1 Prioritizing ecosystems to be monitored

Rather than attempting to track vegetation across all ecosystems within SCPN parks, limited funding requires us to narrow the focus to selected predominant ecosystems. Depending on park size and complexity, the network monitors one to several ecosystems within most park units (see table 2). Working with park staff and researchers, we choose which upland ecosystems to monitor using the following 5 criteria:

- ecosystems that are relatively intact
- ecosystems that cover a significant portion of the park,
- ecosystems of particular management interest (e.g., where restoration actions or other active management are planned)
- ecosystems whose dynamics are not well known, and are not currently being studied or monitored

**Table 2. The target ecosystems and selected ecological sites for integrated upland monitoring in 12 SCPN parks**

| Park | Target ecosystems | Selected ecological site(s) | Ecological site ID | Associated soil components |
|------|-------------------|------------------------------|---------------------|-----------------------------|
| AZRU | grassland | Limy | R037XA003NM | Avalon, Blackston, |
| BAND | pinyon-juniper woodland | Mesa Top Pinyon-Juniper[1] | – | Palatka, Canuela, Adornado, Hackroy, Nyjack, Armenta |
|      | mixed conifer forest[2] | – | – | – |
| CHCU | grassland | Sandy Loam Upland | R037XA030NM | Chacoan, Shiprock |
| ELMA | ecosystem to be determined | – | – | – |
| ELMO | ecosystem to be determined | – | – | – |
| GLCA | desert shrubland[2] | Desert Sand | R035XY115UT | Sheppard |
|      | ecosystem to be determined | – | – | – |
|      | ecosystem to be determined | – | – | – |
| GRCA | mixed conifer forests | Loamy Hills and Loamy Hills Cold | F035XI902AZ F035XI903AZ | Kanabownits, Kaiparowits, Kippers |
|      | pinyon-juniper woodlands | Limestone Upland | F035XF619AZ | Chunkmonk, Wodomont, Toqui |
| MEVE | pinyon-Juniper woodland | Loamy Mesa Top (Pinyon-Juniper) | R036XY142CO | Morefield, Roubideau |
|      | pinyon-juniper woodlands[2] | Shallow Loamy Mesa Top (Pinyon-Juniper) | – | Longburn, Arabrab |
| PEFO | grassland | Sandy Loam Upland | R035XA117AZ | Clovis, Palma, Fruitland, Sheppard |
|      | grassland | Clayey Fan | R035XB239AZ | Jocity, Claysprings |
| PETR | grassland | Malpais | R042XA056NM | Alemeda |
| WACA | ecosystem to be determined | – | – | – |
| WUPA | grassland | Limy Upland | R035XB208AZ | Tuweep |
|      | shrubland | Sandstone Upland | R035XB215AZ | Epikom |

[1]Sites that have been altered or combined and do not correspond directly to ecological sites.
[2]In development.

- ecosystems that are of particular regional conservation value or are potentially threatened

We then identify ecological sites described by the Natural Resource Conservation Service that correspond to the ecosystems of interest.

### 3.1.2 Developing the final sampling frame

Development of the spatial design entails defining the sampling frame, a physical representation of the target population. The final sampling frame is the area from which sampling sites are randomly selected, and therefore the area to which statistical inferences can be made. For most SCPN parks, we use ecological sites as the basis for defining the initial sampling frame. Ecological sites are developed by the Natural Resources Conservation Service (NRCS) in association with soil survey data (U.S. Department of Agriculture 2003). An ecological site is a landscape division with specific physical characteristics that differs from other landscape divisions in its ability to produce distinctive types and amounts of vegetation, and in its response to management (Society for Range Management Task Group on Unity in Concepts and Terminology 1995). Ecological sites have characteristic soils, hydrology, plant communities, and disturbance regimes and responses (U.S. Department of Agriculture 2003).

We chose to base initial sampling frames on soils-based ecological sites for several reasons:

- The close association of vegetation to

soil types ensures relatively homogenous vegetation within a sampling frame, thus minimizing variability, and making it easier to detect trends over time.

- It is important to base sampling frames on features that are stable over time. If a sampling frame was based instead on a more transitory classification, such as a vegetation map, problems might arise when the vegetation changed, for example, in response to a disturbance such as fire.

- Ecological sites can often be distinguished from each other on the basis of parent material and landscape position (Bestelmeyer et al. 2004), which is a useful feature in field verification and implementation.

- When fully developed, the ecological site description contains a state-and-transition model which describes the vegetation dynamics within a site in response to various stressors; these models will greatly facilitate identification and interpretation of observed variability in the field during monitoring, and provide the basis for interpreting monitoring results within the context of ecological condition.

Because of high variability in biotic and abiotic components of upland ecosystems across SCPN parks, individual sampling frames will, in most cases, be composed of single ecological sites within a park. For some parks, the upland target population consists of 2 to 3 closely related ecological sites and vegetation types. For example, the Loamy Hills and Loamy Hills-Cold ecological sites comprise the initial sampling frame for the mixed conifer forests of the North Rim of GRCA. We will use probability-based sampling to make valid inferences for each ecological site within a particular park.

To determine the target populations and corresponding sampling frames, we begin by holding discussions with park staff and local experts to identify and locate the ecosystems with the highest priority for monitoring. During these meetings, we review soil data and ecological sites derived from NRCS soil map units using Geographical Information Systems (GIS) technology to locate areas of highest interest. We discuss how well the surrogate soil map units represent the location, distribution, and occurrence patterns of the target populations. We conclude by selecting one or more ecological sites to represent the initial sampling frames.

We then conduct initial field reconnaissance of the selected ecological sites at randomly selected points. The field objectives are to

- evaluate the feasibility of identifying the ecological site using the stated NRCS biophysical characteristics

- observe the variation in plant species composition, topography, and soil features across the ecological site

- make a preliminary assessment of the errors associated with the ecological site delineation

Depending on existing park conditions, several adjustments are made to the initial sampling frame, based on a variety of factors:

- To ensure that the 0.5 ha plot is entirely within the ecological site, we apply a 50 m buffer around the ecological site boundary.

- To reduce the effect of human disturbances, we eliminate areas that are within 100 m of a road or developed areas.

- To further reduce the effects of other human disturbances, we eliminate areas from the frame that have been or are scheduled for management treatments, such as mechanical thinning treatments in forests.

- To avoid sampling-induced erosion, we eliminate areas that exceed 20 to 30% slope using the National Elevation Dataset (10 m resolution) : 30% slope was used in montane ecosystems, and 20% was used in dryland ecosystems.

- For some target populations that include recently burned forested areas (e.g., mixed conifer at GRCA), we use burn severity data to eliminate areas classified as having had moderate to high burn severity because these early-successional areas were considered to be non-target.

- For some parks, we may eliminate areas that require an excessive amount of travel for sampling (e.g., areas that are more than 2 hiking hours away from a trailhead or access point).

These and other factors are evaluated for each selected ecological site, and adjustments are made using GIS to derive the final sampling frames. This selection process and the necessary adjustments have been completed for a variety of parks. Descriptions of park and ecosystem specific spatial designs are provided in Appendix A.

### 3.1.3 Selecting sites within final sampling frames

To randomly select sites that are spatially-balanced within each final sampling frame, we use the Generalized Random-Tessellation Stratified (GRTS) design (Stevens and Olsen 2004). We use the spsurvey package (Kincaid 2011) within R software to run GRTS designs to select points to serve as the centers for each sampling site (or plot). In most ecological sites we install 30 plots; however, in sites of small spatial extent we may install a reduced set of 6 plots, and in ecological sites that are highly variable we may install 45 plots. Power analysis will assist us in determining the final number of plots needed to detect trends. We intentionally overdraw the GRTS sample to accommodate errors in the final sampling frame and other factors that may cause points to be eliminated. The GRTS points are evaluated in numerical order to determine the first 30 (or 6 or 45) points that meet the target population and sampling frame criteria. GRTS points may be rejected in the field because the sampling site is determined to be non-target (i.e., wrong ecological site, disturbed, or too steep). Points may also be rejected by park staff if they fall in the vicinity of archaeological sites or other sensitive resources. If a GRTS point is rejected, the next point in the GRTS sequence is evaluated as its replacement.

## 3.2 Response design

The response design describes the layout of the field plot and the methods of data collection. This protocol systematically describes the process of data collection at each sample site. Each procedure is described in detail in the SOPs (Standard Operating Procedures). The response design includes various measurements of vegetation composition and structure, soil stability and hydrologic function in permanently marked 0.5 ha plots (fig. 2).

Centered within the plot are three 50 m transects. The following data are collected from within five 10 m² quadrats placed along each transect (see *4 Field methods* for a detailed description):

- cover of all herbaceous and shrub species
- frequency of all herbaceous and shrub species in 5 nested quadrats
- counts of tree seedlings by size class
- cover of plant functional categories
- cover of soil surface features (in 1 m² quadrat)

Photopoints are taken at the ends of each transect. A 0.1 ha. overstory tree plot is positioned between 2 of the transects.

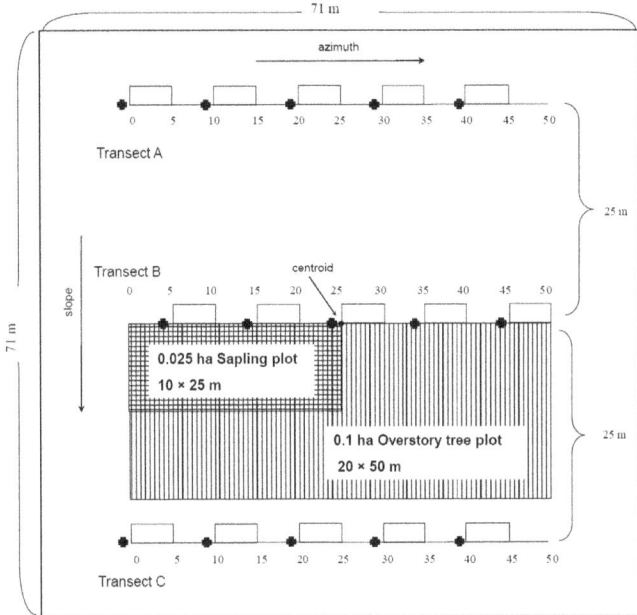

Figure 2. Standard plot layout. The plot is 0.5 ha, measuring 71 × 71 m. Three 50 m transects, spaced 25 m from each other, run perpendicular to the slope. Five nested quadrats are arranged along each transect. A 20 × 50 m (0.1 ha) overstory tree plot is located downslope of the middle transect. A 10 × 25 m (0.025 ha) understory tree plot is located in the corner of the overstory plot.

Sapling data is collected within a 0.025 ha subplot within the tree plot. Canopy closure is measured with a spherical densiometer at points along the transects. Soil stability data is collected from random points along the transects. Basal and canopy gaps are measured along the transects to provide an estimate of the amount of bare soil subject to wind and water erosion. Tree canopy cover is also measured along the transect. An ecological site assessment is performed in which the topography, soils, and vegetation are described. Disturbances inside and outside the plot are documented.

Some procedures are implemented at all sites, and some are pertinent only to specific ecological sites (see *4.3 Sampling procedures*, below).

## 3.3 Revisit design

The revisit design describes the frequency and pattern of monitoring visits to the field plots. A pilot period is typically implemented prior to finalizing the revisit design, in which we will sample 10 plots in an ecological site for 3 to 5 consecutive years (more plots are sampled for sites we expect to be highly variable, following the GRTS spatial allocation design). We will then analyze these data to determine spatial and temporal variation for several key metrics. We will conduct power analyses (using a variety of change detection and error levels) to provide insight into trend detection and to help us select a final revisit design that best addresses our monitoring objectives. However, for certain sites we may be able to infer spatio-temporal patterns from other similar ecological sites and avoid this time consuming pilot sampling.

Our general revisit design (table 3) is a connected design in both spatial and temporal aspects that balances the allocation of effort between addressing temporal (year to year) variability and spatial variability within the ecological site. Variability within an ecological site is dependent both on its inherent heterogeneity and on its spatial extent (larger areas are likely to be more variable). For those ecological sites with greater variability, we will compensate by increasing the number of plots in each panel to maintain a similar level of accuracy in our statistical estimates of ecological site conditions.

To determine which plots will be sampled and when, we assign sequential sets of sampling points from the GRTS output to individual panels. For example, in our 3 panel design, the first 10 points of the GRTS output are assigned to panel 1, points 11 to 20 to panel 2, and points 21 to 30 to panel 3. Use of the GRTS points in sequential order should provide the best spatial balance in the resulting panels.

**Table 3. Example of panel design used for a single ecological site. "X" represents 10 plots for most ecological sites, for a total of 30 plots across 3 panels. For more variable ecological sites, "X" represents 15 plots for a total of 45 plots across 3 panels**

| Panel | Year | | | | | | | | | | |
|-------|------|------|------|------|------|------|------|------|------|------|------|
|       | 1    | 2    | 3    | 4    | 5    | 6    | 7    | 8    | 9    | 10   | 11   |
| 1     | X    |      | X    |      |      |      | X    |      | X    |      |      |
| 2     |      |      | X    |      | X    |      |      |      | X    |      | X    |
| 3     | X    |      |      |      | X    |      | X    |      |      |      | X    |
| sum/yr | 2X  | 0    | 2X   | 0    | 2X   | 0    | 2X   | 0    | 2X   | 0    | 2X   |

# 4 Field methods

## 4.1 Preparing for the field season

Field visit logistics must to be arranged well before the start of the field season. This includes creating a field schedule, hiring the field crew, renewing research permits, organizing and purchasing field equipment, and arranging transportation and accommodations (see *SOP #1* and appendix B).

A field schedule will be developed each season. The revisit plan (see 3.3. *Revisit design*) outlines the ecological sites and plots to be visited each year. When planning the field season, this sequence must be reviewed, and a schedule created listing sampling dates for each park. When a draft schedule is complete, it should be sent to park staff. For parks where new plots are to be established, the final sampling frame must be finalized, GRTS points must be evaluated, and any necessary field reconnaissance must be completed. Current research permits should be reviewed to ensure that they are up-to-date. New permits should be applied for in parks where field work is beginning.

Once the field schedule has been developed, the crew must be hired. The SCPN is accomplishing the field work associated with this protocol through a cooperative agreement with Northern Arizona University (NAU). Supervised by the NAU principal investigator with field oversight by the project manager and botanist, the NAU upland crew will consist of 3-5 crew members, including a crew leader. Ample time should be allowed to accommodate university hiring procedures and paperwork. Once the crew is hired, the members must be trained in monitoring procedures and plant identification. (See *7.2 Crew qualifications and training* and *SOP #2*.)

All necessary equipment and supplies should be organized and made ready for the field season (see *SOP #1* and the yearly project list in appendix B). Any missing or broken equipment should be repaired or replaced. Rebar and rebar caps must be ordered; rebar caps must be stamped. Copies of the field datasheets, revisit reports of previous years' data, and maps should all be printed. GRTS points should be loaded into the GPS units.

## 4.2 Timing of monitoring

Sampling for monitoring begins in April (table 4) at the low-elevation desert ecological sites (e.g., Glen Canyon NRA), followed by sampling in high-elevation mixed conifer forests (e.g., Grand Canyon NP and Bandelier NM) pinyon-juniper woodlands (e.g., Bandelier NM, Grand Canyon NP, and Mesa Verde NP), and grasslands/shrublands (e.g., Petrified Forest NP, Chaco Culture NHP). Ideally, plots should be sampled when grasses are flowering and biomass is at its peak. Plots should be visited at approximately the same time each year, although changes in weather patterns (e.g., delay in monsoons) may justify changes in the sampling time. In some years, certain ecological sites may not receive enough precipitation to make monitoring worthwhile.

**Table 4. Timing of sample collection**

| Ecosystem | Index period |
| --- | --- |
| Desert and Lowland Systems | April–early June |
| Mixed Conifer Forests | June–July |
| Pinyon-Juniper Woodlands | August–September |
| Grassland and Shrublands | August–October |

## 4.3 Sampling procedures

This section systematically describes the process of data collection at each sample site. The individual field procedures are described in more detail in *SOPs # 3–8*. The protocol includes various measurements of vegetation and soils in permanently marked 0.5 ha plots.

While some sampling procedures are used at all sites, others are only pertinent to certain ecological sites. Table 5 shows which SOPs are to be used at which sites. Some procedures are only used for establishing plots. Many procedures are used during each site visit. Other procedures are not used for every visit. For example, it is not

Table 5. Summary of protocols used, including the ecological sites where each is performed, most efficient number of people needed and time required

| Activity | SOP | Ecological sites | Location | Crew size | Estimated time required |
|---|---|---|---|---|---|
| Ecological site assessment[1] | 4 | all | 71 × 71 m plot (0.5 ha) | 1 | 45 minutes |
| Plot establishment[1] | 5 | all | 71 × 71 m plot (0.5 ha) | 3–5 | 0.75–2.5 hours |
| Site disturbance/burn severity | 5 | all | 71 × 71 m plot (0.5 ha) and surrounding area | 1 | 5 minutes |
| Photopoints | 5 | all | photopoints at endpoints of 3 transects | 1 | 15 minutes |
| Frequency/cover of shrub & herbaceous species, and functional groups[2] | 6 | all | five 10 m² quadrats along each of three 50 m transects | 2 | 1.5-4 hours |
| Soil surface features[2] | 6 | all | | | |
| Tree seedlings[2] | 6 | forest, woodland | | | |
| Overstory trees | 7 | forest, woodland | 20 × 50 m (0.1 ha) subplot | 2–3 | 30–75 minutes 0.5–1.5 hours |
| Saplings | 7 | forest, woodland | 10 × 25 m (0.025 ha) subplot | 2 | 15 minutes |
| Canopy closure | 7 | forest | 5 points along each of three 50 m transects | 1 | 30–45 minutes |
| Canopy cover | 7 | woodland | three 50 m transects | | |
| Basal gaps Canopy gaps (optional) | 8 | woodland, shrubland, grassland | three 50 m transects | 2 | 20–60 minutes[3] |
| Soil aggregate stability (subsurface is optional) | 8 | woodland, shrubland, grassland | 6 random points along each of 3 transects | 1 | 45 minutes[3] |

[1]These procedures are conducted once at the time of plot setup.
[2]These 3 procedures are completed at the same time.
[3]Optional methods are not included in time estimates.

necessary to collect tree measurements on back-to-back visits as these measurements are not expected to substantially vary on an annual basis.

It takes 1 to 2.5 hours for a 4-person crew to conduct the ecological site assessment and establish a plot. Forested and woodland plots take longer because it is often difficult to sight across the plot and string tapes through large junipers and treefalls. It then takes 2 to 4.5 hours to complete sampling procedures at the site.

### 4.3.1 Collecting data efficiently
It is important to maximize efficiency when collecting field data. Key considerations include determining the number of crew members to perform each procedure, and the order in which the various procedures are performed

For the establishment and monitoring of forest and woodland plots, crews of 4 to 5 members are most efficient, with 2 people collecting the quadrat data, and the other crew members working in pairs and separately on the other protocols. A third person may be useful in the establishment of tree plots. For the establishment and monitoring of grassland/shrubland plots, crews of 2 to 3 members are most efficient.

For some procedures it is most efficient to have 2 people collecting the data—a recorder and an observer. These procedures include measuring quadrats, basal and canopy gaps, and trees. The recorder is responsible for ensuring that all collected data are complete, including plot metadata. The observer is responsible for data accuracy (species identification, cover estimates, tree measurements, etc.). To ensure consistent observations and minimize observer fatigue and boredom, pairs are typically rotated among jobs, and the tasks of observer and recorder are also alternated. For other procedures, such as measuring soil aggregate stability, collecting photopoints, and most of the ecological site assessments, it is most efficient for one person to collect the data.

One-person tasks can often be combined to maximize efficiency. For example, when establishing the plot, the person pounding in the rebar can also GPS the rebar and take photos at the photopoints. Such steps not only save time, but minimize trampling of the plot.

### 4.3.2 Assessing the ecological site

The ecological site assessment serves 2 purposes. First, it provides the physical and biological basis for accepting or rejecting a potential plot site for monitoring. Second, it provides a record of topographical, soil, biological, and physical characteristics of the plot that can be used to interpret the vegetation and soils monitoring data. This procedure is generally conducted once prior to plot establishment (See *SOP # 4* for the methods used to conduct an ecological site assessment.) It can be conducted either immediately prior to plot establishment, or during an earlier screening visit to the site. Before a plot is established, some parks require that sites are cleared by an archaeologist.

First, the crew navigates to the GRTS point using a Global Positioning System (GPS), (see *SOP #3* for details), temporarily marking the point with a pin flag or rebar. This point is to become the centroid (center point) of the plot if it is to be established. The assessment is conducted for the 0.5 ha area surrounding the point. The topography is described or measured in terms of landform, slope complexity, slope shape, percent slope, and aspect (see appendix C for common landforms). The aspect is used to determine the azimuth of the transects for the plot establishment procedure to follow. A soil profile is taken in which texture, color, rock fragments and effervescence are described for each 10 cm increment of a 1 meter soil core, and the probable soil component is identified.

The vegetation is assessed and matched with the appropriate US National Vegetation Classification Standard (NVCS) association taken from the NPS vegetation map. Major disturbances in and around the site are assessed. If the soil and vegetation appear to match the target ecological site, and there are no major disturbances, the site is accepted for plot establishment. If the plot establishment does not immediately follow assessment, the centroid point should be permanently marked with rebar.

### 4.3.3 Establishing the plot

Plots are 0.5 hectares, measuring 71 by 71 meters, with the GRTS point as the centroid of the plot. Three 50-meter transects are located within the plot, spaced 25 meters apart and running perpendicular to the slope (fig. 2). (See *SOP #5* for details about establishing plots.)

Rebar with stamped rebar caps are used to monument the plot centroid and the transect endpoints. In most locations, rebars without caps monument the transect midpoints. Locations of the transect endpoints and the centroid are documented with GPS (see appendix D). When possible, 2 witness trees are tagged for each transect end point. The transects are delineated by 50 m tapes.

### 4.3.4 Describing site disturbance

Both natural and human disturbances within the plot and in the area surrounding the plot are described. The objective of this procedure is to provide a basis for interpreting anomalies in the vegetation data. The type and size of disturbances are described and mapped on a plot diagram. During plot revisits, only new disturbances are described (See *SOP #5* for details on documenting site disturbance.)

When site visits occur within 2 years of a wildfire or prescribed fire, a more detailed burn severity assessment is conducted. In this assessment, the percentage of the plot composed of areas of different levels of burn severity for the tree canopy and the understory/substrate are estimated.

### 4.3.5 Photopoints

Photopoints are established at the ends

of each transect for a total of 6 points per plot. The photographer stands 5 meters back from the rebar that marks the beginning or end of the transect, and takes a photograph looking inward, down the measuring tape. If there is a major obstacle (e.g., tree) blocking the view, the location of the photopoint is offset. (See *SOP #5* for details on taking photographs for photopoints.)

### 4.3.6 Measuring shrub and herbaceous vegetation, tree seedlings, and soil surface features

Foliar cover and frequency by species, cover of plant functional groups, tree seedling density, and cover of soil surface features are all measured in quadrats. There are five 10 m² rectangular quadrats evenly spaced along each of the 50 m transects, and 5 levels of nesting within the quadrats: 0.01 m², 0.1 m², 1 m², 5 m², and 10 m². (fig. 3). (See *SOP #6* for details on collecting data for vegetation frequency and cover, and tree seedlings.) Table 6

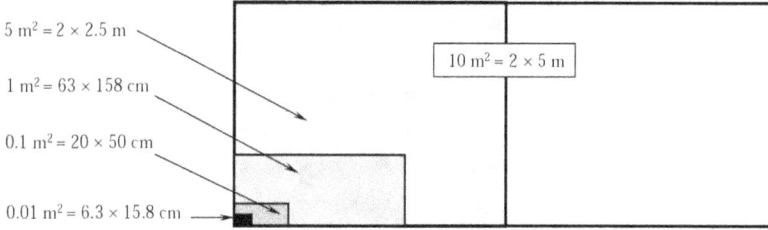

5 m² = 2 × 2.5 m
1 m² = 63 × 158 cm
0.1 m² = 20 × 50 cm
0.01 m² = 6.3 × 15.8 cm
10 m² = 2 × 5 m

**Figure 3. Arrangement and sizes of nested frequency quadrats.**

**Table 6. Quadrat scale and type of measurement for shrub and herbaceous vegetation, soil surface features, functional groups, and tree seedlings**

| | Measurement | Location of measurement |
|---|---|---|
| Herbaceous and shrub species | presence | all nested quadrats |
| | % cover | 10 m² quadrats |
| Soil surface features[1] | % cover | 1 m² quadrats |
| Functional groups[2] | % cover | 10 m² quadrats |
| Tree seedlings | count by species and size class | 1 m² quadrats |

[1]Soil surface features include: Live plant base; Dead herbaceous base; Dead woody base; Duff and litter; Undifferentiated crust; Bare ground; Woody debris (>2.5 cm); Fine gravel (0.2 to <2 cm); Coarse gravel (2 to <7.5 cm); Cobble (7.5 to < 25 cm); Stone, boulder (≥ 25 cm); Cyanobacteria; Lichen; Moss
[2]Functional groups include: Total live foliar cover (Shrubs, Perennial grasses/graminoids, Annual grasses, Forbs, Cacti/succulents); Standing dead herbaceous; Standing dead woody

summarizes how the various types of data are collected in the quadrats.

***Nested frequency data*** are collected in each of the quadrats. Beginning with the 0.01 m² quadrat, all vascular plant species rooted in that quadrat are recorded. The crew then subsequently samples the larger quadrats (0.1 m², followed by 1 m², 5 m² and 10 m²), recording species that did not already occur in the smaller nested quadrats. Larger quadrats capture less common species, while smaller quadrats capture the dominant species, such that changes in frequency over time can be detected. Identification is to the species level whenever possible. (Procedures for processing of unknown species are outlined in *4.2.12 Recording and collecting unknown species*, and detailed in *SOP #6*).

***Foliar cover*** is then estimated in the 10 m² quadrat. Each species is assigned a cover class according to Table 7. These cover classes are modified from the North Carolina Vegetation Survey (Peet et al. 1998), with more divisions among the smaller classes. Cover estimates are based on a vertical projection of live cover, both photosynthetic and non-photosynthetic, onto the ground surface. Dead material is only included if it was from the current growing season. All species with live foliar cover in the quadrat are included in cover estimates, whether they are fully rooted in the quadrat or not.

***Cover of functional groups*** is estimated in the 10 m² quadrat (fig. 3) using the same cover classes (table 7). Functional group estimates are the vertical projection of each group, and account for overlapping species' canopies. Dead cover from previous growing seasons is included in the *Standing dead herbaceous* and *Standing dead woody* categories.

***Tree seedlings*** are counted in the 10 m² plot, and are grouped according to species and size class.

***Cover of soil surface features*** is collected in the 1 m² plot due to the small scale heterogeneity of these features. The same cover classes are used (See table 7.)

**Table 7. Cover classes used for quadrat sampling**

| Cover class | Cover | Cover class | Cover |
|---|---|---|---|
| 1 | <0.1% | 7 | 10 to <15% |
| 2 | 0.1 to <0.5% | 8 | 15 to <25% |
| 3 | 0.5 to <1% | 9 | 25 to <35% |
| 4 | 1 to <2% | 10 | 35 to <50% |
| 5 | 2 to <5% | 11 | 50 to <75% |
| 6 | 5 to <10% | 12 | 75–100% |

Data are collected in this manner for all 5 quadrats on each of the 3 transects.

### 4.3.7 Measuring overstory trees and saplings

Procedures used to measure trees are modified from the Fire Monitoring Handbook (U.S. Department of Interior 2003). Tree data are collected in a 20 × 50 m (0.1 ha) plot, immediately downslope of the middle transect. Trees are divided into 2 strata—overstory and saplings. Overstory trees are measured in the 0.1 has plot and are defined as all trees with a diameter ≥15 cm measured at 137 cm above ground level (diameter at breast height or DBH). Saplings are measured in a 10 m × 25 m subplot within the tree plot and are defined as trees with a DBH ≥2.5 cm and <15 cm. Due to their shrubby, branching habit, diameter at root crown (DRC) is used for measuring *Juniperus* spp. (see figure 2 for plot layout and *SOP # 7* for details on measuring trees).

All living overstory trees within the 0.1 ha plot are given a brass tag with an ID number. Species, diameter, and status of the tree are recorded and the location of the tree is indicated on the tree map. Standing dead trees are measured and mapped during the initial visit, but are not tagged.

Saplings are neither tagged nor mapped, but are tallied by species and size class. The size classes are: 2.5 to <5.0 cm DBH, 5.0 to <10.0 cm DBH, and 10.0 to <15.0 cm DBH (or DRC when measuring junipers).

### 4.3.8 Canopy closure and canopy cover

We measure canopy closure to monitor changes in the forest canopy using a spherical densiometer. Measurements are taken at 5 fixed points along each transect. Four samples are taken at each point in each of 4 directions: facing the transect end, the transect start, upslope and downslope. Line intercept transects of live tree foliar cover are used to measure tree canopy in pinyon-juniper woodlands (see *SOP #7* for details on collecting canopy closure and canopy cover data).

### 4.3.9 Basal and canopy intercepts

Procedures to measure basal and canopy gaps were modified from Herrick et al. (2005a). Line intercept methods are used to measure basal gaps and canopy gaps along the transects. Basal gaps are the bare ground between plant bases; large gaps between plant bases are important indicators of increased potential for runoff and water erosion. Canopy gaps are the spaces between shrub and perennial herbaceous plant canopies; large gaps in the canopy indicate increased potential for wind erosion (Herrick et al. 2005a, b). Both basal gap intercepts and canopy gap intercepts are optional methods. (See *SOP #8* for details of collecting gap information along transects.)

### 4.3.10 Soil aggregate stability

Soil stability is measured by collecting 18 soil samples from random points along the transects. Small soil samples approximately 2-3 mm thick and 6-8 mm in diameter are excavated and placed on small sieves. The sieves are submerged in a water-filled compartmentalized box for 5 minutes, then raised out of the water and resubmerged 5 times in rapid succession. Stability is determined by how quickly the soil samples lose their structural integrity in this process. Each sample is rated based on a 6-point scale (see *SOP #8* for details on testing for soil aggregate stability).

### 4.3.11 Revising the standard plot layout

This protocol describes the standard plot layout used for the majority of the ecological sites. However, it may become necessary to change aspects of the plot layout, or the methodologies, to accommodate unique features in some of the ecological sites. For example, in open savanna or grasslands that are being invaded by junipers, it is desirable to include a tree plot. If tree density is generally low, the tree plot can be expanded to include the entire area between Transects A and C (0.25 acres). Additional alternations may be necessary as new ecological sites are added to this monitoring program. Decisions to modify the plot layout are made by the project manager, and should remain consistent across the ecological site.

### 4.3.12 Recording and collecting unknown species

Species not immediately identified in the field are to be collected, documented with a written description, assigned an unknown species code, and recorded on the datasheet, with the assigned code. Specimens are to be collected outside the plot, only if there are at least 10 individuals, and placed in a plant press for later examination. If the species is too rare to collect, photos should be taken, and the location of the plant in the plot will be noted on the datasheet, with the hope that its identity can be resolved in subsequent visits. **Under no circumstances are rare, threatened and/or endangered species to be collected**. (See *SOP #6* for details on processing and documentation of unknown species.)

Collected specimens are discarded following identification, or mounted on acid-free herbarium paper and kept in insect-proof cabinets as part of the SCPN reference collection. The SCPN reference collection is a working collection to be used for training of field crews in the identification of Colorado Plateau plant species. If parks require voucher specimens of selected species for park herbaria, they may request additional collections.

# 5 Data management

Data management requirements for monitoring protocols include procedures to collect, enter, document, archive, and distribute data. The project manager and botanist will ensure the integrity and security of the data during a given field season by adhering to standard operating procedures (SOPs). Additional details are in the SCPN data management plan (Tancreto and Hendrie 2006).

Project information management may be best understood as an ongoing process, as shown in Figure 4. Yearly data management tasks are shown in the yearly project list (appendix B).

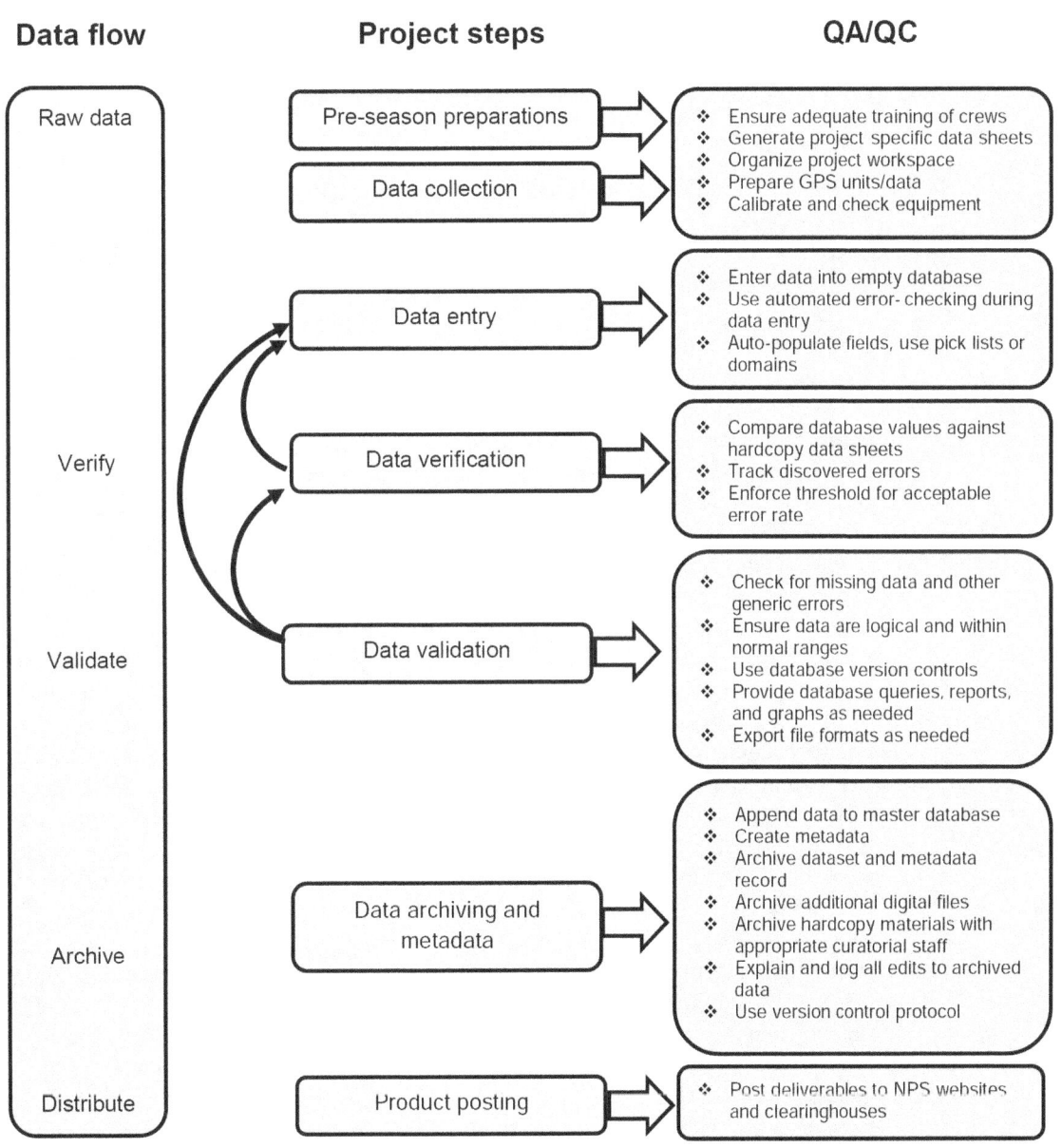

**Figure 4. Schematic diagram of the overall data management procedures to be carried out during the project stages associated with the typical data flow**

## 5.1 Pre-season preparations

Prior to the field season, the SCPN data manager reserves a section of the network file server for the project and establishes permissions so that project staff members have access to needed files within this workspace (see *SOP #10* in this protocol, and appendix F in the SCPN data management plan). Automated back-up procedures run on a daily schedule.

The GIS specialist and botanist work together to ensure that all maps, target coordinates, and other GPS layers are loaded on a sufficient number of GPS units prior to each trip. The GIS specialist also provides paper maps to aid in navigating.

## 5.2 Recording data

All data collected in the field will be recorded on paper datasheets until an electronic data collecting system is implemented. Before leaving a plot, the crew leader is responsible for ensuring that all forms have been filled out completely and that the information on each form is logical and legible. Upon returning from each field trip, datasheets will be scanned to PDF files. If changes are made to paper datasheets, they should be re-scanned. The botanist is responsible for safekeeping and organization of the datasheets until data entry and verification procedures have been completed, at which point the datasheets are stored in the network office.

Appendix D describes how to use the GPS unit to document and re-locate plot points. The GIS specialist will download GPS data from the GPS units at the end of each field trip and store them in the raw GPS files workspace (see appendix F in the SCPN data management plan). The GIS specialist will then process the raw GPS data and store them in the project geodatabase organized by park unit. The data manager will upload corrected coordinate information into the integrated upland database and create any GIS datasets. The botanist and GIS specialist will periodically review the processed GPS data to ensure that any errors or inconsistencies are identified early.

## 5.3 Digital image procedures

Digital images include photopoints, unknown plant photos, photos of the ecological sites, and photos of the crew at work. Digital images are downloaded from cameras at the end of each field trip and stored in the project workspace (see appendix F in the SCPN data management plan). Data images are linked to the project database. Other images will be entered into the network image database. (See the SCPN data management plan for more details.)

## 5.4 Data entry, verification, and validation

### 5.4.1 Data entry

Integrated upland monitoring data are managed through the SCPN Integrated Upland Monitoring Database, a relational database based on the Inventory and Monitoring (I&M) program's Natural Resources Database Template (NRDT) (http://science.nature.nps.gov/im/apps/template/index.cfm). The database design follows the NRDT's hierarchical datatable organization (see appendix E). The database is divided into 2 components: the "working database" for entering, editing, and error-checking data for the current season, and the "master database" that contains the complete set of certified data for the monitoring project.

During the field season, the crew is provided with a copy of a working database into which they enter and edit data for the current season (refer to *SOP #11*). The botanist is responsible for ensuring that multiple copies of the database are not created, with edits inadvertently occurring in multiple database files. The integrated upland monitoring data recorded on the paper forms will be entered into this database. If there is time, this can be undertaken throughout the field season. Otherwise, it should occur immediately following the field season. Data entry should be completed by someone who participated in data collection, or is familiar with the project and data. The primary goal of data entry is to transfer the data from paper into the database with 100% accuracy. The botanist ensures that data are entered completely and properly into the database.

It is recommended that a backup copy of the database is created every time new data are entered. This ensures that the initial data entry starting point can be recovered should irreversible errors or problems occur during the data entry session. Any time a revision of the protocol requires a revision to the database, a complete copy of the database will be made and stored in an archive directory.

### 5.4.2 Data verification

The integrated upland database application incorporates quality assurance/quality control (QA/QC) strategies to ensure data quality. The database design and the allowable value ranges assigned to individual fields within the data tables help to minimize the potential for data entry errors and/or the transcription of erroneously recorded data.

*SOP #11* describes the steps that the project manager, botanist, and data management staff will take to ensure that the data records within a given season's dataset are verified (i.e., database values are compared against hard-copy datasheets). The overall goal is to check at least 25% of records, correct and track any errors discovered, and enforce a threshold for an acceptable error rate. If, among the records checked, more than 0.1% are found to contain errors, then all of the records within that season's dataset are reviewed. The GIS specialist will verify the geospatial component of the integrated upland database each field season (see the SCPN data management plan).

Record-reviewing tools are built into the integrated upland database (see *SOP #11*). Documented error rates are noted in the dataset metadata, along with details about any all-record review, if the error threshold is exceeded, and the resulting actions (e.g., percent of records corrected, nature of the errors, and any necessary re-entry of data).

### 5.4.3 Data validation

The project manager, botanist, and data management staff collectively validate (i.e., ensure that the data make sense) a given season's dataset. Some validation

methods have been incorporated into the integrated upland database (see *SOP #12*). Other, more specific, validation routines are worked out with the protocol project manager and/or project staff and incorporated into the database as appropriate. Data management staff will work closely with the project manager to provide any needed database queries, reports, graphs, or export file formats to assist with the overall validation.

Once validated, the data manager reviews the dataset and requests revisions or corrections, if necessary. Once approved, the dataset is considered certified and the data manager will upload the dataset to the master project database.

## 5.5 Archiving data

Metadata can be defined as structured information about the content, quality, condition, and other characteristics of a given dataset. Additionally, metadata provide the means to catalog and search among datasets, thus making them available to a broad range of potential data users. Metadata for all protocol monitoring data will conform to Federal Geographic Data Committee standards.

Metadata are created annually for both tabular and spatial data. Specific procedures for creating, parsing, and posting the metadata record are provided in the SCPN data management plan. Final metadata records are posted to the online NPS Integrated Resource Management Applications (IRMA) (https://irma.nps.gov), satisfying requirements of Executive Order 12906 (http://www.archives.gov/federal-register/executive-orders/pdf/12906.pdf).

Secure data archiving is essential for protecting data files from corruption (SCPN data management plan). Once the master project dataset and metadata are considered final, the data manager will place a copy of the dataset and the metadata record into the appropriate folder within the archive directory on the network server. These archived files will be stored in read-only format. Any subsequent changes made to this database must be documented in an edit log and in the metadata. In addition to the database copy in its native format, all tables will be archived in a comma-delimited ASCII format that is platform-independent by using the Access_to_ascii.mdb utility developed by the Central Alaska Network.

Additional digital files to be archived include all digital photos associated with that field season, and any digital files associated with data analysis products and project reporting.

Digital materials can be made available to park curators upon request. Hard-copy materials (e.g., datasheets, field note-books, photo prints, reports) are currently stored in the network office but will be moved to an NPS-approved repository for permanent storage.

## 5.6 Data maintenance

Any editing of archived data must be documented in the edit log and accompanied by an explanation that includes pre- and post-edit data descriptions (Tessler and Gregson 1997). Datasheets can be reconciled to the database through the use of the edit log.

Prior to any major changes of a dataset, a copy is stored with the appropriate version number to allow for tracking changes over time. Each additional version will be assigned a sequentially higher number. Frequent users of the data are notified of the updates and provided with a copy of the most recent version.

Full metadata records are available through IRMA. Records for reports and other publications are created in the Data Store section (https://irma.nps.gov/App/Reference/Search) of IRMA. Digital report files, in PDF format, are then uploaded and linked to the IRMA record. Species observations are extracted from the database and entered into the NPSpecies section of IRMA, which is the NPS database and application for maintaining park-specific species lists and observation data (https://irma.nps.gov/App/Species/Search).

Data requestors should contact the data manager who will fulfill any data requests. Only validated datasets should be shared outside NPS. See the SCPN data management plan for more details.

# 6 Data analysis and reporting

The primary focus of data analysis is to estimate vegetation and soil parameters and conduct trend analyses, including testing hypotheses to determine if changes have occurred. Analyses to determine trend and changes in soil and vegetation attributes will be performed following completion of full cycles of the revisit design. Because these designs vary by park, trend analyses will be conducted periodically (e.g., every 5, 7, or 10 years).

The objectives for data analysis include

- determining status and trends for single metrics and indices of vegetation and soil
- determining community-level status and trends in vegetation composition and structure

- determining relationships among vegetation patterns and measures associated with soil stability and upland hydrologic function

Metrics commonly used to evaluate vegetation and soils in upland communities are described in Table 8.

To provide further interpretation of the current condition and trends of targeted ecological sites, observed status and trend estimates may be compared, where possible, to data from reference sites and/or ecological thresholds. Data from other vital signs monitoring (e.g., climate, landscape vegetation patterns) should also be explored to identify relationships with vegetation and soil features in order to pursue an integrated approach to monitoring ecosystem condition within targeted ecological

**Table 8. Suggested integrated upland metrics**

| Metric type | Metric | Description |
|---|---|---|
| Herbaceous and shrub species abundance | species cover | mean percentage of a quadrat covered by a species based on cover class midpoints |
| | functional group cover | mean percentage of a quadrat covered by a functional group based on cover class midpoints |
| | species frequency | mean percentage of quadrats or plots containing a species |
| Species diversity (herbaceous and shrub species) | species richness | number of species in a plot or ecological site |
| | Shannon diversity index | a measure of species diversity that takes into account the relative abundance of each species |
| | species evenness | a measure of the degree to which all species are equal in abundance |
| | Beta diversity | a measure of within-ecological site heterogeneity |
| Tree abundance | tree basal area | total cross-sectional area of a tree species (by species) per hectare |
| | tree density | total number of tree stems per unit area |
| | seedling density | total number of individuals per unit area |
| | canopy cover | percentage of transect cover in tree canopy |
| | canopy closure | mean percentage of sky obscured by the tree canopy when viewed from a single point |
| Soil stability and hydrologic function | relative cover of gaps by size class | percentage of transects covered in basal or canopy gaps of different sizes |
| | median gap size | median size of a basal or canopy gap |
| | gap number | number of basal or canopy gaps |
| | mean surface soil aggregate stability | a quantitative test that describes the degree to which t soil particles are bound together |
| | cover of soil surface features | mean quadrat cover based on cover class midpoints |

sites. Post-hoc domain approaches can be used by dividing the ecological sites into smaller units for analysis. Such approaches may be used in the following situations: where there is more than one vegetation type in an ecological site, where portions of the ecological site have received management treatments (e.g., mechanical thinning), or where natural disturbance (e.g., fire) has occurred in a portion of the plots within an ecological site.

A common first step in data analysis is to conduct exploratory analyses designed to elucidate underlying trends and patterns in central tendencies and distributions. Trends are often detected by simply graphing parameter means and variances over time; box and whisker plots are useful for evaluating distributions. Parameter variability can also be examined by calculating the coefficients of variation (CV) within ecological sites. Another pre-analysis step is to conduct tests for normality and homogeneity of variances. For statistical tests requiring normal distributions, data that fail the normality test will be transformed (e.g., using a (x + 1) or log (x +1) transformation). If transformed data still fail normality tests, they can be compared using nonparametric methods, such as Kruskal-Wallis ANOVA on ranks. Outlier analysis can be conducted on both raw and transformed data to identify atypical observations that may profoundly influence statistically-derived relationships and results.

## 6.1 Determining trends in single metrics and indices

For detecting trends in univariate metrics and indices within the target ecological site, we will use an expanded linear regression model that includes 4 components of variation: site, year, interaction, and residual (Larsen et al. 1995, 2004). This expanded model is appropriate because the sampling design is a complex survey design that includes multiple sites and years, and the design is unbalanced (i.e., not all plots are sampled each year). The general hypothesis tested for a given metric is that the linear trend slope across sampling periods (comprised of the average of the plot-specific trends) is zero. A

mixed-effects model will be used to assess trends. In the model, time is treated as the fixed effect, and site and year are the random effects. Site refers to the plot, and year is the same as time. Both site and year are treated as categorical variables. The output from the model is a measure of the intercept and slope, the significance of the slope and intercept being different from zero, and measures of the variance and covariance of the regression parameters. A significant slope indicates a significant trend. Trend assessments are performed separately for each metric within a target ecological site. In general, the reporting unit for metrics and indices is the ecological site.

## 6.2 Variance estimation and power analysis

Periodic evaluations of the variance components in the linear regression models should be conducted in order to evaluate the efficacy of the implemented survey design in light of the sampling objectives. Variance estimation is a useful exercise to identify the main sources of variation that may hinder detection of trends; this knowledge may lead to adjustments in the sampling design to better meet the sampling objectives. Variance estimation is based on all data collected to date, not just observations of the current monitoring event. Because of the increasing precision offered by accumulated observations over time, the utility of variance estimates will increase over time as the number of sampled plots increases. One procedure for determining variance components is based on maximum likelihood estimation (Larsen et al. 2004), such as the Methods of Moments Estimation (available in statistical programs such as SAS).

After obtaining variance estimates, a power analysis can be conducted to evaluate the power of the sampling design to detect the desired minimum level of change (or trend). Statistical power is the ability to detect change when it has actually occurred, given a fixed sample size, change detection level, and specified error rates. Power analysis is commonly conducted to determine the adequacy of sample sizes in meeting the stated monitoring objective(s). It is important to remember that power estimates are based on the variance estimates derived from past and present data and, because of the uncertainty of future trends, cannot be estimated with great accuracy (Lesica and Steele 1996). Various procedures to calculate power for trend are presented in Urquhart et al. (1998), Urquhart and Kincaid (1999), and in Monte Carlo simulation approaches (e.g., Sims et al. 2006; Garman 2008).

## 6.3 Using Bayesian methods to detect trends

Detecting trends using traditional methods may be problematic because of numerous sources of uncertainty, including spatial, temporal, and measurement variation. For selected parameters, we will use an alternative approach to determine trends that is designed to address the difficulties arising from uncertainties. Bayesian methods provide a way to express uncertainty (using probabilities) in parameter estimates, and to determine the probability that a hypothesis of interest is true given a set of data (Ellison 1996). Bayesian statistics are based on Bayes' theorem (Bayes 1763), which expresses the probability of one event given, or conditional, on another event. In trend assessment, Bayesian methods can be used to identify the probability of different slope-parameter values, given the observed data (Gelman et al. 2000; Wade 2000). For testing the null hypothesis of no linear trend slope, Bayesian methods determine the probability of this hypothesis being true, given the observed data. Reasons for using Bayesian methods to assess the probability of different slope values are (1) that trends may be revealed sooner than through use of conventional statistics, and (2) the approach may provide insights into trends for key parameters that are known to have low to moderate statistical power.

Performing a Bayesian analysis starts with quantifying information (known or unknown) about a parameter; this quantity is called the prior, or prior probability distribution. Prior information can be from other surveys or experiments, mod-

els, published literature, or expert opinion. Next, a likelihood distribution is generated from sampled data, which provides the probability of observing the data for every possible parameter value. Then, a posterior (or posterior probability) is calculated by combining the likelihood function with the prior distribution to generate a new distribution, which is used to make inferences about the parameter. The posterior distribution allows assessments of the probabilities of user-selected parameter and slope values. One objective for trend assessment is to derive the probability of different levels of slope declines or increases. In cases where conventional statistics fail to reveal significant trends, relatively high probabilities (e.g., >0.70) of trends using Bayesian methods may warrant special attention. For more detail and explanations of Bayesian methods, see Gelman et al. (2000) and Wade (2000).

## 6.4 Analyzing multivariate community measures

Several questions of interest regarding multivariate analysis of vegetation composition address changes in similarity of species composition within and among plots sampled through time and include:

- Is species composition (at both the plot and ecological site level) changing or remaining stable through time?

- If species composition is found to be unstable, then is there directional change? Directional change could consist of a community that is responding to a particular disturbance (e.g., long-term drought) by manifesting a divergence of species, or the community appears to be in recovery by resulting in a convergence of species (Philippi et al. 1998).

A general approach for multivariate hypothesis testing has been described by several authors (Clarke and Green 1988; Clarke 1993; Anderson 2001) and includes these steps:

1. Choose an appropriate distance measure to serve as the basis of analysis (e.g., Bray-Curtis or Euclidean).

2. Perform ordination to visualize patterns of resemblance among observations based on their community composition.

3. Conduct a multivariate nonparametric test to detect differences among groups or directional change.

Two cautionary notes regarding these steps are (1) that no universal agreement exists on which dissimilarity metric performs best under all conditions, so its selection should be based on the expected forms of compositional differences (Philippi et al. 1998), and (2) while ordinations are useful for detecting general patterns of temporal change in multivariate community data by reducing the dimensionality of the data (Anderson 2001), they are not essential for performing statistical tests.

With multiple years of data, one approach to assess species compositional change at both the plot and ecological site level is to choose a similarity distance measure (e.g., Euclidean) and apply the mixed effects linear regression model (discussed above) to assess trend. In this case, site (or plot) is used as a covariate, and Euclid-ean distance (the dependent variable) is calculated between each plot for the sampled years, and for all possible time lags. Time is expressed as a time lag from 1 to n time lags, and includes all possible 1-yr, 2-yr, ..., 5-yr, etc. lags. A square root transformation is applied to the time lags to address the potential bias provided by the smaller number of points at the largest time lags. Some potential outcomes of this analysis are shown in Figure 5. Collins (2000) used time lag regression analysis to detect directional change in grasslands subjected to varying fire frequencies.

Numerous ordination methods are also available to assess trends in vegetation community composition and structure. Ordination methods are designed to represent multivariate data structures in low-dimensional space. Typically, this low dimensional space reduces the noise associated with multivariate data and ideally represents interpretable environmental gradients or trends. Ordination methods are operations performed on the community data matrix. For vegetation communities, this matrix is typically composed of species cover values for each plot by sampling period. Ordination techniques

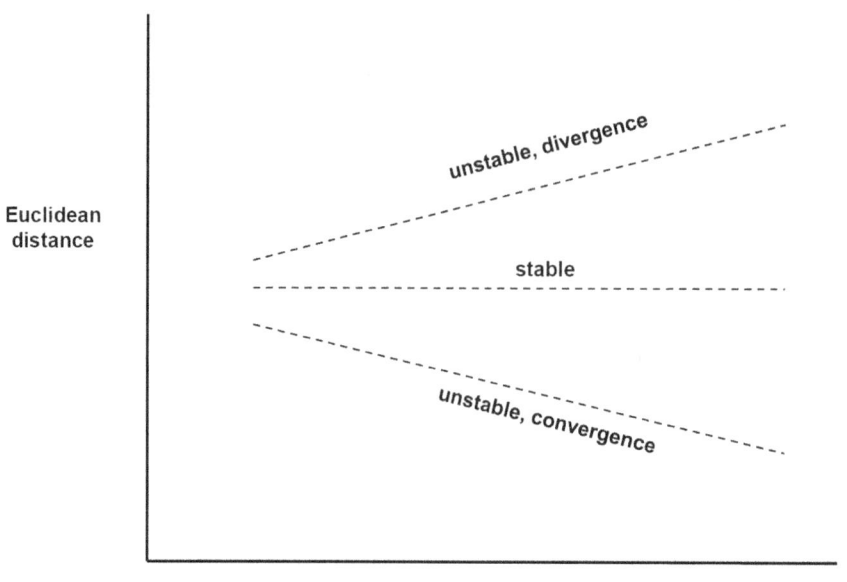

Figure 5. Conceptual model of community stability and directional change using time lag regression analysis (adapted from Philippi et al. 1998, and Collins 2000)

arrange the samples in terms of their similarity of species composition or associated environmental gradients. Ordination analyses generate diagrams, where each point corresponds to a plot within an ecological site, and the distances between the points approximate the degree of similarity between the sites (the closer the points, the more similar). For example, 2 plots with exactly the same species composition and abundance would occupy the same point or position in ordination space. Trends in vegetation communities within an ecological site can be examined using a host of techniques that analyze these relative distances in ordination space; we discuss only a few here.

Polar ordination involves the calculation of Bray-Curtis distances (Bray and Curtis 1957) and is a common technique to assess changes in species composition over time. This is a measure of dissimilarity that arranges samples between endpoints (or poles) with values ranging from 0 (identical samples) to 1 (complete dissimilarity). Many studies (e.g., Motzkin et al. 1999; Rodriguez et al. 2003) have used the Bray-Curtis distance measure to provide input values for conducting another ordination technique, Nonmetric Multi-Dimensional Scaling (NMDS). NMDS calculates a set of metric coordinates for samples using the rankings of distances between species. The Bray-Curtis similarity coefficients (and other indices including Morisita's and Jaccard's index) are appropriate for use as inputs to NMDS ordinations. A stress coefficient is computed, which measures the mismatch between a new ranked ordination and the original Bray-Curtis distances. Successive ordinations are conducted iteratively until the "stress" appears to reach a minimum. NMDS is an appropriate technique for biotic data (typically nonlinear) because it makes no assumptions about the underlying data structure.

NMDS ordinations can be used in several ways to evaluate spatial and temporal differences in similarity of species composition of plots within an ecological site. With several years of monitoring data, an "overall" NMDS can be performed that includes all plots and sampling years for a given ecological site. Vectors can be used to connect plots through time, and the various time trajectories, synchronicity, and magnitude of change among plots can be evaluated to determine if plots are changing in a consistent manner, or have dissimilar patterns. To further detect spatial differences, a "time series" of NMDS can be performed using all plot data for individual sampling years (or time periods), and the relative positions of particular plots in ordination space can be monitored. If individual plots are found to be grouped together through time, or occupy the same ordination space through time, this provides some evidence for a site or spatial difference among the plots.

Conversely, if there is no spatial patterning in ordination space for individual plots through time (i.e., the arrangement of plots appears random), then there may not be a site difference. This procedure can also be applied in a "plot series" manner to evaluate temporal change. For each plot, NMDS ordinations can be performed using data from all sampled years. When evaluating the series of ordinations by plot, if the relative positions of sampling years are found grouped together (or if an individual year occupies a unique position among all plots), this provides evidence for temporal differences. Conversely, evidence for a temporal trend may be lacking if the arrangement of sampling years in ordination space appears random when viewed across all plots.

If the ordination results indicate either spatial or temporal differences in species composition within an ecological site, significant differences in species composition can be tested with a multivariate analysis of similarity. ANOSIM (Analysis of Similarities; Clarke and Warwick 1994) is a nonparametric permutation procedure that can be applied to a similarity matrix (e.g., Bray-Curtis). Although there are no true plot replicates for species composition, a global R-statistic from ANOSIM can be obtained (using the PRIMER software; Clarke and Gorley 2006) in a two-way crossed approach (similar to the 2-way ANOVA) to test for both a spatial and temporal effect.

The R-statistic is a relative measure of dissimilarity of samples; higher R-values indicate greater dissimilarity (Clarke and Warwick 1994). A randomization process (e.g., Monte Carlo) is then used to assess the probabilities of gaining particular R values, and thus derive a significance level for the test. To provide further interpretation of any observed temporal or spatial differences in vegetation composition, an analysis of similarity percentages (SIMPER) can be conducted (in PRIMER) to identify the individual species that contribute the most to the dissimilarity patterns.

## 6.5 Exploring relationships among variables

To more fully interpret the trends observed in the vital signs from the analyses described above, it would be helpful to determine if the response patterns of vegetation and soil attributes are related to each other and to indicators from other vital signs monitoring, such as climate and landscape pattern variables. By identifying links among variables, we can pursue an integrated approach to monitoring ecosystem condition that involves key components, stressors, and processes at multiple scales.

Correlation and regression analysis can be used to detect relationships among vegetation and soil features and other indicators. Correlation analysis is used to identify the vegetation and soil variables that are most closely related to each other, and to other variables. The strength of the relationship between variables be obtained using Pearson's product-moment correlation analysis (and Spearman's rank correlation as a nonparametric method). Regression methods can be used to further analyze relationships between a response variable (e.g., total plant cover) and one or more explanatory variables (e.g., basal gap, canopy gap). The effects of continuous variables (e.g., plant cover, litter cover) on a categorical response variable (e.g., soil aggregate stability) can be explored with logistic regression analysis (e.g., Mittelbach et al. 2001).

Ordination techniques that arrange species abundance data or habitat variables in terms of their similarity can also be used; selecting an appropriate method depends upon the study objectives and the underlying data structure. Some methods (e.g., principal components analysis, PCA) assume a linear data structure and are often appropriate for abiotic data. Biotic data, however, are usually nonlinear and use of ordination techniques based on unimodal models of species abundances (e.g., Detrended Correspondence Analysis or DCA, and Canonical Correspondence Analysis or CCA) is common in ecological studies. CCA is a direct gradient analysis technique that seeks to maximize the dispersion of species and samples (or plots) in ordination space by constructing linear combinations of environmental variables (ter Braak 1987). For example, de Gruchy et al. (2005) used CCA to identify several biophysical factors (i.e., disturbance type, nutrient levels, biomass) that best explained the composition of both native and exotic plant species across various habitats in a Canadian national park. Two commonly used indirect gradient analysis techniques, DCA and NMDS, may also be appropriate for our sampling units (or plots) because they were not formally partitioned along an environmental gradient. NMDS (discussed in the previous section) does not assume an underlying data structure, and thus may be a good choice when factors determining species composition are unknown. One can use the NMDS ordination axes to further understand relationships among species composition and other biotic or abiotic variables by conducting correlation and regression techniques among the axes and other variables (e.g., Motzkin et al. 1999; Rodriguez et al. 2003). DCA, in contrast to NMDS, is based on an underlying unimodal model for species distributions. DCA is a common technique to summarize vegetation patterns and to relate those patterns to environmental features (e.g., Collins 2000; Schade et al. 2003).

Model selection is another analytical approach that can be used to better understand the dynamic relationships among vegetation and soil components, ecosystem drivers, and stressors. A suite of models can be developed that represent competing hypotheses of ecologically meaningful relationships. Numerous models can be considered, each with different combinations of independent variables and interaction terms. Model selection is based on the principle of parsimony, where the "optimal" model should contain only enough significant parameters to account for the variation in the data. The relative strength of these competing models can be compared with information-theoretic approaches (Burnham and Anderson 2002), such as Akaike's Information Criterion (AIC) (Akaike 1973). AIC values can be generated using the mixed-effects model (described previously), and AIC values for each model (adjusted for number of independent variables) are compared to determine the best-fit model. Models can be based on measures of climate and other indicators, including land cover and land condition. For example, Frescino et al. (2001) modeled spatially-explicit data of precipitation, elevation, and geology with satellite data to predict forest composition and structural diversity in the Uinta Mountains in Utah. The combination of variables to consider will develop over time with experience, and as other monitoring data becomes available. Initially, consideration of precipitation and vegetation greenness measures are obvious choices in building models to explain the observed trends in vegetation and soil parameters.

## 6.6 Data reporting

Consistent analysis and reporting of data is critical for any monitoring program and provides resource managers with information on the current status and trends over time of park vegetation and soils.

This information is necessary for natural resource planning and management. For example, monitoring data may suggest that managers need to implement management actions to restore ecosystems, or may guide adaptive management of ecosystems. SCPN will undertake 2 types of analyses and reporting to provide upland vegetation monitoring results to the park resource managers: (1) data summaries that are compiled into annual reports, and (2) analyses of long-term monitoring data.

### 6.6.1 Annual data summaries
After the data are validated, routine data summaries are prepared to describe the current status of the upland ecosystems monitored in each park. The various metrics are generally averaged across plots within an ecological site. These summaries can be generated as customized database reports and sent to the parks as annual reports. When appropriate, the data summarized for the season can be compared to previous years' data. The reports should be completed no later than May of the year following the field season. Appendix F is a sample report, and *SOP #13* describes data summary and reporting.

### 6.6.2 Long-term monitoring reports
A primary purpose of the network is to design and implement long-term ecological monitoring to evaluate the integrity of park ecosystems and contribute to the understanding of ecosystem processes. Periodic trend reports are fundamental to communicating monitoring results to park management. The objectives of these reports are to identify significant trends in key metrics, and to identify when key metrics exceed known thresholds. Trend reports will be prepared every 5 to 10 years, depending upon the revisit design for a particular ecosystem.

# 7 Personnel requirements and training

## 7.1 Roles and responsibilities

The program manager is responsible for the overall management and supervision of the network monitoring program. Serving in the role of project manager, the plant ecologist is responsible for the overall management and supervision of integrated upland monitoring, and will work with the program manager to coordinate the involvement of other network staff. The roles and responsibilities for all pertinent SCPN staff are summarized in Table 9.

The SCPN is accomplishing the field work associated with this protocol through a cooperative agreement with

**Table 9. Key roles and responsibilities for implementing integrated upland monitoring**

| Position | Roles and responsibilities |
|---|---|
| Program Manager | The program manager is responsible for the overall management and supervision of the program. Duties include overseeing the development and testing of monitoring protocols, hiring and supervising network staff, managing the implementation of monitoring projects, and ensuring that the data are appropriately analyzed, reported and made available for park planning and management. |
| Project Manager | The project manager is the network plant ecologist, and is responsible for implementing the integrated upland monitoring project. Duties include working collaboratively with park staff to understand management issues and information needs, development of protocols, obtaining research permits, data summary and analysis and report writing. The project manager works closely with the data manager, GIS specialist, quantitative ecologist and botanist to ensure that high-quality standards are achieved and maintained in collecting, processing, analyzing upland vegetation and soils data. The project manager is responsible for hiring the crew and ensuring that field crew members are appropriately trained. The project manager will serve as the point of contact concerning data content and will work to establish partnerships as appropriate. |
| Data Manager | The data manager is responsible for the information and data stewardship of the integrated upland monitoring project. The data manager designs databases, writes the data management plan and protocols, and works with the project manager and network staff to ensure that the datasets are fully documented, validated, certified and archived. The data manager, in collaboration with the project manager and the botanist, develops data-entry forms and other database features as part of quality assurance and automates report generation. The project manager and the data manager share responsibility for preparing data for analysis. The data manager populates NPS servicewide databases, maintains digital document libraries, and maintains the network website. |
| GIS Specialist | The GIS specialist is responsible for managing the spatial data and providing GIS support to the integrated upland monitoring project. Duties include managing, documenting and distributing spatial data resulting from the monitoring project, maintaining a library of relevant park spatial data, and working with the project manager and quantitative ecologist in developing the final sampling frames. |
| Quantitative Ecologist | The quantitative ecologist works with the program manager and project manager to develop spatial and temporal sampling designs for the project, develop sound statistical approaches to analyzing monitoring data, and provide analytic support to the project. |
| Botanist | The botanist is responsible for leading day-to-day field operations, and providing taxonomic expertise to the field crew. Duties include training the field crew, maintaining up-to-date species lists for all park units, creating keys and other plant identification aids, organizing field equipment, ensuring that data collection procedures and standards are maintained on a day-to-day basis, and assisting with the development of final sampling frames. The botanist works with the project manager to hire field crews, arrange field schedules and logistics, and purchase and maintain field equipment and supplies. |
| Integrated Upland Crew Members | The field crew will consist of from 3–5 members. They are responsible for field data collection, data entry, and data verification. Other duties include equipment maintenance and assisting with field logistics. |

Northern Arizona University (NAU). Overseen by the project manager and botanist, the NAU upland crew will consist of 3-5 crew members. At minimum, the field crew will consist of one research specialist (GS-7 equivalent) with expertise in botany or ecology who will act as a crew leader, and 2 research technicians (GS-5 equivalent) with a background in biology or ecology. Additional personnel will be hired as needed.

## 7.2 Crew qualifications and training

Competent, well-qualified, and detail-oriented observers are essential for the collection of credible, high-quality vegetation data. Crew members must be skilled in identifying plant species and accurately estimating species cover to reduce observer bias. Observer bias in the estimation of cover and the misidentification of species can affect the ability to detect trends in vegetation over time. Crew members should also have good organizational skills, memory retention and the ability to work methodically and consistently under difficult conditions. Crew members should be physically fit and experienced with backcountry hiking and camping.

Training is essential for developing skilled field observers. Prior to the field season, all crew members will read and become familiar with the SCPN integrated upland monitoring protocol, as well as the SCPN safety plan (in preparation). Crew members should also familiarize themselves with the flora of individual parks. Reference plant specimens and keys for difficult and uncommon species will be provided. Crew members will be trained in cover estimation at the start of the field season, and throughout the field season observers' cover estimates will be compared to ensure consistency. (*SOP #2* provides more detail.)

# 9 Literature cited

Akaike, H. 1973. Information theory and an extension of the maximum likelihood principle. In: Petran, B. N. and F. Csaki. (editors). International Symposium on Information Theory. 2nd ed. Akademiai Kiadi, Budapest, Hungary.

Anderson, M. J. 2001. A new method for non-parametric multivariate analysis of variance. Austral Ecology 26: 32–46.

Bayes, T. 1763. An essay towards solving a problem in the doctrine of chances. Philosophical Transactions, Royal Society of London. 53: 370–418.

Belnap, J., R. Prasse, and K. T. Harper. 2003. Influence of biological soil crusts on soil environments and vascular plants. Pages 281-300, in J. Belnap, and O. L. Lange (eds.) Biological Soil Crusts: Structure, Function, and Management (2nd ed.) Springer-Verlag, Berlin, Germany.

Bestelmeyer, B. T., J. E. Herrick, J. R. Brown, D. A. Trujillo, and K. M. Havstad. 2004. Land management in the American Southwest: A state and transition approach to ecosystem complexity. Environmental Management 34: 38–51.

Bray, J. R. and J. T. Curtis. 1957. An ordination of the upland forest communities of southern Wisconsin. Ecological Monographs 27: 325–349.

Breshears, D. D., N. S. Cobb, P. M. Rich, K. P. Price, C. D. Allen, R. G. Balice, W. H. Romme, J. H. Kastens, M. L. Floyd, J. Belnap, J. J. Anderson, O. B. Myers, C. W. Meyer. 2005. Regional vegetation die-off in response to global-change-type drought. Proceedings of the National Academy of Sciences, 102: 15144–15148.

Brotherson, J. D., W. E. Evenson, S. R. Rushforth, J. Fairchild, and J .R. Johansen. 1985. Spatial patterns of plant communities and differential weathering in Navajo National Monument, Arizona. The Great Basin Naturalist 45: 1–13.

Burnham, K. P. and D. R. Anderson. 2002. Model selection and multimodal inference: A practical information-theoretic approach. Springer, New York, New York.

Clark, J. S. 1991. Disturbance and population structure on the shifting mosaic landscape. Ecology 72: 1119–1137.

Clarke, K. R. 1993. Non-parametric multivariate analyses of changes in community structure. Australian Journal of Ecology 18: 117–143.

Clarke, K. R. and R. N. Gorley. 2006. PRIMER v6: User manual/Tutorial. PRIMER-E, Plymouth, UK.

Clarke, K. R. and R. H. Green. 1988. Statistical design and analysis for a 'biological effects' study. Marine Ecology Progress Series 46: 213–226.

Clarke, K. R. and R. M. Warwick. 1994. Change in marine communities: an approach to statistical analysis and interpretation. Bourne Press, Bournemouth, UK.

Collins, S. 2000. Disturbance frequency and community stability in native tallgrass prairie. The American Naturalist 155: 311–325.

Davenport, D. W., D. D. Breshears, B. P. Wilcox and C. D. Allen. 1998. Viewpoint: Sustainability of pinyon-juniper ecosystems —A unifying perspective on soil erosion thresholds. Journal of Range Management 51: 231–240.

de Gruchy, M. A., R. J. Reader, and D. W. Larson. 2005. Biomass, productivity, and dominance of alien plants: A multihabitat study in a national park. Ecology 86: 1259-1266.

Ellison, A. M. 1996. An introduction to Bayesian inference for ecological research and environmental decision-making. Ecological Applications 6: 1036–1046.

Elzinga, C. L., D. W. Salzer, and J. W. Willoughby. 1998. Measuring & monitoring plant populations, BLM Technical Reference 1730-1.

Faber-Langendoen, D., D. L. Tart, and Ralph H. Crawford. 2009. Contours of the revised U.S. National Vegetation Classification Standard. Bulletin of the Ecological Society of America 90: 87–93.

Frescino, T. S., T. C. Edwards, Jr., and G. G. Moisen. 2001. Modeling spatially explicit forest structural attributes using generalized additive models. Journal of Vegetation Science 12: 15–26.

Garman, S. 2008. CSDSim: A simulation approach for trend detection. On CD-ROM.

Gelman, A., J. B. Carlin, H .S. Stern, and D. B. Rubin. 2000. Bayesian data analysis. Chapman & Hall/CRC, New York, New York.

Glenn-Lewin, D. C., and E. van der Maarel. 1992. Patterns and processes of vegetation dynamics. Pages 11–59 in D. C. Glenn-Lewin, R. K. Peet and T. T. Beblen, eds. Plant Succession, Theory and Prediction. Chapman and Hall, London, United Kingdom.

Hall, Frederick C. 2001. Photo point monitoring handbook. Gen. Tech. Rep. PNW-GTR-526. Portland, OR: U.S. Department of Agriculture, Forest Service, Pacific Northwest Research Station. Available from www.fs.fed.us/pnw/pubs/gtr526/.

Havstad, K. M., J. E. Herrick, and W. H. Schlesinger. 2000. Desert rangelands, degradation and nutrients. Pages 77–87 in O. Arnalds and S. A. Archer eds., Rangeland desertification. Kluwer Academic Publishers, Dordrecht, The Netherlands.

Herrick, J. E., J. R. Brown, A. J. Tugel, P. L. Shaver, and K. M. Havstad. 2002. Applications of soil quality monitoring and management: Paradigms from rangeland ecology. Agronomy Journal 94: 3–11.

Herrick, J. E., and W. E. Whitford. 1995. Assessing the quality of rangeland soils: challenges and opportunities. Journal of Soil and Water Conservation 50: 237–242.

Herrick, J. E., J. W. Van Zee, K. M. Havstad, J. M. Burkett, and W. G. Whitford. 2005a. Monitoring manual for grassland, shrubland and savanna ecosystems. Volume I: Quick start. USDA-ARS Jornada Experimental Range, Las Cruces, New Mexico.

Herrick, J. E., J. W. Van Zee, K. M. Havstad, J. M. Burkett, and W. G. Whitford. 2005b. Monitoring manual for grassland, shrubland and savanna ecosystems. Volume II: Design, supplementary methods and interpretation. USDA-ARS Jornada Experimental Range, Las Cruces, New Mexico.

Jennings, S. B., N. D. Brown, and D. Sheil. 1999. Assessing forest canopies and understory illumination: canopy closure, canopy cover and other measures. Forestry 72(1): 59–73.

Karlen, D. L., M. J. Mausbach, J. W. Doran, R. G. Cline, R. F. Harris, and G. E. Schuman. 1997. Soil quality: A concept, definition and framework for evaluation. Soil Science Society of America Journal 61: 4–10.

Kincaid, T. M. 2011. Probability survey design and analysis functions: User guide for spsurvey, version 2.2. Available at http://www.epa.gov/nheerl/arm/analysispages/software.htm.

Larsen, D. P., P. R. Kaufmann, T. M. Kincaid, and N. S. Urquhart. 2004. Detecting persistent change in the habitat of salmon-bearing streams in the Pacific Northwest. Canadian Journal of Fisheries and Aquatic Sciences 61: 283–291.

Larsen, D. P., N. S. Urquhart, and D. L. Kugler. 1995. Regional scale trend monitoring of indicators of trophic conditions of lakes. Water Resources Bulletin 31: 117–140.

Lesica, P. and B. M. Steele. 1996. A method for monitoring long-term population trends: An example using rare arctic-alpine plants. Ecological Applications 6: 879–887.

Miller, M. E. 2005. The structure and functioning of dryland ecosystems – conceptual models to inform long-term ecological monitoring. Scientific Investigations Report 2005-5197. U. S. Geological Survey, Moab, Utah.

Miller, M. E., D. Witwicki, and R. Mann. 2006. Field-based evaluations of sampling methods for long-term monitoring of upland ecosystems on the Colorado Plateau–2005 Annual Report. USGS, Flagstaff, Arizona.

Mills, E. L., J. H. Leach, J. T. Carlton, and C. L. Secor. 1993. Exotic species in the Great Lakes: A history of biotic crisis and anthropogenic introductions. Journal of Great Lakes Research 19: 1–54.

Mittelbach, G. G., C. F. Steiner, S. M. Scheiner, K. L. Gross, H. L. Reynolds, R. B. Waide, M. R. Willig, S. I. Dodson, and L. Gough. 2001. What is the observed relationship between species richness and productivity? Ecology 82: 2381–2396.

Motzkin, G., P. Wilson, D. R. Foster, and A. Allen. 1999. Vegetation patterns in heterogeneous landscapes: The importance of history and environment. Journal of Vegetation Science 10: 903–920.

NatureServe. 2003. International Ecological Classification Standard: International Vegetation Classification. Natural Heritage Central Databases, NatureServe, Arlington, Virginia.

NatureServe Ecology. 2012. Terrestrial ecological systems and land cover of the conterminous United States. Version 2.8. NatureServe. Arlington VA USA. Digital map.

Noon, B. R. 2003. Conceptual issues in monitoring ecological resources. Pages 27-72 in Monitoring Ecosystems: Interdisciplinary Approaches for Evaluating Ecoregional Initiatives. D.E . Busch and J. C. Trexler (eds.). Island Press, Washington, D.C.

Norfleet, M. L., C. A. Ditzler, W. E. Puckett, R. B.Grossman, and J. N. Shaw. 2003. Soil quality and its relationship to pedology. Soil Science 168: 149–155.

Norton, J. B., J. A. Sandor, and C. S. White. 2003. Hillslope soils and organic matter dynamics within a native American agroecosystem on the Colorado Plateau. Soil Science Society of America Journal 67: 225–234.

Peet, R. K. 1992. Community structure and ecosystem function. Pages 103–151 in D. C. Glenn-Lewin, R. K. Peet and T. T. Beblen, eds. Plant succession, Theory and Prediction. Chapman and Hall, London, United Kingdom.

Peet, R. K., T. R. Wentworth and P. S. White. 1998. A flexible, multipurpose method for recording vegetation composition and structure. Castanea 63(3): 262– 274.

Philippi, T. E., P. M. Dixon, and B.E. Taylor. 1998. Detecting trends in species composition. Ecological Applications 8: 300–308.

Pickett, S. T. A. and M.L. Cadenasso. 2005. Vegetation succession. Pages 178–198, in E. van der Maarel (ed.) Vegetation Ecology. Blackwell, New York.

Raunkier, C. 1934. The life forms of plants and statistical plant geography. Clarendon Press, Oxford, United Kingdom.

Rodriguez, C., E. Leoni, F. Lezama, and A. Altesor. 2003. Temporal trends in species composition and plant traits in natural grasslands of Uruguay. Journal of Vegetation Science 14: 433– 440.

Schade, J. D., R. Sponseller, S. L. Collins, and A. Stiles. 2003. The influence of Prosopis canopies on understory vegetation: Effects of landscape position. Journal of Vegetation Science 14: 743–750.

Schoeneberger, P. J., D. A. Wysocki, E. C. Benham, and W. D. Broderson, eds. 2002. Field book for describing and sampling soils, Version 2.0. Natural Resources Conservation Service, National Soil Survey Center, Lincoln, Nebraska.

Seager, R., M. Ting, I. Held, Y. Kushnir, J. Lu, G. Vecchi, H. Huang, N. Harnik, A. Leetmaa, N. Lau, C. Li, J. Velez, and N. Naik. 2007. Model projections of an imminent transition to a more arid climate in southwestern North America. Science 316: 1181–1184.

Sims, M., S. Wanless, M. P. Harris, P. I. Mitchell, and D. A. Elston. 2006. Evaluating the power of monitoring plot designs for detecting long-term trends in the numbers of common guillemots. Journal of Applied Ecology 43: 537–546.

Society for Range Management Task Group on Unity in Concepts and Terminology. 1995. New concepts for assessment of rangeland condition. Journal of Range Management 48: 271–282.

Stevens, D. L. and A. R. Olsen. 2004. Spatially balanced sampling of natural resources. Journal of the American Statistical Association 99: 262-278.

Tancreto, N. J., and M. N. Hendrie. 2006. Supplement V: Data management plan for the Southern Colorado Plateau Network. In Thomas, L.P., M.N. Hendrie (editor), C.L. Lauver, S.A. Monroe, N.J. Tancreto, S.L. Garman, and M.E. Miller. 2006. Vital Signs Monitoring Plan for the Southern Colorado Plateau Network. Natural Resource Report NPS/SCPN/NRR-2006/002. National Park Service, Fort Collins, Colorado, USA.

ter Braak, C. J. F. 1987. The analysis of vegetation-environment relationships by canonical correspondence analysis. Vegetation 69: 69–77.

Tessler, S., and J. Gregson. 1997. Draft data management protocol. National Park Service I&M Program. Available from http://www1.nrintra.nps.gov/im/dmproto/joe40001.htm. (accessed 9 August 2006).

Thomas, L. P., M. N. Hendrie (editor), C. L. Lauver, S. A. Monroe, N. J. Tancreto, S. L. Garman, and M. E. Miller. 2006. Vital signs monitoring plan for the Southern Colorado Plateau Network. Natural Resource Report NPS/SCPN/NRR-2006/002. National Park Service, Fort Collins, Colorado.

Urquhart, N. S. and T. M. Kincaid. 1999. Designs for detecting trend from repeated surveys of ecological resources. Journal of Agricultural, Biological, and Environmental Statistics 4: 404-414.

Urquhart, N. S., S. G. Paulsen, and D. P. Larsen. 1998. Monitoring for policy-relevant regional trends over time. Ecological Applications 8: 246-257.

U.S. Department of Agriculture. Natural Resources Conservation Service. 2003. National range and pasture handbook. U.S. Department of Agriculture, Washington, D.C.

U.S. Department of the Interior. National Park Service. 2003. Fire monitoring handbook. Fire Management Program Center, Boise Idaho.

van der Maarel, E. 2005. Vegetation ecology –an overview. Pages 1-51 in van der Maarel, E. (ed.) Vegetation ecology.Blackwell, Oxford, United Kingdom.

Vankat, J. L. 2006. Montane and subalpine terrestrial ecosystems of the Southern Colorado Plateau—Literature review and conceptual models. Southern Colorado Plateau Network Vital Signs Monitoring Plan Montane Ecosystem Model Supplement, Flagstaff, Arizona.

Wade, P. R. 2000. Bayesian methods in conservation biology. Conservation Biology 14: 1308–1316.

West, N. E., and Young, J. A. 2000. Intermountain valley sand lower mountain slopes. Pages 256–284 in M. G. Barbour and W. D. Billings, editors. North American Terrestrial Vegetation. Cambridge University Press, Cambridge, United Kingdom.

# Standard Operating Procedures

The 14 standard operating procedures (SOPs) included here provide details on all activities necessary to conduct integrated upland monitoring for the Southern Colorado Plateau Network of the National Park Service.

## Contents

# Standard Operating Procedure #1: Preparations for the Field Season and Equipment Needed

## Version 1.00

## Revision History Log

| Previous version number | Revision date | Author | Changes made | Section and paragraph | Reason | Approved by | New version number |
|---|---|---|---|---|---|---|---|
| | | | | | | | |
| | | | | | | | |
| | | | | | | | |
| | | | | | | | |
| | | | | | | | |
| | | | | | | | |
| | | | | | | | |
| | | | | | | | |

Only changes in this specific SOP will be logged here. Version numbers increase incrementally by hundredths (e.g., version 1.01, version 1.02) for minor changes. Major revisions should be designated with the next whole number (e.g., version 2.0, 3.0, 4.0). Record the previous version number, date of revision, author of the revision; identify paragraphs and pages where changes are made, who approved the revision, and the reason for making the changes along with the new version number.

This standard operating procedure (SOP) describes pre-season procedures for the SCPN integrated upland monitoring project. The procedures described here are primarily the responsibility of the project manager and botanist. Included in this SOP are descriptions of general preparations, staffing, field season scheduling considerations, permitting, and a list of necessary supplies and equipment for sampling. A complete yearly project task list is provided in Appendix B. The procedures described here should begin no later than 4 months prior to the field season.

## General preparations and review

1. Review monitoring narrative and all SOPs. The project leader and botanist should be thoroughly familiar with the objectives described in the SCPN integrated upland monitoring protocol and have a solid working knowledge of the conceptual models that summarize existing knowledge and hypotheses concerning the structure and functioning of upland ecosystems of the Colorado Plateau. They should review the narrative and all SOP's prior to the field season to ensure that they can provide guidance to the crew on all sampling procedures.

2. Review year-end report from previous year. At the end of the field season, the project manager will write a report outlining issues and problems encountered during the field season, including suggestions for improving methods and/or efficiency. At the start of each new field season, this report will be reviewed and any proposed changes will be implemented as appropriate.

3. Initiate planning. The project manager should initiate discussions of specific sampling objectives, staffing, budget, and vehicle needs with SCPN staff. Goals for the upcoming season and a realistic timeline to meet the goals should be established.

4. Develop a field schedule. The field schedule will begin in April or May with lower elevation sampling sites. Sampling will continue through late October. Sites will be sampled based on peak phenology and logistical considerations. Sites will be sampled at approximately the same time every year. The schedule will be based on the revisit design, and should provide an initial plan for the entire season, but allow flexibility for unforeseen conditions. Reasons for mid-season schedule changes include permitting delays, monsoon timing, snowmelt timing, park closures, road closures, and backcountry road conditions. The number of sites being sampled and staffing constraints will also affect scheduling.

5. Begin hiring process. The project manager should begin the hiring process in January or February. See *SOP #2 Hiring and Training the Field Crew*.

6. Obtain permits. The project manager should obtain all necessary permits well in advance of the field season. These include Scientific Research and Collecting Permits, as well as backcountry hiking and camping permits (where necessary). Scientific Research and Collecting Permits should be obtained for each park using the National Park Service Research Permit and Reporting System website, http://science.nature.nps.gov/research. Research permits may require archaeological clearance of sampling sites, requiring preliminary, plot-screening visits with qualified park staff. Other permits should be obtained through park natural resource staff or rangers.

7. Arrange housing and transportation logistics. Contact appropriate park staff to arrange park housing or campground use. Discuss vehicle needs with program manager and administrative assistant. If additional vehicles are necessary, contact NAU transportation contacts or private rental companies to arrange for short-term and long-term rental.

8. Prepare supplies and equipment. Review inventory lists of field equipment from the previous fall. Check all equipment to ensure that it is in optimal working condition. Working with the administrative assistant, order necessary equipment including replacements for damaged gear. Check availability of field guides, datasheets, field notebooks, GPS units, maps, camping gear, and safety equipment. For a complete list of supplies and equipment, see Table 1-1 below.

9. Notify data manager, GIS specialist and program assistant of needs for the coming season. These needs include maps and GIS support, and revisit reports (see below). Initiate computer access for the field crew, and ensure the project workspace is ready for use. Initiate building key requests.

10. Prepare datasheets. Print datasheets for the field season and organize into packets for each ecological site to be sampled. Additional datasheets should be printed on waterproof paper.

11. Work with the data manager to prepare revisit reports. These reports should contain data collected on previous plot visits including GPS coordinates, directions, transect azimuth, witness tree data, rebar offsets, photopoint offsets, in-plot and off-plot disturbances, species occurrences by quadrat, tree measurements, tree maps and canopy closure offsets.

12. Prepare ecological site folders. The project manager and/or botanist should create field folders for each ecological site to be sampled during the field season, or update existing folders to make sure that all of the listed paperwork items are included (table 1-1). The following items are included in these folders: ecological site description, soil descriptions, maps, park and ecological site species lists, copy of the permit, list of the UTM coordinates of plots, revisit reports and any other pertinent park specific information.

**Table 1-1. Equipment list, providing the quantity of each item needed according to which procedures are used, as indicated by the associated SOP. Visits vary by which SOP applies, thus not all supplies are needed for every visit.**

| Item | All visits | SOP #3 | SOP #4 | SOP #5 | SOP #6 | SOP #7 | SOP #8 | Notes |
|---|---|---|---|---|---|---|---|---|
| Compass | | 1 | 1 | 1 | | | | SOP 5: per observer |
| Chaining pins | | | | 8-12 | | | | |
| 50 m tapes | | | | 3-5 | | 1-2 | | |
| Clinometer | | | 1 | | | | | optional |
| Sighting rod | | | 1 | | | | | |
| Ecological site folder | | | 1 | | | | | |
| 2 mm soil sieve | | | 1 | | | | | |
| 1 M HCL | | | 1 | | | | | |
| Distilled deionized water | | | 1 | | | | 1 | |
| Soil auger | | | 1 | | | | | |
| Soil tarp | | | 1 | | | | | |
| Rebar | | | 1 | 8 | | | | optional, include additional short rebar in ecological sites with shallow soils |
| 3 lb hammer | | | 1 | 1 | | | | |
| GPS unit (mapping grade) | | | 1 | 1 | | | | |
| Tree tags | | | | 12 | | X | | SOP 5: for witness trees in forest & woodland plots; SOP 7: sufficient for all trees in plot |
| Hammer | | | | 1 | | 1 | | for witness trees in forest & woodland plots |
| 3" nails | | | | 12 | | X | | SOP 5: for witness trees in forest & woodland plots; SOP 7: sufficient for all trees in plot |
| Rebar caps | | | | 7 | | | | pre-stamped |
| Rebar cap pad | | | | 1 | | | | |
| Camera | | | | 1 | | | | |
| Monopod | | | | 1 | | | | |
| Drill with ½-inch bit | | | | 1 | | | | optional, requires preapproval from park |
| 1 m² quadrat frame | | | | | 1-2 | | | depending on crew size |
| 10 m² quadrat frame | | | | | 1-2 | | | depending on crew size |
| Cover class guide squares | | | | | 1 | | | per observer |
| 30 cm ruler | | | | | 1 | | | per observer |
| Plant press | | | | | 1 | | | with ample supplies for pressing plants |
| Hand lens | | | | | 1 | | | per observer |
| Zippered plastic bags | | | | | 1 | | | per observer |
| Unknown species book | | | | | 1 | | | for unknown species |

# Table 1-1. (continued)

| Item | All visits | SOP #3 | SOP #4 | SOP #5 | SOP #6 | SOP #7 | SOP #8 | Notes |
|---|---|---|---|---|---|---|---|---|
| Park/ecological site species list (in ecological site folder) | | | | | | | | per observer |
| Diameter tape | | | | 1 | | 1 | | |
| Meter stick | | | | 1 | | 1 | | |
| Apron | | | | | | 1 | | for forest plots |
| Calipers | | | | | | 1 | | optional for forest plots |
| Convex spherical densiometer | | | | | | 1 | | |
| Rangefinders | | | | | 1 | 1 | | |
| Soil stability kit | | | | | | | 1 | |
| Stopwatch | | | | | | | 1 | |
| Random number table | | | | | | | 1 | |
| Clipboards | X | | | | | | | |
| Pencils, erasers, extra lead | X | | | | | | | |
| Permanent markers | X | | | | | | | |
| Datasheets | X | | | | | | | including *waterproof* versions |
| Copy of SOPs | X | | | | | | | |
| Flagging, pin flags | X | | | | | | | |
| Maps | X | | | | | | | showing roads and trail access, plot locations |
| GPS (for navigation) | X | | | | | | | with background maps, plot coordinates |
| Revisit report | X | | | | | | | only for revisits |
| Floras | | | | | X | | | as applicable |
| Extra batteries | X | | | | | | | |
| First aid kit | X | | | | | | | |
| Satellite phone | X | | | | | | | or other back up communication device |
| Emergency contact list | X | | | | | | | |
| Park contact list | X | | | | | | | |
| Rain gear | X | | | | | | | personal gear |
| Sunhat | X | | | | | | | personal gear |
| Drinking water | X | | | | | | | personal gear |
| Snacks | X | | | | | | | personal gear |
| Sunscreen | X | | | | | | | personal gear |
| Laser pointer (optional) | | | | | | 1 | | |
| Multi-tool | X | | | | | | | personal gear |

# Standard Operating Procedure #2: Hiring and Training the Field Crew

**Version 1.00**

**Revision History Log**

| Previous version number | Revision date | Author | Changes made | Section and paragraph | Reason | Approved by | New version number |
|---|---|---|---|---|---|---|---|
| | | | | | | | |
| | | | | | | | |
| | | | | | | | |
| | | | | | | | |
| | | | | | | | |
| | | | | | | | |
| | | | | | | | |
| | | | | | | | |

Only changes in this specific SOP will be logged here. Version numbers increase incrementally by hundredths (e.g., version 1.01, version 1.02) for minor changes. Major revisions should be designated with the next whole number (e.g., version 2.0, 3.0, 4.0). Record the previous version number, date of revision, author of the revision; identify paragraphs and pages where changes are made, who approved the revision, and the reason for making the changes along with the new version number.

This standard operating procedure (SOP) describes the steps for hiring and training seasonal field personnel to collect data for the SCPN integrated upland monitoring project. Hiring an experienced and qualified field crew is a critical component of collecting accurate, high-quality data. Once hired, the crew must be properly trained in monitoring protocols and plant identification.

## 1 Hiring the field crew

The SCPN integrated upland field crew is overseen by the SCPN project manager and botanist, and will consist of 3 to 5 individuals who are responsible for carrying out integrated upland monitoring across SCPN parks. Current operational plans call for accomplishing field monitoring through a cooperative agreement with Northern Arizona University (NAU). Due to the wealth of students, graduates, and NAU-affiliated staff with ecological and botanical experience and skills, this arrangement is conducive to hiring a well-qualified crew. The field crew will include at least one Research Specialist (GS-7 equivalent) with expertise in botany and ecology who will act as the crew leader, and 2 Research Technicians (GS-5 equivalent) with a background in biology or ecology. Other personnel will be hired as needed. See Table 2-1 for detailed descriptions of the integrated upland field crew positions. The NAU positions are temporary, up to 8 months long, with full time work not exceeding 19 weeks per NAU fiscal year (which ends June 30th). The process of recruiting and hiring field crews should begin in January.

## 2 Technical training

Field crew members must be familiar with all sampling methods related to collecting vegetation and soils data (outlined in *SOPs #4–#8*). During the training period, crew members are given sufficient time to read through the protocol. The project manager and/or botanist will conduct a pre-season training exercise so that crew members have an opportunity to practice all field procedures included in the protocol. Items covered in the training include plot establishment, procedures for quadrat sampling, cover class estimation, and measurement of trees, basal gaps, canopy closure and canopy cover. Because it is important that cover class estimations are consistent and accurate throughout the field season, one specific focus of the training will be practicing cover estimation to ensure that crew members

**Table 2-1. Integrated upland crew positions**

**Research Specialist**

Minimum qualifications:
- Bachelor's degree in biology, botany, ecology, soil science or environmental sciences AND 2 years of related research experience; OR
- Six years research or work experience in biology, botany, ecology, soil science or environmental sciences or related research experience, OR
- Any equivalent combination of experience, training, and/or education.

Desired qualifications:
- Two years of specialized experience as a Biological Technician with duties similar to those of this position.
- Experience with Microsoft Word, Excel, and Access software.
- Field experience working in remote backcountry settings and harsh field conditions.

Knowledge, skills and abilities:
- Knowledge in the following subject areas related to the Colorado Plateau: upland ecosystems with an emphasis on vegetation, flora and soils.
- Experience with methods, procedures, and techniques for collection of vegetation and ecological data.
- Ability to recognize and adapt to unusual conditions or data encountered in the normal course of work.
- Skills conducting field research in ecological, biological, or environmental topics.
- Extreme attention to detail, organization and record keeping.
- Skills using Microsoft Office software.
- Experience using GPS units. Skill in leading others in a field setting.
- Ability to work effectively with people from a variety of culturally diverse backgrounds.
- Ability to work in remote backcountry settings with little supervision.

**Research Technician**

Minimum qualifications:
- Bachelor's degree in biology, botany, ecology, soil science, or environmental sciences; OR
- Four years research or work experience in biology, botany, ecology, soil science or environmental sciences; OR,
- Any equivalent combination of experience, training, and/or education.

Desired qualifications:
- Two years of specialized experience as a Biological Technician with duties similar to those of this position.
- Experience with Microsoft Word, Excel, and Access software.
- Field experience working in remote backcountry settings and harsh field conditions.

Knowledge, skills and abilities:
- Familiarity with Colorado Plateau upland ecosystems, with emphasis on vegetation, flora and soils.
- Familiarity with the methods, procedures, and techniques of collection of vegetation and ecological data.
- Ability to recognize and adapt to unusual conditions or data encountered in the normal course of work.
- Skills conducting field research in ecological, biological, or environmental topics.
- Extreme attention to detail, organization, and record keeping.
- Experience with GPS units.
- Skills using Microsoft Office software.
- Ability to work in remote backcountry settings.
- Ability to work effectively with people from a variety of culturally diverse backgrounds.

have achieved a sufficient level of accuracy and precision. Crew members are encouraged to continue a dialogue concerning any aspect of the sampling methods throughout the field season, and to revisit the protocol as necessary.

An important component of pre-season training is familiarizing crew members with the plant species occurring in SCPN parks. Prior to the field season, crew members will review park species lists, regional field guides, websites, floras, and the SCPN working herbarium to improve their floristic knowledge. Once field work is underway, the SCPN botanist will provide oversight and ongoing training in field identification skills. Crew members should ask for identification assistance whenever necessary.

SCPN field crews should be familiar with the rules, regulations and guidelines of SCPN, as well as individual park units. The SCPN safety plan (in preparation) should be reviewed by each crew member and a copy will be provided in every vehicle. Crew members will be briefed on maintaining good working relationships with park staff, adhering to permit requirements, backcountry hiking and camping guidelines, check-in requirements, and emergency procedures for each park where they will be working.

Field work in SCPN parks often occurs in remote locations and can be extremely physically demanding. All field crew members should be prepared for difficult field conditions. Field work also requires physical capacity for backpacking to remote field sites and long days of hiking in rugged, steep terrain. Field crews may remain in the field for long periods of time, experiencing extreme and highly variable weather. The remote nature of this work requires the ability to function as a member of a crew and to independently exercise good judgment in difficult situations. Crew members should have prior experience working and camping in backcountry situations. Competency in Wilderness First Aid and CPR is recommended, and it is required that at least one person on each crew will have completed basic first aid and CPR training.

# Standard Operating Procedure #3: Navigation to the Plot and Recording its Location

## Version 1.00

### Revision History Log

| Previous version number | Revision date | Author | Changes made | Section and paragraph | Reason | Approved by | New version number |
|---|---|---|---|---|---|---|---|
| | | | | | | | |
| | | | | | | | |
| | | | | | | | |
| | | | | | | | |
| | | | | | | | |
| | | | | | | | |
| | | | | | | | |
| | | | | | | | |

Only changes in this specific SOP will be logged here. Version numbers increase incrementally by hundredths (e.g., version 1.01, version 1.02) for minor changes. Major revisions should be designated with the next whole number (e.g., version 2.0, 3.0, 4.0). Record the previous version number, date of revision, author of the revision; identify paragraphs and pages where changes are made, who approved the revision, and the reason for making the changes along with the new version number.

This standard operating procedure (SOP) describes how to use the global position system (GPS) to navigate to, and collect data from, upland monitoring plots. This is generalized information not specific to a particular GPS unit or system. For specific GPS unit information, see Appendix D.

## 1 Pre-visit

Prior to a site visit, a shapefile is loaded into a minimum of 2 GPS units by the GIS specialist or an assistant. This file contains the centroid points and transect endpoints for all plots to be visited (for a site revisit), or a consecutive series of Generalized Random Tessellation Stratified (GRTS) points for a plot establishment visit. Available background files, such as topographical and ecological site maps, are added to the units as applicable. In addition, fine and coarse scale hard-copy maps are generated for field use. The project manager and the botanist are responsible for notifying the GIS specialist in advance about impending fieldwork to ensure there is sufficient time to complete these tasks.

## 2 Navigating to a plot centroid

Different users prefer different methods of navigating, and there are few set rules for this section. Crew members may use any GPS unit, a compass and maps, or written directions to get to within striking distance of a plot.

If this is a plot establishment visit, a mapping grade GPS unit should be used for the final navigation to the centroid point if possible. Once the location of the centroid is determined as accurately as possible, place the center rebar at the point indicated by the GPS, driving it in partially and marking it with a pin flag for added visibility. In some cases, the center rebar may be already installed. The final point may not be exactly placed due to GPS error; however, a small displacement is acceptable because these errors are assumed to be random and therefore unbiased with respect to the sampling frame.

If this is a revisit, use the GPS to locate the plot centroid and mark it with a pin flag or flagging. Use either the GPS, witness trees or measuring and pacing along the known transect azimuth to locate all transect endpoints and mark these with pin flags or flagging tape.

## 3 Recording exact plot location during plot establishment

Once the plot centroid has been located, set the mapping grade GPS unit at the centroid and allow it to acquire satellites. When the unit is ready, collect a point using the proper method for that specific type of GPS unit. Label the point using the convention [<plot ID><transect point>] (e.g., L05BC) in the proper park and ecological site file. Record points at the plot centroid and at all transect endpoints. If any of the rebars are offset, use the GPS to record the location of the rebar. When finished, double check to ensure that all 7 points have been recorded.

## 5 Downloading data

When the crew returns to the office, the data on the GPS must be downloaded and processed by the GIS specialist or an assistant.

# Standard Operating Procedure #4: Ecological Site Assessment

**Version 1.00**

**Revision History Log**

| Previous version number | Revision date | Author | Changes made | Section and paragraph | Reason | Approved by | New version number |
|---|---|---|---|---|---|---|---|
| | | | | | | | |
| | | | | | | | |
| | | | | | | | |
| | | | | | | | |
| | | | | | | | |
| | | | | | | | |
| | | | | | | | |
| | | | | | | | |

Only changes in this specific SOP will be logged here. Version numbers increase incrementally by hundredths (e.g., version 1.01, version 1.02) for minor changes. Major revisions should be designated with the next whole number (e.g., version 2.0, 3.0, 4.0). Record the previous version number, date of revision, author of the revision; identify paragraphs and pages where changes are made, who approved the revision, and the reason for making the changes along with the new version number.

This standard operating procedure (SOP) gives step-by-step instructions for describing physical and biotic characteristics of potential field sites for long-term ecological monitoring. These data are generally collected on a one-time basis, prior to plot establishment, but may be collected at infrequent intervals thereafter to determine if aspects of this assessment have changed over time. All or a portion of this SOP may be conducted on a visit prior to plot establishment. Equipment needs for this procedure are listed in *SOP #1*, Table 1-1.

This SOP is associated with the *Ecological Site Assessment Datasheet*, and is used to help determine whether the potential plot is located on the target ecological site, and whether it meets the acceptance criteria for sampling. The ecological site assessment also provides information on the edaphic and biological characteristics of the plot that may provide important information for interpreting monitoring data. The ecological site assessment is generally performed by the project manager or botanist to ensure consistency and quality control. This assessment should cover the 0.5 ha area (71 × 71 m) that the plot will occupy. The datasheet is divided into several sections: *Initial assessment*, *Topographic assessment*, *Vegetation assessment*, *Soil profile assessment* and *Ecological site assessment*. The datasheet is laid out such that all sections should be filled out before determining that a plot is accepted. If one section indicates a reason for rejecting the site, then the other sections do not have to be filled out. For example, it is not necessary to conduct the soil profile characterization if the slope indicates the wrong ecological site.

## 1 General plot information

Fill out the top of the *Ecological Site Assessment Datasheet* at the end of this SOP, following these guidelines:

- **Park code.** Use the 4-letter code for the park unit.
- **GRTS.** Initial site number assigned during random placement generation.
- **Plot ID.** A pre-assigned unique alphanumeric code number is provided for each plot. The letter designates the ecological site, and the number is assigned consecutively with plot establishment. This is filled out only if the plot is accepted. If plot establishment does not immediately follow the ecological site assessment, the Plot ID must be filled in at the time of plot establishment.

- Date. MM/DD/YYYY (e.g., 04/14/2008).
- Recorder. Write the first initial and last name of the person recording data.

## 2 Initial assessment

The initial assessment portion is designed to be filled out in situations where the decision to reject the plot is determined based on factors external to the Ecological Site determination. If the plot is rejected during archaeological screening, check the box marked **Reject plot—archaeological site**. If there is a major disturbance (such as a road or fuel treatment) that necessitates plot rejection, check the box marked **Reject plot—major disturbance** and briefly describe type and scale of disturbance in the **Description** section below (minor disturbances that do not result in plot rejection will be described on the *Site Disturbance Datasheet*; see *SOP #5*). Examples of acceptable levels of disturbance include cattle grazing at GLCA, low severity fire in mixed conifer forests, animal trails and burrows, and mechanical thinning in BAND; unacceptable levels of disturbance include high severity fire in mixed conifer forests, powerline access roads and foot trails. If, upon hiking to the plot, it is determined that access to the plot exceeds the 2-hour maximum or the plot is inaccessible, check the box marked **Reject plot—access** and provide details in the **Description** field below. If there is any other cause to reject the plot based on initial assessment that is not listed above, check the box marked **Reject—other** and explain the reason and rationale in the **Description** section.

If the plot is rejected during initial assessment, there is no need to fill out the rest of the datasheet, but the datasheet should be maintained as a record of plot rejection.

## 3 Topography assessment

### 3.1 Landform

Determine whether or not the site is on the expected landform for the ecological site of interest. Landforms commonly encountered on the Colorado Plateau include alluvial fans, cuestas, hillslopes, mesas, plateaus, sand sheets, and structural benches. Definitions of common landforms on the Colorado Plateau and a list of landscapes and landforms by geomorphic environment are listed in Appendix C. Additional landforms are described in the Natural Resources Conservation Service (NRCS) *Field Book for Describing and Sampling Soils* (Schoeneberger et al. 2002), and definitions are provided on the NRCS website, http://soils.usda.gov/technical/handbook/contents/part629glossary1.html. Write the appropriate landform on the datasheet.

### 3.2 Hillslope position

Select the hillslope position that describes the location of the site and circle it on the datasheet. Possible hillslope positions include summit, shoulder, backslope, footslope, and toeslope (see fig. 4-1). If the 0.5 ha plot occupies 2 or more hillslope positions, circle all that are applicable. Hillslope position may not be relevant in some cases, such as for mesa tops. In such cases, circle "N/A" on the datasheet.

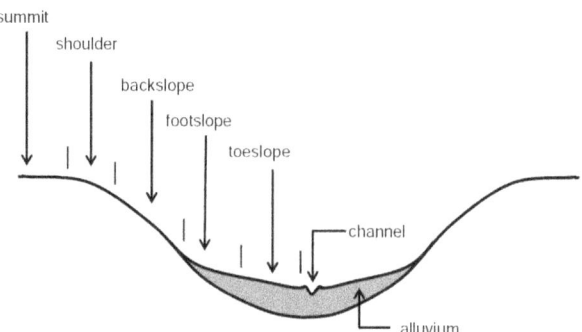

Figure 4-1. NRCS figure for determining hillslope position (adapted from Schoeneberger et al. 2002)

### 3.3 Slope complexity

This refers to the relative uniformity of the ground surface leading downslope and across the plot. Is the ground undulating or smooth? Figure 4-2 illustrates examples of simple versus complex slopes. Decide which best describes the site and circle the appropriate category on the datasheet. Circle "N/A" on the datasheet if there is no slope.

### 3.4 Slope shape

Determine the slope curvature (linear, concave, or convex) for down slope and across slope (fig. 4-3). Circle the appropriate categories on the datasheet. Circle "N/A" on the datasheet if there is no slope.

### 3.5 Percent slope and aspect

Slope and aspect measurements are taken from locations based on approximate positions of the 3 not-yet-installed

simple vs. complex

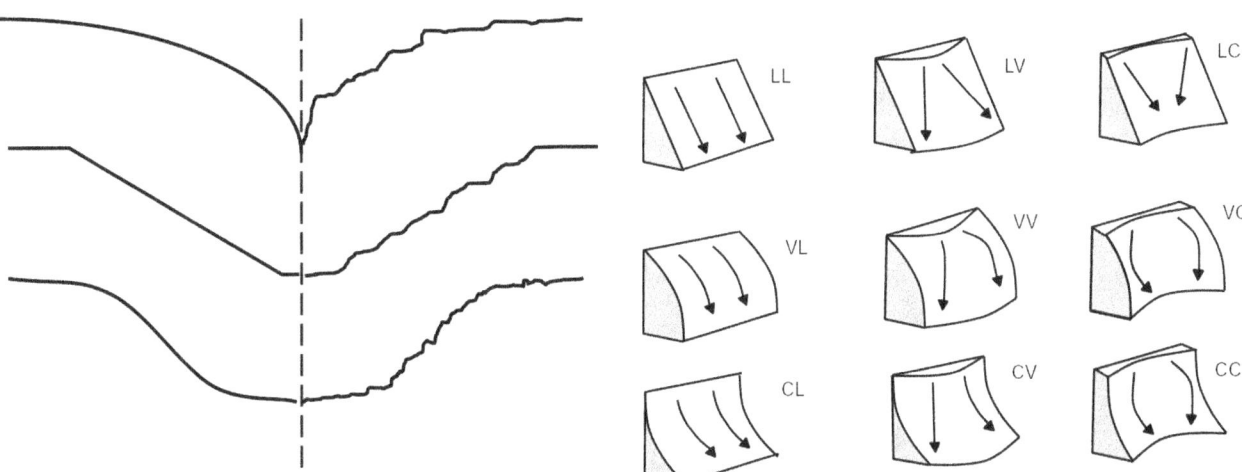

Figure 4-2. NRCS figure for determining hillslope complexity (adapted from Schoeneberger et al. 2002)

Figure 4-3. NRCS figure for determining slope shape (adapted from Schoeneberger et al. 2002). The first letter measures downslope, and the second letter measures across slope, where L=linear, V=convex, and C=concave.

sampling transects (Transects A, B, C are laid out parallel to each other and perpendicular to the slope, with A at the most upslope position). The crew imagines a transect with an azimuth approximately parallel to the slope contour and its midpoint at the plot centroid—this is the approximate B transect. Two crew members step 1–2 meters downslope from this envisioned transect at the centroid, then pace approximately 30 meters towards the transect start, walking parallel to the slope contour. At that point, the 2 crew members will be standing together, just outside of the approximate location of the start of the B transect.

Next, one crew member paces upslope approximately 30 meters to a location approximately 5 meters upslope from the approximate location of the start of Transect A. At the same time, the second crew member paces approximately 30 meters downslope to a location about 5 meters downslope from the approximate location of the start of Transect C. In some forests and woodlands, it may not be possible to see each other from such a distance. In these instances, the 2 crew members should maximize distance while still being visible to each other. When performing these measurements, the crew members should do their best not to trample areas to be sampled along the 3 transects. Figure 4-4 illustrates the transect layout for a plot, and the approximate locations of the 2 crew members, symbolized by X and Y in the figure.

Upslope and downslope crew members align themselves to be parallel to the direction of the slope. The upslope person measures percent slope with a clinometer by sighting to the

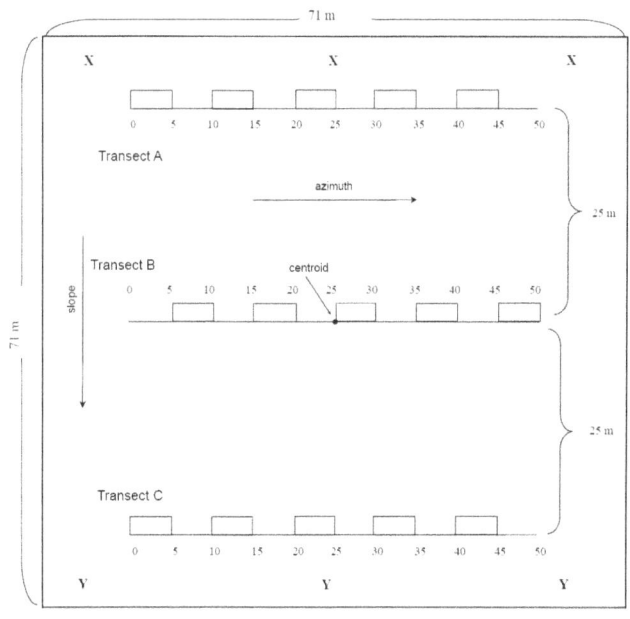

Figure 4-4. Plot layout diagram, showing locations for measuring slope and aspect (indicated by "X" and "Y")

person directly downslope. The upslope observer must predetermine where their eye-level falls on the downslope crew member, or use a sighting rod. The aspect observer measures the direction of the steepest portion of the slope from where they are standing. It is useful to visualize the direction water would flow through the plot. Aspect can be measured by the upslope or downslope crew member using a compass. If the downslope person measures aspect, they need to backsight with the compass or subtract 180 from their reading, as aspect is recorded facing downslope. Record **Percent slope** and **Aspect** measurements in their respective "S" (for Start) boxes . Two more readings will be undertaken in the same manner, with the 2 crew members pacing 30 m across slope to the approximate midpoint or center of the transect locations and entering their measurements in the "C" box (for Center), and then pacing an additional 30 m across the slope to the approximate finish and recording their measurements in the "F" box (for Finish). If a portion of the slope is substantially steeper than the overall slope, this portion should be measured separately and the slope should be noted in the **Comments** section. Compass readings are taken with no correction for declination. Declination will be corrected during data management. The aspect and slope are considered for the area within the plot. The slope and aspect of the larger landscape outside the plot should be ignored.

Calculate the **Mean** of the 3 values for each category and record. In cases where the aspect measurements straddle 360, add 360 to the small values before calculating the mean (i.e., 349, 350, and 6 should be calculated from 349, 360 and 366). Figure 4-5 shows plot layout and aspect measurement against a hypothetical contour map.

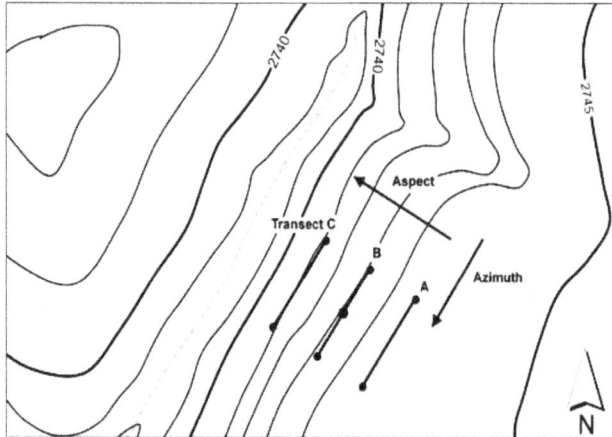

Figure 4-5. Example of a hypothetical plot layout on a contour map

### 3.5 Target match
Determining whether the site is suitable for monitoring is based on 2 criteria: whether the site is too steep for monitoring, and if the topography of the site matches the description of the ecological site.

Sites with steep slopes are not suitable for monitoring as human traffic on these sites causes soil disturbance and erosion. We use a threshold of 30% slope for forested sites, and 20% for all other sites. If the site exceeds this threshold, it will be rejected.

Ecological site descriptions include a topographic characterization that includes the landform, hillslope position, and range of slopes on which the ecological site occurs. Compare the data in the topographic assessment with the ecological site description. If they are reasonably close, then it is considered a target match, e.g., the site has a slope of 12%, and the ecological site description has a range of 2–10% slope. Large deviations from the ecological site description are not considered a target match, e.g., the site occurs on a backslope but the description says the site should occur on mesa tops.

If the data from topographic assessment does not reasonably match the topography of the ecological site description, or the any one of the 3 slope measurements exceed the 20% or 30% threshold, then circle "No" in **Target match**. Otherwise, circle "Yes."

## 4 Vegetation assessment
We characterize vegetation at the plot level to assess whether observed vegetation conforms reasonably well to the expected vegetation associated with the target ecological site. This will contribute to determining whether the plot is in the target ecological site and should be accepted for monitoring.

Additionally, through the NPS Inventory and Monitoring Program, vegetation maps are being completed for all park units with significant natural resources, using the U.S. National Vegetation Classification Standard (NVCS). By describing the vegetation of each plot using NVCS, we can link plot level vegetation data to each park unit's current vegetation map.

## 4.1 Dominant physiognomic class

Physiognomy describes the external or overall appearance of the vegetation, and is the result of growth forms of the dominant plants, along with structural characteristics such as plant height, stratification and horizontal spacing. See Table 4-1 for definitions of the dominant types. Check the box in front of the dominant physiognomic class of the plot. If a second physiognomic class is co-dominant in the plot, note it in the comments section at the bottom of the *Vegetation assessment* block.

## 4.2 Upland cover by vegetation association

Record the **Vegetation association**(s) present in the plot, drawing from a list of plant associations taken from the most recent park vegetation map, if available (included in the ecological site folder). Assign each association a **Cover class** based on the datasheet key drawn from Table 4-2. Note that these cover classes differ from those used in quadrat sampling in *SOP #6*. Note any discrepancies, or add additional associations in the **Comments** section at the bottom of the *Vegetation assessment* block of data.

## 4.3 Upland cover and dominant species by vegetation stratum

Record up to 3 **Dominant species** of tree (where applicable) using the 6-letter species code and assign a **Cover class** for the tree stratum using the vegetation characterization cover class codes provided on the datasheet. Do the same for the shrub layer and the herbaceous understory layer. Record any relevant **Comments**.

**Table 4-1. Dominant physiognomic types**

| Physiognomic class | Canopy cover and type | Canopy height |
|---|---|---|
| Forest | 60–100% tree | >5 m |
| Woodland | 25 to <60% tree | >5 m |
| Sparse Woodland | 10 to <25% tree | >5 m |
| Shrubland | 25–100% shrub | 0.5–5 m |
| Sparse Shrubland | 10 to <25% shrub | 0.5–5 m |
| Dwarf Shrubland | 25–100% shrub | <0.5 m |
| Sparse Dwarf Shrubland | 10 to <25% shrub | <0.5 m |
| Herbaceous | 10–100% herbaceous | <0.5 m |
| Sparsely Vegetated | <10% vascular vegetation | <0.5 m |

**Table 4-2. Canopy cover classes**

| Cover class | Percent canopy cover |
|---|---|
| 1 | <1% |
| 2 | 1 to <5% |
| 3 | 5 to <10% |
| 4 | 10 to <25% |
| 5 | 25 to <50% |
| 6 | 50 to <75% |
| 7 | 75–100% |

## 4.4 Target match

Consider any differences you might see between observed vegetation and expected vegetation for that ecological site. Examine *Potential vegetation* and *Dynamics* columns in the ecological site descriptions, if available. Look specifically for evidence of vegetation listed as *Potential vegetation* for the ecological site. Familiarize yourself with the range of variation in the plant community due to natural and/or anthropogenic disturbances. Soil, landscape, and climate characteristics are primary determinants of ecological sites. Existing vegetation should be used with great caution as a clue in determining whether you are on the target ecological site. Observed vegetation may differ from expected vegetation due to effects of land use, natural disturbances such as fire, or climate. In answering this question, it is important to consider the full range of potential vegetation dynamics on a site—including natural post-disturbance successional processes, typical fluctuations in relation to climate, and possible degradational changes associated with invasive species, overgrazing, and/or major soil loss or redistribution. If observed vegetation is within the range of potential dynamics (natural and anthropogenic) for this ecological site, then circle "Yes" for vegetation **Target match** on the datasheet. However, if observed vegetation appears to be beyond the realm of potential dynamics, circle "No".

NOTE: in some instances, the final sampling frames have been modified to exclude early successional states of vegetation based on park management priorities. For example, severely burned areas are excluded from final sampling frames in mixed conifer forests at GRCA and from final sampling frames in the pinyon-juniper woodlands at MEVE.

Use the following examples to help you decide departures within the range of potential dynamics:

- In reference condition, potential vegetation for the target ecological site is co-dominated by sagebrush and native perennial grasses, but observed vegetation is dominated by invasive annuals (e.g., cheatgrass), or juniper with evidence of past sagebrush presence.

- Potential vegetation for the target ecological site is a mixed conifer forest but the observed vegetation is an aspen forest. The aspen forest may be a post-fire successional stage.

Use the following examples to help you decide departures beyond the range of potential dynamics:

- Potential vegetation for the target ecological site is desert grassland dominated by black grama, and observed vegetation is a montane shrubland dominated by Gambel oak and serviceberry.
- Potential vegetation for the target ecological site is galleta grassland, however it lies near an archaeological site and seems to be anthropogenically influenced. Dominant vegetation includes wolfberry and fourwing saltbush.

## 5 Soil profile assessment

The soil profile data should be collected in a location that represents the predominant soil-geomorphic setting associated with the plot, but that is away from the transects. The default location is approximately 2 meters downslope from the centroid so as to avoid impacts to on-site dynamics near the transects, however it should be moved to avoid areas with disturbed soil, areas near trees and small areas of atypical shallow soils or exposed bedrock. Using the 3" soil auger, auger 10 cm increments, placing each increment on the soil tarp, until you reach bedrock or root restricting layers, e.g., a calcic hardpan, or until you reach a maximum depth of 1 meter. Characterize each 10 cm increment of the profile for texture, soil color, quantity and size of rock fragments, and degree of effervescence. Record this information on the datasheet for each soil depth increment.

In certain instances, soil profile characterization will not be conducted (e.g., in parks that do not allow soil disturbance). In these instances, only collect soil information from the top 2 centimeters of the soil surface.

### 5.1 Soil texture

Soil texture refers to the particle size distribution of the fine earth fraction of soil (sand, silt, and clay particles <2 mm in diameter). Sieve each 10 cm increment of soil through a 2 mm soil sieve. Place rock fragments in a pile adjacent to the sieved soil to help estimate percentage rock particles (see below). Collect a small amount of sieved soil in your hand and add water slowly. Knead the water and soil in your hand and use the key in Figure 4-6 to determine the soil texture. The texture triangle (fig. 4-7) is also helpful for understanding the relationship between different soil particle sizes in determining soil texture. Write the soil **Texture** for each depth increment on the datasheet.

If sand is a major part of the soil texture (e.g., loamy sand or sandy loam), include "fine" or "coarse" in the soil texture if appropriate (medium is not indicated, but implied through lack of an indicator). "Fine" is used when the predominant size class of sand is <0.25 mm, and "coarse" is used when the predominant size class of sand is >0.5 mm (see fig. 4-8).

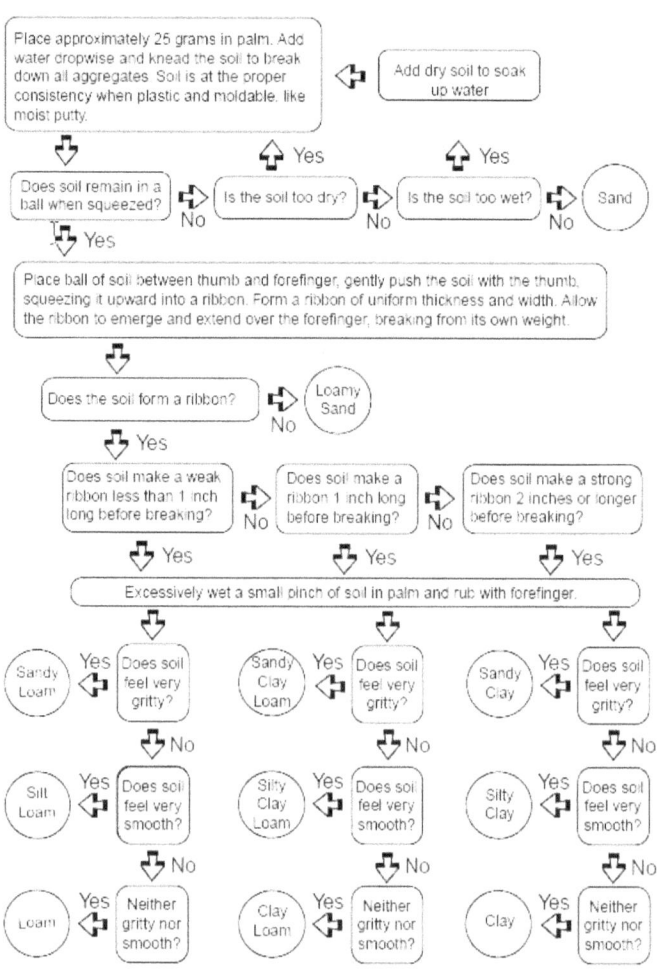

Figure 4-6. Soil texture key. Begin in the top left corner and answer the yes/no questions to determine soil texture. (Source: NRCS, available from http://soils.usda.gov/education/resources/lessons/texture/)

## 5.2 Color

Briefly describe the color of the soil. This is most important for describing changes in the color within the soil profile. Often described by using general terms, such as dark brown, yellowish brown, etc., soil colors are also described more technically by using Munsell soil color charts. These charts separate color into 3 components: hue (relation to red, yellow and blue), value (lightness or darkness) and chroma (paleness or strength). It is not necessary to use a Munsell chart to describe soil color, but you should limit soil colors to gray, black, white, red, brown, or yellow, and limit modifying terms to light or dark and reddish, yellowish, bluish or greyish. Record the **Color** for each depth increment on the datasheet.

## 5.3 Rock fragment modifiers

Soil types are further described by rock fragment quantity and size (e.g., gravelly sandy loam), which are recorded in the **Rock fragments** column on the datasheet.

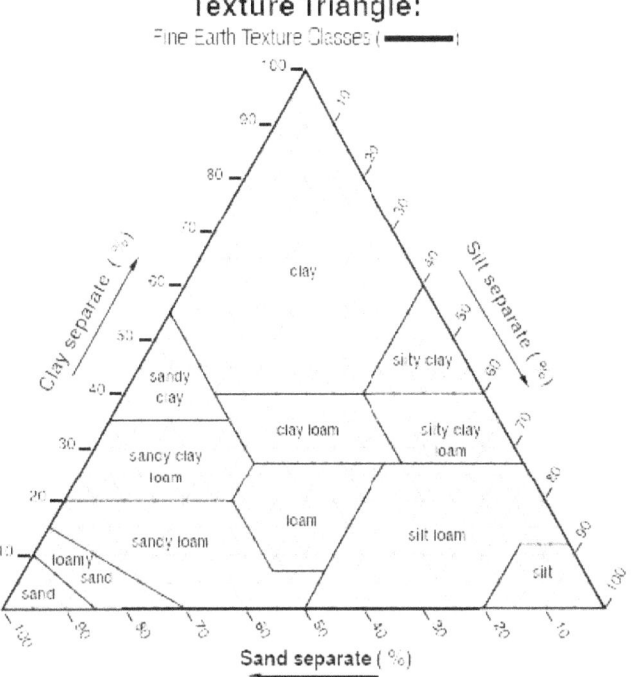

**Texture Triangle:**
Fine Earth Texture Classes

Figure 4-7. Soil texture triangle (based on Schoeneberger et al. 2002)

| fine earth | | | | | rock fragments | | | |
|---|---|---|---|---|---|---|---|---|
| clay | silt | sand | | | gravel | | cobbles | stones, boulders |
| | | fine | medium | coarse | fine | coarse | | |

0.0002 mm   0.002 mm    0.05 mm       0.25 mm      0.5 mm     2 mm       2 cm        7.5 cm        25 cm

Figure 4-8. Sizes of soil particles and rock fragments (adapted from Schoeneberger et al. 2002)

First, compare the amount of rock fragments with the amount of sieved soil on the tarp to determine the percent of rock fragments by volume. Less than 15% rock fragments by volume is not described; in this case write "N/A" in the space for rock fragments. If there is more than 15% rock fragments by volume, use the following categories to determine the appropriate rock fragment size, and quantity if appropriate:

*Size.* Use the rock fragment size chart in Figure 4-8 to determine the largest dominant fragment. The largest dominant fragment is the largest rock fragment class present, unless a smaller size class is present in substantial quantity. A smaller fragment size class must exceed 2 times the volume of a larger fragment before it is considered dominant.

*Rock quantity adjective.* Determine the approximate rock fragment content percent by volume for the largest dominant type of fragment, and refer to Table 4-3 for the appropriate rock fragment quantity adjective. Rock fragments 15 to <35% by volume require only fragment size (e.g., gravelly loam). Use the quantity adjectives "very" and "extremely" to describe soils with 35 to <60% and 60 to <90% rock fragments respectively (e.g., very gravelly loam and extremely gravelly loam). If there is 90% or more of rock fragment, then soil is described by only the rock fragment size (e.g., gravel) and not by the fine earth. Record quantity and size modifiers in the **Rock fragments** column on the datasheet for each depth increment.

**Table 4-3. NRCS texture modifiers to describe the amount of rock fragments in soil (adapted from Schoeneberger et al. 2002)**

| Fragment content % by volume | Rock fragment modifier usage | Example |
|---|---|---|
| <15 | no texture adjective is used—noun only | loam |
| 15 to <35 | use adjective for appropriate size | gravelly loam |
| 35 to <60 | use "very" with an appropriate size adjective | very gravelly |
| 60 to <90 | use "extremely" with an appropriate size adjective | extremely gravelly |
| ≥90 | use appropriate noun for the dominant size class in lieu of texture of fine earth component | gravel |

## 5.4 Effervescence

The degree of effervescence relates to the quantity and surface area of carbonate compounds in the soil. Apply a few drops of 1 M HCl to the fine soil fraction, and use Table 4-4 to determine the effervescence class. More bubbles indicate higher amounts of carbonate compounds in the soil. Record the **Effervescence** class for each depth increment on the datasheet.

## 5.5 Soil depth

Measure or estimate the depth to bedrock or a root restricting layer. Use Table 4-5 to determine the depth class, and circle your choice on the datasheet. In instances where you have not dug a soil profile, you will have to do your best to assign a soil depth class based on your observations of bedrock exposures or naturally occurring profile exposures in the area. Circle the appropriate **Soil depth** value on the datasheet.

## 5.6 Probable soil component and target match

Use the information on the datasheet, ecological site description, and soil series descriptions to determine the probable soil component. Record the **Probable soil component** on the datasheet (or write "unknown" if the soil component cannot be determined), then consider whether this matches the target soil component(s).

**Table 4-4. Effervescence classes determined by dropping 1 M HCl on the fine soil fraction (adapted from Schoeneberger et al. 2002)**

| Effervescence class | Criteria |
|---|---|
| Noneffervescent | no bubbles form |
| Very slightly effervescent | few bubbles form |
| Slightly effervescent | numerous bubbles form |
| Strongly effervescent | bubbles form low foam |
| Violently effervescent | bubbles form a noisy thick foam |

**Table 4-5. Depth to root restricting layer in centimeters (cm) for depth classes**

| Depth class | Centimeters |
|---|---|
| Very shallow | <25 |
| Shallow | 25 to <50 |
| Moderately deep | 50 to <100 |
| Deep | 100 to <150 |
| Very deep | ≥150 |

To determine if the soil is a target match, compare the information you collected on the datasheet with the characteristics of the soil components of the target ecological site in the ecological site description. Do the observed soil and landscape characteristics reasonably match those associated with the target soil component and ecological site? Large departures in ecologically significant characteristics, such as depth and texture, or presence of an argillic or calcic horizon, are grounds for answering "No" to this question. Examples of large departures include a target soil that is deep and the observed soil is very shallow or shallow; or a target soil is a sandy loam while the observed soil is a gravelly clay loam. Examples of relatively minor departures include a target soil that is shallow while the observed soil is very shallow; and a target soil that is a gravelly clay loam while the observed soil is a very gravelly sandy clay loam.

If you suspect several soil components to be present on the plot, but the most dominant component matches the target component, indicate a positive match by circling "Yes" for **Target match** and note the probable occurrence of other components in the **Comments** section. If the soil component does not match the target ecological site, or if non-target components are dominant, circle "No" and add narrative explaining your choice.

## 6 Ecological site determination and site selection

The responses to the above assessments for topography, vegetation and soil (sections 2 through 5) determine whether the site matches the target ecological site. Plots are rejected if they do not match the target ecological site (wrong slope, slope position, landform, soil, soil depth, or vegetation), or if >20% of the plot is contained by another ecological site or an impermeable obstruction or cliff. Plots are also rejected for other reasons addressed in the initial assessment: if the plot contains a disturbance, natural or human, that has the potential to substantially alter the vegetation structure, composition and/ or dynamics of the plot; if the hiking time to the plot exceeds 2 hours or is otherwise inaccessible; or for certain parks, is in proximity to an archaeological site.

If the site is accepted in each of these assessments—initial, topography, soils and vegetation—and at least 80% of the plot appears to have suitable soil and vegetation characteristics, then note that the plot is accepted on the datasheet by circling "Yes" for both the **Target match** and **Accept plot** fields. If the **Target match** in any of these individual assessments has the answer "No", then circle "No" for **Target match** and **Accept plots**, and remove the rebar.

Fill in the name of the **Primary ecological site** that you characterized and provide an estimate of the plot area (% **area**) comprised of this site type. For plots with more than one ecological site type, indicate the second-most common (**Other ecological site**) and the plot % **area**. Write "unknown" if you are unable to determine the ecological site from the information you have. Describe your rationale in the **Comments** section.

# Ecological Site Assessment Datasheet

Park code_____ GRTS: _____ Plot ID:_____ Date (MM/DD/YYYY):_____ Recorder:_____

## Initial assessment

| Reject plot--archeological site ☐ | Reject plot--major disturbance(s) ☐ | Reject plot--access ☐ | Reject—other ☐ |
|---|---|---|---|

Description:

## Topography assessment

Landform:

| Hillslope position (circle all that apply) | Summit | | Shoulder | Backslope | Footslope | Toeslope | N/A |
|---|---|---|---|---|---|---|---|
| Slope complexity | Simple | | Complex | NA | | | |
| Slope shape | Down slope: | Linear | | Concave | Convex | N/A | |
| | Across slope | Linear | | Concave | Convex | N/A | |
| Percent slope | S: | C: | | F: | Mean: | | |
| Aspect (°) | S: | C: | | F: | Mean: | | |
| Target match? | Yes | | No | | | | |

Comments:

## Vegetation assessment

### Dominant physiognomic class (check only one)

| Type | Canopy cover & type | Canopy height |
|---|---|---|
| Forest | 60–100% tree | >5 m |
| Woodland | 25 to <60% tree | >5 m |
| Sparse Woodland | 10 to <25% tree | >5 m |
| Shrubland | 25–100% shrub | 0.5–5 m |
| Sparse Shrubland | 10 to <25% shrub | 0.5–5 m |
| Dwarf Shrubland | 25–100% shrub | <0.5 m |
| Sparse Dwarf Shrubland | 10 to <25% shrub | <0.5 m |
| Herbaceous | 10–100% herbaceous | <0.5 m |
| Sparsely Vegetated | <10% vascular veg | <0.5 m |

### Upland cover by vegetation association (park specific from current vegetation map)

| Vegetation association: | Cover class: | Vegetation characterization cover classes | |
|---|---|---|---|
| | | 1 | <1% |
| | | 2 | 1 to <5% |

### Upland cover and dominant species by vegetation stratum

| Stratum | Dominant species | Cover class: | 3 | 5 to <10% |
|---|---|---|---|---|
| Tree | | | 4 | 10 to <25% |
| Shrub | | | 5 | 25 to <50% |
| Herbaceous | | | 6 | 50 to <75% |
| Target match? Yes    No | | | 7 | 75–100% |

Comments:

## Soil profile assessment

| Depth (cm) | Texture | Color | Rock fragments | Effervescence |
|---|---|---|---|---|
| 0–2 | | | | |
| 2–10 | | | | |
| 10–20 | | | | |
| 20–30 | | | | |
| 30–40 | | | | |
| 40–50 | | | | |
| 50–60 | | | | |
| 60–70 | | | | |
| 70–80 | | | | |
| 80–90 | | | | |
| 90–100 | | | | |

| Soil depth | Very shallow (<25 cm) | Shallow (25 to <50 cm) | Moderately deep (50 to <100 cm) | Deep to very deep (≥100 cm) |
|---|---|---|---|---|
| Probable soil component: | | | Target match?   Yes     No | |
| Comments: | | | | |

| Texture | Color | Rock fragments | Effervescence |
|---|---|---|---|
| If soil has sandy texture, add "fine" or "coarse" to description derived from the soil texture key (fig. 4-6 in SOP #4) | Brown Red Yellow Grey White Black | <15%="N/A" 15 to <35%="gravelly", "cobbly", "stony", 35 to <60%=add "very" 60 to <90%=add "extremely" | No bubbles="none" Few bubbles="very slight" Numerous bubbles="slight" Low foam="strong" Noisy thick foam="violent" |

## Ecological site determination and site selection

| Target match?   Yes     No | Accept plot?   Yes     No | |
|---|---|---|
| Primary ecological site: | | % area: |
| Other ecological site: | | % area: |
| Comments: | | |
| | | |
| | | |
| | | |
| | | |
| | | |
| | | |
| | | |
| | | |

# Standard Operating Procedure #5: Plot Establishment and Qualitative Assessments

## Version 1.00

### Revision History Log

| Previous version number | Revision date | Author | Changes made | Section and paragraph | Reason | Approved by | New version number |
|---|---|---|---|---|---|---|---|
|  |  |  |  |  |  |  |  |
|  |  |  |  |  |  |  |  |
|  |  |  |  |  |  |  |  |
|  |  |  |  |  |  |  |  |
|  |  |  |  |  |  |  |  |
|  |  |  |  |  |  |  |  |
|  |  |  |  |  |  |  |  |
|  |  |  |  |  |  |  |  |

Only changes in this specific SOP will be logged here. Version numbers increase incrementally by hundredths (e.g., version 1.01, version 1.02) for minor changes. Major revisions should be designated with the next whole number (e.g., version 2.0, 3.0, 4.0). Record the previous version number, date of revision, author of the revision; identify paragraphs and pages where changes are made, who approved the revision, and the reason for making the changes along with the new version number.

This standard operating procedure (SOP) provides instructions for establishing the integrated upland monitoring plot. It includes instructions on layout and marking the endpoints and midpoints of the 3 transects that comprise a permanent upland monitoring plot during the initial visit, as well as guidance for laying out transect tapes during revisits. It also includes procedures for the qualitative assessments of taking photopoints, evaluating site disturbance, and assessing burn severity. Equipment needs for this procedure are listed in *SOP #1*, Table 1-1. Four datasheets are associated with this SOP: *Plot Establishment Datasheet*, *Photopoint Datasheet*, *Site Disturbance Datasheet*, and the *Burn Severity Datasheet*.

## 1 Plot establishment

Plot establishment may occur immediately following the ecological site assessment, or at a later interval (see *SOP #4*). Plots consist of three 50-meter transects, spaced 25 meters apart (see fig. 5-1). Transects run perpendicular to the slope (parallel to the slope contour), aligned with the azimuth. Following plot layout, the endpoints and midpoints of the transects are permanently marked with rebar fitted with rebar caps which include the plot ID and location code. The endpoints of the transects are mapped with a GPS. In forest and woodland plots, witness trees are tagged at each transect endpoint to aid in re-locating the transects.

### 1.1 Plot layout

Fill out relevant general information at the top of the *Plot Establishment Datasheet* using the following guidelines:

- **Park code**. Use the standard 4-letter code to indicate the park unit.
- **Plot ID**. A pre-assigned unique alphanumeric code number is provided for each plot. The letter designates the ecological site, and the number is assigned consecutively with plot establishment.
- **Date**. MM/DD/YYYY (e.g., 03/14/2008).

The first step is to determine the transect azimuth. Transfer the mean plot aspect value from the *Ecological Site Assessment Datasheet* to the **Mean plot aspect** field of the *Plot Establishment Datasheet*. To determine the **Transect**

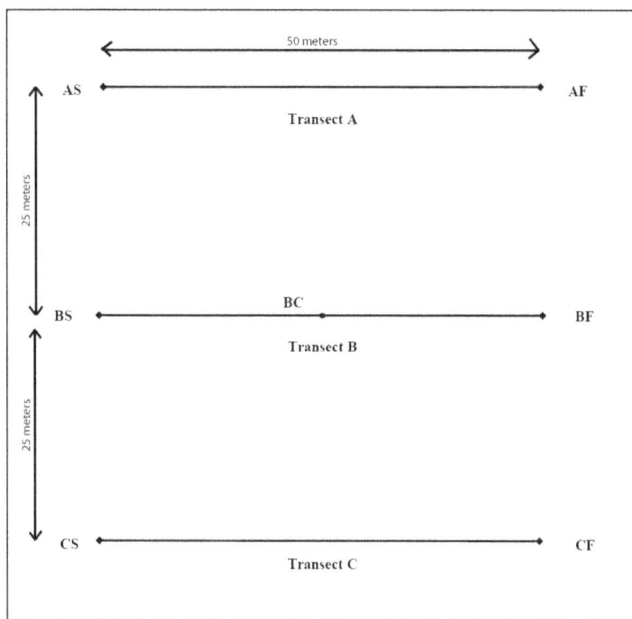

**Figure 5-1. Transect layout for the plot. BC is the plot center.**

azimuth, subtract 90˚ from this value and record on the datasheet. This is the direction, from start to finish, that the transects will be oriented. If the site is completely level, use an established method to choose a random azimuth such as using a random number table, or spinning a compass. Compass readings are taken with no correction for declination. Declination will be corrected during the data management process.

The transects are identified as follows (and as shown in fig. 5-1): A is the upper transect (upslope), B is the center transect, and C is lower transect (downslope). The points along the transects are identified as follows: S for start, (i.e., 0 m); C for center, (i.e., 25 m); and F for finish, (i.e., 50 m). Points along the transect are labeled using the following notation: XY, where X represents the transect and Y represents the point on the transect. The starting point of all transects is to the left when facing upslope.

The following letters, A–E, document the step by step process for laying out tape to delineate each transect , and are illustrated in figs. 5-2a through 5-2f. As a general note, while laying out the tapes, be careful not to trample the area on the upslope side of the transect. Always walk slightly downslope of the transect location. The tape should be taut and as close to the ground as possible to avoid curvature in the line. It is okay to run the tape over low shrubs, but the tape generally should be threaded through any shrubs taller than 0.75 m. In mixed conifer forests, it may be necessary to string the tape more than 0.75 m from the ground surface, for example when the transect crosses deadfalls. If the ground surface is undulating, pin the tape so that it follows the contour of the landscape, and remains no more than than 0.75 m from the ground surface. It may be useful to use a chaining pin at 25 m point, and extra chaining pins should be used to pin down the tape and keep it from moving during windy weather.

**A. Lay out tape on Transect B.** One crew member stands over BC, holding tape #1 and a compass. A second crew member backsights (azimuth minus 180) the azimuth with a compass and pulls the end of the tape towards the start of the transect, until the tape is at exactly 25 m over the BC. The member at the centroid also sights the angle, and helps to guide the other crew member to the right location. Both crew members then double check the angle before crew member 2 secures the end of the tape with a chaining pin. This is point BS. Next, the person holding the tape reel (crew member 1) sites the azimuth and pulls the reel out to the 50 m point (BF), with input from crew member 2 (who may need to move from BS to BC in plots with poor visibility), and then secures the end with a chaining pin. This is BF. Both crew members then ensure that the tape is aligned correctly, as straight as possible, and that the 25 m point is directly over BC (see fig. 5-2a). For the plot to be square, it is critical that Transect B is straight.

**B. Locate approximate finish points for Transects A and C.** Use the mean plot aspect to sight a line perpendicular to the transect azimuth. Standing at BF, crew member 1 holds tape #2, while crew member 2 backsights upslope, and pulls the 0 end of the tape upslope 25 meters, guided by crew member 1, until 25 m is directly over BF. Both crew members double check the angle, then crew member 2 attaches the end with a chaining pin. This is AF. Crew member 1 then sights downslope, and, guided by crew member 2, pulls the tape 25 m and attaches the reel of tape #2 with a chaining pin. The 50 m point is CF (see fig. 5-2b).

To ensure that the plot angles are square, a third crew member extends tape #3 diagonally from BC to AF (where crew member 2 is still standing). The distance of this diagonal should be 35.35 m. If this measurement is off by more than 5 cm the 2 crew members should adjust the end of tape #2 so that it intersects with 35.35 m on tape #3. Repeat this procedure to align the CF point (see fig. 5-2c).

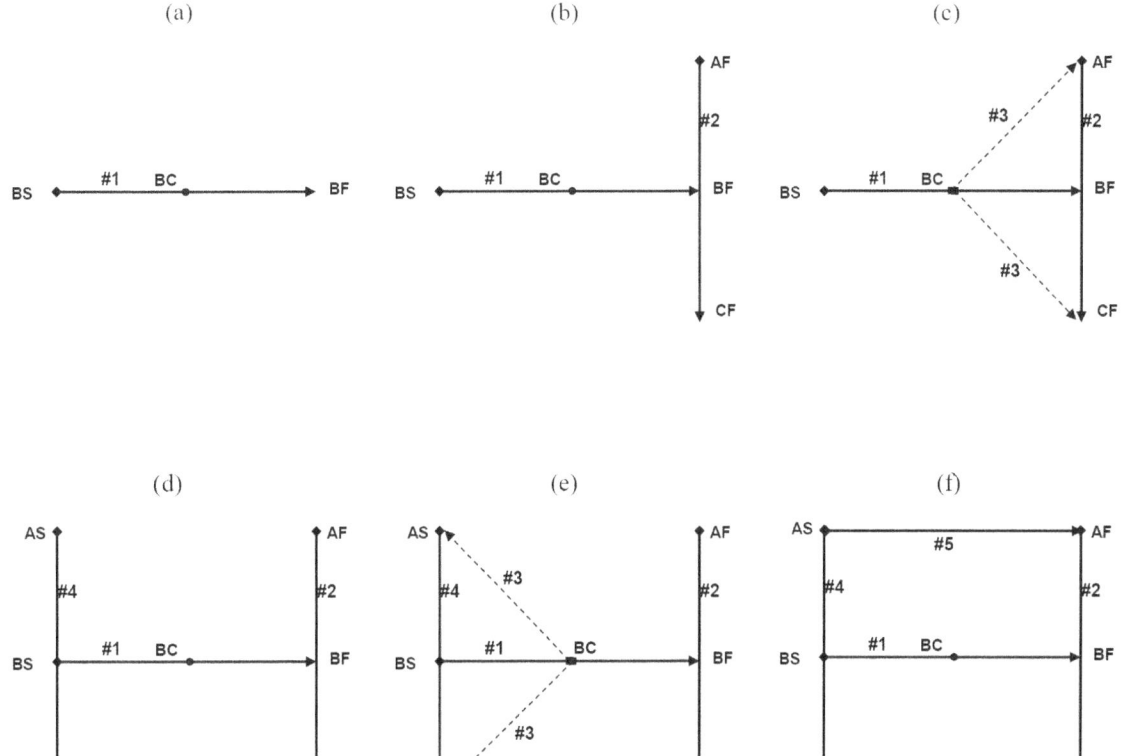

Figure 5-2. Transects are delineated by laying 4 tapes out in the sequence shown above, starting with (a) and ending with (f).

**C. Locate start points for Transects A and C.** Repeat step B to locate AS and CS, starting at BS. Tape #4 is extended from AS to CS with tape #3 used to measure the diagonals. Use extreme care not to trample the areas upslope of AS and CS that will be sampled (see figs. 5-2d and fig. 5-2e).

**D. Lay out tapes on Transect C.** A crew member removes the chaining pin holding down tape #4 near CS, and attaches tape #3 at CS (i.e., the 50 m point on tape #4) with a chaining pin and walks the tape towards CF, securing the end of the tape at CF (i.e., the 50 m point on tape #2) with another chaining pin. This person should walk slightly downslope of the line, so as not to travel in the sampling area. If the pin at CF is not visible, another crew member should stand at CF to direct crew member 1. In plots with dense trees, an additional crew member can be positioned mid-transect to help direct crew member 1. Care taken during this step will save time later, as a crooked tape will need to be restrung. Once the tape is laid out, all participating crew members ensure that Transect C is straight and is situated at the 50 m points of tapes #2 and #4 respectively (not at the pins that are holding down the tapes)(fig. 5-2f.)

**E. Lay out tape on Transect A.** Using tape #5, step D is repeated to lay out Transect A. Tapes #2 and #4 should be left in place if there are trees in the plot to be measured; otherwise the crew can reel up the tapes, ensuring that all transect ends are marked with chaining pins. Note: If the crew is carrying only 4 tapes, tape #4 can be used for laying out Transect A. It is important to leave the chaining pin in place to mark the location of AS before reeling in the tape (see fig. 5-2f).

Once the plot has been laid out, all crew members should check the transects to ensure that they are as straight and low as possible and are pinned down where necessary. If it is windy, use additional chaining pins to hold tapes in place. All personal and sampling equipment should be moved to a location near BS or BF.

## 1.2 Monumenting the plot
Nine 1.2 × 50 cm (0.5" × 20") rebar are used to permanently mark the plot. Seven of these rebar are prestamped to identify plot ID and transect point to aid in relocation of the plot. Install a rebar using a 3 lb hammer at S, C and F points of each transect, leaving approximately 10 cm exposed. If the rebar can't be installed to this depth, try using a short, 25 cm rebar. If it is not possible to sink the rebar at all due to very shallow soil or exposed bedrock exposure, locate the closest possible point *along the transect* to sink the rebar. In the *Transect installation record* section of the datasheet, record the offset location of the rebar next to its point label (e.g., 48.5 if it is 1.5 m from the transect finish). Alternately, a cordless drill can be used to install the rebar at rocky sites if permission has been granted by the park.

Add caps onto the installed rebar at S and F points of all transects and at the centroid (BC). Caps can be hammered on to the ends of the rebar with the 3 lb hammer, padding the rebar cap so as not to mar the writing on the cap. A piece of leather is generally used as padding. Rebar at points AC and CC are not capped.

Caps are labeled the year, "NPS SCPN", and "DO NOT REMOVE", and are stamped prior to plot establishment using a die set with the plot ID and transect position. Be careful to place rebar caps in the correct location as they are very difficult to remove once installed.

Using the mapping grade GPS unit, record a point at each rebar marking the transect ends and the centroid (7 points total). If any of the rebars were offset, use the GPS to record the location of the rebar, regardless of the location along the transect. See *SOP #3* and Appendix D for specific GPS instructions.

## 1.3 Witness trees
In forest and woodland sites, identify 2 trees near each of the transect ends as witness trees. Ideally the trees should be live, large (>15 cm diameter), healthy, within 3 meters of the rebar, and at least 90 degrees from each other with respect to the rebar. While in many cases, one or more of these criteria may be relaxed, all witness trees must be within 10 m of rebar. Select the best and most obvious choices available.

Using a hammer and a 3" nail, install a brass tree tag at breast height and oriented so that it is pointing towards the rebar. The tags are prestamped with "SCPN" and an ID number. If the tree is in the tree plot (see *SOP #7*), the tag should be nailed at breast height (137 cm). Measure the distance from the tree tag to the rebar with a tape, to the nearest 0.1 m, and use a compass to determine the azimuth from the tree to the rebar. Record **Species**, **Tree ID**, **Azimuth** and **Distance** in the *Witness trees* section of the *Plot Establishment Datasheet*.

## 1.4 Directions to plot
Write down any information that will assist in relocating the plot in the *Directions to plot* section of the *Plot Establishment Datasheet*. Because we use UTM coordinates and a GPS unit to relocate the plots, it is not necessary to provide detailed instructions. However, useful tips for return visits may reduce travel time. Potential items to note include: access roads, parking locations, landmarks and obstacles or hazard to avoid.

## 2 Plot revisit
If revisiting a plot, use a GPS unit (*SOP #3*) to navigate to the plot centroid. As a reminder, each monitoring site includes three 50-meter transects spaced 25 meters apart (see fig. 5-1). Use a compass, the transect azimuth from the revisit report, witness trees, GPS and a metal detector, if necessary, to locate all endpoints of the 50 m transects. Use the rebar caps to confirm the transect letter and orientation. Mark the ends of each transect with pin flags or flagging tape as they are located, but avoid trampling excessively along the transects, particularly on the upslope side of transects where quadrats are located. Check the revisit report for any rebar offsets. To lay out the tape in preparation for data collection, begin at the start of each transect (AS, BS and CS) and reel out the tapes towards the finish of each transect (AF, BF and CF, respectively) following the instructions above.

# 3 Photopoints

Photopoints are taken each plot visit where data is collected along the transects, and are documented in the *Photo-point Datasheet*. Six photos are taken during each site visit to provide visual documentation of vegetation structure. For more information on photo point monitoring, see the *USFS Photo Point Monitoring Handbook* (Hall 2001).

## 3.1 General information
Fill out relevant general information at the top of the *Photopoint Datasheet* using the following guidelines:

- **Park code**. Use the standard 4-letter code to indicate the park unit.
- **Plot ID**. A pre-assigned unique alphanumeric code number is provided for each plot. The letter designates the ecological site, and the number is assigned consecutively with plot establishment.
- **Date**. MM/DD/YYYY (e.g., 03/14/2008).
- **Start time**. Record the time (MST) that the transect is started.
- **Photographer**. Record the first initial and last name of the photographer.
- **Camera**. Record the camera type.

## 3.2 Photo number and offset location
If this is a revisit, check the revisit report from the previous visits to determine whether there are photopoint offsets. If offsets are noted, take your photo at the point indicated (see *Photo offsets* below). Otherwise, pace 5 meters back from the end of a transect, set the camera body on top of a monopod adjusted to 1.5 m off the ground (or hold camera at 1.5 m), and aim directly along the transect toward the transect center. The meter tape serves as a reference. The rebar should be visible at the bottom center of the photo (unless the point is offset). The focal point should be near the 25 m point of the transect. Crew members can be working in the photo as long as they don't obstruct the view. Take a photo and examine the resulting image. If the photo is focused, level, and clearly shows the vegetation and site conditions along the transect, record the **Photo number** on the datasheet. If the photo is not adequate, make adjustments and retake the photo. Repeat this procedure for all transect start and finish points

### Photo offsets
If a tree or other obstruction blocks the camera view from the photopoint, move forward. Note the new point on the datasheet, continuing from the default positions of -5 (5 m behind the transect start point) or 55 (5 m behind the transect end point). For example, taking a meter step forward would be recorded as -4 at a transect start point (AS, BS, CS), or 54 at the transect end (AF, BF, CF). Standing at the rebar would be 0 or 50.

## 3.3 Tips for taking good photos
Avoid taking photos into the sun if at all possible. If transects run east-west, try to take the pictures at midday. Be sure to pick a focal point; focusing on the horizon will result in a blurry photo.

# 4 Site disturbance
The plot and the surrounding area is assessed for disturbances.

## 4.1 General information
Fill out the general information at the top of the *Site Disturbance Datasheet* following these guidelines:

- **Park code**. Use the 4-letter code for the park unit.
- **Plot ID**. A pre-assigned unique alphanumeric code is provided for each plot. The letter designates the ecological site, and the number is assigned consecutively with plot establishment.
- **Date**. MM/DD/YYYY (e.g., 03/14/2008).
- **Recorder**. Write down the first initial and last name of the person recording data.
- **Page__ of __**. Note the page number if more than one datasheet is used.

## 4.2 Assess in-plot disturbances

Carefully inspect the area within the plot for any major natural and human disturbances. Major disturbances are those that may impact data collected from the plot (e.g., fire, water erosion, wind erosion, large animal burrows, trails, livestock grazing, livestock trailing, wildlife browse, archaeological sites, wind disturbance, tree die-off, etc.). Do not include disturbances that are smaller than 1 m$^2$.

If disturbances are detected, record the **Disturbance type**, estimated **Size of affected area** (in square meters), **Distance from centroid**, and its **Direction from centroid** (azimuth) on the *Site Disturbance Datasheet*. Provide a thorough **Description** of the disturbances, noting if the disturbance seems to be influencing vegetation composition, soil structure, erosional processes, or fire behavior in the **Potential effects on vegetation, soil, etc.** field. Create a schematic **Illustration of disturbance**, showing size and location, on the back side of the datasheet.

If more than 3 types of disturbances are noted, add the additional data on another datasheet. On plot revisits, review the revisit reports for disturbances noted on previous visits, and only add new disturbances.

## 4.3 Assess off-plot disturbances

Examine the larger area surrounding the plot. If there are any major disturbances that may be influencing the area within the plot (e.g., fire, widespread erosion) record the **Disturbance type** on the datasheet. Size, distance from plot and severity of disturbance should all be considered when deciding whether or not a disturbance is likely to influence the plot. For example, a seldomly used foot trail 5 meters from the edge of the plot could have an impact and should be described on the datasheet. A similar path 200 m from the plot is unlikely to have an effect and does not need to be noted. In contrast, a heavily used OHV trail 200 m from the plot could have an effect and should be described. Record the disturbance as off-plot, regardless if it occurs within the plot as well.

On the *Site Disturbance Datasheet*, provide a thorough **Description** of the disturbance, noting in the **Potential effects on vegetation, soil, etc.** field if the disturbance is influencing or has the potential to influence vegetation composition, soil structure, erosional processes, or fire behavior. Estimate the **Size of affected area**, **Distance from plot**, and **Direction from plot** (azimuth) of the disturbance. Draw a schematic **Illustration of disturbance** on the back side of the datasheet. If more than 3 types of disturbances are noted, add the additional data on another datasheet. If additional disturbances are noted during sampling, remember to add them to the datasheet prior to leaving the plot. On plot revisits, review copies of the previous visits' site disturbance data and only add new disturbances.

## 5 Burn severity

This assessment is conducted during plot establishment or on any plot visit when there has been a prescribed fire or wildfire within the past 2 years. While fires may be described in the *Site Disturbance Datasheet* (see section 4 above), this assessment provides more detail, and should be conducted if the fire occurred within the past 2 years. This assessment should be conducted on all plots in the ecological site if the fire burned through a large portion of the final sampling frame. This assessment describes the burn severity only for the area of the plot.

## 5.1 General information

Fill out the general information at the top of the Burn Severity Datasheet following these guidelines:

- **Park code**. Use the 4-letter code for the park unit.
- **Plot ID**. A pre-assigned unique alphanumeric code is provided for each plot. The letter designates the ecological site, and the number is assigned consecutively with plot establishment.
- **Date**. MM/DD/YYYY (e.g., 03/14/2008).
- **Recorder**. Write down the first initial and last name of the person recording data.

## 5.2 Assess burn severity

### 5.2.1 Fire information

Write down the **Name** of the fire (if known) and **Date of fire** (if known, in month/year form, MM/YYYY), and check the box indicating whether the fire was a prescribed fire or a wildfire.

If the fire impacted a large portion of the final sampling frame but did not impact this plot, check the box for **Plot was not impacted by fire**.

### 5.2.2 Burn heterogeneity

Determine the level of heterogeneity in severity of the burn. This applies to both canopy and understory/substrate. Check the box for whether the heterogeneity is **Low, Medium** or **High**. Low heterogeneity refers to plots where the fire severity is uniform. Medium heterogeneity refers to plots having 2 or 3 distinct areas of differing severities. High heterogeneity refers to plots with more than 3 patches of different severities.

### 5.2.3 Burn severity of canopy

Looking only at overstory trees (≥15 cm diameter), identify areas within the plot where the tree canopy has different levels of scorched needles. Also consider where needles have been consumed, or were scorched and have subsequently fallen. Look for broad patterns across the plot, taking into consideration that the percentage of scorching on individual trees may vary with species and size. Place each identified area into a burn severity class: **Low, Low-Medium, Medium-High** and **High**. See Table 5-1 for definitions of these classes. Estimate the percentage of the plot falling into each burn severity class, using the cover classes in Table 5-2.

### 5.2.4 Burn severity of understory/substrate

Looking at the soil surface, woody debris, and herbaceous and shrub vegetation, identify areas within the plot with different levels of burn severities. These areas may differ from the areas that were identified in the burn severity of canopy. Look at broad patterns of severities across the plot. Place each identified area into a burn severity class: **Low, Low-Medium, Medium-High** and **High**. See Table 5-3 for definitions of these classes. Estimate the percentage of the plot falling into each burn severity class, using the cover classes in Table 5-2. Note the criteria for your rating in the **Comments**. This portion of the assessment becomes increasingly more difficult to conduct since time of the fire. If you cannot determine the levels of burn severity for the understory/substrate, note this in the **Comments**.

## 6 Minimizing site impacts

In any long term monitoring project, care must be taken to avoid sampling impacts which may influence the vegetation and soils of the site. This is especially important if the site has significant biological crust or other "impact sensitive" features. In these cases, special care should be taken to minimize trampling. Crew members should avoid stepping on biological soil crusts; instead they should utilize game trails or paths and rocks, whenever possible.

**Table 5-1. Burn severity classes for tree canopy**

| | |
|---|---|
| Low | 0 to <25% scorched canopy |
| Low-Medium | 25 to <75% scorched canopy and needle consumption |
| Medium-High | 75 to <100% scorched canopy and needle consumption |
| High | 100% needle consumption |

**Table 5-2. Cover classes for burn severity assessment**

| | |
|---|---|
| 1 | <1% |
| 2 | 1 to <5% |
| 3 | 5 to <10% |
| 4 | 10 to <25% |
| 5 | 25 to <50% |
| 6 | 50 to <75% |
| 7 | 75–100% |

**Table 5-3. Burn severity classes for understory/substrate**

| | |
|---|---|
| Low | Most foliage and twigs remain intact, small organic material on ground is scorched but not entirely consumed; mineral soil is rarely exposed. |
| Low-Medium | Woody debris and the majority of the shrub/herbaceous layer are scorched to partially burned; most fine organic materials are partially burned; mineral soil is intermittently exposed. |
| Medium-High | Most woody debris <7.5cm diameter is entirely consumed; most organic matter is entirely consumed. Mineral soil is exposed, but remains intact. Possible vigorous vegetative regrowth may be evident. |
| High | All woody debris is entirely consumed, with the exception of an occasional large log. All litter and duff are consumed, exposing bare mineral soil. Substantial soil erosion may be evident. |

Carry all supplies you will need with you when you begin a task. For example, when collecting quadrat data you should carry with you, in addition to the frame and datasheets, an extra pencil or two, unknown species sheets, species list, and any water or snacks you may want. This will eliminate the need to walk back and forth along the line, thereby reducing trampling.

When locating a plot centroid with the GPS, stop well outside of the plot boundary (approximately 35 m from the centroid) and set down all equipment. One person can then walk to the centroid and install or mark the rebar. When locating the transect endpoints, stay outside of the transect line, looking inward, towards the centroid for the rebar. As you lay out the transects, always be sure to walk well below the line, and watch where you place your feet to avoid stepping on plants or areas of well-developed biological soil crusts. When crossing over a transect line, look at the tape and be sure to cross at a point that will not be within a quadrat (e.g., between 6–9 m or 26–29 m along the A line).

When installing plots, pay particular attention to the start of Transects A and C and the finish of Transect B, as quadrats are located at these points. These areas are often trampled when laying out the line, with significant impacts to the data collected. When extending a diagonal, travel to a point below the transect endpoint to minimize trampling.

These practices are essential at "impact sensitive" sites, but should not be limited to them. All crew members should be aware of their personal impacts to sampling plots and always exercise care to minimize them.

# Plot Establishment Datasheet

Park code:_____   Plot ID:_____   Date (MM/DD/YYYY):_____

## Transect installation record

| Mean plot aspect (°) (facing downslope): | | Transect azimuth (°) (facing transect finish): | |
|---|---|---|---|

If rebar is offset, record the location along the transect where the rebar is installed.

| AS | | AC | | AF | |
|---|---|---|---|---|---|
| BS | | BC | | BF | |
| CS | | CC | | CF | |

Comments:

## Witness trees

| Point | Species | Tree ID | Azimuth (°) | Distance (m) |
|---|---|---|---|---|
| AS | | | | |
| AS | | | | |
| AF | | | | |
| AF | | | | |
| BS | | | | |
| BS | | | | |
| BF | | | | |
| BF | | | | |
| CS | | | | |
| CS | | | | |
| CF | | | | |
| CF | | | | |

Comments:

## Directions to plot

# Photopoint Datasheet

Park code:_____Plot ID: _____ Date (MM/DD/YYYY):_____

Start time (MST):_____ Photographer: _____

Camera: _____

| Photopoints | | |
|---|---|---|
| Transect location | Photo number | Offset location (if altered from -5 or 55)<br>If offset, record the location along the transect where the photo is taken. |
| AS | | |
| AF | | |
| BS | | |
| BF | | |
| CS | | |
| CF | | |
| Comments: | | |
| | | |
| | | |
| | | |

# Site Disturbance Datasheet

Park code:_____Plot ID:_____ Date (MM/DD/YYYY):_____

Recorder:_____                    Page _____ of _____

## In-plot disturbance

| | 1 | 2 | 3 |
|---|---|---|---|
| Disturbance type | | | |
| Size of affected area (m$^2$) | | | |
| Distance from centroid (m) | | | |
| Direction from centroid (°) | | | |
| Description | | | |
| Potential effects on vegetation, soil, etc. | | | |

## Off-plot disturbance

| | 1 | 2 | 3 |
|---|---|---|---|
| Disturbance type | | | |
| Size of affected area (m$^2$) | | | |
| Distance from plot (m) | | | |
| Direction from plot (°) | | | |
| Description | | | |
| Potential effects on vegetation, soil, etc. | | | |

**Example disturbances** (include only disturbances >1 m$^2$ in size that may influence data collected in plot):
archeological site, livestock trailing, livestock grazing, severe wildlife browsing, animal burrows, severe erosion, tree die-off, tree blowdown, human-made structures, invasive plants, fire, etc.

**Illustration of disturbance**

AS _____ AF

BS _____ BF

CS _____ CF

# Burn Severity Datasheet

Park code:_____ Plot ID:_____ Date (MM/DD/YYYY):_____ Recorder:_____

## Fire information

| Name | | Date of fire (MM/YYYY) | |
|------|--|------------------------|--|

Type (check one)  ☐ Wildfire  ☐ Prescribed

☐ Plot was not impacted by fire

Comments:

## Burn heterogeneity

| | | |
|--|--|--|
| ☐ | Low | uniformly affected by fire |
| ☐ | Medium | 2 or 3 discrete areas of differing severities |
| ☐ | High | patchy distribution of differing severities |

Comments:

## Burn severity of tree canopy
In first column, indicate % total plot area for each severity class, using cover classes.

| | | | Cover class | Range |
|--|--|--|-------------|-------|
| | Low | 0 to <25% scorched canopy | 1 | <1% |
| | Low-Medium | 25 to <75% scorched canopy and needle consumption | 2 | 1 to <5% |
| | Medium-High | 75 to <100% scorched canopy and needle consumption | 3 | 5 to <10% |
| | High | 100% complete consumption of needles | 4 | 10 to <25% |
| Comments: | | | 5 | 25 to <50% |
| | | | 6 | 50 to <75% |
| | | | 7 | 75–100% |

## Burn severity of understory/substrate
In first column, indicate % of total plot area for each severity class, using cover classes.

| | | |
|--|--|--|
| | Low | Most foliage and twigs remain intact, small organic material on ground is scorched but not entirely consumed; mineral soil is rarely exposed. |
| | Low-Medium | Majority of shrub/herbaceous layer, woody debris is scorched to partially burned; most fine organic materials are partially burned; mineral soil is intermittently exposed. |
| | Medium-High | Most woody debris <7.5cm diameter is entirely consumed; most organic matter is entirely consumed. Mineral soil is exposed, but remains intact. Possible vigorous vegetative regrowth may be evident. |
| | High | All woody debris is entirely consumed, with the exception of an occasional large log; all litter and duff are consumed, exposing bare mineral soil. Substantial soil erosion may be evident. |

Comments:

# Standard Operating Procedure #6: Shrub and Herbaceous Vegetation

## Version 1.00

### Revision History Log

| Previous version number | Revision date | Author | Changes made | Section and paragraph | Reason | Approved by | New version number |
|---|---|---|---|---|---|---|---|
| | | | | | | | |
| | | | | | | | |
| | | | | | | | |
| | | | | | | | |
| | | | | | | | |
| | | | | | | | |
| | | | | | | | |
| | | | | | | | |

Only changes in this specific SOP will be logged here. Version numbers increase incrementally by hundredths (e.g., version 1.01, version 1.02) for minor changes. Major revisions should be designated with the next whole number (e.g., version 2.0, 3.0, 4.0). Record the previous version number, date of revision, author of the revision; identify paragraphs and pages where changes are made, who approved the revision, and the reason for making the changes along with the new version number.

This standard operating procedure (SOP) provides step-by-step instructions for determining species frequency and estimating species cover, functional group cover, soil surface feature cover, and tree seedling density in quadrats located along three 50 m transects. Instructions for naming and documenting unknown species are included. Species frequency and species and functional group cover data provide measurements of the herbaceous and shrub strata and plant community composition and structure. Tree seedling density data provide information on a portion of the tree strata of plant community composition and structure, and are coupled with other tree data collected using *SOP #7*. Soil surface feature data provide a means for interpreting some of the patterns found in the vegetation data, and may be used to examine hydrologic function (e.g., amount of bare soil that may be subject to erosion); these data may be coupled with soil data collected in *SOP #8*.

Equipment required for this procedure are listed in *SOP #1*, Table 1-1. This SOP is associated with the *Nested Quadrat Datasheet* and the *Unknown Species Datasheet*.

## 1 Sampling teams
Quadrat sampling is performed by a two-person team: one "observer" to report frequency, cover, and seedling density; and one "recorder" to write down these data. The sampling team should maintain their roles for a given transect to maintain consistency, but switch roles between transects to avoid fatigue.

## 2 Sampling procedures
Herbaceous and shrub vegetation data are collected at 5 spatial scales in each of a total of 15 nested 10 m² rectangular quadrats that are located at 10 m intervals along the upslope side of three 50 m transects (fig. 6-1). On Transects A and C, quadrats begin at 0 m, 10 m, 20 m, 30 m, and 40 m; quadrats are offset along transect B and begin at 5 m, 15 m, 25 m, 35 m and 45 m. When sampling each transect, ensure that you are at the right point along the transect. The datasheet columns are labeled with the starting points "0/5" (meaning the 0 or the 5 starting point), "10/15", "20/25", "30/35" and "40/45", to serve as reminders. Data collected in these quadrats include: species frequency, species percent foliar cover, cover of functional groups, cover of soil surface features and density of tree seedlings (table 6-1).

**Table 6-1. Measurements taken in each quadrat**

|  | Measurement | Location of measurement |
|---|---|---|
| Herbaceous and shrub species | presence | all nested quadrats |
|  | % cover | 10 m² quadrats |
| Soil surface features[1] | % cover | 1 m² quadrats |
| Functional groups[2] | % cover | 10 m² quadrats |
| Tree seedlings | count by species and size class | 1 m² quadrats |

[1]Soil surface features include: Live plant base; Dead herbaceous base; Dead woody base; Litter, duff; Undifferentiated crust; Bare ground; Woody debris (>2.5 cm); Fine gravel (0.2 to <2 cm); Coarse gravel (2 to <7.5 cm); Cobble (7.5 to < 25 cm); Stone, boulder (>= 25 cm); Cyanobacteria; Lichen; Moss

[2]Functional groups include: Total live foliar cover (Shrubs, Perennial grasses/graminoids, Annual grasses, Forbs, Cacti/succulents); Standing dead herbaceous; Standing dead woody

## 2.1 Review plants in the area

The crew should review and identify unfamiliar species upon arrival at the plot. All crew members should pay attention to plants encountered during plot set up, and discuss identification of any species about which they have questions. This will increase efficiency during sampling and reduce misidentifications.

## 2.2 Assemble and layout quadrat frames

The quadrat frames are constructed such that the areas within the frame are 1 m² and 10 m². Prior to sampling, assemble the 1 m² sampling frame by connecting the PVC sides with the elbows. The 1 m² frame is marked with colored tape designating 0.01 m² and 0.1 m² nested quadrats within (fig. 6-2). Make sure that the corner of the frame with these markings is located at the lower left of the quadrat. (fig. 6-2). Extend the tent poles that comprise the 10 m² frame and make sure that all the connections are pushed tightly together.

At the location of the first quadrat of the transect, align the 1 m² PVC frame so that the inside lower left corner of the quadrat frame is located at the 0 or 5 m point on the transect tape. If vegetation prevents the frame from lying flat on the ground, keep it as parallel to the ground as possible. It may be necessary to hold the frame parallel to the ground while determining if a plant at the edge of the frame is within the quadrat.

Next, set up the 10 m² quadrat using tent poles. The 10 m² frame consists of 3 collaps-

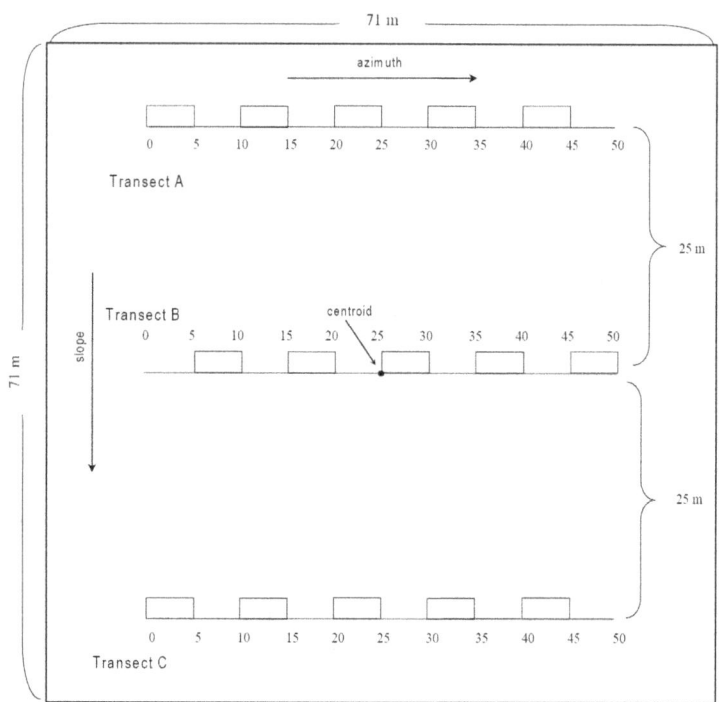

**Figure 6-1. Standard macroplot and transect layout for upland monitoring**

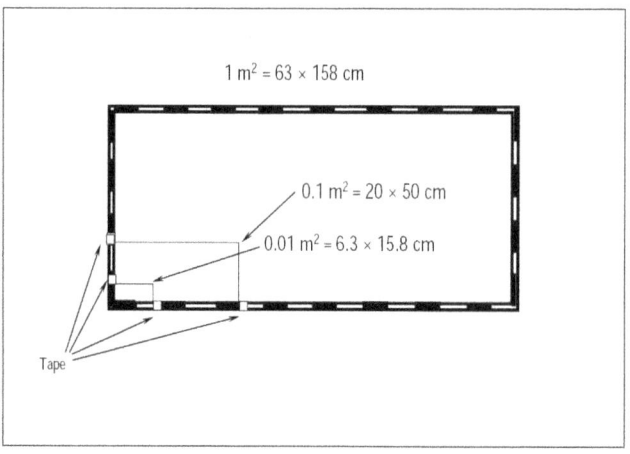

**Figure 6-2. Alignment of nested frequency quadrats on the 1 m² sampling frame. Notice that the 0.01 m² and 0.1 m² quadrats are defined by the inside edge of the tape on the 1 m² sampling frame.**

ible tent poles—2 which are 2 m long and 1 which is 5 m long. Line up the first 2 m tent pole perpendicular to the transect at the appropriate starting point (0 or 5 m), and the second perpendicular pole 5 m farther along the transect (at 5 or 10 m). Place the 5 m pole parallel to the transect and abutting the upslope ends of the two 2 m poles. If there is a tree trunk or some other obstruction, the tent poles can be folded back, so that at least part of the quadrat can be delineated. Ensure that the frames are properly oriented and square; it is important to be diligent about the placement of the quadrats frames to ensure consistent sampling from year to year.

## 2.3 Begin data collection

At this point, you are ready to begin sampling the first quadrat and populating the *Nested Quadrat Datasheet*. When setting up and sampling the plot, minimize trampling within and around the plot. Stepping within the 10 m² quadrat area should be avoided unless absolutely necessary. In such instances, minimize damage to vegetation by stepping on rocks, logs or other resistant surfaces. Always avoid stepping inside the 1 m² quadrat.

### 2.3.1 General information

Fill out the relevant information at the top of the *Nested Quadrat Datasheet*. Use one sheet for each transect, following these guidelines:

- **Park code**. Use the standard 4-letter code to indicate the park unit.
- **Plot ID**. A pre-assigned unique alphanumeric code number is provided for each plot. The letter designates the ecological site, and the number is assigned consecutively with plot establishment.
- **Date**. MM/DD/YYYY (e.g., 07/14/2008).
- **Observer**. Record the first initial and last name of the person reporting quadrat data.
- **Recorder**. Record the first initial and last name of the person recording data.
- **Transect**. Circle A, B or C.
- **Start time**. Record the time (MST, in twenty-four-hour format) that the transect is started.
- **End time**. Record the time (MST, in twenty-four-hour format) that the transect is finished.

### 2.3.2 Sample the 1 m² quadrat for soil surface features

The observer begins with the 1 m² frame to collect soil surface feature cover data (*Cover of soil surface features* section of the datasheet, also listed in table 6-1), making ocular estimates of percent cover of each feature using cover classes from Table 6-2. Soil surface features include anything taking up space on the soil surface: bare ground, duff and litter, woody debris, undifferentiated soil crusts, cyanobacteria, moss, lichens, various size classes of rock, and live and dead plant bases. Soil surface features cover estimates are additive with the sum of the cover estimates equaling 100%. See Table 6-1 for the soil surface features that are documented.

Follow these rules:

- Tree stems *are* included in cover estimations in the **Live plant base** and **Dead woody base** categories.
- **Dead woody base** includes dead shrubs, dead cactus or succulents as well as dead trees. If a portion of a plant base is dead, split the estimate between cover of dead portions as **Dead woody base** or **Dead herbaceous base**, and cover of **Live plant base**.
- **Woody debris** includes downed, detached stems over 2.5 cm in width, tree bark at least 2.5 cm wide by 2.5 cm thick, and only includes the area in direct contact with the ground. Rotting logs are considered woody debris until they become unconsolidated, at which point they are considered **Litter/duff**.
- Dead or live branches still attached to a shrub or tree, but lying on the ground, should be ignored as a surface feature; instead the ground cover beneath an attached branch (e.g., **Bare ground** or **Litter/duff**) should be estimated.
- Moss or lichen that occur on rocks or downed wood should not be considered in cover estimation, but rather the underlying material defines the surface feature.
- Dead herbaceous bases that were alive in the current growing season should be counted as **Live plant base**.

Once the observer is finished estimating all soil surface features that occur in the quadrat, the recorder double checks that soil surface feature estimates account for all features observed, and sum to 100% accounting for cover classes.

### 2.3.3 Sample nested frequency

Species frequency is assessed at the following 5 spatial scales: $0.01 \text{ m}^2$, $0.1 \text{ m}^2$, $1 \text{ m}^2$, $5 \text{ m}^2$ and $10 \text{ m}^2$. These quadrats begin in the lower left corner of the $1 \text{ m}^2$ frame. See Figure 6-3 for the sizes and arrangement of the nested quadrats. The sides of nested quadrats all have a 2:5 ratio, with the exception of the $5 \text{ m}^2$ quadrat.

Data collection begins in the smallest quadrat. The corners of the $0.01 \text{ m}^2$ quadrat are marked with colored tape on the sides of the $1 \text{ m}^2$ sampling frame. The *inside* edges of the tape (closest to the corner of the $1 \text{ m}^2$ sampling frame) define the quadrat (fig. 6-2). The observer identifies to species (when possible) all live vascular plants rooted (at least partially) within the $0.01 \text{ m}^2$ quadrat and reports them to the recorder, who lists them in the "species" column of the datasheet using the 6-letter species code. The recorder then makes a check mark in the **.01** $(\text{m}^2)$ column for each species reported.

**Table 6-2. Cover classes for estimating cover of plant species, functional groups, and soil surface features**

| Cover class | Cover |
|---|---|
| 1 | <0.1% |
| 2 | 0.1 to <0.5% |
| 3 | 0.5 to <1% |
| 4 | 1 to <2% |
| 5 | 2 to <5% |
| 6 | 5 to <10% |
| 7 | 10 to <15% |
| 8 | 15 to <25% |
| 9 | 25 to <35% |
| 10 | 35 to <50% |
| 11 | 50 to <75% |
| 12 | 75–100% |

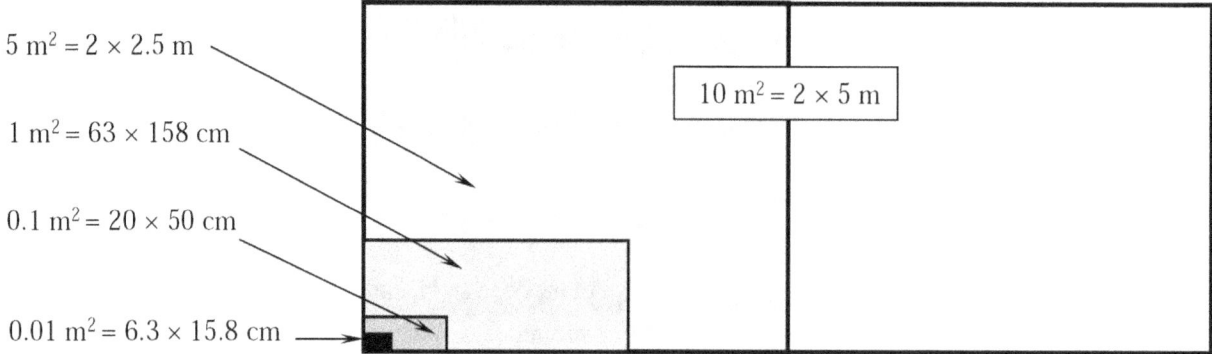

$5 \text{ m}^2 = 2 \times 2.5 \text{ m}$

$10 \text{ m}^2 = 2 \times 5 \text{ m}$

$1 \text{ m}^2 = 63 \times 158 \text{ cm}$

$0.1 \text{ m}^2 = 20 \times 50 \text{ cm}$

$0.01 \text{ m}^2 = 6.3 \times 15.8 \text{ cm}$

**Figure 6-3. Nested frequency quadrat sizes and alignment. The nested quadrats are aligned at the lower left corner to the appropriate sampling point on the transect line.**

Species codes consist of the first 3 letters of the genus and the first 3 letters of the specific epithet. When using codes during revisits, double check all codes against the ecosite species list to ensure it is the correct code for the species. In the few instances of duplicate codes, a new code is created by the botanist for one of the species, which is included on the ecological site species list. For example, ERIDIV is the code for *Erigeron divergens*, and ERIVAR is the code for *Eriogonum divaricatum*. If in doubt, write out the full scientific name. Tree species are not included during quadrat sampling, and should be ignored, because they are captured later in the tree sampling procedure (*SOP #7*). The *Nested Quadrat Datasheet* lists species which are and are not considered trees. Senesced plants that were alive earlier in the current growing season are counted as live plants for the purpose of frequency. For unknown species, record the species on the datasheet by its unknown code (see section 3 below, *Unknown species*).

Once all plant species have been identified within the 0.01 m² quadrat, the observer moves on to the next larger quadrat (0.1 m²), and identifies all species that did not occur in the 0.01 m² quadrat, while the recorder writes down the species code on the datasheet and check marks the **0.1** (m²) column. This process proceeds with the 1 m² quadrat, the 5 m² quadrat, and finally the 10 m² quadrat. Within each consecutively larger nested quadrat, the observer only reports new occurrences. When completed, each species code will be listed only once, and each listed code will have only one checkmark—in the smallest nested quadrat column in which it occurred. For example, if *Poa fendleriana* is present in the 0.1 m² quadrat, and occurs again in the 10 m² quadrat, the observer will report it for the 0.1 m² quadrat and the recorder will only place a check mark in the **0.1** (m²) column.

Unless this is the first visit to a plot, the sampling team will be provided with a revisit report. This report provides the names, but not the frequency or associated cover values, of species previously recorded in a given quadrat for comparison to those currently recorded. During a revisit, when the observer has completed the species frequencies for the entire set of nested quadrats, the recorder scans the revisit report's quadrat species list to identify species not recorded, or possible identification errors. If a perennial species is included on the revisit report, but is not currently present, the observer should double check the entire quadrat to ensure the species has not been overlooked or misidentified. The recorder should then make any changes necessary to the datasheet. In the **Comments** field, the recorder should write any comments that could be pertinent to future sampling or data management, including clarifications of species identifications and whether previously found individuals were dead or missing,

### 2.3.4 Sample cover by species in 10 m² quadrat
Immediately following frequency sampling, an ocular estimate of foliar cover is made within the 10 m² quadrat for each species listed on the datasheet, using one of 12 cover classes (see table 6-2). The observer estimates the vertical projection of live cover, both photosynthetic and non-photosynthetic, onto the ground surface for each species and the recorder writes the value in the **CC** column (for cover class). The empty space between leaves is not included in the cover estimates, nor is dead material that was not alive in the current growing season. All species with cover in the quadrat are included in cover estimates, whether they are rooted in the quadrat or not. For species that are not rooted in the quadrat (i.e., that have no frequency), the recorder should write the species code in the "species" column and the appropriate cover class code in the **CC** column, and then draw a horizontal line through the frequency columns to indicate that the species had no frequency in the quadrat. Cover estimates of tree species (overstory, saplings or seedlings) are not included, but epiphytic species up to 2 meters in height are included (e.g., mistletoe). The recorder should ensure that all species have a cover value, and prompt the observer for any species missed.

The observer should use the taped guides on the frames, plastic cards that represent 1% and 0.1%, and the 1 m² frame (10%) to increase accuracy and consistency in cover class estimation. The recorder should play an active role, double checking the cover classes provided by the observer, and looking for species that were overlooked. If the recorder disagrees with an observer's cover class, the two should discuss it. Discussion helps keep everyone on the same page and ensures that cover classes are being applied consistently by the whole crew.

### 2.3.5 Sample 10 m² cover by functional groups
After completing cover estimation for all species in the quadrat, the observer estimates **Total live foliar cover** and cover for the 7 functional groups (shrubs, perennial grasses/graminoids, annual grasses, forbs, cacti/succulents, standing dead herbaceous, standing dead woody), using the cover classes provided in Table 6-2. For all functional groups, except **Standing dead herbaceous** and **Standing dead woody**, this estimate is a vertical projection of total live cover, both photosynthetic and non-photosynthetic, onto the ground surface. For the standing dead groups, it is the vertical projection of dead (from previous years) leaves or stems. **Standing dead woody** includes dead shrubs, cacti and succulents, but dead trees should be ignored. If there is a question about which functional group a species belongs to, the ecosite species list contains this information.

Functional group cover estimates are important because they account for overlapping canopies and dead material not assessed by individual species' cover. Functional groups should be additive based on component species, except when there are overlapping canopies. Similarly, the 5 living functional groups should add up to the total live foliar cover, except when there are overlapping canopies. The recorder should maintain awareness of values, and indicate to the observer if there are large deviations from a general additive formula.

## 2.3.6 Sample 10 m² tree seedling density

After completing cover estimates, live tree seedlings (if present) are tallied in the 10 m² quadrat to provide a measure of tree seedling density. Tree seedlings are defined as all stems <2.5 cm diameter. *Juniperus* spp. are measured using diameter at root crown (DRC), and all other species are measured using diameter at breast height (DBH, at 137 cm). Seedling density is sampled wherever tree seedlings are present. There are 2 sections of the datasheet for tree seedling data; the bottom front side is the *Tree seedling check* section, and the back side is the *Tree seedling tally* section.

*Seedling check.* If there are no tree seedlings anywhere along the transect being sampled, check the **Seedlings not present** box on the front of the datasheet. If seedlings are present along the transect, but there are no seedlings present in the quadrat being sampled, check the **Seedlings not present** box for the appropriate quadrat. If there are seedlings present in the quadrat, fill out the *Tree seedling tally* section on the reverse side of the datasheet according to the instructions below.

*Tree seedling tally.* Record the 6-letter code of each new species of tree seedling that occurs in the quadrat. Count and record the number of seedlings of each species in each size class. Non-juniper tree seedlings are tallied for each of 3 size classes: 1 (0 to <15 cm height), 2 (15 to <137 cm height) and 3 (≥137 cm height and <2.5 cm DBH; see table 6-3). Juniper seedlings are classified by diameter at root crown (DRC), as opposed to height, and are assigned to either of 2 juniper-only size classes: 4 (<0.5 cm DRC), or 5 (0.5 to <2.5 cm DRC).

**Table 6-3. Size classes for tree seedlings**

| Seedling size class | Size |
|---|---|
| 1 | 0 to <15 cm height |
| 2 | 15 to <137 cm height |
| 3 | ≥137 cm height and <2.5 cm DBH |
| 4 (*Juniperus* only) | <0.5 cm DRC |
| 5 (*Juniperus* only) | 0.5 to <2.5 cm DRC |

## 2.3.7 Complete sampling at all quadrats along the transect

Once the first quadrat is complete, repeat steps 2.3.2 through 2.3.6 for the remaining 4 quadrats along the transect. Sample quadrats in order while moving down the transect, ensuring that all locations are sampled, as indicated in Figure 6-1. When finished with the fifth quadrat, record **End time** at the top of the data sheet.

## 2.3.8 Sample the other transect(s)

Once the team finishes sampling all 5 quadrats on a transect, they collect the equipment and move to the next transect line. The observer and recorder should switch roles, obtain a new datasheet, and repeat the sampling procedures for the new transect(s).

# 3 Unknown species
## 3.1 Verify unknown status

Plants of unknown identity are brought to the attention of all crew members with botanical expertise. Park- and plot-specific species lists and field keys may aid in field identification. If the identity of a plant cannot be determined in the field, the plant is documented as an unknown and the *Unknown Species Datasheet* is completed.

## 3.2 Document unknown species

The following instructions provide guidance for populating fields in the *Unknown Species Datasheet*, for specimen collection, and for species determination.

### 3.2.1 General information

Fill out relevant information at the top of the *Unknown Species Datasheet* using the following guidelines:

- **Park code.** Use the standard 4-letter code to indicate the park unit.
- **Plot ID.** A pre-assigned unique alphanumeric code number is provided for each plot. The letter designates the ecological site, and the number is assigned consecutively with plot establishment.

- **Date**. MM/DD/YYYY (e.g., 07/14/2008).

- **Observer**. Record the first initial and last name of the person filling out the datasheet.

- **Transect**. Circle A, B or C (if unknown plant occurs on more than one transect, indicate all transects on which it occurs).

- **Quadrat**. Circle point on transect where quadrat begins (if unknown plant occurs in more than one quadrat, do not circle).

### 3.2.2 Provide a plant description

Assign a unique Unknown ID (<parkcode><date><unknown number>, e.g., GRCA 20070824_2) for each new unknown plant species encountered during sampling, and enter it on the datasheet. Start over with the number "1" for the unknown number part of the ID on each new date.

If you have some information on the unknown plant you can record what you know. If the **Family** or **Genus** of the plant is known or the **Species** is suspected, fill out these fields. It is encouraged to record guesses if you have them; adding a question mark can help indicate uncertainty. Take one or more photographs of the plant and record **Photo numbers**.

Next, indicate the life-form of the plant by checking the box indicated: graminoid, forb, subshrub, shrub, succulent, tree, or vine. Subshrub is used for a partially woody plant that falls between a forb (just woody at base) and shrub (woody throughout).

The **Salient features** entry is the most critical part of this datasheet. Specimens can look very different after pressing and drying, so taking the time to thoroughly record what you observe in the field is important. Record the most diagnostic features of the unknown plant, taking care to describe leaf architecture, branch arrangement, flower color (which often changes as the specimen dries). For grasses and forbs, note whether it is annual or perennial and rhizomatous or not. An example entry might read, "perennial forb ca. 0.5 m tall, with glandular inflorescence, 5 blue petals and big, opposite pinnatifid leaves". If you will be collecting the plant, don't record things such as leaf size, or stamen arrangement, which can be determined in the lab.

Finally, indicate whether or not the plant will be collected as an herbarium-quality voucher specimen by checking the indicated box after the entry, *Collected*?. If yes, the *Label information* section of the datasheet will need to be populated (see below).

### 3.2.3 Collect a specimen

If at least 10 individuals are present at the site, collect a specimen from outside the plot. Try to find the best specimen available, preferably with flowers and/or fruit. If the unknown plant is at an unfavorable stage for identification, look around for last year's dried remnants which may include flowering stalks or fruit. Collect the whole plant if herbaceous (including the root), or a representative branch if woody. The plant should be placed either in a zippered plastic bag with a little water and kept in the shade and as cool as possible for identification following the day's fieldwork, or carefully pressed in a field plant press. The bag or newspaper housing the specimen should be labeled with the **Unknown ID** and collector's initials using a permanent marker. A small, partial sample of the species should also be taped on to the *Unknown Species Datasheet*, to be referred to throughout sampling in a given park or ecological site. This will ensure consistency in applying **Unknown ID**s and properly recording unknowns during sampling.

Plants not immediately field-pressed should be keyed out and pressed as soon as possible. Specimens kept in bags should be kept in the shade, and transferred to coolers or refrigerators as soon as possible. When pressing plants originally collected in bags, it is important to remember to label the newspaper surrounding the specimen with the correct unknown species ID (transferred from the bag). If making a herbarium-quality voucher, collect duplicates.

*Unknown species of small population size*. If less than 10 individuals are present at the site, do not collect a specimen, but do take extra time to ensure that the salient features are thoroughly described and the specimen is adequately photographed. This information is crucial to determining the species and/or relocating the plant for identification.

### 3.2.4 Label information

If the collected specimen is of sufficient quality to serve as a voucher, and there is a sufficient population, collect at least 2 individuals. Describe the dominant species in the area in the **Growing with** field on the datasheet. Describe the habitat in the **Habitat description** field. Take a GPS reading and record the **UTM coordinates**. If unable to take a GPS reading of the plant's location, include a locality description in the UTM field.

### 3.2.5 Make a determination

If the specimen is successfully keyed following collection, the **Scientific name, Date**, and the person it was **Determined by** should be recorded in the *Determination* section of the *Unknown Species Datasheet*. The correct scientific name can then be used in subsequent sampling efforts.

Unknown species datasheets should be kept in a binder in the field and taken out when sampling. Following a sampling trip, datasheets should be scanned and saved, and datasheets should be returned to binder. When species are determined, datasheets in the binder must be updated.

# Nested Quadrat Datasheet

Park code:_____ Plot ID:_____ Date (MM/DD/YYYY):_____
Observer:_____ Recorder:_____ Transect:  A   B   C
Start time (MST):_____ End time (MST):_____

Comments:_____
_____
_____

**Nested frequency and cover** (checkmark the appropriate quadrat size column for each species; record cover class—**CC**)

| Quadrat (m) | 0/5 | | | | | | 10/15 | | | | | | 20/25 | | | | | | 30/35 | | | | | | 40/45 | | | | | |
|---|---|---|---|---|---|---|---|---|---|---|---|---|---|---|---|---|---|---|---|---|---|---|---|---|---|---|---|---|---|---|
| **Species** | .01 | 0.1 | 1 | 5 | 10 | CC | .01 | 0.1 | 1 | 5 | 10 | CC | .01 | 0.1 | 1 | 5 | 10 | CC | .01 | 0.1 | 1 | 5 | 10 | CC | .01 | .1 | 1 | 5 | 10 | CC |
| | | | | | | | | | | | | | | | | | | | | | | | | | | | | | | |
| | | | | | | | | | | | | | | | | | | | | | | | | | | | | | | |
| | | | | | | | | | | | | | | | | | | | | | | | | | | | | | | |
| | | | | | | | | | | | | | | | | | | | | | | | | | | | | | | |
| | | | | | | | | | | | | | | | | | | | | | | | | | | | | | | |
| | | | | | | | | | | | | | | | | | | | | | | | | | | | | | | |
| | | | | | | | | | | | | | | | | | | | | | | | | | | | | | | |
| | | | | | | | | | | | | | | | | | | | | | | | | | | | | | | |
| | | | | | | | | | | | | | | | | | | | | | | | | | | | | | | |
| | | | | | | | | | | | | | | | | | | | | | | | | | | | | | | |
| | | | | | | | | | | | | | | | | | | | | | | | | | | | | | | |
| | | | | | | | | | | | | | | | | | | | | | | | | | | | | | | |
| | | | | | | | | | | | | | | | | | | | | | | | | | | | | | | |
| | | | | | | | | | | | | | | | | | | | | | | | | | | | | | | |
| | | | | | | | | | | | | | | | | | | | | | | | | | | | | | | |
| | | | | | | | | | | | | | | | | | | | | | | | | | | | | | | |
| | | | | | | | | | | | | | | | | | | | | | | | | | | | | | | |

| Cover of soil surface features | 0/5 | 10/15 | 20/25 | 30/35 | 40/45 |
|---|---|---|---|---|---|
| Live plant base | | | | | |
| Dead herbaceous base | | | | | |
| Dead woody base | | | | | |
| Litter & duff | | | | | |
| Undifferentiated crust | | | | | |
| Bare ground | | | | | |
| Woody debris (>2.5 cm diam) | | | | | |
| Fine gravel (0.2 to <2 cm) | | | | | |
| Coarse gravel (2 to <7.5 cm) | | | | | |
| Cobble (7.5 to <25 cm) | | | | | |
| Stone, boulder (≥25 cm) | | | | | |
| Cyanobacteria | | | | | |
| Lichen | | | | | |
| Moss | | | | | |

| Cover class | |
|---|---|
| 1 | <0.1% |
| 2 | 0.1 to <0.5% |
| 3 | 0.5 to <1% |
| 4 | 1 to <2% |
| 5 | 2 to <5% |
| 6 | 5 to <10% |
| 7 | 10 to <15% |
| 8 | 15 to <25% |
| 9 | 25 to <35% |
| 10 | 35 to <50% |
| 11 | 50 to <75% |
| 12 | 75–100% |

| Tree seedling check (see reverse for tally) | | | | | |
|---|---|---|---|---|---|
| Seedlings not present on transect? | | | | | |
| | 0/5 | 10/15 | 20/25 | 30/35 | 40/45 |
| Seedlings not present | | | | | |
| **Cover of functional groups** | | | | | |
| Total live foliar cover | | | | | |
| Perennial grasses/graminoids | | | | | |
| Shrubs | | | | | |
| Forbs | | | | | |
| Annual grasses | | | | | |
| Cacti/succulents | | | | | |
| Standing dead herbaceous | | | | | |
| Standing dead woody | | | | | |

**Nested frequency and cover**—page 2 (checkmark the appropriate quadrat size column for each species; record cover class—**CC**)

| Quadrat (m) | 0/5 | | | | | | 10/15 | | | | | | 20/25 | | | | | | 30/35 | | | | | | 40/45 | | | | | |
|---|---|---|---|---|---|---|---|---|---|---|---|---|---|---|---|---|---|---|---|---|---|---|---|---|---|---|---|---|---|---|
| **Species** | .01 | .1 | 1 | 5 | 10 | CC | .01 | .1 | 1 | 5 | 10 | CC | .01 | .1 | 1 | 5 | 10 | CC | .01 | .1 | 1 | 5 | 10 | CC | .01 | .1 | 1 | 5 | 10 | CC |
| | | | | | | | | | | | | | | | | | | | | | | | | | | | | | | |
| | | | | | | | | | | | | | | | | | | | | | | | | | | | | | | |
| | | | | | | | | | | | | | | | | | | | | | | | | | | | | | | |
| | | | | | | | | | | | | | | | | | | | | | | | | | | | | | | |
| | | | | | | | | | | | | | | | | | | | | | | | | | | | | | | |
| | | | | | | | | | | | | | | | | | | | | | | | | | | | | | | |
| | | | | | | | | | | | | | | | | | | | | | | | | | | | | | | |
| | | | | | | | | | | | | | | | | | | | | | | | | | | | | | | |
| | | | | | | | | | | | | | | | | | | | | | | | | | | | | | | |
| | | | | | | | | | | | | | | | | | | | | | | | | | | | | | | |
| | | | | | | | | | | | | | | | | | | | | | | | | | | | | | | |
| | | | | | | | | | | | | | | | | | | | | | | | | | | | | | | |
| | | | | | | | | | | | | | | | | | | | | | | | | | | | | | | |
| | | | | | | | | | | | | | | | | | | | | | | | | | | | | | | |
| | | | | | | | | | | | | | | | | | | | | | | | | | | | | | | |
| | | | | | | | | | | | | | | | | | | | | | | | | | | | | | | |
| | | | | | | | | | | | | | | | | | | | | | | | | | | | | | | |
| | | | | | | | | | | | | | | | | | | | | | | | | | | | | | | |
| | | | | | | | | | | | | | | | | | | | | | | | | | | | | | | |
| | | | | | | | | | | | | | | | | | | | | | | | | | | | | | | |
| | | | | | | | | | | | | | | | | | | | | | | | | | | | | | | |
| | | | | | | | | | | | | | | | | | | | | | | | | | | | | | | |
| | | | | | | | | | | | | | | | | | | | | | | | | | | | | | | |

**Trees are:**
ABICON
ABILAS
PINEDU
PICENG
PICPUN
PINPON
POPTRE
PSEMEN
JUNDEP
JUNMON
JUNOST

**Trees are not:**
Quercus
ROBNEO

**Tree seedling tally** (tally individuals for each species under the correct size class column)

| Quadrat (m) | 0/5 | | | | | 10/15 | | | | | 20/25 | | | | | 30/35 | | | | | 40/45 | | | | |
|---|---|---|---|---|---|---|---|---|---|---|---|---|---|---|---|---|---|---|---|---|---|---|---|---|---|
| **Species** | 1 | 2 | 3 | 4 | 5 | 1 | 2 | 3 | 4 | 5 | 1 | 2 | 3 | 4 | 5 | 1 | 2 | 3 | 4 | 5 | 1 | 2 | 3 | 4 | 5 |
| | | | | | | | | | | | | | | | | | | | | | | | | | |
| | | | | | | | | | | | | | | | | | | | | | | | | | |
| | | | | | | | | | | | | | | | | | | | | | | | | | |
| | | | | | | | | | | | | | | | | | | | | | | | | | |
| | | | | | | | | | | | | | | | | | | | | | | | | | |
| | | | | | | | | | | | | | | | | | | | | | | | | | |
| | | | | | | | | | | | | | | | | | | | | | | | | | |

| | Size class | Size |
|---|---|---|
| Seedlings | 1 | 0 to <15 cm height |
| | 2 | 15 to <137 cm height |
| | 3 | ≥137 cm height and <2.5 cm DBH |
| *Juniperus* seedlings only | 4 | <0.5 cm DRC |
| | 5 | 0.5 to <2.5 cm DRC |

# Unknown Species Datasheet

Park code:_____ Plot ID:_____ Date (MM/DD/YYYY):_____

Observer:_____ Transect:  A  B  C  Quadrat:  1  2  3  4  5

| **Plant description** |
|---|
| Unknown ID (<parkcode><date><#>) : |
| Family:               Genus:                              Species: |
| Photo number(s): |
| **Life-form:**    graminoid ☐    forb ☐    subshrub ☐    shrub ☐    cactus/succ ☐    tree ☐    vine ☐ |

| Salient features | |
|---|---|
| | |
| | |
| | |
| | |
| | |
| | |

**Collected?** Yes ☐  No ☐      If collected as voucher, fill out *Label information* section below

| **Label information** | |
|---|---|
| Growing with: | |
| Habitat description: | |
| **UTM coordinates:** | E                           N |

| **Determination** |
|---|
| Scientific name: |
| Determined by:                                           Date: |

# Standard Operating Procedure #7: Trees

**Version 1.00**

**Revision History Log**

| Previous version number | Revision date | Author | Changes made | Section and paragraph | Reason | Approved by | New version number |
|---|---|---|---|---|---|---|---|
|  |  |  |  |  |  |  |  |
|  |  |  |  |  |  |  |  |
|  |  |  |  |  |  |  |  |
|  |  |  |  |  |  |  |  |
|  |  |  |  |  |  |  |  |
|  |  |  |  |  |  |  |  |
|  |  |  |  |  |  |  |  |
|  |  |  |  |  |  |  |  |

Only changes in this specific SOP will be logged here. Version numbers increase incrementally by hundredths (e.g., version 1.01, version 1.02) for minor changes. Major revisions should be designated with the next whole number (e.g., version 2.0, 3.0, 4.0). Record the previous version number, date of revision, author of the revision; identify paragraphs and pages where changes are made, who approved the revision, and the reason for making the changes along with the new version number.

This standard operating procedure (SOP) provides instructions for collecting data for overstory trees, saplings, canopy closure and tree canopy cover. This SOP is generally used in forests and woodlands, but is also used in grassland and shrubland sites where trees have become established. The methods vary slightly depending on species composition and forest structure. Due to their shrubby, multi-stemmed growth form, individuals of *Juniperus* spp. are measured using diameter at root crown (DRC), as opposed to diameter at breast height (DBH). DBH is used for all other tree species. Because of this difference, a different datasheet is used for plots containing overstory juniper trees. In areas where trees are sparse, the tree plot is sometimes expanded to include the entire area between the transects, and the *Expanded Tree Map Datasheet* is used. There are 2 ways to measure canopy in this SOP: canopy closure and canopy cover. Canopy closure is generally used in forests, while canopy cover is generally used in woodlands.

Portions of this SOP were modified from the NPS *Fire Monitoring Handbook* (USDI National Park Service 2003). Equipment needs for this procedure are listed in *SOP #1*, Table 1-1. Eight datasheets are associated with this SOP: *Forest Tree Datasheet, Standard Tree Map Datasheet, Expanded Tree Map Datasheet, Pinyon-Juniper Tree Datasheet, Canopy Closure Datasheet, Forest Tree Revisit Datasheet, Pinyon-Juniper Tree Revisit Datasheet* and the *Tree Canopy Cover Datasheet*.

All of the datasheets have a top section that generally requires the same basic information to be recorded, following these guidelines:

- **Park code**. Use the standard 4-letter code to indicate the park unit.
- **Plot ID**. A pre-assigned alphanumeric code unique number is provided for each plot. The letter designates the ecological site, and the number is assigned consecutively with plot establishment.
- **Date**. MM/DD/YYYY (e.g., 03/14/2008).
- **Observer**. Record the first initial and last name of the person collecting the measurements.
- **Recorder**. Record the first initial and last name of the person recording the data (if different from observer).

- **Start time**. Record the time (MST, in twenty-four-hour format) that the measurements are started.

- **End time**. Record the time (MST, in twenty-four-hour format) that the measurements finished.

## 1 Overstory tree and sapling measurements in forests

Datasheets: *Forest Tree Datasheet, Standard Tree Map Datasheet, Expanded Tree Map Datasheet, Forest Tree Revisit Datasheet*

This section describes sampling procedures in plots not containing overstory junipers.

### 1.1 General information

Fill out the relevant information at the top of the *Forest Tree Datasheet, Standard* (or *Expanded*) *Tree Map Datasheet*, and the *Forest Tree Revisit Datasheet* (if this is a revisit).

Two categories of trees are considered for the *Forest Tree Datasheet*. Overstory trees have a diameter ≥15 cm. Saplings have a diameter ≥2.5 cm and <15 cm.

### 1.2 Sampling procedure for overstory trees

Tree measurements are generally conducted by 2 people: a recorder and an observer. A third person can be used to map the trees, or nail tree tags. Data is collected in a 20 × 50 m (0.1 ha) sub-plot (tree plot) located immediately downslope from the middle transect (Transect B, see fig. 7-1). To outline the tree plot, the sampling team runs 2 tapes 20 m downslope, perpendicular to the middle transect from BS towards CS and BF towards CF (see fig. 5-1 in *SOP #5* for codes). In plot establishment visits, these tapes will already be in place. The layout of the tapes can vary depending on the number of available tapes and density of trees. Additional tapes can be strung to assist with the mapping, or tapes can be moved as the sampling team proceeds through the plot. Within the tree plot, all live trees ≥15 cm diameter are tagged, measured, and mapped.

**Figure 7-1. Plot layout for tree measurements. Overstory trees are measured in a 20 × 50 m plot located downslope from Transect B. Saplings are measured in a 10 × 25 m subplot. Canopy closure is measured along the transects, one meter left of the quadrats, noted by black octagons.**

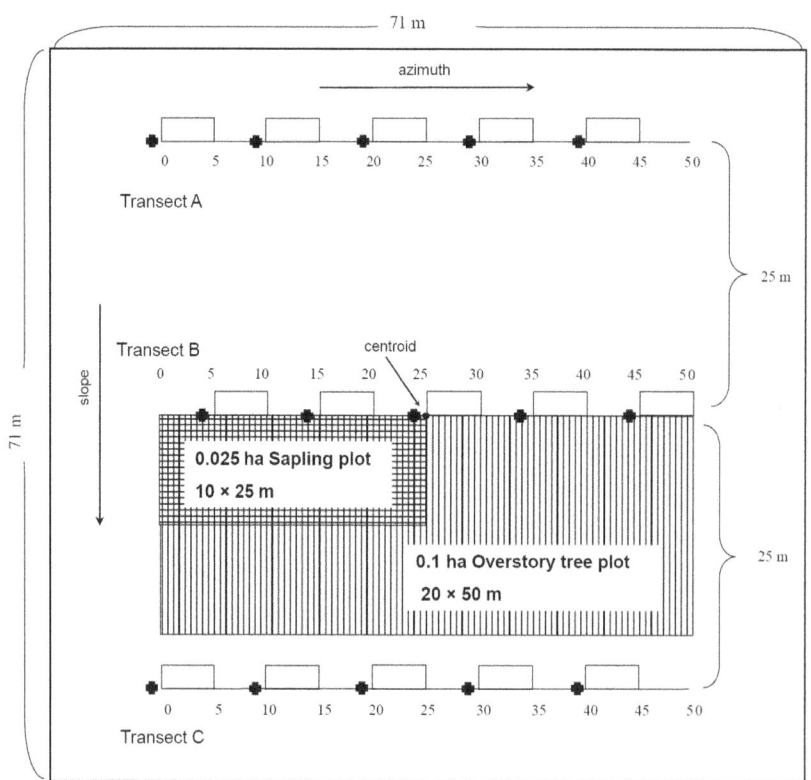

The size of the tree plot is variable. In ecological sites where overstory tree density is low, the tree plot may be expanded to the 50 × 50 m (0.25 ha) area delineated by Transects A and C. The size of the sapling subplot may similarly be expanded (see section 1.3 below). The size of the tree and sapling plots is determined by the project manager, and the applied consistently across the ecological site.

### 1.2.1 Tag overstory trees

If this is the establishment visit to a plot, all living trees ≥15 cm are tagged with brass ID tags stamped with "SCPN" and a sequential ID number prior to being measured. The tags are nailed into the tree at breast height (137 cm). Tags should be oriented to face the plot centroid, except in areas where tags would be visually obtrusive (i.e., near a trail or road), or if the tree was already tagged as a witness tree. The observer drives a 3" (or larger) nail into the tree at an angle through the hole in the tag, such that the tag hangs down and away from the tree and leaves several centimeters of nail exposed, to allow for tree growth.

### 1.2.2 Measure diameter of overstory trees

All trees ≥15 cm DBH should be measured to the nearest 0.1 cm (1 mm). The observer wraps a diameter tape around each bole just above the nail at breast height (137 cm). The tape should be perpendicular to the bole, tight, and with no twists. The recorder notes the tree **ID #**, **Species**, and **DBH** on the datasheet. Species codes are used to record species, following the convention of using the first 3 letters of the genus and the first 3 letters of the specific epithet.

Standing dead trees (snags) should be measured and recorded with a tree ID # of 0, but they are not tagged. Make appropriate **Comments** if the stem of the dead tree is rotten, decomposing, missing bark or has other conditions that make the current diameter much smaller than when the tree was living.

When measuring trees follow these rules:

- Include trees on plot boundaries if more than 50% of their bases are within the plot.
- For trees on slopes, measure DBH while standing at the midslope side of the tree.
- For trees forked below breast height and clonal tree species (other than *Juniperus* spp.) , treat each bole as an individual tree, tagging and measuring all stems ≥15 cm at breast height.
- If an irregularity (e.g., swelling, damage) occurs at breast height, place the tag above or below the irregularity, keeping the tag between 1 and 2 m in height if at all possible. Make a note of the altered height under **Comments**.
- If a branch or tree is leaning, measure it at 137 cm along the bole, keeping the tape perpendicular to the bole.
- *Robinia neomexicana* and *Quercus* spp. are not measured as trees, but are considered shrubs.
- If a diameter tape is not available, you may use a regular tape to measure the circumference, and calculate the diameter by dividing the circumference by $\pi$.

The NPS *Fire Monitoring Handbook* provides more details on sampling trees with irregularities. Record miscellaneous overstory tree information that may be helpful for resampling or interpreting the data in the *Comments* field of the *Forest Tree Datasheet*.

### 1.2.3 Measure tree height and crown base height of overstory trees

Two optional measurements of overstory trees include tree height and crown base height (CBH). These data are typically collected in collaboration with park fire ecology programs, as they are needed for input into fire behavior models. Tree height, however, is also a useful metric for assessing tree size and growth. Measurements for tree height and CBH are both taken using a laser rangefinder.

To measure tree height, the crew member finds a location where there is an unobstructed view of the entire tree, and points the laser at the bottom of the tree and then at the top of the tree. The rangefinder calculates the tree height from these 2 readings. CBH is calculated in a similar fashion. The crown base of a tree is defined as the lowest height above the ground on an individual tree, above which there is sufficient canopy fuel to propagate fire vertically. See the FIREMON protocols for more details in collecting these data (http://www.frames.gov/documents/projects/firemon/ TDv3_Methods.pdf). Enter data into the **Height** and **CBH** columns of the datasheet.

## 1.2.4 Assign tree status and note damage to overstory trees

Assign each tree a **Status** code, indicating whether the tree is alive or dead (see table 7-1). During plot establishment, all trees should have a code of 1, 2, 5 or 6. A code of 6 is used if it is unclear if the tree is living or not (e.g., a scorched conifer following a fire). Record any significant damage to a living tree. The observer should scan each tree for signs of damage, including, but not limited to, recent fire scars, lighting strike scars, mistletoe infestation, or broken or dead tops. The recorder notes these observations in the **Comments** section.

**Table 7-1. Status codes for overstory trees**

| Code | Status | Description |
|------|--------|-------------|
| 1 | Live | Tree is alive above breast height. |
| 2 | Standing dead | Tree is dead and is standing at least at breast height. |
| 3 | Dead and down | Tree is dead and has been snapped off below breast height or uprooted. |
| 4 | Dead but sprouting | Tree has been snapped or uprooted, but is sprouting below breast height. |
| 5 | Cut | Tree has been cut with a saw. |
| 6 | Status unclear | Tree may be dead, very unhealthy, or without leaves due to drought, fire or insect damage. |

## 1.2.5 Map overstory trees

Immediately after a tree is measured, the recorder, or a third person, notes its location on the *Standard Tree Map Datasheet*. The origin (0,0) of the map is the start of Transect B (BS). On the datasheet, the tape that runs from BS towards CS represents the X axis; the B transect represents the Y axis. (The *Standard Tree Map Datasheet* has an alternate labeling of the X axis for plot establishment visits where tapes are already laid out from AS to CS, and AF to CF. When the tapes are laid out in this fashion, the tapes along the X axis of the tree plot run from 25 to 45 meters.)

The mapper walks along the B transect to obtain the Y coordinate, and the perpendicular lines to obtain the X coordinate. Large dots are drawn at the approximate location of the live trees (to the nearest meter) on the map. The ID # is written next to the dot. An alternative version of this datasheet, the *Expanded Tree Map Datasheet*, is provided for the expanded 50 × 50 m tree plot.

## 1.2.6 Remeasure overstory trees on subsequent visits

Since trees grow relatively slowly, it may not be necessary to remeasure trees on each plot visit; however, assessments of tree mortality should be conducted. Revisit sampling is therefore divided into 2 types: mortality assessments, in which overstory trees are assessed only for mortality, and growth assessments, in which all living trees (with codes 1 and 6) in the tree plot are remeasured and ingrowth is assessed. Checkmark the appropriate box at the top of the datasheet. The revisit report will contain a *Forest Tree Revisit Datasheet* that lists all live trees at the last census with tree **ID #**, **Species**, **Status**, **DBH**, blanks for the updated tree status (**New status**), the **New DBH**, and **Comments**.

For mortality assessments, the observer uses the tree map (included in the revisit report) and the tree tags to locate each tree on the *Forest Tree Revisit Datasheet*, verify the **Species** and assign a **New status**. Missing tags should be replaced, and the new ID # recorded in the **Comments** section of the datasheet. For growth assessments, in addition to verifying the species and assigning an updated tree status code, the observer also remeasures each tree's diameter. The recorder enters the **New DBH** on the *Forest Tree Revisit Datasheet*. Once a tree has been assigned a tree status code of something other than 1 or 6, the tag should be removed and the tree is no longer tracked. If a tree has died, locate the tree on a copy of a tree map from the previous visit and put an "X" through the tree ID number.

During a revisit growth assessment, it is also necessary to record tree ingrowth. The observer should check the plot for any trees that have grown large enough to be included as overstory trees, (≥15 cm DBH). Ingrowth trees must be tagged, and measured. Starting at the first blank row on the *Forest Tree Revisit Datasheet*, record **ID #**, **Species** and **DBH**, assign a tree **Status** code of 1, and note any damage in the **Comments** field. Mark the location of these new trees on the copy of the tree map.

## 1.3 Sampling procedure for saplings

### 1.3.1 Establish sapling sub-plot

Saplings (trees that are ≥2.5 cm DBH and <15 cm DBH) are measured in a 10 × 25 m subplot nested within the over-story tree plot, downslope of the first half of the B transect (see fig. 7-1). The sampling team runs one tape such that it defines the 10 × 25 m subplot. In ecological sites where the tree plot has been expanded to 0.25 ha, the sapling plot is expanded to 25 × 25 m.

### 1.3.2 Measure and record sapling tree data

Once the subplot is established, observer reports sapling trees by species and size class. The recorder enters the **Species** code and the number of trees by size class for that species in the appropriate **Tally** column in the *Saplings* section of the *Forest Tree* or *Pinyon-Juniper Tree Datasheet*. For tallying saplings, follow the system illustrated in Figure 7-2. There should be one row only for each species. Saplings are not tagged. There are 3 sapling size classes: 2.5 to <5.0 cm DBH, 5.0 to <10.0 cm DBH, and 10.0 to <15.0 cm DBH. It is easiest to use calipers or a 30 cm ruler to measure saplings, but a DBH tape can also be used. Measure all tree species at DBH, with the exception of junipers, which are measured at DRC.

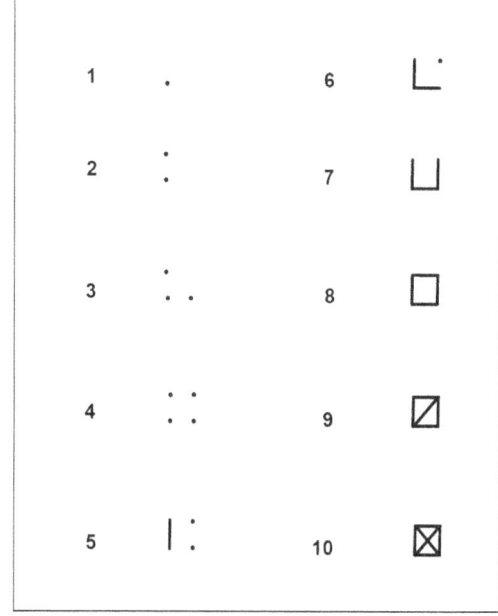

Figure 7-2. Sapling tally recording method. Use dots and lines to tally saplings on the forest tree or pinyon-juniper tree datasheets.

Follow these rules:

- For tree species forked below breast height, individually measure and tally each stem (≥2.5 cm and <15 cm).

- If the main stem of a tree has died or has fallen, but the tree is sprouting from the base, count the individual sprouts for each size class.

- Include clarifying **Comments** on the datasheet, especially for resprouting trees.

- *Quercus* spp. and *Robinia neomexicana* are considered shrubs, therefore are not tallied.

- Trees <2.5 cm DBH are considered seedlings, and are measured in the quadrats instead (see *SOP # 6 Shrub and Herbaceous Vegetation*).

When all saplings have been measured and tallied, the recorder adds up the tally and records it in the **Sum** column for each species and size class.

### 1.3.3 Remeasure saplings on subsequent visits

Saplings are measured in the same way during growth assessment revisits, and recorded in the *Saplings* section on the *Forest Tree Revisit Datasheet*.

## 1.4 Overstory tree and sapling measurements in pinyon-juniper woodlands

Datasheets: *Pinyon-Juniper Tree Datasheet, Standard Tree Map Datasheet* or *Expanded Tree Map Datasheet, Pinyon-Juniper Tree Revisit Datasheet*.

The *Pinyon-Juniper Tree Datasheet* is used anytime there are one or more juniper overstory trees in the tree plot. Due to their typical multi-stemmed growth habit, *Juniperus* tree species are measured using diameter at root crown (DRC) for both overstory trees and saplings. It is not necessary to nail tree tags in junipers at breast height, rather, nail the tag into large, healthy stems where they are most easily accessible and visible , but still oriented towards plot center. Otherwise, the procedures for measuring overstory trees and saplings, collecting tree status, filling in datasheets, and mapping trees for pinyon-juniper woodlands are identical to those measurements in forests. Tree height is an optional measurement; crown base height is not measured in pinyon-juniper forests. The *Pinyon-Juniper Tree Datasheet* and either the *Standard Tree Map Datasheet* or the *Expanded Tree Map Datasheet* (as appropriate), should be used to record the data in pinyon-juniper woodlands.

There are 2 methods for measuring DRC: the tape method and the stick method. All species except *Juniperus monosperma* should be measured by wrapping a diameter tape around the stem at the root crown when possible. The DRC is recorded in the **DRC/DBH** column.

The stick method should always be used for *Juniperus monosperma*, due to its generally multi-stemmed form. It should also be used for other junipers when using a diameter tape is not feasible because of lateral branches or diagonal branches (<45°) at ground level. Two measurements are taken when using the stick method: the diameter of the maximum stem width (excluding lateral and diagonal branches), and a second horizontal measurement perpendicular to this measurement (again excluding the lateral and diagonal branches) (fig. 7-3). When using this method, the largest DRC measurement is recorded in the **DRC/DBH** column and the second measurement is recorded in the **DRC2** column.

If only one diameter measurement is recorded, it is presumed that the tape method was used. If 2 diameter measurements are taken, it is presumed that the stick method was used.

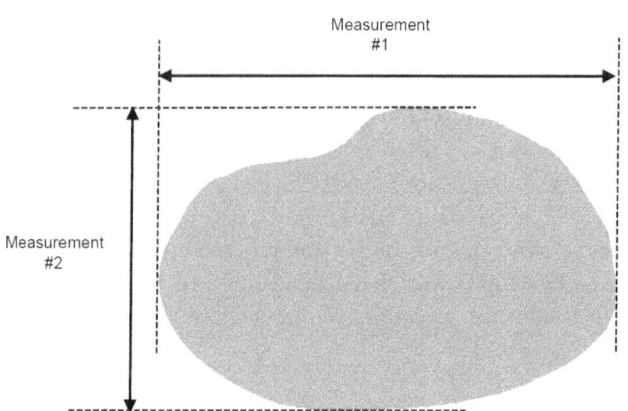

**Figure 7-3. The stick method for measuring diameter at root crown (DRC) for juniper trees requires 2 separate horizontal measurements that are then averaged for the final DRC value. The first measurement is the diameter of the greatest stem width (excluding lateral and diagonal branches). The second measurement is perpendicular to this measurement (again excluding the lateral and diagonal branches).**

Follow these rules (and see fig. 7-4) for determining which method to use and where to measure:

- Use the tape method for junipers other than *Juniperus monosperma* when feasible (fig. 7-4a).
- Use the stick method for *J. monosperma*, and when other junipers have lateral or diagonal branches (fig. 7-4b).
- When one or more stems of *J. monosperma* are joined below ground as a clone, they should be measured as one using the stick method. (fig. 7-4c)
- When one or more stems of junipers other than *J. monosperma* are joined below ground as a clone, each stem should be tagged and measured separately (fig. 7-4d).
- When a *J. monosperma* has a dead stem that is joined below ground to other live stems, the dead stem should not be included in the DRC (fig. 7-4e).
- When the tree has a root collar, or swelling associated with the roots, the diameter should be measured just above the collar (fig. 7-4f).
- When a single stem is leaning, measure the diameter perpendicular to the trunk (fig. 7-4g).
- Overstory trees are those >15 cm DRC (diameter at root crown). For stems where a meter stick is used to measure DRC, the mean of the 2 measurements is used to determine if the tree meets the ≥15 cm threshold.
- *Pinus edulis* and all other non-juniper tree species are measured at breast height. Their diameters should be recorded in the **DRC/DBH** column.
- Snags are measured but not tagged, as with the forest tree procedures.
- When it is not clear how a tree should be measured, make notes in the **Comments** field of the datasheet to clarify how a tree was measured. This helps to ensure that the tree will be measured consistently in following visits.

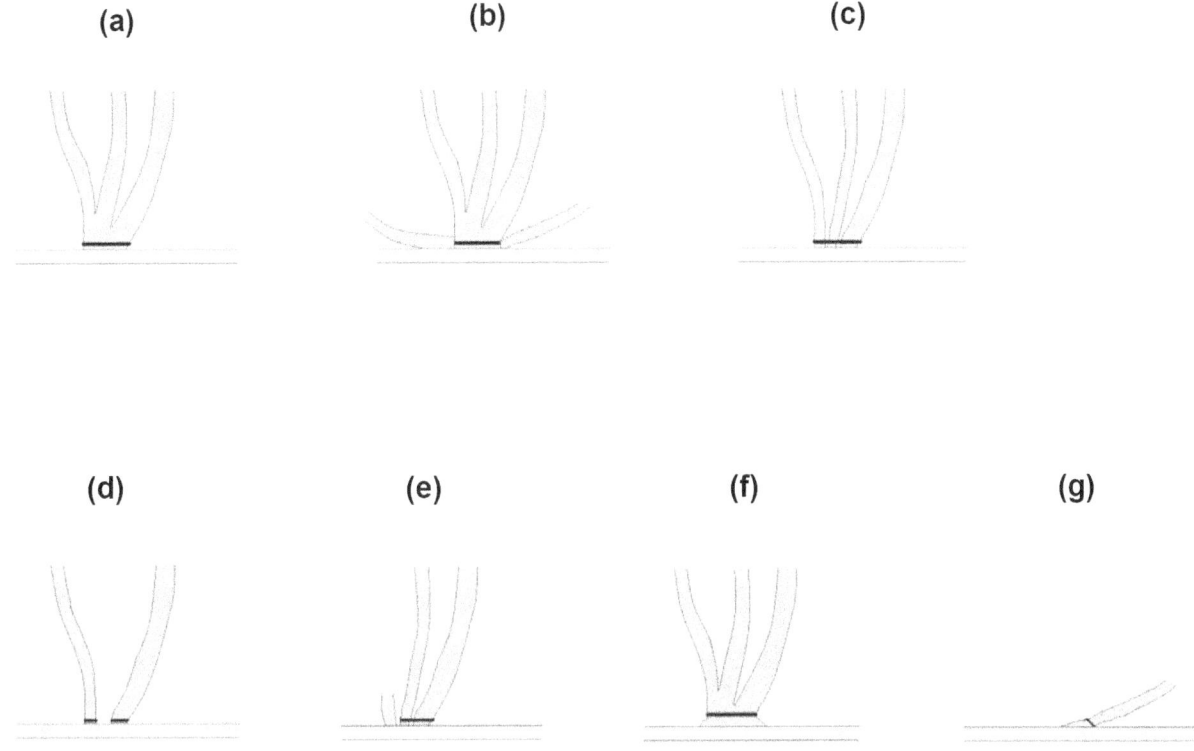

Figure 7-4. How to measure diameter at root crown (DRC) for a variety of situations. The thick black line indicates where the stem should be measured. a) Standard measurement—a diameter tape is used to measure just above the soil line. b) Lateral branches and diagonal branches <45° are not included—these individuals require 2 measurements with a meter stick. c) For *Juniperus monosperma*, all stems that join beneath the soil line are measured together and require 2 measurements with meter stick. d) For all species except *Juniperus monosperma*, all stems that join beneath the soil line are measured separately. e) Dead branches that join beneath the soil line are not included. f) Stems should be measured above the root collar. g) Single leaning stems should be measured perpendicular to the stem.

Saplings are also measured at DRC using the above methods. When using the stick method, determine the size class by taking the mean of the 2 measurements.

For revisits in pinyon-juniper woodland plots, the observer should follow the same mortality, growth, and ingrowth assessment instructions as for forest trees, using the *Pinyon-Juniper Tree Revisit Datasheet*. This datasheet will provide tree **ID #**, **Species**, **Status**, **DRC** (and **DRC2**, depending on methods), with blanks for the updated tree status (**New status**), the **New DRC** (and **DRC2**), and **Comments**. Be sure to use the same method used during the previous growth measurement (i.e., if the tree was measured using the stick method, do not use the tape method during remeasurement).

## 2 Canopy closure
Datasheet: *Canopy Closure Datasheet*

Canopy closure refers to the proportion of the sky hemisphere obscured by vegetation when viewed from a single point (Jennings et al. 1999). Canopy closure is measured at 5 fixed points along each of the 3 transects in forested ecological sites and in certain high-canopy pinyon-juniper woodlands.

### 2.1 General information
Fill out relevant information at the top of the *Canopy Closure Datasheet*.

## 2.2 Locate points along transect

Sampling occurs at 5 points along each transect, for a total of 15 points per plot (fig. 7-1). Sampling points are offset 1 m from quadrat locations to avoid trampling damage in the quadrats. Along transect lines A and C, sampling points are located at -1, 9, 19, 29 and 39 m; along Transect B, sampling points are located at 4, 14, 24, 34 and 44 m. If a point is occupied by a tree stem, the observer should move towards the transect's start (away from the quadrat) a sufficient distance so that the tree's trunk is not visible in the densiometer, and note the new sampling location (based on meters from start) in the **Comments** section of the *Canopy Closure Datasheet*. On site revisits, check the revisit report for canopy closure offsets, so that future sampling will be conducted using the offset points.

## 2.3 Measure canopy closure

Four measurements are taken at each sampling point along the transect using a convex spherical densiometer. Beginning at the -1 m point of Transect A, the observer faces the transect finish, holding the densiometer in front of them above the point at elbow height, far enough away from their body (30 to 46 cm) so that their head is just outside the grid. The instrument should be kept level using the leveling bubble. The observer imagines 4 equally spaced dots in each square of the grid, (see fig. 7-5), and systematically counts either the number of dots intersected by canopy OR the number not covered by canopy. In either case, it is the number of dots covered that must be recorded on the datasheet. When canopy cover is low, it is quicker to count covered dots and record that number. When canopy cover is high, it is easier to count dots not covered and subtract the total from 96.

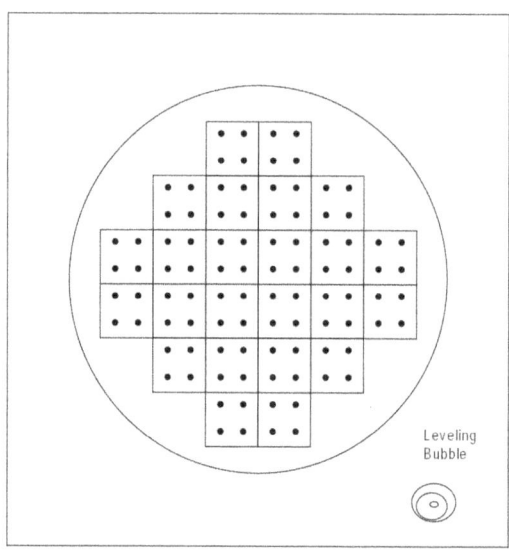

**Figure 7-5. Diagram of spherical densiometer**

It is important for the observer to imagine 4 equally spaced dots, and not divide the squares into sections or use any other way of estimating coverage inside the squares. Deciding whether or not an imaginary dot is covered is a simple objective decision, and is less susceptible to bias. Only green foliage should be counted as cover; branches, boles and scorched needles should not be counted as cover. Record number of dots covered. Dot numbers are converted to percent canopy cover ([#dots covered/96]*100) during the data management process. Record this first measurement in the **Finish** column.

While keeping the densiometer in the same spot, the observer turns their body clockwise 90 degrees from the previous measurement (i.e., facing downslope) then repeats the measurement of canopy closure and records this value on the datasheet in the space column **Down**. The observer repeats the procedure 2 more times to complete the **Start** and **Up** measurements, then moves to the next sampling point along the transect and repeats the 4 measurements. Once all the transect points have been completed, the observer repeats the procedure for the B and C transects.

## 3 Tree canopy cover
Datasheet: *Tree Canopy Cover Datasheet*

Tree canopy cover is an optional measurement taken in pinyon-juniper woodlands, where canopy closure may not provide an adequate metric due to the height and shape of the canopy.

## 3.1 General information
Fill out relevant information at the top of the *Tree Canopy Cover Datasheet*. Data for all 3 transects is recorded on the same datasheet, but the start of each new transect's data must be clearly identified either at the top of the datasheet column or at the location on the datasheet where the transition to a new transect occurs.

## 3.2 Sampling procedure for canopy cover

Beginning at the start of Transect A, using a long, straight object such as the 2 m tent pole or monopod, or a laser pointer to assist in projecting the transect line upward, the observer walks on the downslope side of the transect and records the start and end of any cover of live tree foliage or branches that intersects the line. Record the **Start** and **End** of canopy intersect locations to the nearest centimeter. Follow these rules:

- Include cover only for species listed as trees on the nested quadrat datasheet.
- Tree canopy occurs any time an entire 20 cm segment of tape edge is diffusely (at least 50%) covered by live or dead tree canopy, based on a vertical projection from canopy to ground.
- There is no minimum or maximum height requirement for tree canopy cover.
- If tree canopy exceeds the beginning or end of the transect line, start the canopy at 0, or end the canopy at 5000; do not record anything outside of the actual transect length.
- Exclude canopy intercepts of less than 20 cm.
- Exclude dead branches from canopy measurements.

Follow the above procedure to complete canopy cover sampling on Transects B and C, starting in a new column and recording the transect letter each time. Record **End time**. Record any relevant comments in the **Comments** section.

# Forest Tree Datasheet

Park code:_____ Plot ID:_____ Date (MM/DD/YYYY):_____

Observer:_____

Recorder:_____

Start time (MST): _____End time (MST): _____

| Status codes: 1=Live 2=Standing dead 3=Dead & down |
| --- |
| 4=Dead but sprouting 5=Cut 6=Status unclear |

**Overstory trees**

| ID # | Species | DBH (cm) | Height (m) | CBH (m) | Status | Comments |
| --- | --- | --- | --- | --- | --- | --- |
| | | | | | | |
| | | | | | | |
| | | | | | | |
| | | | | | | |
| | | | | | | |
| | | | | | | |
| | | | | | | |
| | | | | | | |
| | | | | | | |
| | | | | | | |
| | | | | | | |
| | | | | | | |
| | | | | | | |
| | | | | | | |
| | | | | | | |
| | | | | | | |
| | | | | | | |
| | | | | | | |
| | | | | | | |
| | | | | | | |
| | | | | | | |
| | | | | | | |
| | | | | | | |
| | | | | | | |
| | | | | | | |
| | | | | | | |
| | | | | | | |
| | | | | | | |
| | | | | | | |
| | | | | | | |
| | | | | | | |
| | | | | | | |
| | | | | | | |
| | | | | | | |
| | | | | | | |
| | | | | | | |
| | | | | | | |
| | | | | | | |
| | | | | | | |
| | | | | | | |
| | | | | | | |

## Overstory trees—page 2

| ID # | Species | DBH (cm) | Height (m) | CBH (m) | Status | Comments |
|------|---------|----------|-----------|---------|--------|----------|
|      |         |          |           |         |        |          |
|      |         |          |           |         |        |          |
|      |         |          |           |         |        |          |
|      |         |          |           |         |        |          |
|      |         |          |           |         |        |          |
|      |         |          |           |         |        |          |
|      |         |          |           |         |        |          |
|      |         |          |           |         |        |          |
|      |         |          |           |         |        |          |
|      |         |          |           |         |        |          |
|      |         |          |           |         |        |          |
|      |         |          |           |         |        |          |
|      |         |          |           |         |        |          |
|      |         |          |           |         |        |          |
|      |         |          |           |         |        |          |
|      |         |          |           |         |        |          |
|      |         |          |           |         |        |          |
|      |         |          |           |         |        |          |
|      |         |          |           |         |        |          |
|      |         |          |           |         |        |          |
|      |         |          |           |         |        |          |
|      |         |          |           |         |        |          |
|      |         |          |           |         |        |          |
|      |         |          |           |         |        |          |
|      |         |          |           |         |        |          |
|      |         |          |           |         |        |          |
|      |         |          |           |         |        |          |
|      |         |          |           |         |        |          |
|      |         |          |           |         |        |          |

## Saplings

| DBH: | 2.5 to <5.0 cm | | 5.0 to <10.0 cm | | 10.0 to <15.0 cm | | |
|------|------|-----|------|-----|------|-----|----------|
| Species | Tally | Sum | Tally | Sum | Tally | Sum | Comments |
|      |       |     |       |     |       |     |          |
|      |       |     |       |     |       |     |          |
|      |       |     |       |     |       |     |          |
|      |       |     |       |     |       |     |          |
|      |       |     |       |     |       |     |          |
|      |       |     |       |     |       |     |          |
|      |       |     |       |     |       |     |          |
|      |       |     |       |     |       |     |          |
|      |       |     |       |     |       |     |          |
|      |       |     |       |     |       |     |          |
|      |       |     |       |     |       |     |          |

# Standard Tree Map Datasheet

Park code:_____ Plot ID:_____ Date (MM/DD/YYYY):_____

Observer:_____ Recorder:_____

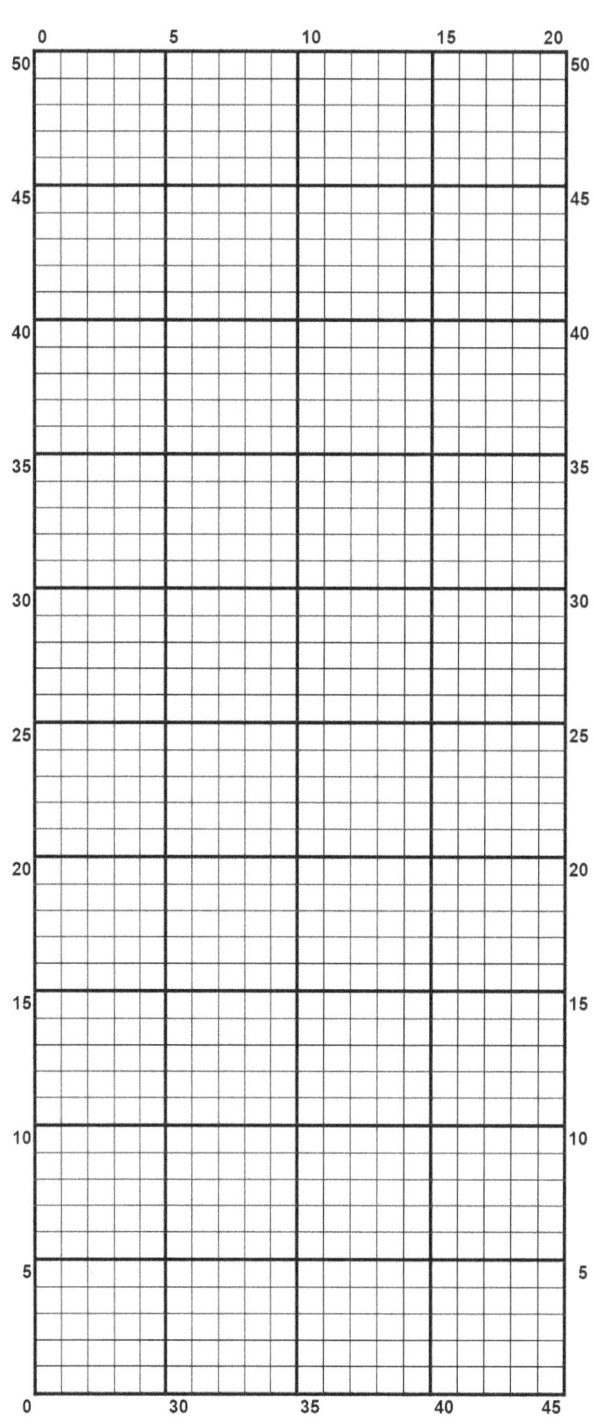

# Expanded Tree Map Datasheet

Park code:_____ Plot ID:_____ Date (MM/DD/YYYY):_____
Observer:_____ Recorder:_____

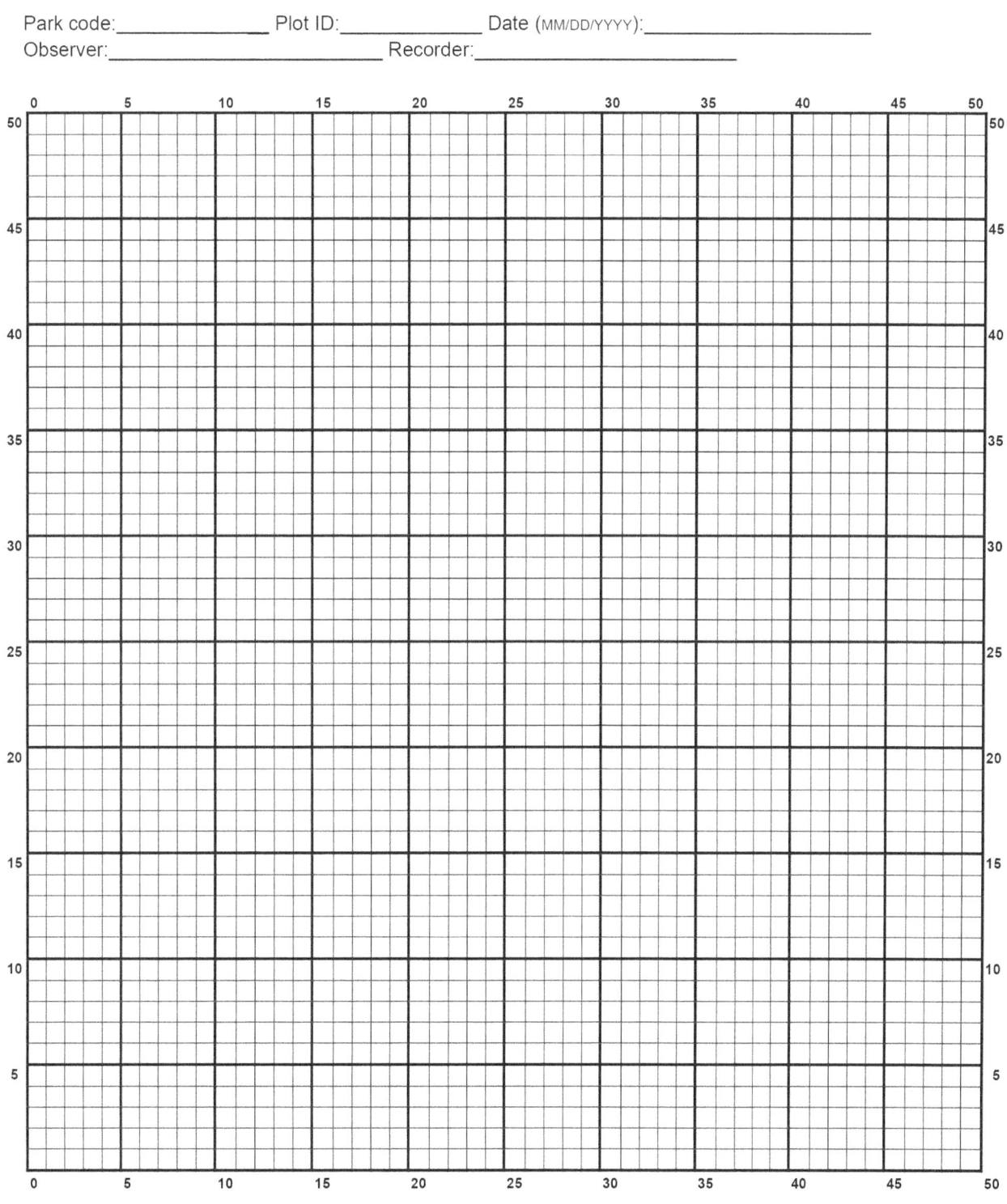

# Pinyon-Juniper Tree Datasheet

Park code:_____ Plot ID:_____ Date (MM/DD/YYYY):_____

Observer:_____

Recorder:_____

Start time (MST): _____ End time (MST): _____

| Status codes: 1=Live, 2=Standing dead, 3=Dead & down, 4=Dead but sprouting, 5=Cut, 6=Status unclear |
| --- |

**PJ overstory trees** (DBH for *Pinus*, DRC for *Juniperus*; record DRC 2 only for *Juniperus* measured using stick method)

| ID # | Species | DRC/DBH (cm) | DRC 2 (cm) | Height (m) | Status | Comments |
|------|---------|--------------|------------|------------|--------|----------|
|      |         |              |            |            |        |          |
|      |         |              |            |            |        |          |
|      |         |              |            |            |        |          |
|      |         |              |            |            |        |          |
|      |         |              |            |            |        |          |
|      |         |              |            |            |        |          |
|      |         |              |            |            |        |          |
|      |         |              |            |            |        |          |
|      |         |              |            |            |        |          |
|      |         |              |            |            |        |          |
|      |         |              |            |            |        |          |
|      |         |              |            |            |        |          |
|      |         |              |            |            |        |          |
|      |         |              |            |            |        |          |
|      |         |              |            |            |        |          |
|      |         |              |            |            |        |          |
|      |         |              |            |            |        |          |
|      |         |              |            |            |        |          |
|      |         |              |            |            |        |          |
|      |         |              |            |            |        |          |
|      |         |              |            |            |        |          |
|      |         |              |            |            |        |          |
|      |         |              |            |            |        |          |
|      |         |              |            |            |        |          |
|      |         |              |            |            |        |          |
|      |         |              |            |            |        |          |
|      |         |              |            |            |        |          |
|      |         |              |            |            |        |          |
|      |         |              |            |            |        |          |
|      |         |              |            |            |        |          |
|      |         |              |            |            |        |          |
|      |         |              |            |            |        |          |
|      |         |              |            |            |        |          |
|      |         |              |            |            |        |          |
|      |         |              |            |            |        |          |
|      |         |              |            |            |        |          |
|      |         |              |            |            |        |          |
|      |         |              |            |            |        |          |
|      |         |              |            |            |        |          |
|      |         |              |            |            |        |          |

**PJ overstory trees**—page 2  (DBH for *Pinus*, DRC for *Juniperus*; record DRC 2 only for *Juniperus* measured using stick method)

| ID # | Species | DRC/DBH(cm) | DRC 2 (cm) | Height (m) | Status | Comments |
|------|---------|-------------|------------|------------|--------|----------|
|  |  |  |  |  |  |  |
|  |  |  |  |  |  |  |
|  |  |  |  |  |  |  |
|  |  |  |  |  |  |  |
|  |  |  |  |  |  |  |
|  |  |  |  |  |  |  |
|  |  |  |  |  |  |  |
|  |  |  |  |  |  |  |
|  |  |  |  |  |  |  |
|  |  |  |  |  |  |  |
|  |  |  |  |  |  |  |
|  |  |  |  |  |  |  |
|  |  |  |  |  |  |  |
|  |  |  |  |  |  |  |
|  |  |  |  |  |  |  |
|  |  |  |  |  |  |  |
|  |  |  |  |  |  |  |
|  |  |  |  |  |  |  |
|  |  |  |  |  |  |  |
|  |  |  |  |  |  |  |
|  |  |  |  |  |  |  |
|  |  |  |  |  |  |  |
|  |  |  |  |  |  |  |
|  |  |  |  |  |  |  |
|  |  |  |  |  |  |  |
|  |  |  |  |  |  |  |
|  |  |  |  |  |  |  |
|  |  |  |  |  |  |  |
|  |  |  |  |  |  |  |
|  |  |  |  |  |  |  |
|  |  |  |  |  |  |  |
|  |  |  |  |  |  |  |
|  |  |  |  |  |  |  |
|  |  |  |  |  |  |  |
|  |  |  |  |  |  |  |
|  |  |  |  |  |  |  |

**Saplings** (use DRC for *Juniperus*, DBH for *Pinus*)

| DRC/DBH: | 2.5 to <5.0 cm | | 5.0 to <10.0 cm | | 10.0 to <15.0 cm | | |
|----------|------|-----|------|-----|------|-----|----------|
| Species | Tally | Sum | Tally | Sum | Tally | Sum | Comments |
|  |  |  |  |  |  |  |  |
|  |  |  |  |  |  |  |  |
|  |  |  |  |  |  |  |  |
|  |  |  |  |  |  |  |  |

# Canopy Closure Datasheet

Park code: _____ Plot ID: _____ Date (MM/DD/YYYY): _____ Observer: _____

Start time (MST): _____ End time (MST): _____ Recorder (if used): _____

## Transect A

| Transect position (If offset, note new position) | Finish | Down | Start | Up |
|---|---|---|---|---|
| -1 | | | | |
| 9 | | | | |
| 19 | | | | |
| 29 | | | | |
| 39 | | | | |

## Transect B

| Transect position (If offset, note new position) | Finish | Down | Start | Up |
|---|---|---|---|---|
| 4 | | | | |
| 14 | | | | |
| 24 | | | | |
| 34 | | | | |
| 44 | | | | |

## Transect C

| Transect position (If offset, note new position) | Finish | Down | Start | Up |
|---|---|---|---|---|
| -1 | | | | |
| 9 | | | | |
| 19 | | | | |
| 29 | | | | |
| 39 | | | | |

Comments:

# Forest Tree Revisit Datasheet

Park code:_____ Plot ID:_____ Date (MM/DD/YYYY):_____

Observer:_____

Recorder:_____

| Status codes: 1=Live 2=Standing dead 3=Dead & down |
| 4=Dead but sprouting 5=Cut 6=Status unclear |

Start time (MST): _____End time (MST): _____

Mortality assessment ☐ Growth assessment ☐

| Overstory trees | | | | | | |
|---|---|---|---|---|---|---|
| ID # | Species | Status | DBH (cm) | New status | New DBH (cm) | Comments |
| | | | | | | |
| | | | | | | |
| | | | | | | |
| | | | | | | |
| | | | | | | |
| | | | | | | |
| | | | | | | |
| | | | | | | |
| | | | | | | |
| | | | | | | |
| | | | | | | |
| | | | | | | |
| | | | | | | |
| | | | | | | |
| | | | | | | |
| | | | | | | |
| | | | | | | |
| | | | | | | |
| | | | | | | |
| | | | | | | |
| | | | | | | |
| | | | | | | |
| | | | | | | |
| | | | | | | |
| | | | | | | |
| | | | | | | |
| | | | | | | |
| | | | | | | |
| | | | | | | |
| | | | | | | |
| | | | | | | |
| | | | | | | |
| | | | | | | |
| | | | | | | |
| | | | | | | |
| | | | | | | |

## Overstory trees—page 2

| ID # | Species | Status | DBH (cm) | New status | New DBH (cm) | Comments |
|------|---------|--------|----------|------------|--------------|----------|
|  |  |  |  |  |  |  |
|  |  |  |  |  |  |  |
|  |  |  |  |  |  |  |
|  |  |  |  |  |  |  |
|  |  |  |  |  |  |  |
|  |  |  |  |  |  |  |
|  |  |  |  |  |  |  |
|  |  |  |  |  |  |  |
|  |  |  |  |  |  |  |
|  |  |  |  |  |  |  |
|  |  |  |  |  |  |  |
|  |  |  |  |  |  |  |
|  |  |  |  |  |  |  |
|  |  |  |  |  |  |  |
|  |  |  |  |  |  |  |
|  |  |  |  |  |  |  |
|  |  |  |  |  |  |  |
|  |  |  |  |  |  |  |
|  |  |  |  |  |  |  |
|  |  |  |  |  |  |  |
|  |  |  |  |  |  |  |
|  |  |  |  |  |  |  |
|  |  |  |  |  |  |  |
|  |  |  |  |  |  |  |
|  |  |  |  |  |  |  |
|  |  |  |  |  |  |  |
|  |  |  |  |  |  |  |
|  |  |  |  |  |  |  |
|  |  |  |  |  |  |  |
|  |  |  |  |  |  |  |

## Saplings

| DBH: | 2.5 to <5.0 cm | | 5.0 to <10.0 cm | | 10.0 to <15.0 cm | | |
|------|----------------|--|-----------------|--|------------------|--|--|
| Species | Tally | Sum | Tally | Sum | Tally | Sum | Comments |
|  |  |  |  |  |  |  |  |
|  |  |  |  |  |  |  |  |
|  |  |  |  |  |  |  |  |
|  |  |  |  |  |  |  |  |
|  |  |  |  |  |  |  |  |
|  |  |  |  |  |  |  |  |
|  |  |  |  |  |  |  |  |
|  |  |  |  |  |  |  |  |
|  |  |  |  |  |  |  |  |
|  |  |  |  |  |  |  |  |

# Pinyon-Juniper Tree Revisit Datasheet

Park code:_____ Plot ID:_____ Date (MM/DD/YYYY):_____

Observer:_____

Recorder:_____

Start time (MST): _____End time (MST): _____

| Status codes: 1=Live 2=Standing dead 3=Dead & down 4=Dead but sprouting 5=Cut 6=Status unclear |
| --- |

Mortality assessment ☐ Growth assessment ☐

| **Overstory trees** | | | | | | | | |
| --- | --- | --- | --- | --- | --- | --- | --- | --- |
| ID # | Species | Status | DRC (cm) | DRC2 (cm) | New status | New DRC (cm) | New DRC2 (cm) | Comments |
| | | | | | | | | |
| | | | | | | | | |
| | | | | | | | | |
| | | | | | | | | |
| | | | | | | | | |
| | | | | | | | | |
| | | | | | | | | |
| | | | | | | | | |
| | | | | | | | | |
| | | | | | | | | |
| | | | | | | | | |
| | | | | | | | | |
| | | | | | | | | |
| | | | | | | | | |
| | | | | | | | | |
| | | | | | | | | |
| | | | | | | | | |
| | | | | | | | | |
| | | | | | | | | |
| | | | | | | | | |
| | | | | | | | | |
| | | | | | | | | |
| | | | | | | | | |
| | | | | | | | | |
| | | | | | | | | |
| | | | | | | | | |
| | | | | | | | | |
| | | | | | | | | |
| | | | | | | | | |
| | | | | | | | | |
| | | | | | | | | |
| | | | | | | | | |
| | | | | | | | | |

## Overstory trees—page 2

| ID # | Species | Status | DRC (cm) | DRC2 (cm) | New status | New DRC (cm) | New DRC2 (cm) | Comments |
|---|---|---|---|---|---|---|---|---|
| | | | | | | | | |
| | | | | | | | | |
| | | | | | | | | |
| | | | | | | | | |
| | | | | | | | | |
| | | | | | | | | |
| | | | | | | | | |
| | | | | | | | | |
| | | | | | | | | |
| | | | | | | | | |
| | | | | | | | | |
| | | | | | | | | |
| | | | | | | | | |
| | | | | | | | | |
| | | | | | | | | |
| | | | | | | | | |
| | | | | | | | | |
| | | | | | | | | |
| | | | | | | | | |
| | | | | | | | | |
| | | | | | | | | |
| | | | | | | | | |
| | | | | | | | | |
| | | | | | | | | |
| | | | | | | | | |
| | | | | | | | | |
| | | | | | | | | |
| | | | | | | | | |
| | | | | | | | | |
| | | | | | | | | |

## Saplings (use DRC for *Juniperus*, DBH for *Pinus*)

| DRC/DBH: | 2.5 to <5.0 cm | | 5.0 to <10.0 cm | | 10.0 to <15.0 cm | | |
|---|---|---|---|---|---|---|---|
| Species | Tally | Sum | Tally | Sum | Tally | Sum | Comments |
| | | | | | | | |
| | | | | | | | |
| | | | | | | | |
| | | | | | | | |

# Tree Canopy Cover Datasheet

Park code:_____ Plot ID:_____ Date (MM/DD/YYYY):_____

Observer:_____ Recorder:_____

Start time (MST):_____End time (MST):_____

Comments:_____

_____

_____

| Tree canopy cover (record intercepts for juniper and pine canopy to the nearest cm; ignore all shrubs and dead branches) | | | | | | | |
|---|---|---|---|---|---|---|---|
| Transect: | | Transect: | | Transect: | | Transect: | |
| Start | End | Start | End | Start | End | Start | End |
| | | | | | | | |
| | | | | | | | |
| | | | | | | | |
| | | | | | | | |
| | | | | | | | |
| | | | | | | | |
| | | | | | | | |
| | | | | | | | |
| | | | | | | | |
| | | | | | | | |
| | | | | | | | |
| | | | | | | | |
| | | | | | | | |
| | | | | | | | |
| | | | | | | | |
| | | | | | | | |
| | | | | | | | |
| | | | | | | | |
| | | | | | | | |
| | | | | | | | |
| | | | | | | | |
| | | | | | | | |
| | | | | | | | |
| | | | | | | | |
| | | | | | | | |
| | | | | | | | |
| | | | | | | | |
| | | | | | | | |
| | | | | | | | |
| | | | | | | | |
| | | | | | | | |
| | | | | | | | |
| | | | | | | | |
| | | | | | | | |
| | | | | | | | |
| | | | | | | | |
| | | | | | | | |

**Tree canopy cover—page 2** (record intercepts for juniper and pine canopy to the nearest cm; ignore all shrubs and dead branches)

| Transect: | | Transect: | | Transect: | | Transect: | |
|---|---|---|---|---|---|---|---|
| Start | End | Start | End | Start | End | Start | End |
| | | | | | | | |
| | | | | | | | |
| | | | | | | | |
| | | | | | | | |
| | | | | | | | |
| | | | | | | | |
| | | | | | | | |
| | | | | | | | |
| | | | | | | | |
| | | | | | | | |
| | | | | | | | |
| | | | | | | | |
| | | | | | | | |
| | | | | | | | |
| | | | | | | | |
| | | | | | | | |
| | | | | | | | |
| | | | | | | | |
| | | | | | | | |
| | | | | | | | |
| | | | | | | | |
| | | | | | | | |
| | | | | | | | |
| | | | | | | | |
| | | | | | | | |
| | | | | | | | |
| | | | | | | | |
| | | | | | | | |
| | | | | | | | |
| | | | | | | | |
| | | | | | | | |
| | | | | | | | |
| | | | | | | | |
| | | | | | | | |
| | | | | | | | |
| | | | | | | | |
| | | | | | | | |
| | | | | | | | |
| | | | | | | | |
| | | | | | | | |
| | | | | | | | |
| | | | | | | | |
| | | | | | | | |

# Standard Operating Procedure #8: Soil Stability and Hydrologic Function

**Version 1.00**

**Revision History Log**

| Previous version number | Revision date | Author | Changes made | Section and paragraph | Reason | Approved by | New version number |
|---|---|---|---|---|---|---|---|
| | | | | | | | |
| | | | | | | | |
| | | | | | | | |
| | | | | | | | |
| | | | | | | | |
| | | | | | | | |
| | | | | | | | |
| | | | | | | | |

Only changes in this specific SOP will be logged here. Version numbers increase incrementally by hundredths (e.g., version 1.01, version 1.02) for minor changes. Major revisions should be designated with the next whole number (e.g., version 2.0, 3.0, 4.0). Record the previous version number, date of revision, author of the revision; identify paragraphs and pages where changes are made, who approved the revision, and the reason for making the changes along with the new version number.

This standard operating procedure (SOP) gives step-by-step instructions for measuring basal and canopy gap intercepts and soil aggregate stability. Material for this SOP was modified from the *Monitoring Manual for Grassland, Shrubland and Savanna Ecosystems*, Volumes 1 & 2 (Herrick et al. 2005a, b). Basal and canopy gap intercepts are optional measures conducted in woodlands, shrublands and grasslands. The size and distribution of basal gaps are important indicators of the potential for water erosion; the size and distribution of canopy gaps are important indicators of potential wind erosion. The soil stability test quantifies the degree of soil structural development and the soil's resistance to erosion. Equipment needs for this procedure are listed in *SOP #1*, Table 1-1. Two datasheets are associated with this SOP: *Basal and Canopy Gap Intercept Datasheet*, and the *Soil Aggregate Stability Datasheet*.

## 1 Sampling teams
Gap intercept sampling generally requires a two-person team: one "observer" to report gap measurements and one "recorder" to write down measurements. One person can conduct both the observations and recording, albeit at a slower pace. Soil aggregate stability sampling requires only one person.

## 2 Sampling basal gap intercepts (optional)
Fill out general information on the Basal and Canopy Gap Intercept Datasheet, using the following guidelines:

- **Park code.** Use the standard 4-letter code to indicate the park unit.
- **Plot ID.** A pre-assigned unique alphanumeric code number is provided for each plot. The letter designates the ecological site, and the number is assigned consecutively with plot establishment.
- **Date.** MM/DD/YYYY (e.g., 03/14/2008).
- **Transect.** Circle A, B or C.
- **Observer.** Record the first initial and the last name of the person calling out gap measurements.
- **Recorder.** Record the first initial and last name of the person recording data.

- **Start time**. Record the time (MST) that the transect is started.
- **End time**. Record the time (MST) that the transect is finished.

## 2.1 Sample basal gap intercepts

Basal gaps are linear spaces along the transect in which no perennial vegetation is rooted (i.e., they contain no plant bases). Beginning with Transect A, the sampling team stands on the downslope side of the first transect at the 0 m end and works from left to right towards the 50 m end. The observer looks straight down on the tape, uses a meter stick, chaining pin or pin flag as a plumb bob to project a line vertically to the ground on the upslope side of the tape. The observer reports and the recorder records the **Start** and **End** of each gap to the nearest centimeter. The closer the tape is to the ground, the easier it is to accurately determine the start and end of a gap.

Follow these rules:

- A plant base is any non-annual vascular plant stem emerging from the soil surface along the line formed by the upslope edge of the tape that would force an ant walking along the line on the soil to step off the line to get around it.
- Plant bases may be alive or dead, but must be anchored in the ground. Litter is not a plant base.
- Annual species are not included as plant bases, due to their transient nature.

See Table 8-1 and Figure 8-1 for examples of how to collect and record data.

## 2.2 Check data

The recorder should check data to make sure that gaps increase logically. Once the entire transect has been sampled, record **End time**.

## 2.3 Sample remaining transects

Following the above procedure, complete gap intercept sampling on Transects B and C, using a new datasheet for each transect.

**Table 8-1. Example of how basal and canopy gap data from Figure 8-1 should be recorded on the datasheets**

| Basal gaps | | Canopy gaps | |
|---|---|---|---|
| Start (cm) | End (cm) | Type | End (cm) |
| 0 | 11 | G | 31 |
| 12 | 62 | H | 34 |
| 65 | 88 | G | 53 |
| | | S | 70 |
| | | G | 85 |
| | | S | 97 |

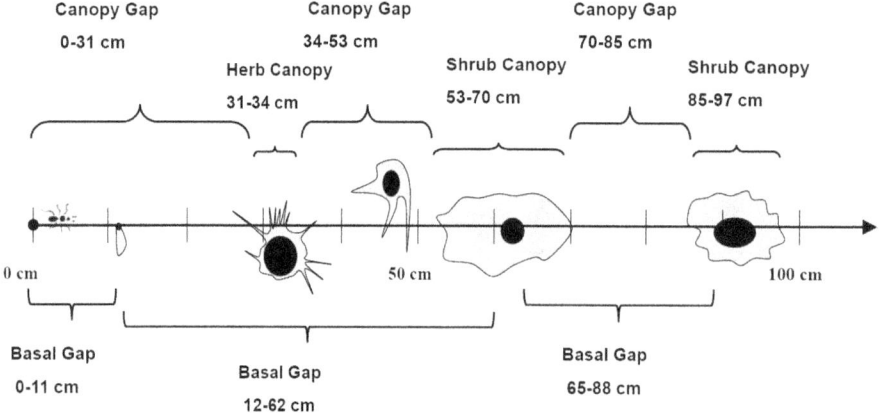

Note: Each hatch mark is 10 cm.

Figure 8-1. Example of basal gaps and canopy gaps. An overhead diagram of a hypothetical transect shows basal gaps (below the transect) and canopy gaps (above the transect). Three basal gaps (0–11 cm, 12–62 cm and 65–88 cm) and 3 canopy gaps (0–31 cm, 34–53 cm and 70–85 cm) are depicted. The herb canopy at 31–34 cm is 3 cm long and occupies >50% of the space. In contrast, the canopies at 11–12 cm and 45–49 cm occupy <50% of the space, therefore are not counted.

# 3 Sampling canopy gap intercepts (optional)

## 3.1 Sample canopy gap intercepts

Use the reverse side of the *Basal and Canopy Gap Intercept Datasheet* to record canopy gap data. Canopy gap measurements are a continuous accounting of the length of the tape, breaking all canopy (<2 m in height) into type categories and specifying where each type ends (and therefore where the subsequent type begins). It includes both length of canopy cover for shrubs (including *Juniperus* spp. and *Pinus edulis* under 2 m), herbaceous plants and cactus/succulents, as well as the length of gaps. To begin, the observer stands on the downslope side of the transect at the 0 m end and works from left to right towards the 50 m end. The observer looks straight down on the tape and use a meter stick or other stiff stick as a plumb bob to project a line vertically to the ground on the upslope side of the tape. The observer reports the canopy type (gap, herbaceous, dead herbaceous, shrub, dead shrub, cactus/succulent or dead cactus/succulent), and the measurement where that canopy ends and a new canopy type begins. The recorder records the canopy type in the **Type** column, and the point on the tape where the canopy type ends in the **End** column, to the nearest centimeter. Segments along a transect fall into 7 distinct types of cover (table 8-2).

**Table 8-2. Types of cover to be measured for canopy gaps**

| Canopy type | Code | Definition |
|---|---|---|
| Canopy gap | G | any area not covered by vegetation |
| Shrub | S | shrub canopy; include *Juniperus* spp. and *Pinus edulis* and any other woody plant in this category |
| Herbaceous | H | any canopy cover of perennial forbs and graminoids; annual herbs are ignored |
| Cactus/ Succulent | C | basal portion of a cactus or succulent. |
| Dead shrub | DS | shrub canopy that is dead; include *Juniperus* spp. and any other woody plant in this category |
| Dead herbaceous | DH | perennial forb and graminoid canopy that is dead |
| Dead cactus/succulent | DC | non-living cactus or succulent |

Follow these rules:

- Include any shrub cover <2 m in height, including *Juniperus* spp. and *Pinus edulis*.
- Record canopy any time a 3 cm segment of tape edge is more than 50% covered by live or dead plant canopy, based on a vertical projection from canopy to ground.
- If shrub and herbaceous vegetation co-occur in a given line segment, record canopy type for the type that has the denser cover.

## 3.2 Check data

The recorder should check to ensure that all data is logical:

- canopy gaps proceed from 0–5000 cm
- classes are all valid
- 2 of the same class are not consecutive

Refer again to Figure 8-1 and Table 8-1 for examples of how to collect and record data. Record **End time**.

## 3.3 Sample remaining transects

Follow the above procedure to complete canopy gap sampling on Transects B and C.

# 4 Soil aggregate stability

Generally only surface samples are collected to measure soil aggregate stability. Subsurface sampling is optional and used to assess soil erodibility after disturbance. If collecting surface samples only, 2 boxes are required—1 for collecting the samples and 1 for conducting the test. If collecting both surface and subsurface samples, 3 boxes are required—2 for collecting the samples and 1 for conducting the tests. The soil stability test must be conducted with dry soil samples. If soils are moist at sampling time, the samples can be left out to air-dry while other procedures are being conducted. If it is raining, or it is not possible for the samples to dry out, the test should not be conducted.

## 4.1 General information

Fill out relevant information at the top of the *Soil Aggregate Stability Datasheet* using the following guidelines:

- **Park code**. Use the standard 4-letter code to indicate the park unit.
- **Plot ID**. A pre-assigned unique alphanumeric code number is provided for each plot. The letter designates the ecological site, and the number is assigned consecutively with plot establishment.
- **Date**. MM/DD/YYYY (e.g., 03/14/2008).
- **Recorder**. Record the first initial and last name of the person conducting the test.

## 4.2 Randomly select 18 sampling points

Use a random numbers table to select 18 random points along the transects, 6 points for each transect, to the nearest 0.1 m. Record sampling locations (points) under **Position** on the datasheet. Decide on a small set distance from the transect to collect the sample from, e.g., a hand span, and use the same distance from the transect for all points along that transect. When selecting the point, it is critical that it is strictly random and unbiased.

## 4.3 Determine the dominant cover type

Determine the dominant cover type over the random point and enter this into the **Veg** (for Vegetation) column on the datasheet. See Table 8-3 for cover type codes. The area to be classified is effectively as large as the sample area (8 mm in diameter)(fig. 8-2).

## 4.4 Collect a surface sample

Collect samples at the exact point. Move the sample point only if it has been disturbed by the sampling crew (i.e., foot print), or the soil surface is obstructed by a rock, a plant base, or embedded litter. Move the point a standard distance (a hand span) along the transect. Do not move the point if there has been a natural disturbance (animal burrow), or a human disturbance not caused by monitoring crew (foot trail).

Figures 8-3 through 8-9 illustrate the steps. Excavate a small trench (10–15 mm deep) in front of the area to be sampled (fig. 8-3). Lift out a soil fragment and trim it (if necessary) to the correct size (figs. 8-4, 8-5). The soil fragment should be 2–3 mm thick and 6–8 mm in diameter (fig. 8-5) —the diameter of a standard pencil eraser. The sample should fit in the dot of Figure 8-2.

**Table 8-3. Dominant cover types for soil aggregate stability samples**

| Code | Description |
|------|-------------|
| NC | no perennial grass, shrub or tree canopy cover |
| G | perennial grass canopy and grass/shrub canopy mixture |
| F | perennial forb |
| S | shrub (includes *Juniperus* spp., *Pinus edulis*, other tree species, dead shrubs, and cacti/succulents) |

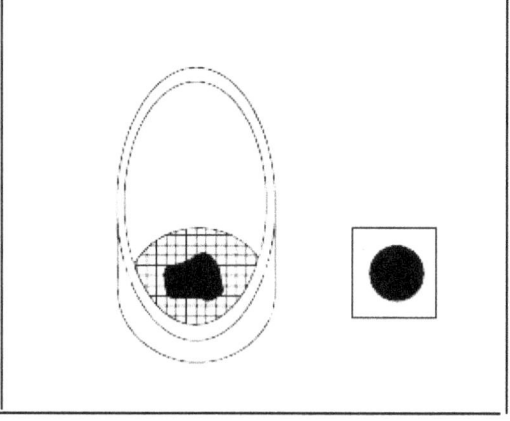

Figure 8-2. Sample in sieve drawn to scale and actual size of sample.

- Minimize shattering by slicing the soil around the sample before lifting, or lifting out a larger sample than required, and trimming it to size in the palm of your hand. If the sample still will not hold together, record a **Rating** of "1" on the datasheet.
- If the soil surface is covered by a lichen or cyanobacteria crust, include the crust in the sample. If the sample is covered by moss, collect the sample from under the moss. If the sample location is covered by thick duff and litter (>2.5 cm) record an "L" for the **Rating**, and do not collect the sample. If the sample location is covered by deep pumice (>2.5 cm), record a "P" for the **Rating**, and do not collect the sample. Gently place the sample in a dry sieve (fig. 8-2), and place the sieve in the appropriate cell of a dry box. Orient the box so that the columns and rows are consistent with the columns and rows of the datasheet.

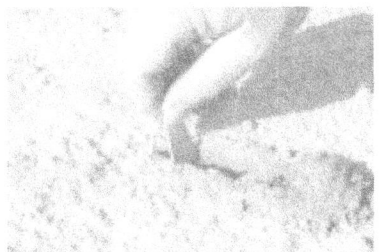
Figure 8-3. Excavate small trench

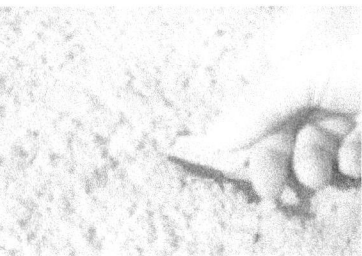
Figure 8-4. Collect surface sample

Figure 8-5. Ensure correct sample size

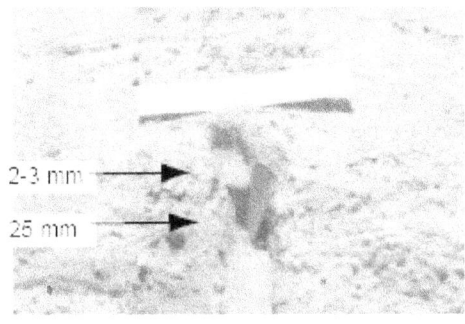

2-3 mm →

25 mm →

Figure 8-6. Excavate trench for subsurface sample

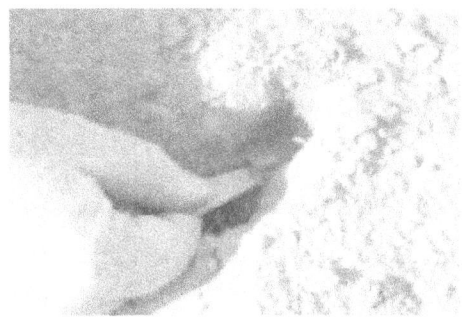
Figure 8-7. Collect subsurface sample

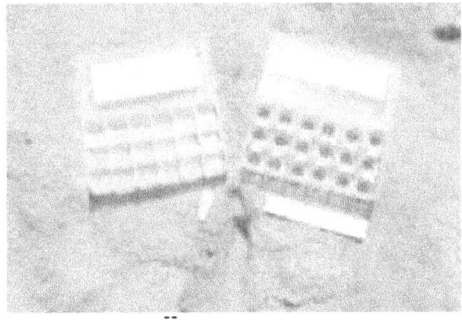
Figure 8-8. Complete soil stability kit with water and samples

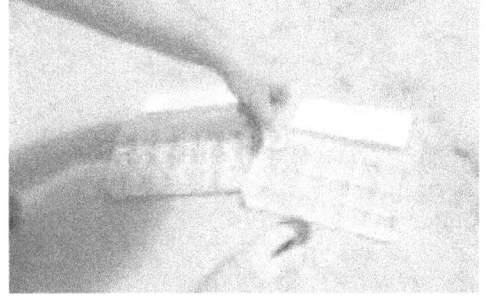
Figure 8-9. Place first sample in water

## 4.5 Collect a subsurface sample (optional)

A subsurface sample is collected directly below the surface sample. Use the flat, square (handle) end of the scoop to gently excavate the previous trench (in front of the surface sample) to a depth of 3–4 cm. Remove soil from directly below the surface sample, so that a "shelf" is created with the top step 2–2.5 cm below the soil surface (fig. 8–6). Use the scoop to lift out a subsurface sample from below (fig. 8-7). The soil fragment should be 2–3 mm thick and 6–8 mm in diameter (fig. 8–5). If you encounter a rock, record "R" in the **Rating** column and move to the next sample. Place the sample in a dry sieve; place sieve in the dry box. Leave box lid open (fig. 8-8).

## 4.6 Test the surface samples

Samples must be dry before testing. If samples are not dry after collecting, allow to air dry. Do not leave lid closed on samples for more than 1 minute on hot or sunny days. Excessive heat can artificially increase or decrease stability. The test should not be conducted if the samples are not dry.

Fill the empty (no sieves) box with deionized or distilled water, bringing the water level in each compartment to near the top. The water should be approximately the same temperature as the soil (fig. 8-8).

Lower the first sieve with the sample into its respective water-filled compartment—upper left corner of sample box to upper left corner of water box (fig. 8-9). One second should elapse from the time the sieve screen touches the water

**Table 8-4. Stability class ratings**

| Code | Description |
|------|-------------|
| 1 | 50% of structural integrity lost (melts) within 5 seconds of immersion in water, OR soil too unstable to sample (falls through sieve) |
| 2 | 50% of structural integrity lost (melts) 5–30 seconds after immersion |
| 3 | 50% of structural integrity lost (melts) 30–300 seconds after immersion, OR <10% of soil remains on the sieve after 5 dipping cycles |
| 4 | 10–25% of soil remains on the sieve after 5 dipping cycles |
| 5 | 25–75% of soil remains on the sieve after 5 dipping cycles |
| 6 | 75–100% of soil remains on the sieve after 5 dipping cycles |

surface to the time it rests on the bottom of the box. Start the stopwatch when the first sample touches the water. Immerse additional samples at a rate of one sample every 15 seconds.

Rate the samples during the first 5 minutes after immersion, based on time to disintegration. Observe the fragments from the time the sample hits the water to 5 min (300 sec), and record a stability class based on Table 8-4.

At 5 minutes, raise the sieve completely out of the water, and then lower it to the bottom without touching the bottom of the tray. Repeat this immersion a total of 5 times. Do this even if you have already rated the sample a 1, 2 or 3 (you are allowed to change your rating if after sieving >10% of soil remains on sieve). It should take one second for each sieve to clear the water's surface and one second to return to near the bottom of the box. Hydrophobic samples (float in water after pushed under) are rated 6. Use Table 8-4 and Figure 8-10 as references. Record the coded stability class on the datasheet under **Rating**.

## 4.7 Test the subsurface samples (optional)
Use the same method for surface samples to test subsurface samples.

**Sequence for stability class = 1.**

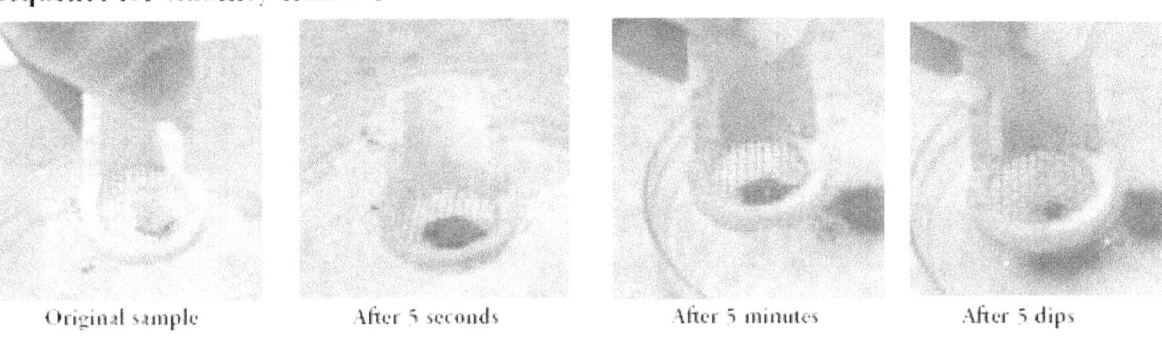

| Original sample | After 5 seconds | After 5 minutes | After 5 dips |

**Sequence for stability class = 4**

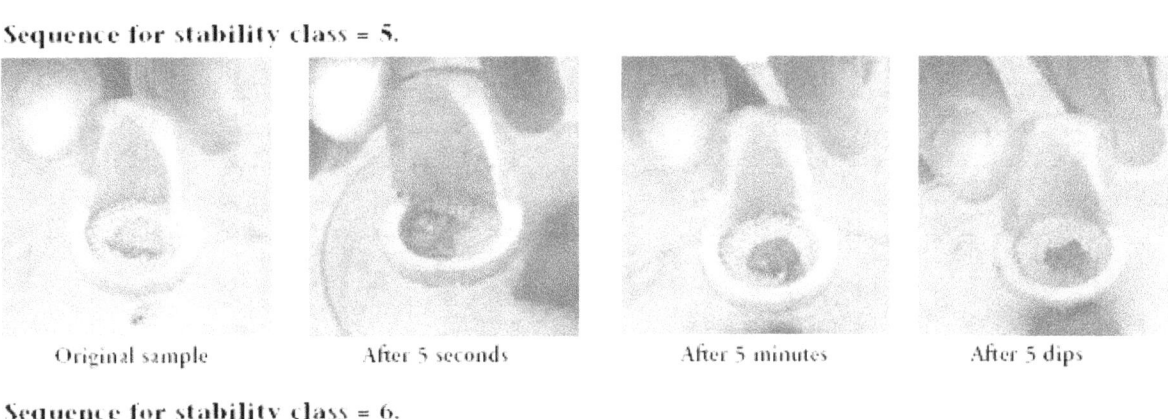

| Original sample | After 5 seconds | After 5 minutes | After 5 dips |

**Sequence for stability class = 5.**

Original sample    After 5 seconds    After 5 minutes    After 5 dips

**Sequence for stability class = 6.**

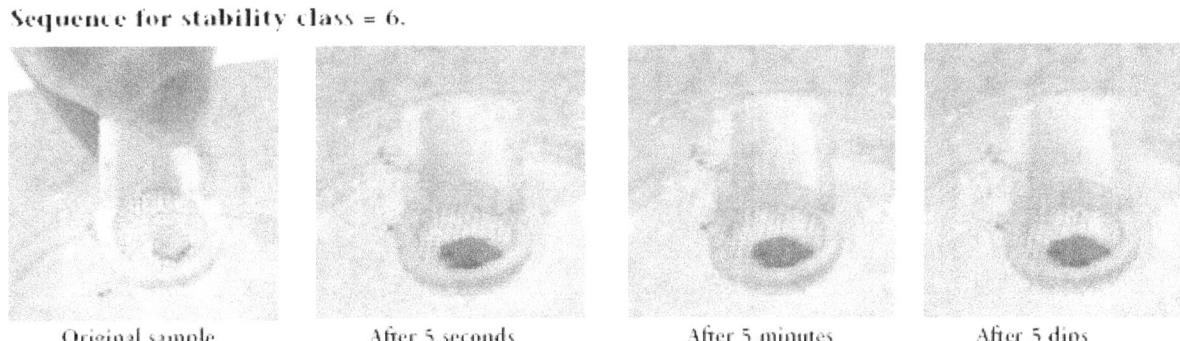

Original sample    After 5 seconds    After 5 minutes    After 5 dips

Figure 8-10. The photos above illustrate the key steps of testing a soil sample for 4 different stability rankings. Important note: Some of the fragments shown in these samples may appear large. They are for illustration only. Be sure to follow the size guidelines in step 4 and Figure 8-2.

# Basal and Canopy Gap Intercept Datasheet

Park code:_____ Plot ID:_____ Date (MM/DD/YYYY):_____

Transect: A  B  C    Observer:_____ Recorder:_____

Start time (MST):_____End time (MST):_____

| Basal gaps | | | | | | | | | |
|---|---|---|---|---|---|---|---|---|---|
| Start (cm) | End (cm) | Start (cm) | End (cm) | Start (cm) | End (cm) | Start (cm) | End (cm) | Start (cm) | End (cm) |
| | | | | | | | | | |
| | | | | | | | | | |
| | | | | | | | | | |
| | | | | | | | | | |
| | | | | | | | | | |
| | | | | | | | | | |
| | | | | | | | | | |
| | | | | | | | | | |
| | | | | | | | | | |
| | | | | | | | | | |
| | | | | | | | | | |
| | | | | | | | | | |
| | | | | | | | | | |
| | | | | | | | | | |
| | | | | | | | | | |
| | | | | | | | | | |
| | | | | | | | | | |
| | | | | | | | | | |
| | | | | | | | | | |
| | | | | | | | | | |
| | | | | | | | | | |
| | | | | | | | | | |
| | | | | | | | | | |
| | | | | | | | | | |
| | | | | | | | | | |
| | | | | | | | | | |
| | | | | | | | | | |
| | | | | | | | | | |
| | | | | | | | | | |
| | | | | | | | | | |
| | | | | | | | | | |
| | | | | | | | | | |
| | | | | | | | | | |
| | | | | | | | | | |
| | | | | | | | | | |
| | | | | | | | | | |
| | | | | | | | | | |
| | | | | | | | | | |
| | | | | | | | | | |
| | | | | | | | | | |

# Basal and Canopy Gap Intercept Datasheet

Park code:_____ Plot ID:_____ Date (MM/DD/YYYY):_____

Transect: A  B  C   Observer:_____ Recorder:_____

Start time (MST):_____End time (MST):_____

| Canopy gaps (G=gap, H=herbaceous, DH=dead herbaceous, S=shrub, DS=dead shrub, C=cactus/succ, DC=dead cactus/succ) | | | | | | | | | | | | | | | | | |
|---|---|---|---|---|---|---|---|---|---|---|---|---|---|---|---|---|---|
| Type | End (cm) | | Type | End (cm) | | Type | End (cm) | | Type | End(cm) | | Type | End (cm) | | Type | End(cm) |
| | | | | | | | | | | | | | | | | | |
| | | | | | | | | | | | | | | | | | |
| | | | | | | | | | | | | | | | | | |
| | | | | | | | | | | | | | | | | | |
| | | | | | | | | | | | | | | | | | |
| | | | | | | | | | | | | | | | | | |
| | | | | | | | | | | | | | | | | | |
| | | | | | | | | | | | | | | | | | |
| | | | | | | | | | | | | | | | | | |
| | | | | | | | | | | | | | | | | | |
| | | | | | | | | | | | | | | | | | |
| | | | | | | | | | | | | | | | | | |
| | | | | | | | | | | | | | | | | | |
| | | | | | | | | | | | | | | | | | |
| | | | | | | | | | | | | | | | | | |
| | | | | | | | | | | | | | | | | | |
| | | | | | | | | | | | | | | | | | |
| | | | | | | | | | | | | | | | | | |
| | | | | | | | | | | | | | | | | | |
| | | | | | | | | | | | | | | | | | |
| | | | | | | | | | | | | | | | | | |
| | | | | | | | | | | | | | | | | | |
| | | | | | | | | | | | | | | | | | |
| | | | | | | | | | | | | | | | | | |
| | | | | | | | | | | | | | | | | | |
| | | | | | | | | | | | | | | | | | |
| | | | | | | | | | | | | | | | | | |
| | | | | | | | | | | | | | | | | | |
| | | | | | | | | | | | | | | | | | |
| | | | | | | | | | | | | | | | | | |
| | | | | | | | | | | | | | | | | | |
| | | | | | | | | | | | | | | | | | |
| | | | | | | | | | | | | | | | | | |
| | | | | | | | | | | | | | | | | | |

# Soil Aggregate Stability Datasheet

Park code:_____Plot ID: _____ Date (MM/DD/YYYY):_____

Recorder: _____

Is this a subsurface sample?   Yes   No

| Sample # | Start / Dip time | Position (to 0.1 m) | Veg | Rating | Sample # | Start / Dip time | Position (to 0.1 m) | Veg | Rating | Sample # | Start / Dip time | Position (to 0.1 m) | Veg | Rating |
|---|---|---|---|---|---|---|---|---|---|---|---|---|---|---|
| **Transect A** | | | | | **Transect B** | | | | | **Transect C** | | | | |
| 1 | 0:00/5:00 | | | | 1 | 0:15/5:15 | | | | 1 | 0:30/5:30 | | | |
| 2 | 0:45/5:45 | | | | 2 | 1:00/6:00 | | | | 2 | 1:15/6:15 | | | |
| 3 | 1:30/6:30 | | | | 3 | 1:45/6:45 | | | | 3 | 2:00/7:00 | | | |
| 4 | 2:15/7:15 | | | | 4 | 2:30/7:30 | | | | 4 | 2:45/7:45 | | | |
| 5 | 3:00/8:00 | | | | 5 | 3:15/8:15 | | | | 5 | 3:30/8:30 | | | |
| 6 | 3:45/8:45 | | | | 6 | 4:00/9:00 | | | | 6 | 4:15/9:15 | | | |

Comments:

**Veg codes**

| | |
|---|---|
| NC | no perennial canopy |
| G | perennial grass/grass shrub mix |
| F | perennial forb |
| S | shrub/cactus/succulent |

**Rating**   **Criteria**

| | |
|---|---|
| 1 | 50% of structural integrity lost (melts) within 5 seconds of immersion OR too unstable to sample |
| 2 | 50% of structural integrity lost (melts) 5–30 seconds after immersion |
| 3 | 50% of structural integrity lost 30–300 seconds after immersion OR <10% remains on sieve after 5 dipping cycles |
| 4 | 10–25% of soil remains on sieve after 5 dipping cycles |
| 5 | 25–75% of soil remains on sieve after 5 dipping cycles |
| 6 | 75–100% of soil remains on sieve after 5 dipping cycles |
| L | deep litter (>2.5 cm) |
| P | deep pumice (>2.5 cm) |
| R | rock (subsurface sample only) |

# Standard Operating Procedure #9: After the Field Season

**Version 1.00**

**Revision History Log**

| Previous version number | Revision date | Author | Changes made | Section and paragraph | Reason | Approved by | New version number |
|---|---|---|---|---|---|---|---|
| | | | | | | | |
| | | | | | | | |
| | | | | | | | |
| | | | | | | | |
| | | | | | | | |
| | | | | | | | |
| | | | | | | | |
| | | | | | | | |

Only changes in this specific SOP will be logged here. Version numbers increase incrementally by hundredths (e.g., version 1.01, version 1.02) for minor changes. Major revisions should be designated with the next whole number (e.g., version 2.0, 3.0, 4.0). Record the previous version number, date of revision, author of the revision; identify paragraphs and pages where changes are made, who approved the revision, and the reason for making the changes along with the new version number.

This standard operating procedure (SOP) describes post-season procedures for the SCPN integrated upland monitoring project. The procedures include management of field equipment and datasheets, review of the field season, and preparation of the Investigator's Annual Report.

## 1 Returning field equipment

- **Clean all equipment before storage**. Crew members should ensure that all equipment used during the field season is clean and fully operational. Any problems with equipment should be reported to the project manager or botanist.
- **Inventory field equipment**. Crew members should inventory all equipment as it is returned to storage. Any damaged equipment should be set aside to be repaired or replaced; all other equipment should be properly stored.
- **Repair/replace damaged equipment**. When possible, damaged equipment should be repaired. Otherwise, damaged equipment should be replaced to ensure that all necessary equipment is on hand and functional prior to the next field season.
- **Clean vehicles**. All field vehicles should be thoroughly cleaned—inside and out.

## 2 Datasheets and data management

- **Proof datasheets**. Each datasheet should be proofed in the field, prior to leaving the plot to ensure that there are no missing data and that data are logical and legible. When returning from the field, the datasheets should be reproofed.
- **Scan and archive original datasheets**. Datasheets are digitally scanned. Separate data files should be created for each ecological site. Before being scanned, the datasheets should be consistently arranged in the order of the SOPs. After being scanned they are filed by ecological site.
- **Mark corrections on original datasheets with pen**. If changes to data on the datasheets need to be made subse-

quent to data collection, they should be made by drawing a horizontal line through the original value, and writing the new value adjacent to the original value, with the date and initials of the person making the change. Corrected errors and changes made on a datasheet should be circled. A short explanation of the change should be included in the margin of the datasheet, along with the date and initials of the person who made the correction. Any datasheets that have been corrected should be rescanned if the change was made after the scanning and archiving process. It may be best to wait until after the data validation process (see *SOP #12*) before the datasheets are rescanned.

- **Organize photos**. Organize photos from the season's photopoints and rename by park, plot ID, and location (e.g., BAND_P17_AF). Review and organize additional photos of fieldwork and landscapes, and place in appropriate folder for the current year.

## 3 Review of field season

The project manager and the botanist should perform a review of the field season before the departure of the temporary field crew. This can be done individually or as a group. The review should focus on aspects of the field season that went well and aspects that could be improved. Specific topics should include planning, scheduling, logistics (travel, lodging, meals), protocols, efficiency, field conditions, and safety, and any other relevant topic.

The project manager will prepare a brief report based on the field season review. The report will be reviewed prior to the next field season to refine protocols, if needed.

## 4 Reporting scientific research and collecting activities

**Prepare and submit reports**. Prepare and submit Investigator's Annual Reports for each park via the NPS Research Permit and Reporting System (RPRS) web site: http://science.nature.nps.gov/research, per permit requirements. These are brief reports that describe the accomplishments of the field season.

# Standard Operating Procedure #10: Project Workspace

**Version 1.00**

**Revision History Log**

| Previous version number | Revision date | Author | Changes made | Section and paragraph | Reason | Approved by | New version number |
|---|---|---|---|---|---|---|---|
| | | | | | | | |
| | | | | | | | |
| | | | | | | | |
| | | | | | | | |
| | | | | | | | |
| | | | | | | | |
| | | | | | | | |
| | | | | | | | |

Only changes in this specific SOP will be logged here. Version numbers increase incrementally by hundredths (e.g., version 1.01, version 1.02) for minor changes. Major revisions should be designated with the next whole number (e.g., version 2.0, 3.0, 4.0). Record the previous version number, date of revision, author of the revision; identify paragraphs and pages where changes are made, who approved the revision, and the reason for making the changes along with the new version number.

This standard operating procedure (SOP) describes how and where data and other records, both digital and hard-copy, are stored for the project. Guidelines for structuring and accessing digital data are provided, as well as specific standards for digital file and folder naming. The archiving and management of records should be carefully accomplished based on the direction provided by this SOP.

## 1 File directory structure

A section of the network file server is reserved for the integrated upland monitoring project. The space will include a working file section as well as an archival section. Permissions allow project staff members to have access to needed files within this workspace. Prior to each season, the SCPN data manager will create a network account for each new staff member to give them access to the project workspace.

The file structure within this workspace is shown in Figure 10-1. Year-specific folders are included where needed. This will make it easier to identify and move these files to the project archives at the end of each season.

## 2 Naming conventions
### 2.1 Folder naming standards
Folders are named like this example, "BAND_20081001" and in all cases, should follow these guidelines:

- Use a 4-letter park code (e.g., BAND).
- Do not use spaces or special characters in the folder name.
- Use the underscore ("_") character to separate words in folder names.
- Try to limit folder names to 20 characters or fewer.
- Dates should be formatted YYYYMMDD (e.g., 20081001 is October 1, 2008).
- Name subfolders "old" or "temp" to indicate a temporary nature, and that they should eventually be removed after project completion.

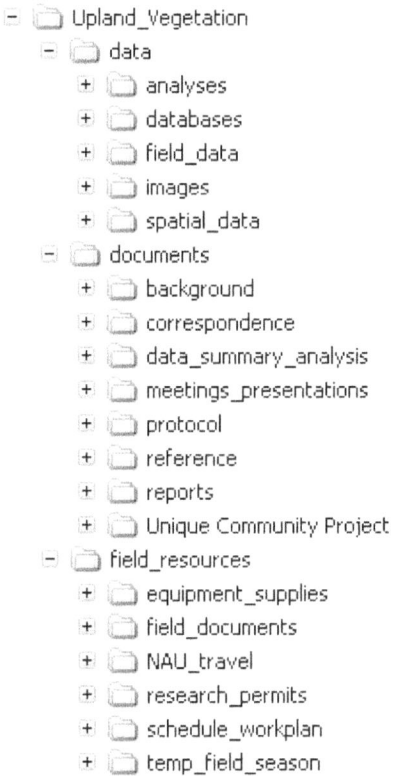

**Figure 10-1. Example of file directory structure**

## 2.2 File naming standards

Files are named like these examples, "BAND_ 20081001_taxa.xls", "GLCA_20081026.jpg", and in all cases, should follow these guidelines:

- Use a 4-letter park code (e.g., BAND).
- Do not use spaces or special characters in the file name.
- Use the underscore ("_") character to separate file name components.
- Dates should be formatted as YYYYMMDD (e.g., 20081001 is October 1, 2008).
- Use leading zeroes for numbers 1 through 9, for sorting purposes.
- File names should be as short as possible, but include all mandatory information.
- The file name should be unique so that another electronic file is not likely to have the same name on the SCPN file server.
- Do not use version numbers or tags on working documents (e.g., version1, final, etc.). The file date (YYYYM-MDD) will be used as your file version.

## 3 Archival and records management

All project files should be reviewed and organized by the project manager on a regular basis. Decisions on what to retain and what to destroy should be made following the guidelines stipulated in NPS Director's Order 19 (http://www.nps.gov/policy/DOrders/DOrder19.htm). This order provides a schedule for how long various kinds of records should be retained.

## 3.1 Digital data

Once the master project dataset and metadata are considered final, the data manager will place a copy of the dataset and the metadata record into the appropriate folder within the archive directory on the network server. These archived files will be stored in read-only format. Any subsequent changes made to this dataset must be documented in an edit log and in the metadata. In addition to archiving the dataset copy in its native format, all tables will be archived in a comma-delimited ASCII format that is platform-independent. This archiving will use the Access_to_ascii.mdb utility developed by the NPS Central Alaska Network. The project name and the term "Arc" should be included in the filename, with ASCII files including a .txt file extension and Access files including an .mdb file extension (e.g., Int_Up_Arc_20081101.mdb).

Prior to any major changes of a dataset, a copy should be stored with the appropriate version number to allow for tracking of changes over time. Versions of archived datasets should be marked by adding a 3 digit number to the file name, with the first version being numbered 001 (e.g., Int_Up_BE_20081101_v001, for the first version of a back-end data file at the end of the 2008 field season). Each additional version is assigned a sequentially higher number. This should also be documented in the edit log. Frequent users of the data should be notified of the updates and provided with a copy of the most recently archived version. Additional digital files to be archived include all digital photos and any digital files associated with data analysis products and project reporting. Official project reports will be cataloged in the online NPS Integrated Resource Management Applications. All digital materials are stored in the network office and can be made available to park curators upon request.

## 3.2 Hardcopy materials
Hardcopy materials (e.g., datasheets, field notebooks, photo prints, reports) are stored in the network office. Both the project manager and SCPN staff will work with the curatorial staff at the park(s) to achieve timely and efficient archiving of hardcopy materials.

# Standard Operating Procedure #11: Data Entry and Verification

**Version 1.00**

**Revision History Log**

| Previous version number | Revision date | Author | Changes made | Section and paragraph | Reason | Approved by | New version number |
|---|---|---|---|---|---|---|---|
| | | | | | | | |
| | | | | | | | |
| | | | | | | | |
| | | | | | | | |
| | | | | | | | |
| | | | | | | | |
| | | | | | | | |
| | | | | | | | |

Only changes in this specific SOP will be logged here. Version numbers increase incrementally by hundredths (e.g., version 1.01, version 1.02) for minor changes. Major revisions should be designated with the next whole number (e.g., version 2.0, 3.0, 4.0). Record the previous version number, date of revision, author of the revision; identify paragraphs and pages where changes are made, who approved the revision, and the reason for making the changes along with the new version number.

This standard operating procedure (SOP) describes the general procedures for entry and verification of field data from paper datasheets into the digital working project database. For related guidance, and a clarification of the distinction between the working database and the master database, refer to chapter 5 of the protocol narrative (*Data Management*).

## 1 Data entry overview

The primary goal of data entry is to transcribe the data from paper into the computer with 100% accuracy. Data entry should occur as soon as possible after data collection is completed. It can begin during the field season, if office time is available; otherwise it should be conducted immediately following the field season. Data entry should be completed by the people who collected the data or someone who is familiar with the project and data collection methods. It is the project manager and data manager's shared responsibility to ensure that all data entry staff understand how to enter data. Data enterers are responsible for being familiar with the field datasheets, the database, and any standard codes for data entry.

Each data entry form has built-in quality-assurance components, such as pick lists and validation rules to test for missing data or illogical combinations. Users are strongly encouraged to use only the pre-built forms in order to provide the maximum level of quality assurance.

As data are being entered, the person entering the data should visually review each data form to make sure that the data entered on screen match the datasheet values. This should be done for each record prior to moving to the next form for data entry. At regular intervals and at the end of the field season, the integrated upland staff and data manager should inspect the data that have been entered to check for completeness and to identify avoidable errors.

## 2 Database instructions
### 2.1 Getting started
The Integrated Upland Monitoring Database is fully documented in Appendix E. The database consists of 2 parts: a

front-end and a back-end. The front-end is the user interface, containing the data entry forms and queries; the back-end consists of the data tables. The working back-end database file has "_BE_" as part of its name, and should be stored on the server in the project workspace (see *SOP #10*) so that others can enter data into the same back-end file. Section 2.2.2.1 below (*Connect data tables*) describes how to connect the front-end with the back-end. For enhanced performance, users should copy the front-end database onto their workstation hard drive and open it there. This front-end copy may be considered "disposable" because it does not contain any data, but rather acts as an interface with data residing in the back-end working database.

When new versions of the front-end application are released, there should be no need to move or alter the back-end file. Instead, the old front-end file may be deleted and replaced with the new version, which will be named in a manner reflecting the update. When this occurs, the front- end application will prompt the user to update the links to the back-end database file. This update will only need to be done once for each new release of the front-end database.

## 2.2 The application startup menu

The startup menu (fig. 11-1) is the entry point for the application, and opens automatically when the application starts. Double-clicking the network name at the top left of the menu will open the web site for the Southern Colorado Plateau Network. Double-clicking the NPS Arrowhead or the title "National Park Service" at the top right of the menu will open a browser and navigate to the National Park Service web site (www.nps.gov).

At the top right of the menu is an **Exit** button which can be used to close the application.

A set of tabs resides at the lower left corner of the menu. It contains the *Main menu* tab, the *Defaults* tab, and the *About* tab. Each of the tabs will be examined in more detail in the sections that follow.

At the bottom center-right of the menu is a box that displays the current location of the back-end data file to which the application is linked.

### 2.2.1 Main menu tab

The *Main menu* tab of the front-end application (fig. 11-1) has the following functional components:

- **Enter / edit data**. Opens a form to confirm default settings (for example, user) prior to continuing to the integrated upland monitoring data entry screens.
- **Data verification**. Opens the main data entry form in verification mode, and tracks all changes made by the user
- **QA checks**. Opens the data validation tool that checks for missing data and illogical values. See *SOP #12* for details.
- **Back up data**. Creates a date-stamped copy of the back-end database file.
- **Connect data tables**. Verifies the connection to the back-end working database file, and provides the option to redirect or update that connection.
- **Revisit reports**. Creates revisit reports that can be printed for use in the field.

**2.2.1.1 Connect data tables**. The application has a separate front-end (user interface) and back-end (data tables). In order for the application to work properly, the front-end file must be connected to the correct back-end file. Clicking the **Connect data tables** button on the *Main menu* tab opens the *Update Data Table Connections* form (fig. 11-2), which is used to establish the link from the front-end to the back-end.

The name, path, and file name of the current back-end file are displayed. To change the back-end file connection, click the **Browse** button, select a new back-end file, and click the **Open** button. To make the new connection, click the **Update links** button. If the connection is made, a success message will be displayed.

**2.2.1.2 Enter/edit data.** Clicking on **Enter/edit data** on the *Main menu* tab will open the form to set application defaults (fig. 11-3). Once the application defaults are set, the *Data Gateway* form (fig. 11-4) will open.

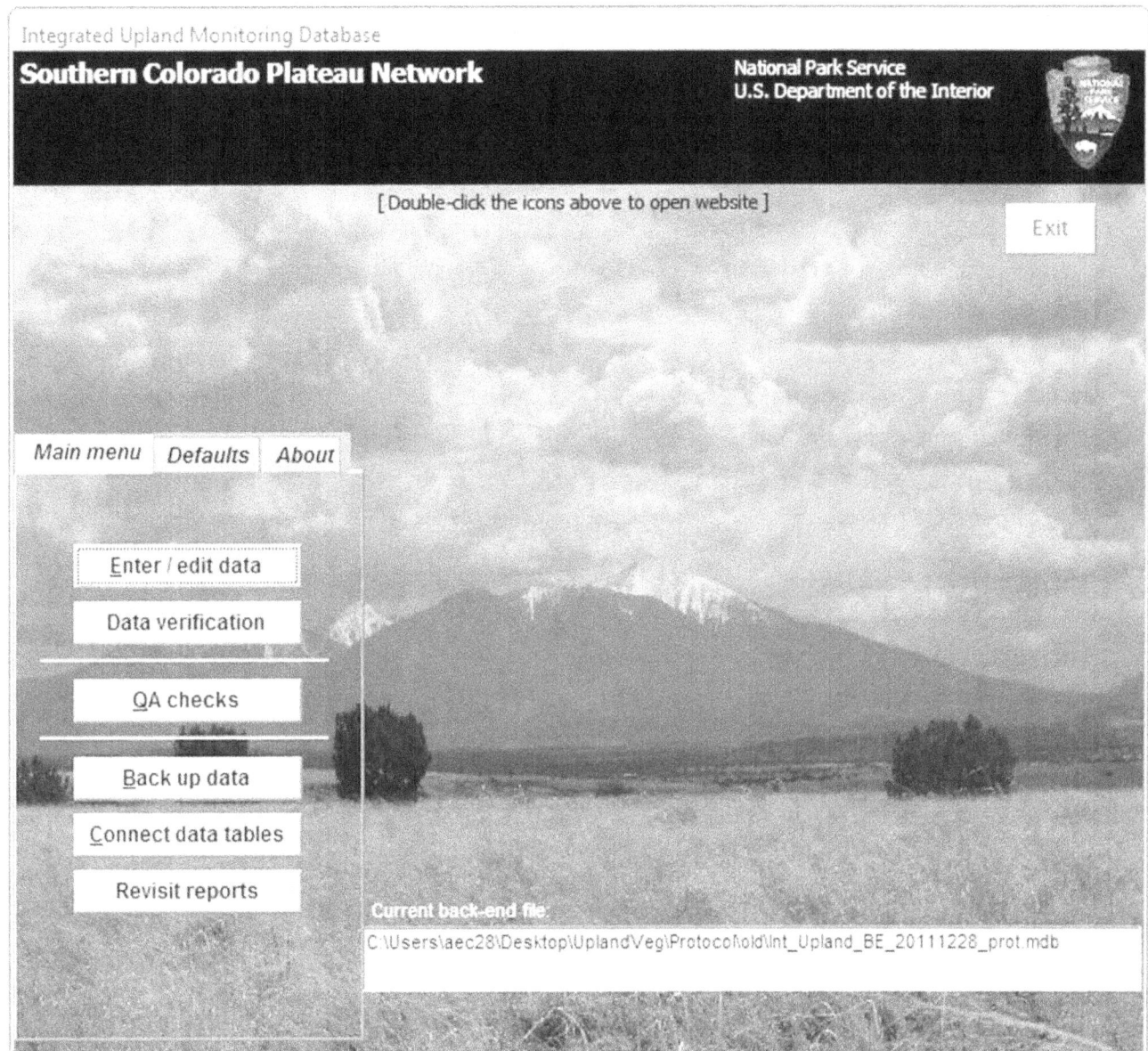

Figure 11-1. The *Main menu* tab of the Integrated Upland Monitoring Database startup menu

*Data Gateway* form

This form displays location and event information to help the user determine which record to edit/view.

*Reviewing existing records.* Filters for **Park Code**, **Plot ID**, **Year**, and **Visit Date** can be set by selecting from the drop-down lists at the top of the form in the *Filters* box. Filters can be removed by clicking the toggle button if it says **Filter Is On**. When the filter is removed, the toggle button will say **Filter Is Off** and all records will be displayed. Alternatively, a specific filter can be removed by deleting the text that is currently displayed in one of the filter controls.

In addition to filters, there are options for sorting the records on the *Data Gateway* form. Double-clicking any of the column headings will cause the records to be sorted in ascending order by that column value. The column heading will change to a bold italic format to indicate that it is the column being used to determine sort order. If the same column is double-clicked a second time, the records will be sorted in descending order by that column value.

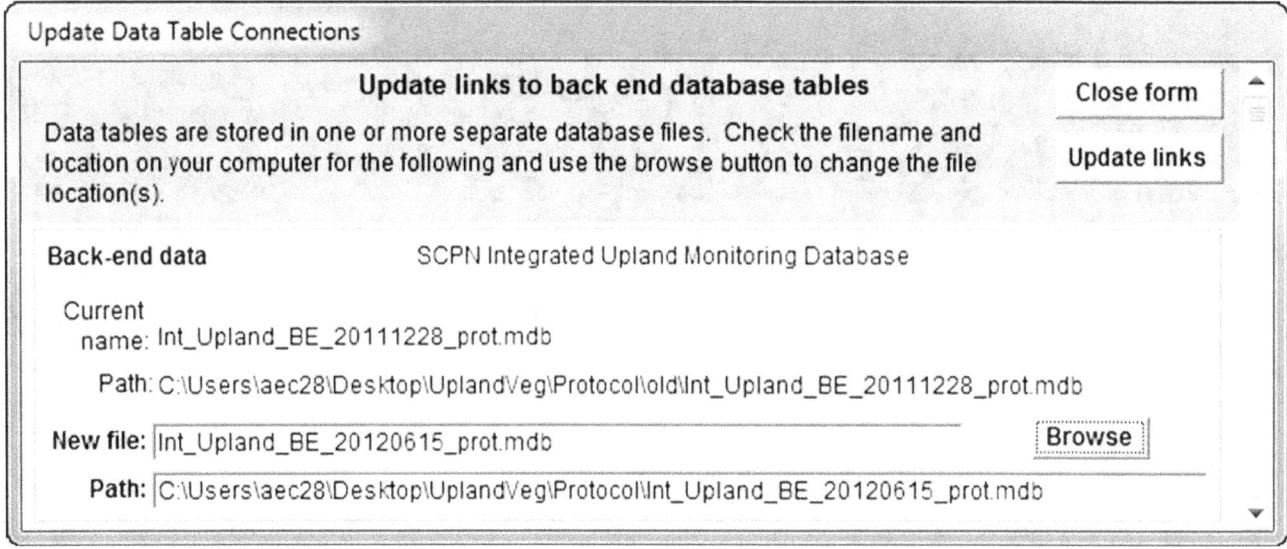

Figure 11-2. *Update Data Table Connections* form opened by clicking the Connect data tables button on the *Main menu* tab

Figure 11-3. *Set application default values* form

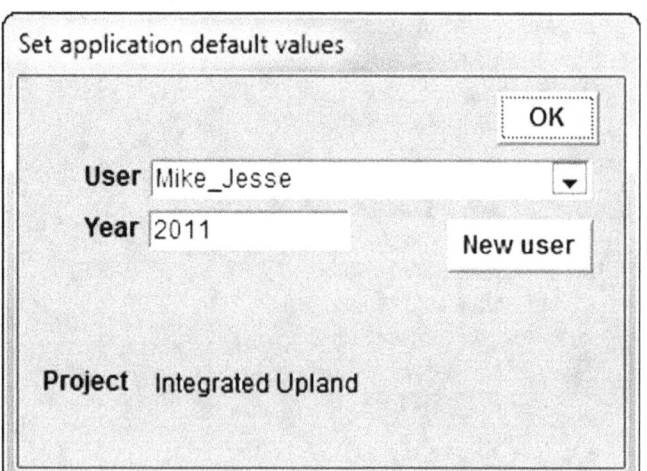

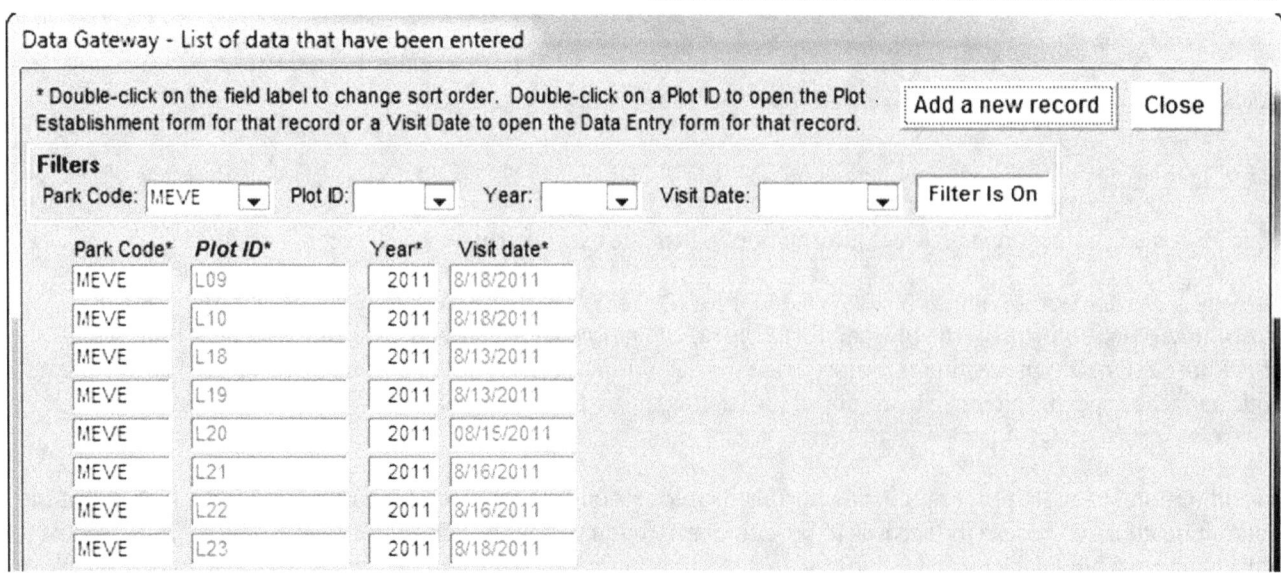

Figure 11-4. *Data Gateway* form

Double-clicking a date in the **Visit date** column will open the *Data Entry* form for that particular record, if there is a need to review or edit the data. If a sampling event record has not been added for a particular location, when that blank cell under **Visit date** is double-clicked, a new data entry record will be opened. Instructions for adding new data records follow.

*Adding new records.* To add a new data entry record, click the **Add a new record** button at the top of the form. Alternatively, once in the *Data Entry* form, clicking the **New Plot Record** button will do the same.

Data Entry form—plot establishment and general information

Data fields and related forms visible at the top of the *Data Entry* form (fig. 11-5) capture general information about the plot and its initial assessment and establishment. In this top area, select a **Park Code** and **Plot ID**, and enter **Start Date**, **End Date**, **Notes**, and **Observers**. **Protocol Name**, **Data Enterer**, and **Data Proofer** are automatically populated.

Park codes and Plot IDs that were previously entered can be selected from a dropdown list; new Plot IDs can be entered by clicking on **Add New Plot ID**, which initiates a new plot record (see below—*Plot Establishment* form).

Information about people who participated in the sampling event can be entered in the *Observer* subform (which covers both observers and recorders). Observers can be selected from the drop-down list. In the **Role**(s) sections, list all roles played by the listed observer. Click **Next Observer** to add another observer, until all observers for the sampling event are entered. If a new observer needs to be entered, click the **Add a person** button to create a new record (see below—*View and edit contact information* form).

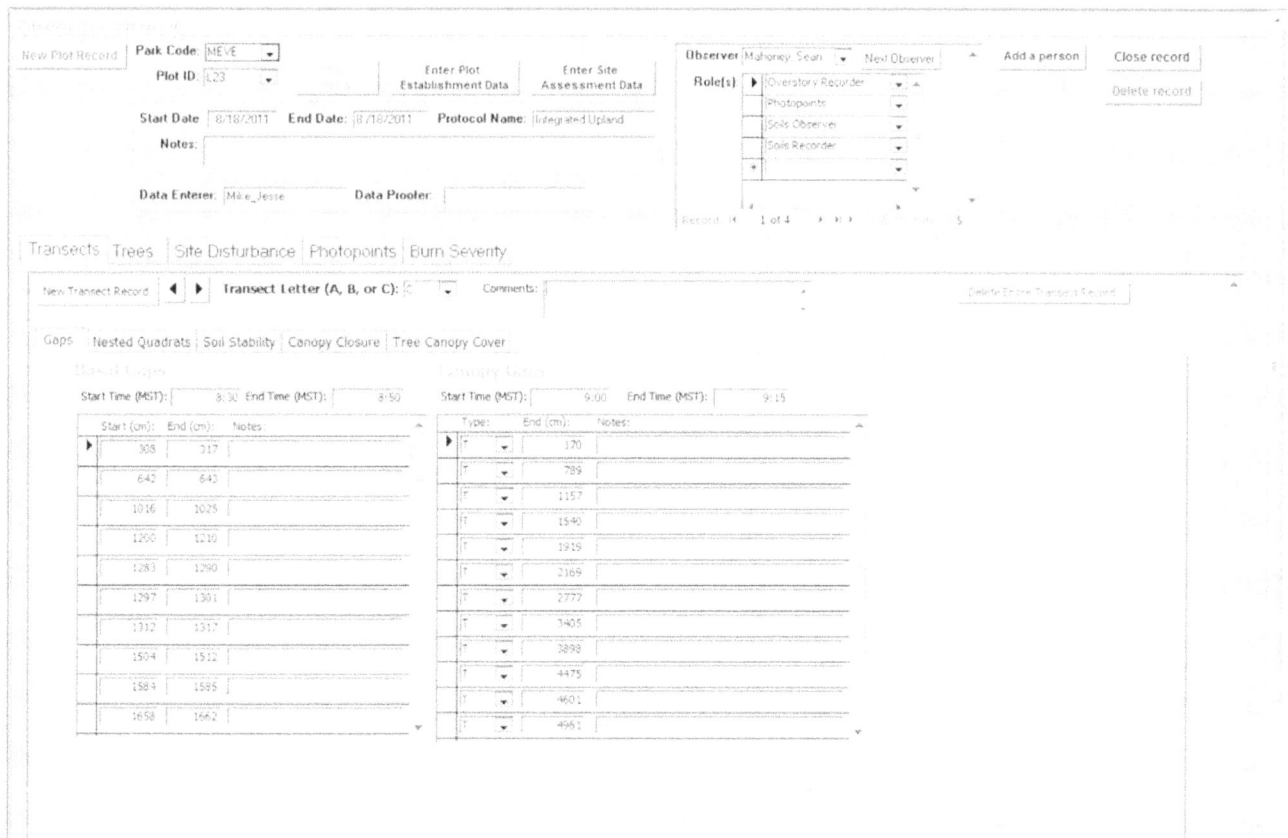

**Figure 11-5.** *Data Entry Form,* accessed through the *Data Gateway* form

## Plot Establishment form

The *Plot Establishment* form (fig. 11-6) records data gathered in the field on the *Plot Establishment Datasheet*. It will open when the **Add New Plot ID** button is clicked to create a new Plot ID value. Likewise, clicking on the **Enter Plot Establishment Data** button (also from the *Data Entry* form) opens the *Plot Establishment* form and allows the user to update existing plot information. Note that the **Enter Plot Establishment Data** button will only be active if a plot has been selected in the **Plot ID** field.

Values entered here include **Plot ID, GRTS Point, Mean Plot Aspect**, and **Transect Azimuth. Park Code** and **Ecological Site** are automatically populated. If any rebar was offset, enter which **Point** and how far it was **Offset**, as well as any **Comments**. Witness trees for all 3 transects should be added here (if applicable). Enter the **Point, Species, Tree ID, Azimuth**, and **Distance**. Add any witness tree **Comments** and **Directions to plot**.

The form includes fields for specific location data (e.g., **UTMX Centroid, UTMY Centroid**), which are downloaded from a GPS and imported into the database table by the data manager or GIS specialist.

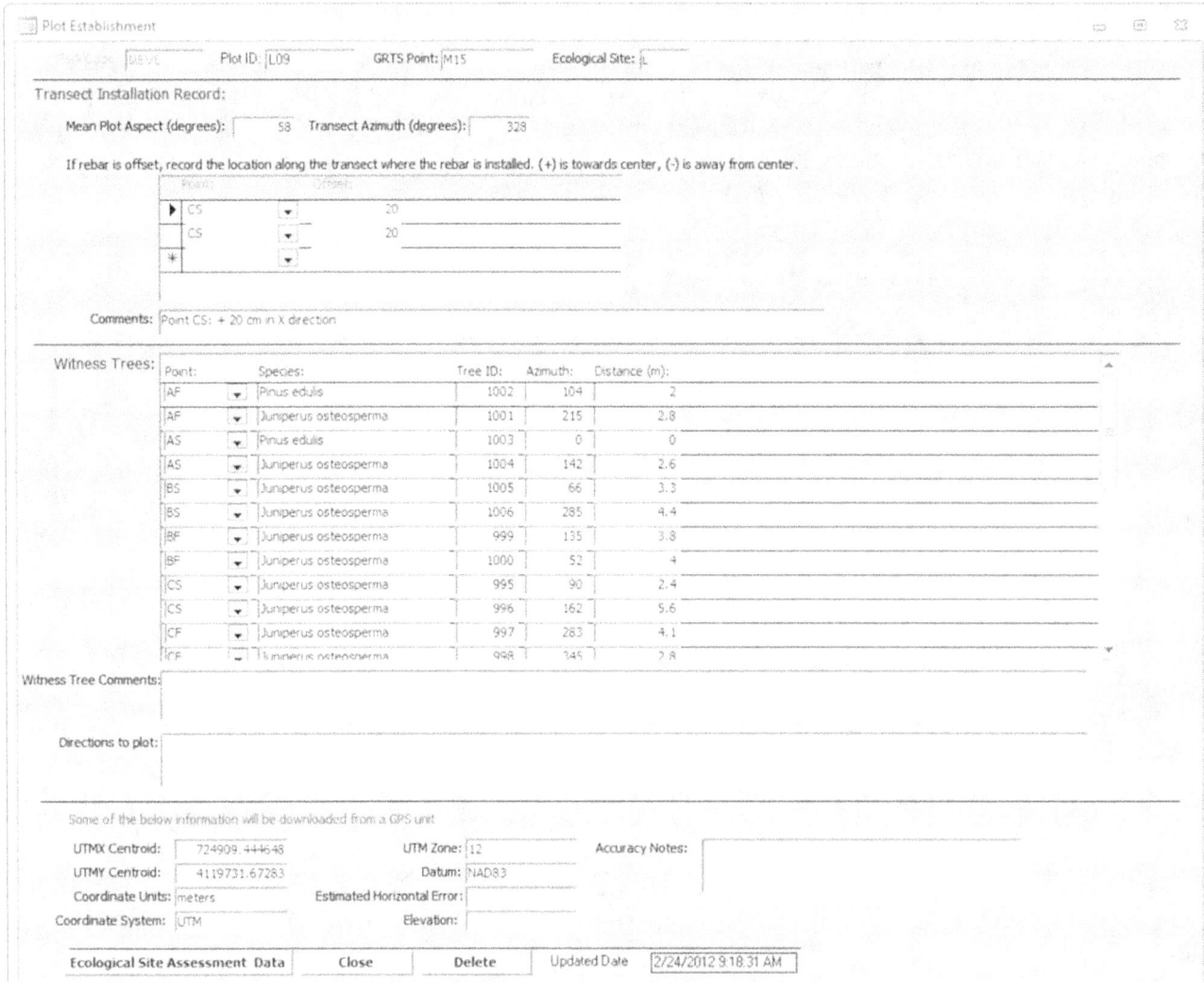

**Figure 11-6.** *Plot Establishment* **form, accessed through the** *Data Entry* **form**

## Ecological Site Assessment form

From the *Plot Establishment* form, click on **Ecological Site Assessment Data** to open the *Ecological Site Assessment* form (fig. 11-7). The user can alternatively click on the **Enter Site Assessment Data** button from the *Data Entry* form, to add or edit ecological site assessment data.

Ecological site assessment data are only entered once per plot, and are derived from field data collected on the *Ecological Site Assessment Datasheet*. In the **Date Surveyed** field, enter the date the ecological site assessment data were collected, as this may have occurred on a different date than plot sampling.

In the *Topography Assessment* section, enter a **Landform, Hillslope Position** (one or more), **Slope Complexity, Slope Shape** (**Down Slope** and **Across Slope**), and the 3 values (**Start, Center, Finish**) of both **Percent Slope,** and **Aspect.** Add **Comments** if needed.

In the *Vegetation Assessment* section, enter the **Dominant Physiognomic Class.** Enter one or more **Vegetation Associations** and their corresponding **Cover Class.** Enter each **Vegetation Stratum** and related **Cover Class,** as well as **Dominant Species** in each stratum. Then enter whether this is a **Target Match** and add any **Comments.**

In the *Soil Profile Assessment* section, enter the soil **Depth, Texture, Color, Rock Fragments,** and **Effervescence.** Enter overall **Soil Depth, Probable Soil Component,** whether it is a **Target Match,** and any **Comments.**

In the *Ecological Site Determination and Site Selection* section, enter whether it was an overall **Target Match,** whether to **Accept Plot,** a description of the **Primary Ecological Site** and % **Area,** a description of the **Other Ecological Site** and % **Area,** as well as any overall **Comments.**

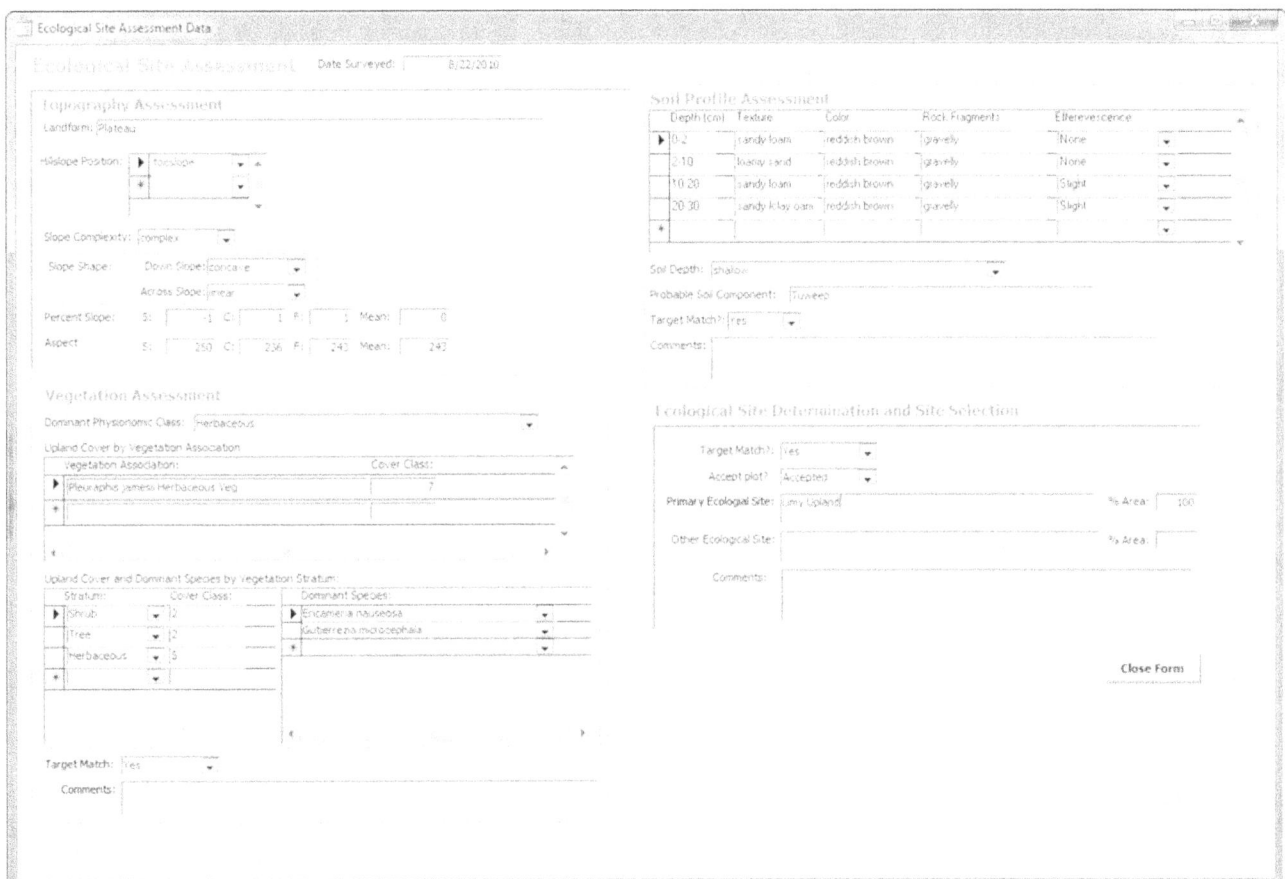

**Figure 11-7.** *Ecological Site Assessment* **form, accessed through the** *Plot Establishment* **form and the** *Data Entry* **form**

## *View and edit contact information* form

The *View and edit contact information* form (fig. 11-8) is used to enter details about individuals who participate in data collection, and who enter information in the database. This form is accessed by clicking the **Add a person** button from the *Data Entry* form. Enter **First Name, Middle Initial, Last Name, Organization, Position/title, Work Phone** and **Extension, Email Address, Address Information**, including **Address Type, Street Address, City, State, Zip Code, Country,** and any **Comments**. Bold fields are required.

Previously entered addresses can be selected from the **Address 1** drop-down list, and the associated **Street Address, City, State Code, Zip Code,** and **Country** values will fill in automatically. The **Organization** and **Position/title** drop-down lists will also allow selection from previously entered values or new entries. The **Contact ID** value, which uniquely identifies a contact, is automatically generated by the application.

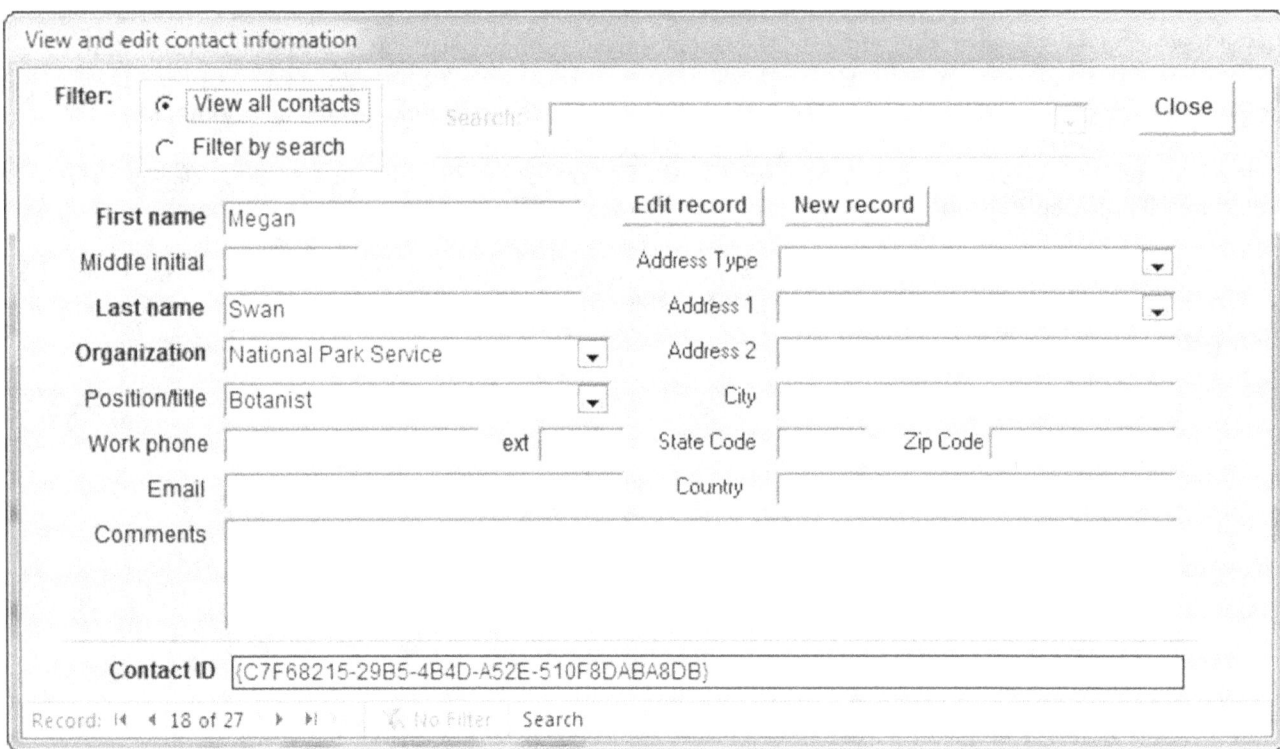

Figure 11-8. *View and edit contact information* form, accessed through the *Data Entry* form

## *Data Entry* form—plot detailed information

The 5 tabs along the bottom half of the *Data Entry* form (*Transects, Trees, Site Disturbance, Photopoints* and *Burn Severity*) capture all the detailed plot measurements, as well as disturbance and photopoint information.

- *Transects* tab and form (fig. 11-9). There are generally 3 transects per plot and a record must be created for each. The **Transect Letter** must be entered. Any **Comments** for the whole transect should be added here. This form includes 5 tabs: *Gaps, Nested Quadrats, Soil Stability, Canopy Closure,* and *Tree Canopy Cover*. When one transect entry is complete, click on **New Transect Record** to enter data for the next transect (data enterers should be careful not to simply choose another Transect letter from the drop-down list, as this will edit the record, not create a new one).

Figure 11-9. *Transects* tab of the *Data Entry* form, showing the *Gaps* tab

○ The *Gaps* tab includes 2 subforms: *Basal Gaps* and *Canopy Gaps*. These capture data collected in the field by the *Basal and Canopy Gaps Datasheet*.

— On the *Basal Gaps* subform (fig. 11-10), enter an overall **Start Time** and **End Time**. Enter **Start, End,** and **Notes** for each basal gap.

— On the *Canopy Gaps* subform (fig. 11-11), enter an overall **Start Time** and **End Time**. Enter a **Type, End,** and **Notes** for each canopy gap. The notes fields can be used to note any errors, such as where the **End** is smaller than the **Start**.

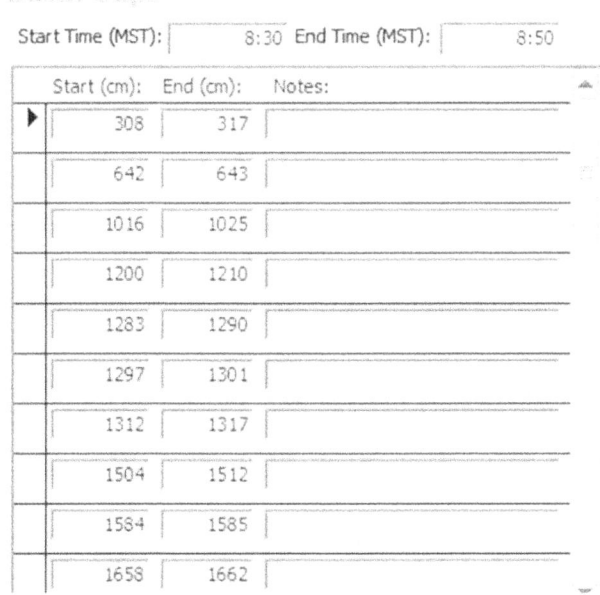

Figure 11-10. *Basal Gaps* subform of the *Gaps* tab

Figure 11-11. *Canopy Gaps* subform of the *Gaps* tab

○ The *Nested Quadrats* tab (fig. 11-12) includes 4 tabs: *Nested Frequency and Cover, Functional Groups, Soil Surface Features,* and *Tree Seedlings*. There are 5 quadrats per transect, and a record must be created for each quadrat. Data for all quadrats on a transect are collected in the field on the *Nested Quadrat Datasheet*. Enter **Start Time** and **End Time** for sampling all quadrats on the transect. The **Quadrat** point must be entered.

When one quadrat entry is complete, click on **New Quadrat Point** to enter the next quadrat (data enterers should be careful not to simply choose another Quadrat from the drop-down list, as this will edit the record, not create a new one).

– On the *Nested Frequency and Cover* tab and form (fig. 11-12), enter **Species**, check the appropriate nested quadrat (**0.01, 0.1, 1.0, 5.0,** or **10.0**), and enter **CC**. If there is a line draw through the frequency columns in the datasheet, but a **CC** value exists, then check **Cover Only.** Add any **Notes**.

– An alternative to repeatedly entering the species (because many of the species exist in all quadrats) is to click the **Plant List** button to open the *Plant List* form (fig. 11-13). The user can list all plants in a plot and use the checkbox to the right of the plant name to mark which plants were recorded for a specific quadrat. Then, click **Add to Current Quadrat to copy** the plant name into the *Nested Frequency and Cover* form (fig. 11-14) and finish the record by filling in cover and frequency fields.

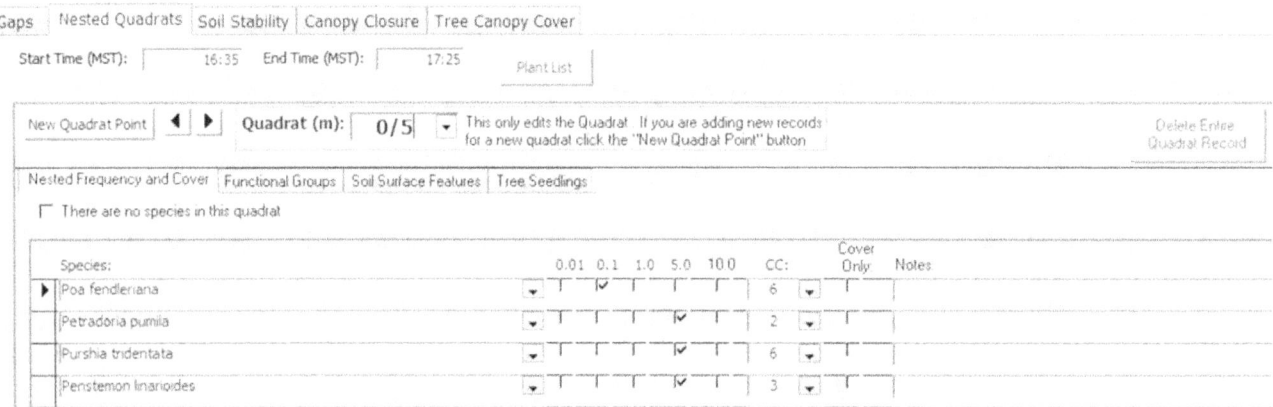

Figure 11-12. *Nested Quadrats* tab showing the *Nested Frequency and Cover* tab open

Figure 11-13. *Plant List* form

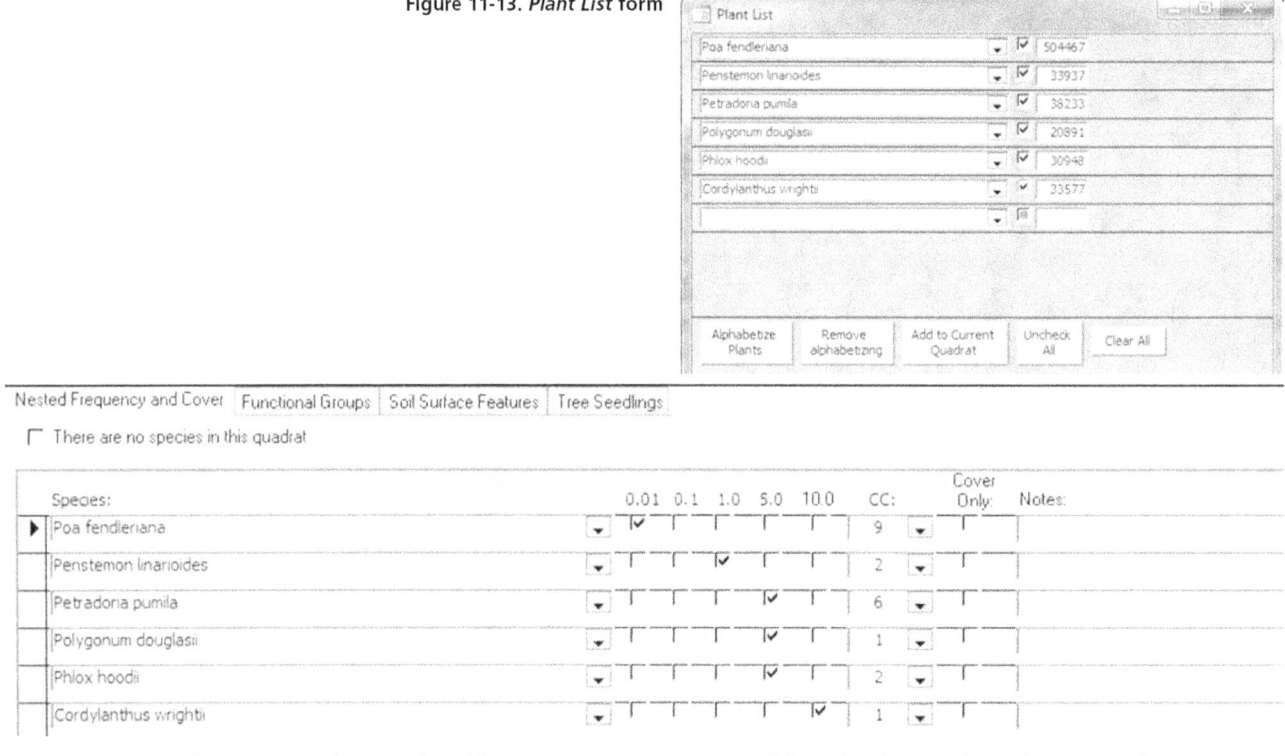

Figure 11-14. *Nested Frequency and Cover* tab and form. Once species are imported from the *Plant List* form, the user needs to update the frequency and cover fields.

- Unknown Species. If a name is entered into the **Species** field of the *Nested Frequency and Cover* or *Plant List* forms (or also the tree species forms), and the plant does not exist in the lookup table that is built into the database, a pop-up message will ask if this is an unknown species. If the species is known but simply missing from the drop-down list, then the user should click "No". The user is then further prompted with the message asking if the name should be added to the plant list. If the user has made a mistake (e.g., a spelling error) then the user should click "No" and is returned to the form to try to enter the name again.

If the species is known but is missing from the list and should be added, the user should click "Yes". This opens the *New Taxon Entry* form (fig. 11-15). Here, the user should enter the **Scientific Name** of the plant, and the **Family Name** if known, and the name will be added permanently to the drop-down list.

If the species is truly unknown, then the user should click "Yes" in the first pop-up form. This will open the *Unknown Species* form (fig. 11-16). The data entered must enter a code into the **Unknown ID** field and checkmark whether the plant was **Collected**. The rest of the form should be populated as much as possible.

**Figure 11-15.** *New Taxon Entry* **form for adding species to the master plant list**

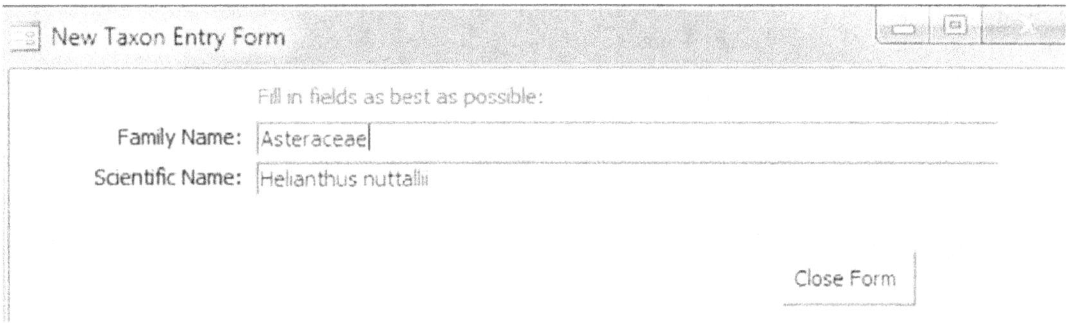

**Figure 11-16.** *Unknown Species* **form**

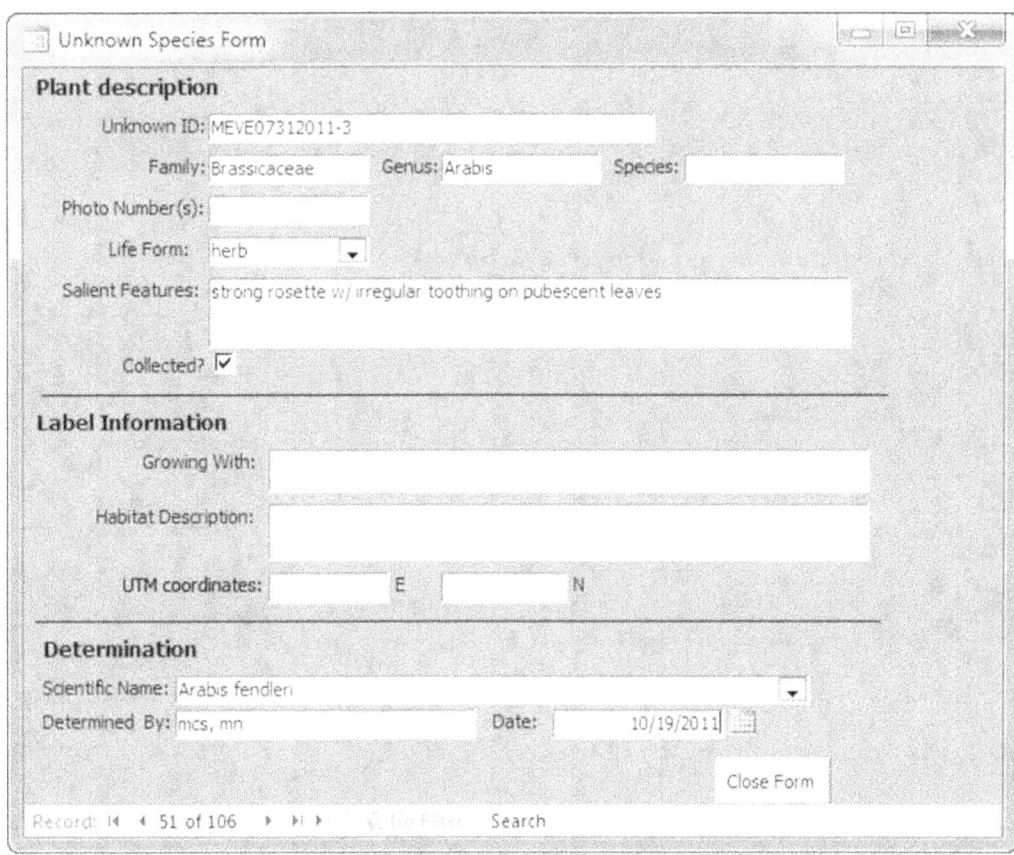

– On the *Functional Groups* tab and form (fig. 11-17), enter **Functional Groups** and the respective **Cover Class** for each quadrat. Alternatively, data can be entered once into the *Functional Group List* form, and copied for multiple quadrats. To do this, the user enters all functional groups for all quadrats into the *Functional Group List*. Then the user checkmarks **Copy** for all functional groups that are associated with the current quadrat. Once the list is complete, click **Add to Current Quadrat** and all checked records in the **Functional Group List** form will be added to the *Functional Groups* form. When the user moves to the next quadrat, the **Functional Group List** remains populated. If no functional groups exist for the current quadrat, check **There are no functional groups in this quadrat**.

– On the *Soil Surface Features* tab and form (fig. 11-18), enter **Soil Surface Features** and the respective **Cover Class** for each quadrat. Alternatively, data can be entered once into the *Soil Surface Feature List* form and then copied for multiple quadrats. To do this, the user enters all soil surface features for all quadrats into the **Soil Surface Feature List**. Then the user checkmarks **Copy** for all soil surface features that are associated with the current quadrat. Once the list is complete, click **Add to Current Quadrat** and all checked records in the **Soil Surface Features List** will be added to the *Soil Surface Features* form. When the user moves to the next quadrat, the **Soil Surface Features List** remains populated.

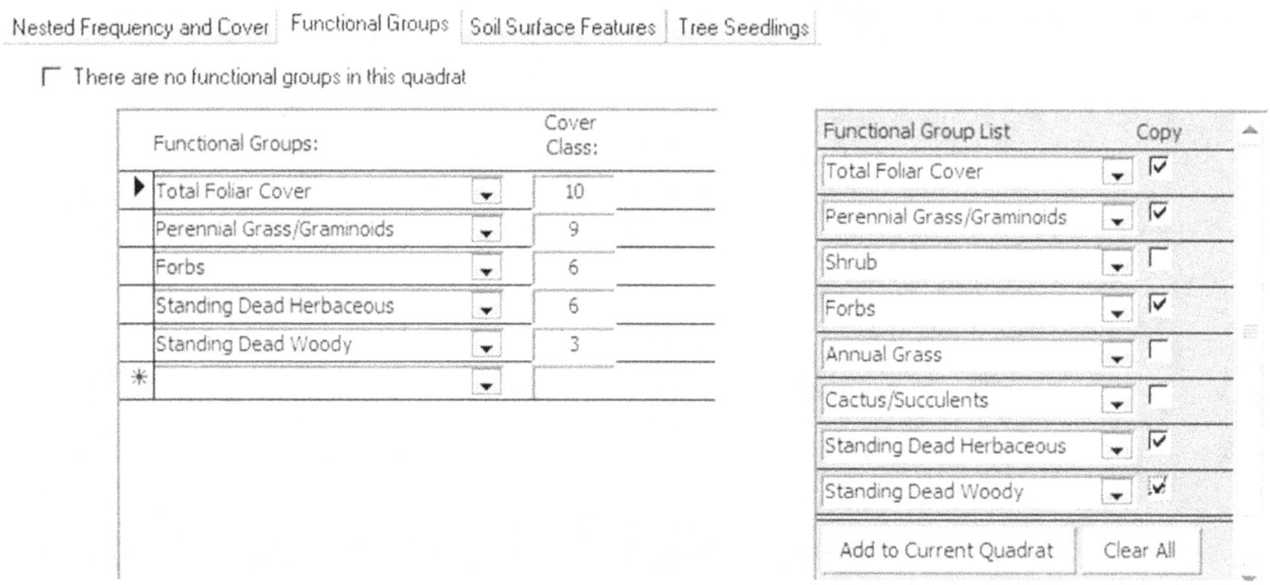

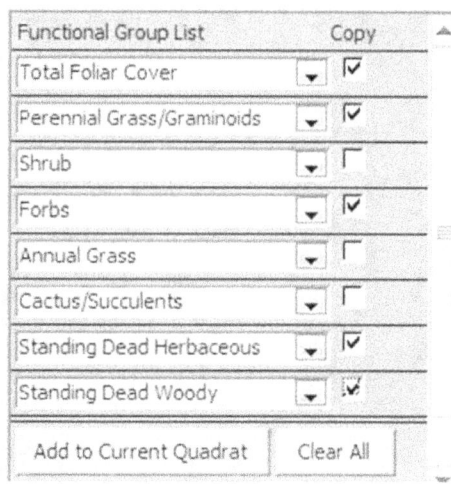

Figure 11-17. *Functional Groups* tab and form of the *Nested Quadrats* tab

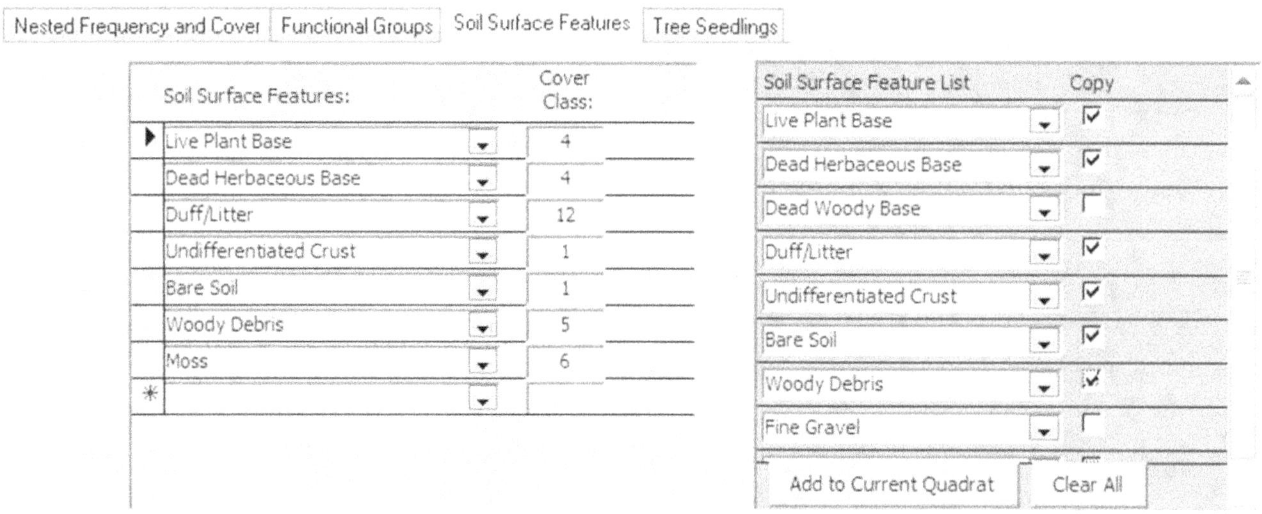

Figure 11-18. *Soil Surface Features* tab and form of the *Nested Quadrats* tab

– On the *Tree Seedlings* tab and form (fig. 11-19), list **Species, Size Class,** and **Tally**. If no seedlings exist for this quadrat, check **There are no seedlings.**

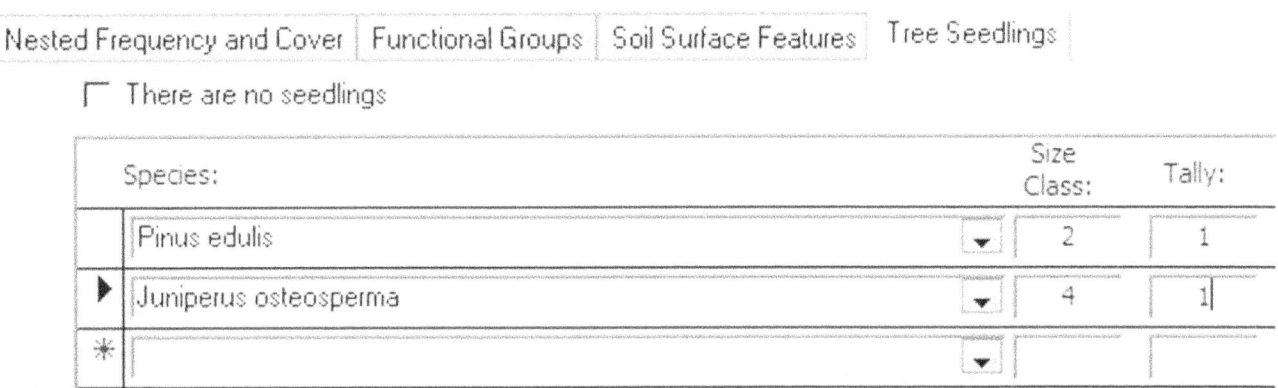

Figure 11-19. *Tree Seedlings* tab and form of the *Nested Quadrats* tab

○ Navigating back up one level, the *Soil Stability* tab and form (fig. 11-20) captures data collected in the field by the *Soil Aggregate Stability Datasheet*. Enter **Sample #, Position, Veg,** and **Rating**.

○ The *Canopy Closure* tab and form (fig. 11-21) captures data collected in the field by the *Canopy Closure Datasheet*. Enter **Start Time** and **End time** for canopy closure sampling. Times are for all 3 transects, but only need to be entered once. Enter **Transect Position, Finish, Down, Start,** and **Up**. Enter any **Comments**.

○ The *Tree Canopy Cover* tab and form (fig. 11-22) captures data collected in the field by the *Tree Canopy Cover Datasheet*. Enter **Start Time** and **End time** for tree canopy cover sampling. Times are for all 3 transects, but only need to be entered once. Enter **Start** and **End**, as well as any **Comments**.

| Gaps | Nested Quadrats | Soil Stability | Canopy Closure | Tree Canopy Cover |

| | Sample #: | Position: | Veg: | Rating: |
|---|---|---|---|---|
| | 1 | 9.2 | NC | 5 |
| | 2 | 16.9 | NC | 3 |
| | 3 | 28.1 | NC | 3 |
| | 4 | 34.2 | S | 3 |
| | 5 | 36.9 | NC | 6 |
| 🖉 | 6 | 43.9 | NC | 3 |
| ✳ | | | | |

Figure 11-20. *Soil Stability* tab and form of the *Transects* tab

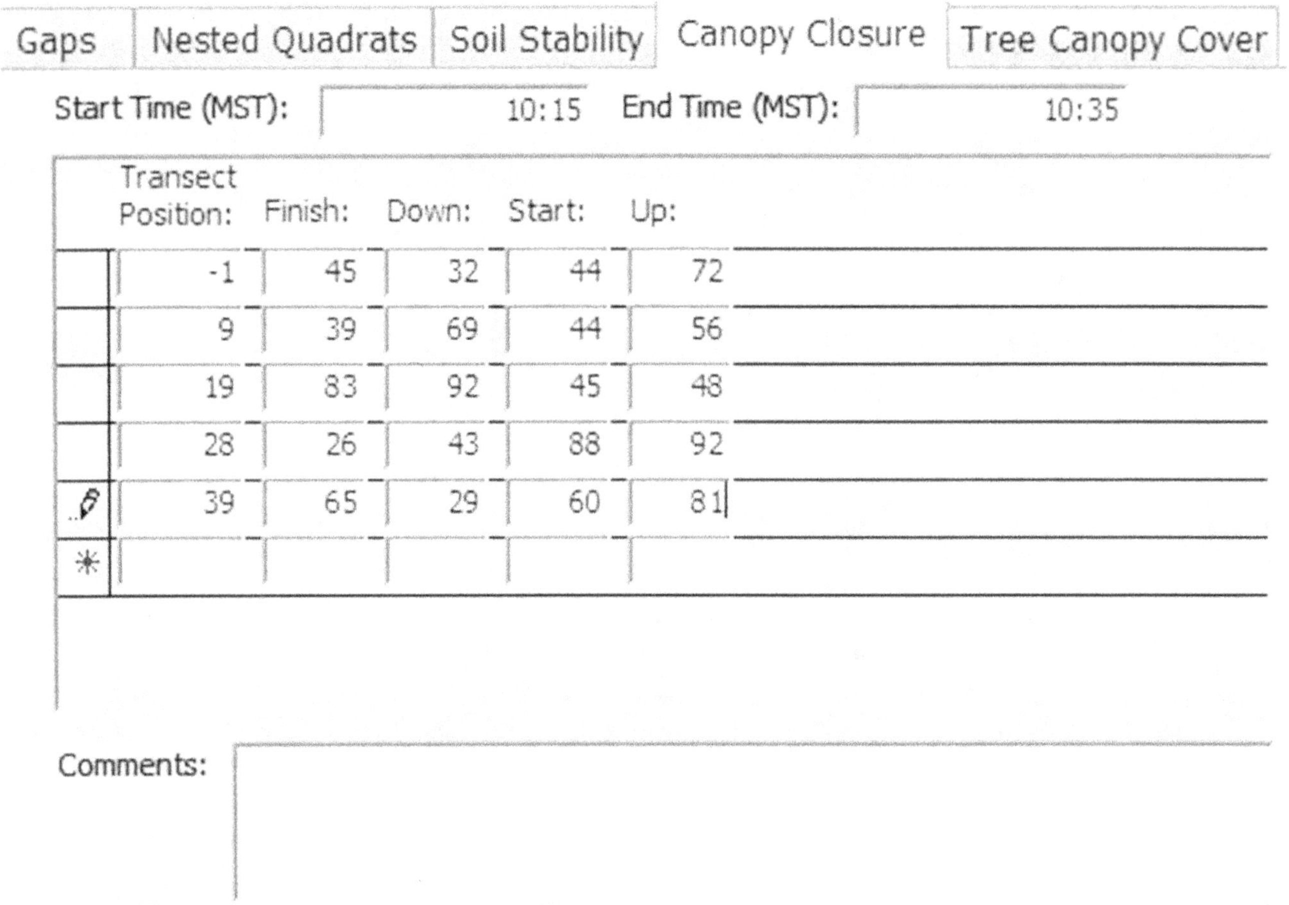

| Gaps | Nested Quadrats | Soil Stability | Canopy Closure | Tree Canopy Cover |

Start Time (MST): 10:15    End Time (MST): 10:35

| Transect Position: | Finish: | Down: | Start: | Up: |
|---|---|---|---|---|
| -1 | 45 | 32 | 44 | 72 |
| 9 | 39 | 69 | 44 | 56 |
| 19 | 83 | 92 | 45 | 48 |
| 28 | 26 | 43 | 88 | 92 |
| 39 | 65 | 29 | 60 | 81 |
| | | | | |

Comments:

Figure 11-21. *Canopy Closure* tab and form of the *Transects* tab

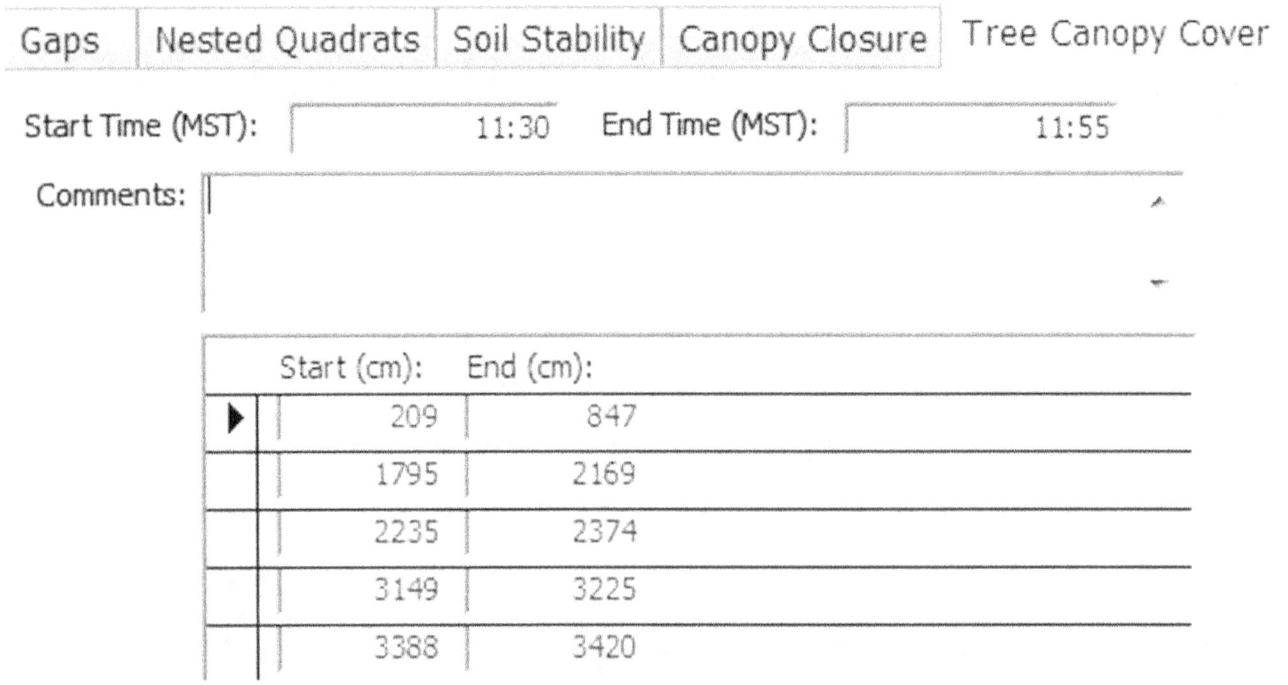

| Gaps | Nested Quadrats | Soil Stability | Canopy Closure | Tree Canopy Cover |

Start Time (MST): 11:30    End Time (MST): 11:55

Comments:

| Start (cm): | End (cm): |
|---|---|
| 209 | 847 |
| 1795 | 2169 |
| 2235 | 2374 |
| 3149 | 3225 |
| 3388 | 3420 |

Figure 11-22. *Tree Canopy Cover* tab and form of the *Transects* tab

- Navigating up to the main level of the *Data Entry* form, the *Trees* tab (fig. 11-23) includes an *Overstory Trees* and a *Saplings* form. Data for the overstory trees are collected in the field on the *Forest Tree Datasheet* or the *Pinyon-Juniper Tree Datasheet*. Enter **Start Time** and **End Time** for tree sampling. In the *Overstory Trees* form, if there are no overstory trees on the plot, check **There are no overstory trees**. Slightly different methods exist depending on the tree species, so there are *Forest Tree Datasheet* and *Pinyon-Juniper Tree Datasheet* tabs and forms.

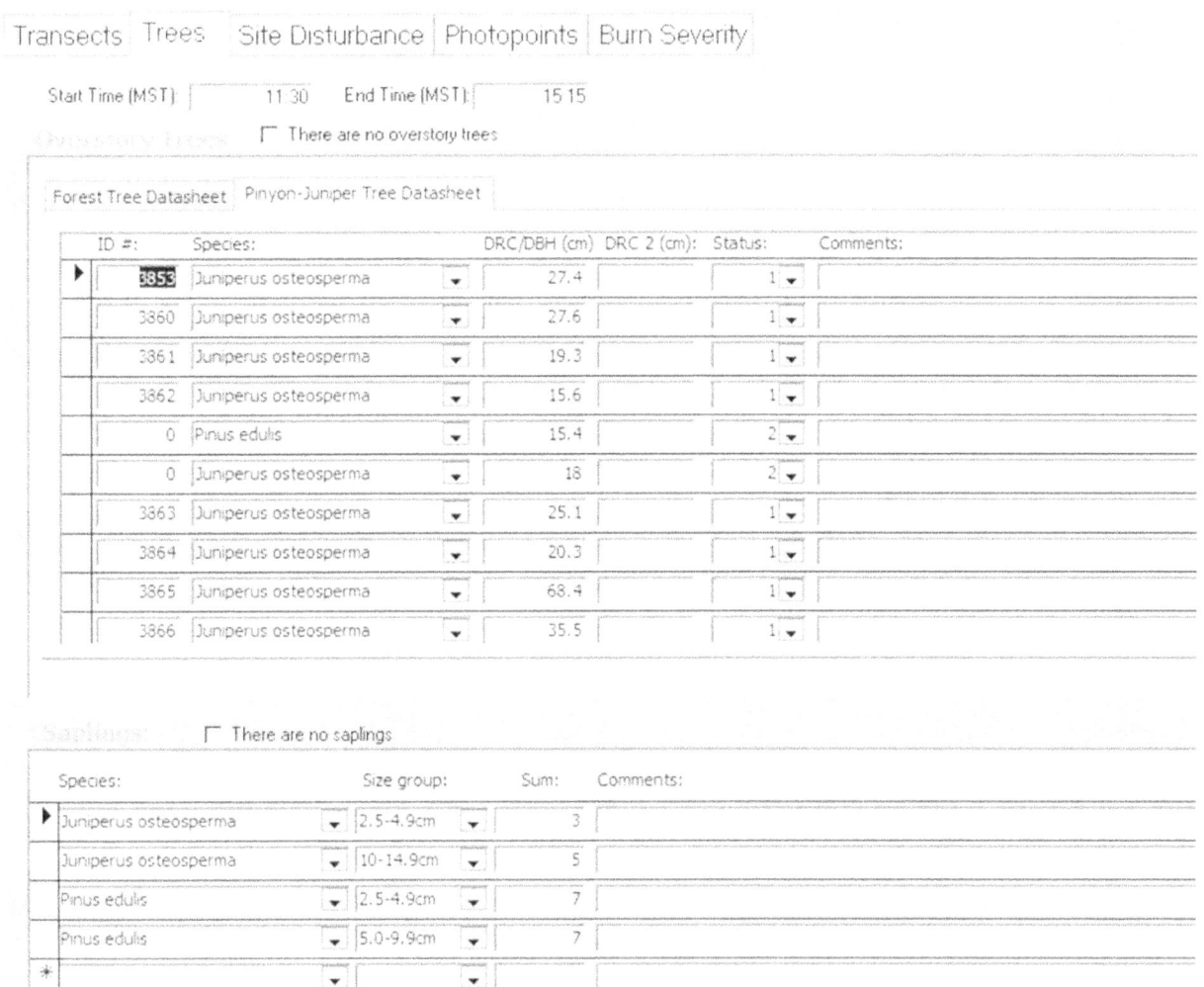

Figure 11-23. *Trees* tab, showing both the *Overstory Trees* and *Saplings* forms

  - On the *Forest Tree Datasheet* tab and form (fig. 11-24), enter **ID #, Species, DBH, Height, CBH, Status,** and any **Comments**.

  - On the *Pinyon-Juniper Tree Datasheet* tab and form (fig. 11-25), enter **ID#, Species, DRC/DBH** (DRC for *Juniperus* or DBH for *Pinus*), **DRC 2, Status,** and **Comments**. Note that if one diameter is recorded, it is entered into the **DRC/DBH** field. **DRC2** is only used when a second diameter is measured, which only occurs for *Juniperus*.

  ○ The *Saplings* form (fig. 11-26) captures data collected in the field from either of the 2 tree datasheets. List sapling information, including **Species, Size group, Sum,** and **Comments**. If there are no saplings on the plot, check **There are no saplings**.

Forest Tree Datasheet | Pinyon-Juniper Tree Datasheet

| ID #: | Species: | | DBH (cm): | Height (m): | CBH (m): | Status: | Comments: |
|---|---|---|---|---|---|---|---|
| 4783 | Abies lasiocarpa | ▼ | 23 | | | 1 ▼ | |
| 4693 | Picea engelmannii | ▼ | 44 | | | 1 ▼ | |
| 4692 | Abies lasiocarpa | ▼ | 30 | | | 1 ▼ | |
| 4788 | Populus tremuloides | ▼ | 45.3 | | | 1 ▼ | |
| 0 | Picea pungens | ▼ | 73 | | | 2 ▼ | |
| 4690 | Abies lasiocarpa | ▼ | 34 | | | 1 ▼ | |

Figure 11-24. *Forest Tree Datasheet* tab and form on the *Overstory Trees* form

Forest Tree Datasheet | Pinyon-Juniper Tree Datasheet

| ID #: | Species: | | DRC/DBH (cm) | DRC 2 (cm): | Status: | Comments: |
|---|---|---|---|---|---|---|
| 0 | Juniperus osteosperma | ▼ | 41 | 34 | 2 ▼ | |
| 4267 | Juniperus osteosperma | ▼ | 35 | 35 | 1 ▼ | |
| 4255 | Juniperus osteosperma | ▼ | 23.5 | | 1 ▼ | |
| 4260 | Pinus edulis | ▼ | 16.6 | | 1 ▼ | |
| 4231 | Juniperus osteosperma | ▼ | 19.6 | | 1 ▼ | |
| 4266 | Juniperus osteosperma | ▼ | 25.6 | | 1 ▼ | |
| 4270 | Juniperus osteosperma | ▼ | 27.7 | | 1 ▼ | |
| 3880 | Pinus edulis | ▼ | 15.4 | | 1 ▼ | |
| 0 | Juniperus osteosperma | ▼ | 55 | 59 | 2 ▼ | |
| 0 | Juniperus osteosperma | ▼ | 56 | 557 | 2 ▼ | |

Figure 11-25. *Pinyon-Juniper Tree Datasheet* tab and form

Saplings: ☐ There are no saplings

| Species: | | Size group: | | Sum: | Comments: |
|---|---|---|---|---|---|
| ▶ Pseudotsuga menziesii | ▼ | 5.0-9.9cm | ▼ | 3 | |
| Abies lasiocarpa | ▼ | 2.5-4.9cm | ▼ | 1 | |
| Abies lasiocarpa | ▼ | 5.0-9.9cm | ▼ | 3 | |
| Picea pungens | ▼ | 2.5-4.9cm | ▼ | 1 | |
| Picea pungens | ▼ | 5.0-9.9cm | ▼ | 2 | |

Figure 11-26. *Saplings* form

- The *Site Disturbance* tab (fig. 11-27) displays an *In-Plot Disturbances* form and an *Off-Plot Disturbances* form, both intended to capture data collected in the field on the *Site Disturbance Datasheet*.
  - In the *In-Plot Disturbances* form, enter **Disturbance Type, Size of Affected Area, Distance from Centroid, Direction from Centroid, Description,** and **Potential Effects on Vegetation, Soil, etc**. If there is more than one disturbance type, click on **Add Another In-Plot Disturbance Record** to create a new record.

- In the *Off-Plot Disturbances* form, enter **Disturbance Type, Size of Affected Area, Distance from Plot, Direction from Plot, Description,** and **Potential Effects on Vegetation, Soil, etc.** If there is more than one disturbance type, click on **Add Another Off-Plot Disturbance Record** to create a new record.

- *Photopoints* tab and form (fig. 11-28). This form captures data collected in the field on the *Photopoint Datasheet*. Enter **Start Time** for taking plot photos. For each transect location, enter a **Photo Number** and edit the default offset **Location** (if appropriate). Add any **Comments** about overall plot photos.

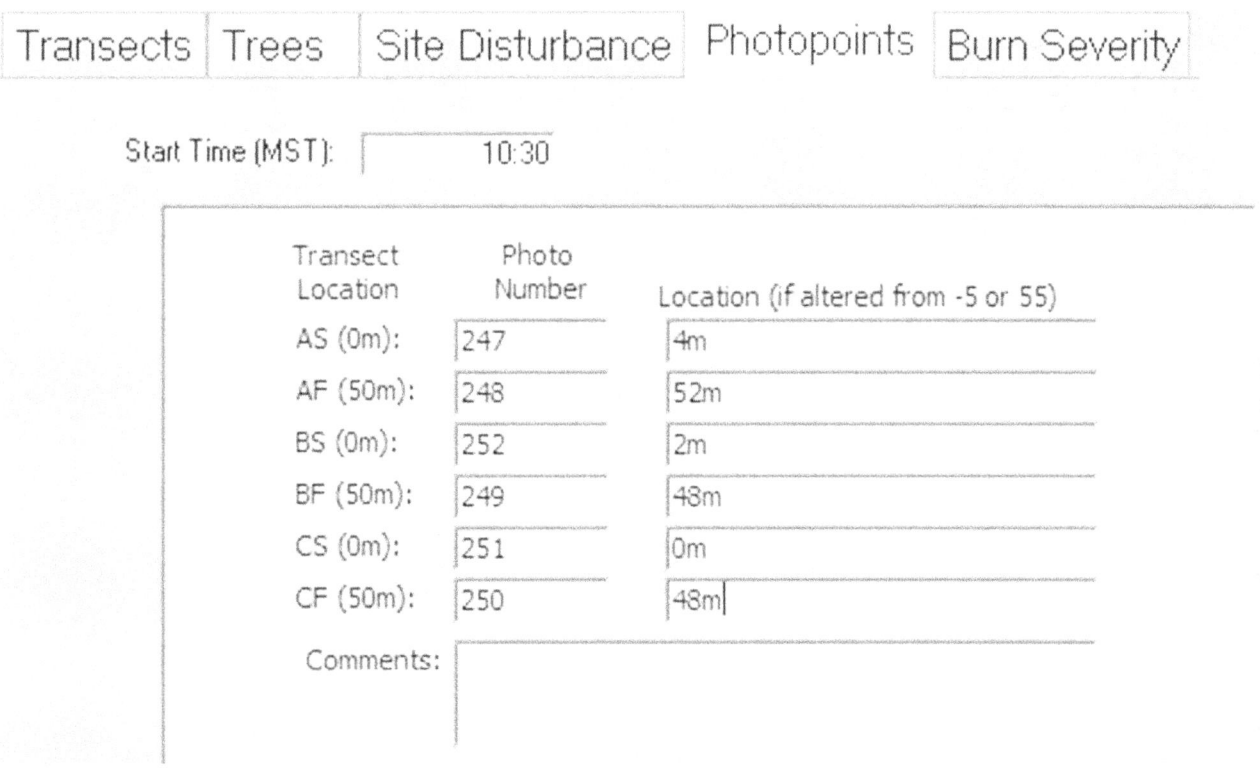

Figure 11-27. *Site Disturbance* tab showing both the *In-Plot Disturbances* and *Off-Plot Disturbances* forms

| Transect Location | Photo Number | Location (if altered from -5 or 55) |
|---|---|---|
| AS (0m): | 247 | 4m |
| AF (50m): | 248 | 52m |
| BS (0m): | 252 | 2m |
| BF (50m): | 249 | 48m |
| CS (0m): | 251 | 0m |
| CF (50m): | 250 | 48m |

Start Time (MST): 10:30

Comments:

Figure 11-28. *Photopoints* tab and form

- The *Burn Severity* tab and form (fig. 11-29) captures data collected in the field on the *Burn Severity Datasheet*. If a plot was within the perimeter of a recent fire, the *Burn Severity* form should be populated. Fill in **Name**, **Date**, and **Type**. If the fire did not affect the plot, check **Plot was not impacted by fire**. Select the appropriate **Burn heterogeneity**. Populate all 4 categories in the following sections: *Burn severity of tree canopy* and *Burn severity of understory/substrate*.

| Transects | Trees | Site Disturbance | Photopoints | Burn Severity |

**Fire Information**

Name  Las Conchas                                    Date  201106

Type  Wildfire  ▾

☐ Plot was not impacted by fire

Low  ▾  **Burn heterogeneity**

Comments

**Burn severity of tree canopy**

7        Low

2        Low-Medium

0        Medium High

0        High

Comments:

**Burn severity of understory/substrate**

2        Low

5        Low-Medium

5        Medium-High

0        High

Comments:  |

Figure 11-29. *Burn Severity* tab and form

**2.2.1.3 Data verification.** Clicking the **Data verification** button from the *Main menu* tab opens the *Data verification switchboard* form (fig. 11-30).

Enter **Start Date** and **End Date**; if no dates are entered, the database will automatically take the earliest and latest dates, respectively. Input the percent of records to be verified and click **Enter**. At a minimum, 25% of the records should be proofed. This will open the *Data verification selection* form (fig. 11-31), which displays the subset of records to be checked.

Selecting a record and clicking **Verify record** opens this record in the *Data Entry* form. If any errors are found, they should be corrected. The **Corrected** box on the *Data verification selection* form will be automatically checked if any errors were corrected. When all records have been checked, click on **Done verifying record**. This navigates back to the *Data verification switchboard*.

Figure 11-30. *Data verification switchboard* opened by the Data verification button on the *Main menu* tab

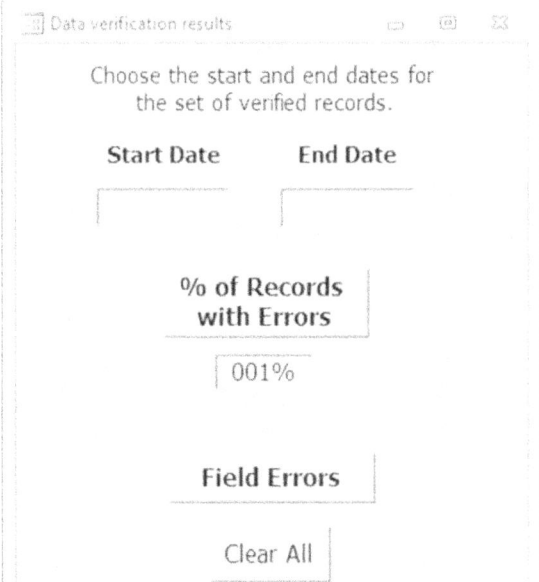

Figure 11-32. *Data verification results* form, accessed through the *Data verification switchboard* form

From the *Data verification switchboard*, click **Error Results** for the *Data verification results* form (fig. 11-32).

Enter **Start Date** and **End Date**. Click on **% of Records with Errors** to see the error rate. If the error rate is greater than 0.1%, the user will be instructed to error check all records. Click on **Field Errors** to see a report of which errors were most frequently corrected (fig. 11-33).

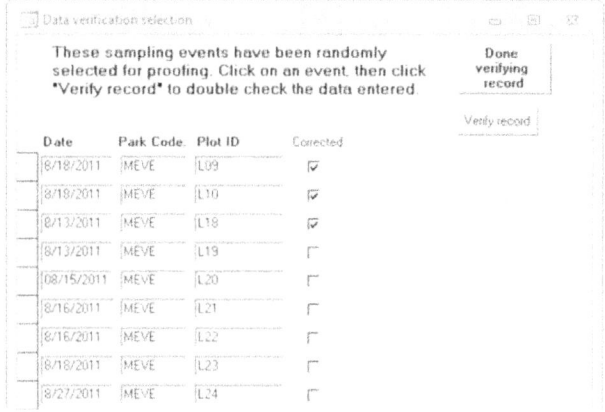

Figure 11-31. *Data verification selection* form, accessed through the *Data verification switchboard* form

## Database Field Errors

| Database Field | Total Errors | Percent of Total Field |
|---|---|---|
| AS Photo Location | 1 | 2% |
| BF Photo Location | 1 | 2% |
| BS Photo Location | 1 | 2% |
| Canopy Cover Position | 5 | 8% |
| CF Photo Location | 1 | 2% |
| CS Photo Location | 1 | 2% |

Figure 11-33. *Database Field Errors* report, accessed through the *Data verification results* form

**2.2.1.4 QA checks.** The **QA checks** button on the *Main menu* tab opens the *Data Validation and Quality Review Tool*. This tool facilitates data validation by showing the results of pre-built queries that check for data integrity, data outliers and missing values, and illogical values. The user may then fix these problems and document the fixes. See *SOP #12* for instructions on this tool.

**2.2.1.5 Back up data.** Clicking the **Back up data** button on the *Main menu* tab will open a **Yes/No** box asking if the user would like to make a backup copy of the data. If **Yes** is selected, the user will be prompted to select a folder in which to place the backup copy. The backup files will be named by adding the current date, time, and user's initials to the end of the back-end file name (e.g., integrated_upland_BE_v1.0_20070605_1711_MS.mdb for a backup file created on June 5, 2007 at 5:11 PM by Megan Swan). Backup copies are used for the current field season only and will not be archived. All such backups may be deleted after the quality review and certification of the data. Clicking the **Save** button creates the backup file and displays a success message.

**2.2.1.6 Revisit reports.** The **Revisit reports** button on the *Main menu* tab opens a report displaying data for each plot that has been entered into the linked back-end database. Reports can be saved as PDFs or printed for field use.

**2.2.2 Defaults tab**
The *Defaults* tab (fig. 11-34) on the database startup menu displays current default values, and check box options for automatic backups on startup or exit, data file compaction on backup, and link verification on startup.

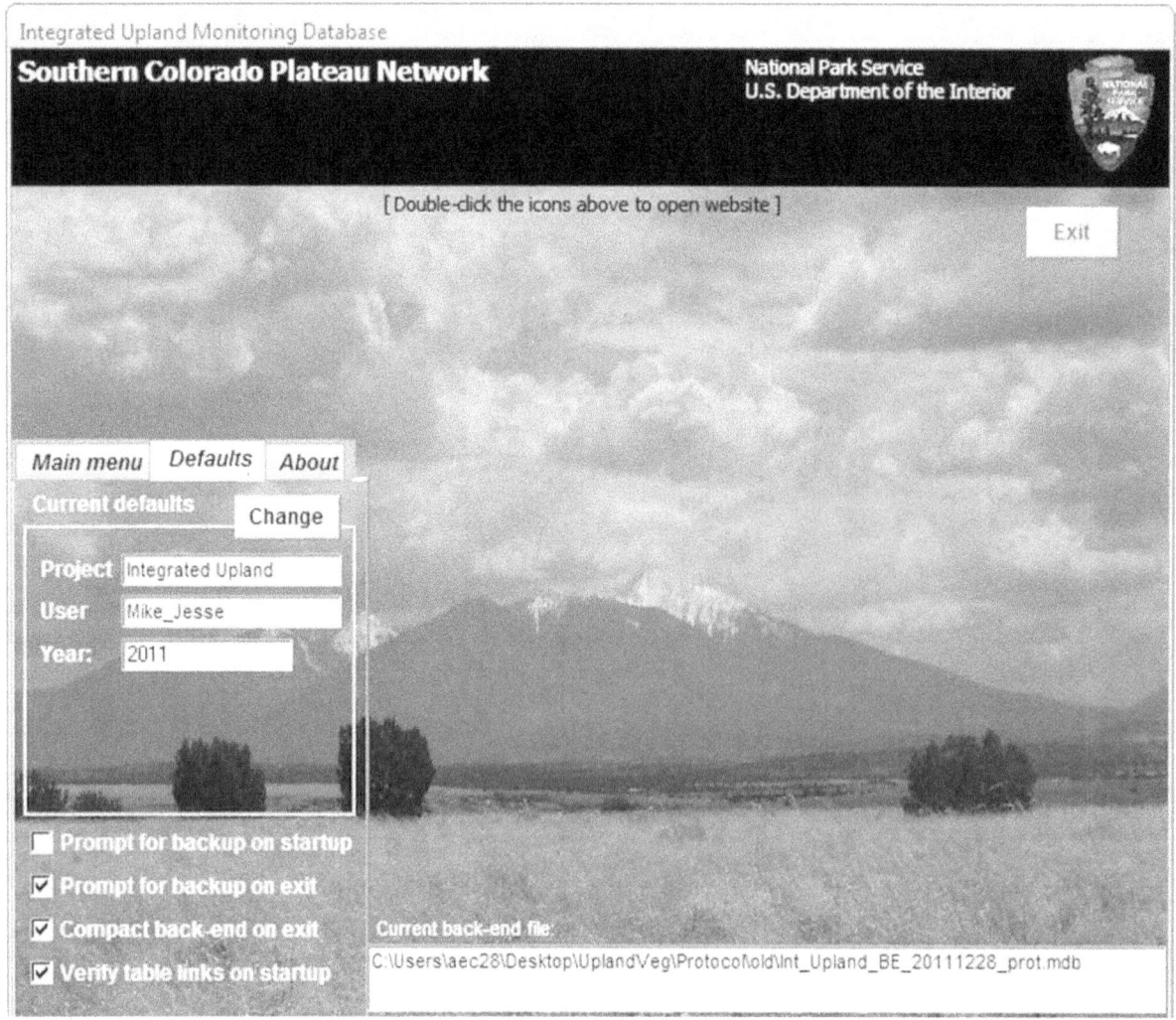

Figure 11-34. *Defaults* tab of the Integrated Upland Monitoring Database startup menu

**2.2.2.1 Current defaults.** The current defaults section of the *Defaults* menu displays values for **Project, User,** and **Year**. To change values, click the **Change** button to bring up the *Set application default values* form (fig. 11-35). **User** and **Year** can be selected from a drop-down list. Click the **New user** button to add a new user (see the *View and edit contact information* form in section 2.2.1.2 of this document for more information). When you have finished entering default values, click the **OK** button to return to the *Defaults* tab.

**2.2.2.2 Automatic backups at startup or exit.** The application can be set to automatically prompt for backups every time it is started, and/or every time it is closed (using the **Exit** button on the main form). Making backups before and after data entry sessions is recommended, in case of database corruption or data entry mistakes. Backups can also be run manually by clicking the **Back up data** button on the *Main menu* tab.

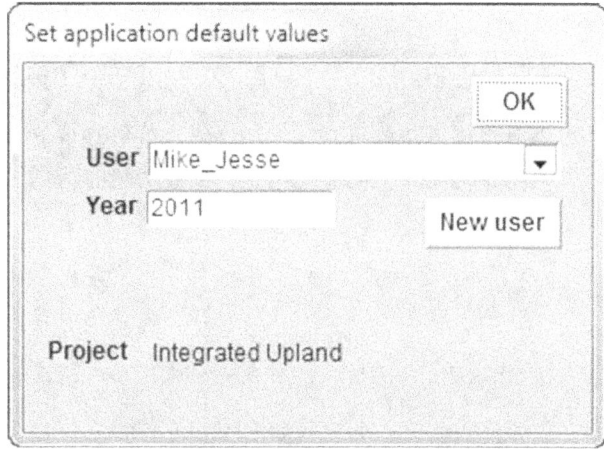

Figure 11-35. *Set application default values* **form**

**2.2.2.3 Compact back-end on exit.** Compaction causes Microsoft Access to optimize the organization of the file, making it smaller and faster at accessing data. Check the option to **Compact back-end on exit** so that the application will compact the linked back-end data file when the application is closed using the **Exit** button on the main form.

**2.2.2.4 Verify table links on startup.** The application is structured with a front-end (user interface) and a back-end (data tables). In order for the application to work properly, the front-end must be linked to the tables in the back-end. When this option is check-marked (recommended), the link to the back-end file(s) will be verified when the application is started.

2.2.3 About tab

The *About* tab (fig. 11-36) presents information about the application, including version number, application author, author organization, author phone, and author email. Buttons for viewing release history and reporting bugs are also provided on the *About* tab.

**2.2.3.1 View release history.** From the *About* tab on the application startup form, clicking the **View release history** button opens the *Application Releases* form (fig. 11-37). This form provides information about all of the different versions of the application that have been released. It is filled in by the application developer before the application is distributed and is therefore read-only.

The *Application Releases* form details specific release information (including version number, date, and known bugs), as well as author information.

**2.2.3.2 Report a bug.** The **Report a bug** button on the *About* tab will prompt the user to contact the application developer with the details of the bug. Developer contact information is located above the **Report a bug** button.

The following information is useful when reporting a bug:

- application name
- application version
- name of the form/report you were on when the bug happened
- action, if any, you took right before the bug occurred
- screen capture of any error messages

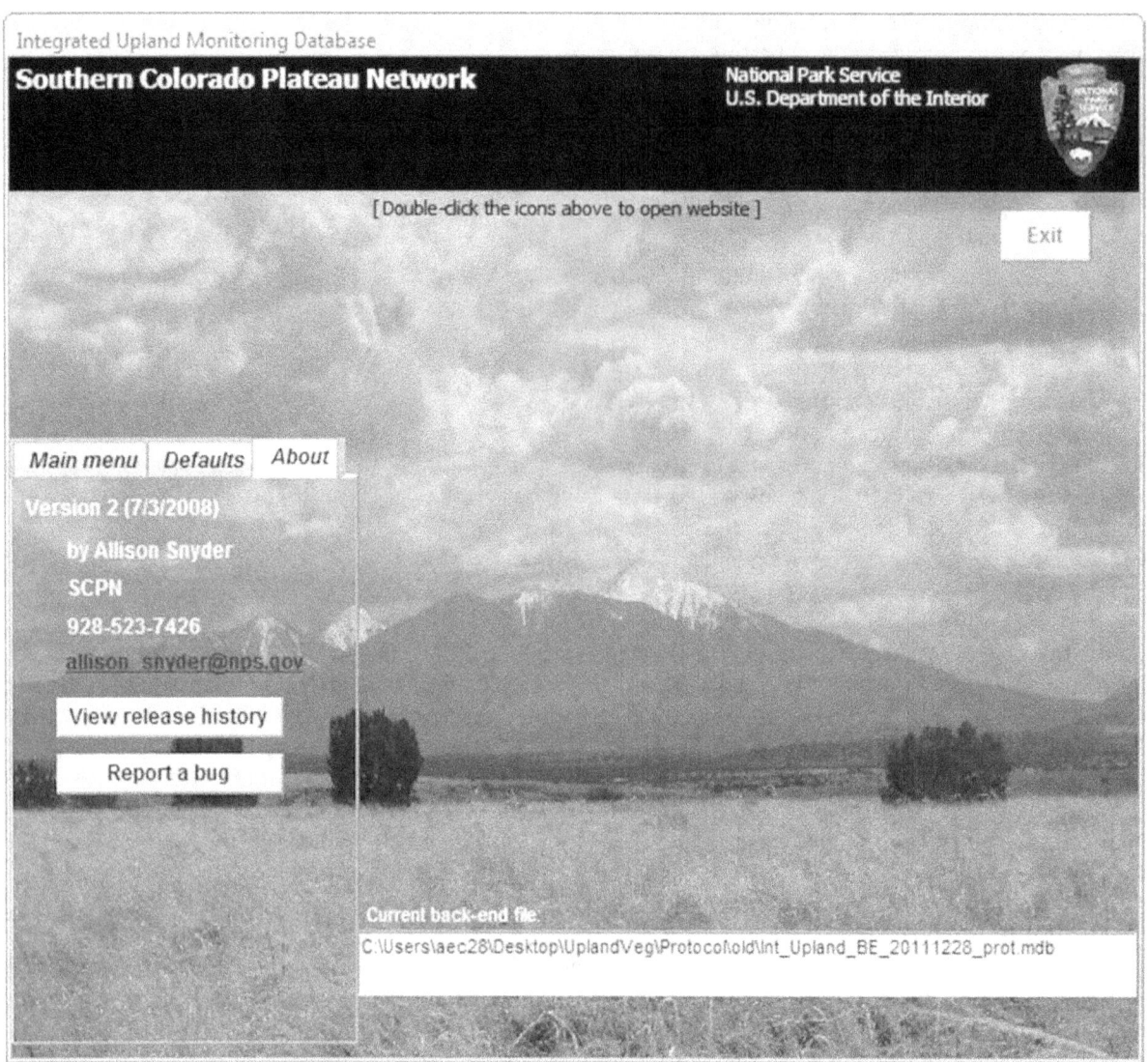

Figure 11-36. *About* tab of the Integrated Upland Monitoring Database startup menu

Figure 11-37. *Application Releases* form, opened by clicking the View release history button on the *About* tab

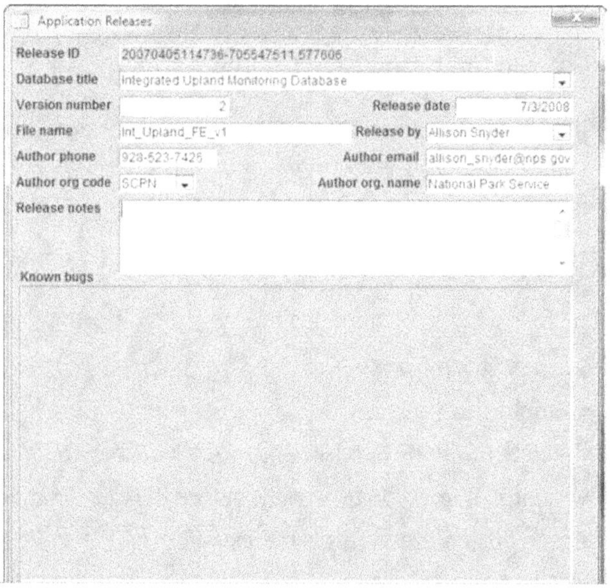

# Standard Operating Procedure #12: Data Quality Review

**Version 1.00**

**Revision History Log**

| Previous version number | Revision date | Author | Changes made | Section and paragraph | Reason | Approved by | New version number |
|---|---|---|---|---|---|---|---|
| | | | | | | | |
| | | | | | | | |
| | | | | | | | |
| | | | | | | | |
| | | | | | | | |
| | | | | | | | |
| | | | | | | | |
| | | | | | | | |

Only changes in this specific SOP will be logged here. Version numbers increase incrementally by hundredths (e.g., version 1.01, version 1.02) for minor changes. Major revisions should be designated with the next whole number (e.g., version 2.0, 3.0, 4.0). Record the previous version number, date of revision, author of the revision; identify paragraphs and pages where changes are made, who approved the revision, and the reason for making the changes along with the new version number.

This standard operating procedure (SOP) describes the procedures for validation of data in the working project database. Data validation is the process of checking data for completeness, structural integrity, and logical consistency. It must be done after every field season's data have been entered and verified. The database application facilitates this process by showing the results of pre-built queries that check for data integrity, data outliers, missing values, and illogical values. The user may then fix these problems and document the fixes.

## 1 Data quality review

Table 12-1 shows an example of the automated validation checks that are performed on the data. These queries return records that need to be fixed or verified. Errors and inconsistencies that cannot be fixed are described in the Notes/Comments field within the table where the error occurs. A description of the resulting errors and why edits were not made is also documented and included in the metadata. The data manager will help construct new database queries or modify existing ones as needed.

The queries are named and numbered hierarchically so that high-order data should be fixed before low-order data. One change in a high-order table may affect many low-order records.

## 2 Using database quality review tools

From the database switchboard, on the Main menu tab, click **QA checks**. This will open the *Data Validation and Quality Review Tool*. Upon opening, the tool automatically runs the validation queries and stores the results in a table built into the front-end database (tbl_QA_Results). Each time the query results are refreshed, or the *Data Validation and Quality Review Tool* is re-opened, the number of records returned and the run times are rewritten so that the most recent result set is always available; any remedy description and the user name for the person making the edits is retained between runs of the queries. The results from the validation queries will be provided in the metadata.

**Table 12-1. Example of validation queries in the integrated upland database**

| Query name | Returns records meeting the following criteria: |
|---|---|
| qry_Val_1a_Plot_Events | Plot records with no related sampling event data |
| qry_Val_1b_Site_Char | Plot records with no related Ecological Site Assessment data |
| qry_Val _1c_Site_Char_veg | Ecological Site Assessment records with no related vegetation data |
| qry_Val_1c_Site_Char_Veg_Assc | Ecological Site Assessment records with no related vegetation association data |
| qry_Val_1c_Site_Char_Veg_Dom | Ecological Site Assessment vegetation records with no related dominant species data |
| qry_Val _1d_Site_Char_soil_prof | Ecological Site Assessment records with no related soil profile |
| qry_Val _1e_Events_Transects | Sampling event records with no related transects |
| qry_Val _1f_Transects | Sampling event records without 3 associated transects |
| qry_Val _1n_Quadrats_Count | Transect records without 5 associated quadrats |
| qry_Val _2a_Plots | Plot records missing GRTS point, slope, aspect, or azimuth- center |
| qry_Val _2k_Events | Sampling event records missing data from any field |
| qry_Val _3a_Photos | Photopoint records missing data from any field except "notes" |
| qry_Val _3b_Site_Dist_On | In-plot disturbance records with a positive response for "disturbance type" but no data for affected area, distance, and effects |
| qry_Val _3f_Trees_Over | Overstory tree records missing status, tree id, dbh, dbh/drc, or species code |
| qry_Val _3h_TreeID_0_Status_2 | Overstory tree records where tree id= 0 and status does not equal 2 |
| qry_Val _3i_Trees_Over_DBH | Overstory trees records where diameter is either <15 cm or >100 cm |
| qry_Val _4d_Quad_Func1 | Quadrat functional group records where category or cover class is null |
| qry_Val_4i_Quad_Nest_Species_NoData | Nested quadrat plot records that list a species but have no cover or frequency data |
| qry_Val _5e_Quad_Surf_TMC<100 | Quadrat surface features where total max cover per quadrat is greater than 100 |

## 2.1 Results summary tab

The *Results summary* tab (fig. 12-1) displays each query with its **Query name, Type,** whether the validation for that query is **Done, N recs,** (number of records returned by the query), the **Last run time,** and a **Description.** Clicking the button to **Refresh results** may need to be done periodically as changes in one part of the data structure may change the number of records returned by other queries.

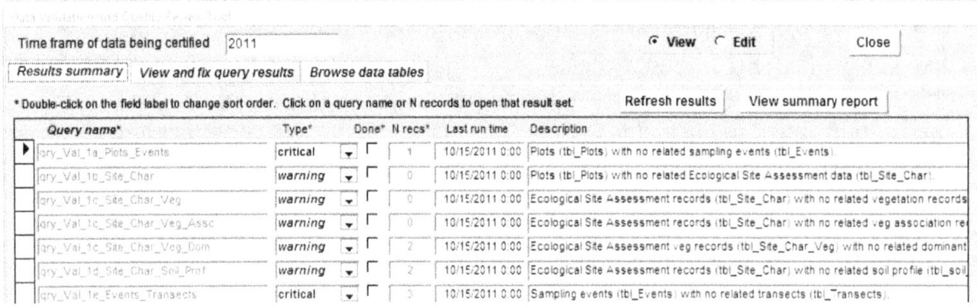

**Figure 12-1. Contents of the *Results summary* tab**

## 2.2 View and fix query results tab

Clicking on a query name in the *Results summary* tab opens the query in the *View and fix query results* tab (fig. 12-2). This form displays the data and allows the user to fix the data and/or to provide details. In the upper right-hand corner, selecting the **Edit** option button allows data editing. Clicking **Design View** will allow the user to see how the query is designed.

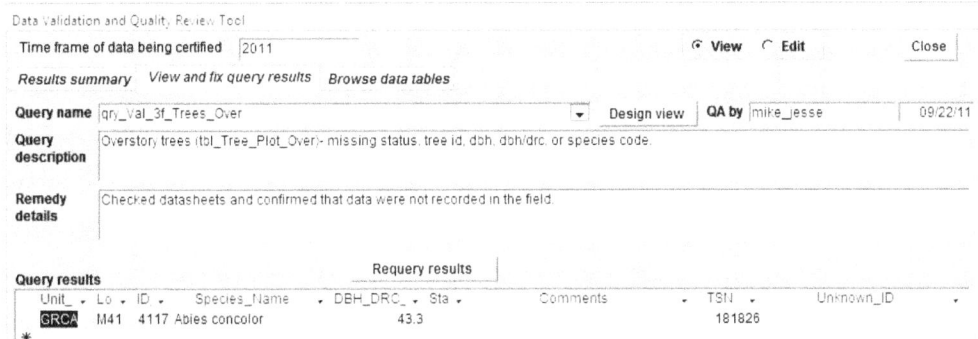

Figure 12-2. Contents of the *View and fix query results* tab

## 2.3 Browse data tables tab

The *Browse data tables* tab (fig. 12-3) enables the user to edit erroneous data directly in the data table, for situations where direct editing is not allowed in the query results form.

The user should toggle between the tabs to complete validation. As edits are made to the data, the user should return to the *Results summary* tab to **Refresh results**. If data are corrected, re-running the query should return no results, and the user can check the **Done** checkbox to show that the data have been validated. Once all queries return zero records, this section of data validation is complete. In some cases, data cannot be fixed and therefore the queries will return records, even though the data validation is complete. All results from validation will be included in the metadata.

Results summary    View and fix query results    *Browse data tables*

Table: tbl_Transect_Basal_Gaps

Warning: This is a last resort! If possible, open the records needing fixes within the data entry form. Also, when making manual edits in data tables, please be sure to update the updated_date and updated_by fields if they are present in the table.

| Transect_ID | Type | Start | End | Note | Order |
|---|---|---|---|---|---|
| {00594CD7-A3AB-432F-AC09-DC8A14766AE6} | G | 0 | 24 | | 210 |
| {00594CD7-A3AB-432F-AC09-DC8A14766AE6} | G | 34 | 306 | | 211 |
| {00594CD7-A3AB-432F-AC09-DC8A14766AE6} | G | 319 | 567 | | 212 |
| {00594CD7-A3AB-432F-AC09-DC8A14766AE6} | G | 575 | 623 | | 213 |
| {00594CD7-A3AB-432F-AC09-DC8A14766AE6} | G | 629 | 796 | | 214 |
| {00594CD7-A3AB-432F-AC09-DC8A14766AE6} | G | 806 | 876 | | 215 |
| {00594CD7-A3AB-432F-AC09-DC8A14766AE6} | G | 877 | 926 | | 216 |
| {00594CD7-A3AB-432F-AC09-DC8A14766AE6} | G | 933 | 958 | | 217 |
| {00594CD7-A3AB-432F-AC09-DC8A14766AE6} | G | 997 | 1032 | | 218 |
| {00594CD7-A3AB-432F-AC09-DC8A14766AE6} | G | 1045 | 1163 | | 219 |
| {00594CD7-A3AB-432F-AC09-DC8A14766AE6} | G | 1168 | 1307 | | 220 |

Figure 12-3. Contents of the *Browse data tables* tab

# Standard Operating Procedure #13: Data Summary and Reporting

## Version 1.00

### Revision History Log

| Previous version number | Revision date | Author | Changes made | Section and paragraph | Reason | Approved by | New version number |
|---|---|---|---|---|---|---|---|
| | | | | | | | |
| | | | | | | | |
| | | | | | | | |
| | | | | | | | |
| | | | | | | | |
| | | | | | | | |
| | | | | | | | |
| | | | | | | | |

Only changes in this specific SOP will be logged here. Version numbers increase incrementally by hundredths (e.g., version 1.01, version 1.02) for minor changes. Major revisions should be designated with the next whole number (e.g., version 2.0, 3.0, 4.0). Record the previous version number, date of revision, author of the revision; identify paragraphs and pages where changes are made, who approved the revision, and the reason for making the changes along with the new version number.

This standard operating procedure (SOP) describes the steps required to prepare and summarize the data for analysis, and provides guidelines for preparing annual summary reports.

## 1 Data summary

The sample unit for all analyses is the plot; hence, all data is summarized at the plot level. For example, for species cover, plot means are calculated from the 15 quadrats, and then a mean and standard deviation for the ecological site are calculated from the plot means. Table 13-1 provides a list of all calculations made for the annual reports.

### 1.1 Shrub and herbaceous cover, frequency and diversity

The quadrat data provides estimates of foliar cover, or abundance, of herbaceous and shrub species. In each quadrat, foliar cover of each species is estimated by cover class, and the mean of the cover class midpoints is calculated to provide the species abundance for the plot. Species frequency is calculated as the percentage of quadrats in which the species occurs in a plot. Mean species abundance and mean species frequency can then be calculated for the ecological site, along with the corresponding standard deviations. For the annual summary reports, species frequency is calculated for the $10m^2$ quadrats, but it can also be calculated for the smaller size quadrats. Species frequency is also calculated at the plot level, i.e., percentage of plots in which a species occurs.

The quadrat data also provides estimates of foliar cover for plant functional groups. As with species data, foliar cover is estimated by cover class, and the mean of the cover class midpoints provides the abundance of functional groups in the plot. Mean abundance and standard deviation of functional groups are calculated for the ecological site.

Various measures of species diversity are calculated for the plot and the ecological site. Species richness refers to the number of species in a given area. Mean species richness (and standard deviation) is calculated for each spatial scale of the nested quadrat ($0.01$ m², $0.1$ m², $1$ m², $5$ m², $10$ m²), and for the 0.5 ha plot. Plot species richness is referred to as alpha diversity. Species richness is also calculated for all plots within an ecological site—this is referred to as gamma diversity. These 2 measures can be used to calculate beta diversity, or within ecological site heterogeneity.

**Table 13-1. Summary calculations for annual summary reports. Since the plot is the sample unit, most metrics are calculated for the plot, and the mean and standard deviations of these metrics are calculated for the ecological site; exceptions are plot frequency, ecological site species richness, and beta diversity.**

| Metric | Description | Units | Calculation |
|---|---|---|---|
| Species Abundance (Foliar Cover) | mean species cover based on cover class midpoints | % | $1/n \sum_{i=1}^{n} c_i$ <br><br> where $c_i$ is the midpoint of the cover class of the species for a quadrat and n is the number of quadrats per plot |
| Cover of Functional Groups | mean functional group cover based on cover class midpoints | % | $1/n \sum_{i=1}^{n} c_i$ <br><br> where $c_i$ is the midpoint of the cover class of the functional group for a quadrat and n is the number of quadrats per plot |
| Quadrat Frequency of Species | mean frequency—percentage of quadrats containing a species | % | $1/n \sum_{i=1}^{n} f_i$ <br><br> where $f_i$ is the frequency of a species in a plot (quadrats occupied divided by quadrats sampled) and n is the number of plots sampled. |
| Plot Frequency of Species | percentage of plots containing a species | % | f (plots occupied by a species divided by plots sampled) |
| Tree Basal Area | total overstory tree basal area, by species and by size class | $m^2/ha$ | $10 \sum_{i=1}^{n} BA_i$ <br><br> where $BA = \pi(DBH_i/2)^2$ <br><br> $BA_i$ is the basal area for each overstory tree, n is the number of overstory trees, and DBH is expressed in meters; presumes trees are sampled in a 1000 $m^2$ subplot |
| Tree Density | total overstory and sapling density, by species, and by size class | stems/ha | #T/0.1 + #t /0.025 <br><br> where #T = number of overstory trees and #t = number of understory trees; presumes overstory trees are sampled in a 1000 $m^2$ subplot, and saplings are sampled in a 250 $m^2$ subplot |
| Seedling Density | total, by species and by size class | stems/ha | $(\sum s) \times 10000/150$ <br><br> where s = number of seedlings in a quadrat |
| Species Richness (S) | the simplest measure of species diversity | number of species | = the total number of species observed per plot ($S_p$) or ecological site ($S_e$) |
| Shannon Diversity Index (H′) | a measure of species diversity that takes into account the relative abundance of each species | | $-\sum_{i=1}^{n} p_i \ln p_i$ <br><br> where $p_i$ is the abundance (cover class midpoint) of each species in an ecological site |
| Species Evenness (E) | a measure of the degree to which all species are equal in abundance | | H′/ ln(S) <br><br> where H′ is the Shannon Diversity Index and S is Species Richness |

**Table 13-1.** *(continued)*

| Metric | Description | Units | Calculation |
|---|---|---|---|
| Beta Diversity ($\beta_w$) | a measure of within-ecological site heterogeneity | | $S_e / (S_p - 1)$ where $S_e$ is the total number of species found in the ecological site and $S_p$ is the mean number of species found per plot |
| Relative Cover of Basal Gaps | relative cover of basal gaps | % | $1/L \sum_{i=1}^{n} g_i$ where $g_i$ is length of each gap and L is the total length of line(s) sampled for the plot |
| Median Basal Gap Size | | cm | if n is odd then Median (M) = ((n + 1)/2)th item term if n is even then Median (M) = [((n)/2)th item term + ((n)/2 + 1)th item term ]/2 where n is the total number of gaps |
| Mean Surface Soil Aggregate Stability | a test to detect changes in the physical, chemical and biological processes that hold soil particles together | | $1/n \sum_{i=1}^{n} a_i$ where $a_i$ is the soil aggregate stability index for a sample and n is the number of samples per plot |
| Cover of Soil Surface Features | mean quadrat abundance based on cover class midpoints | % | $1/n \sum_{i=1}^{n} c_i$ where $c_i$ is the midpoint of the cover class of the surface feature for a quadrat and q is the number of quadrats per plot |
| Number of Gaps by Size Class | | #/transect length | |

Two additional diversity measurements are calculated. The Species Distribution Evenness Index (E) measures the evenness of the distribution among the plots. Shannon diversity (H′) is calculated to provide a measure of species diversity where each species is weighted by its abundance, hence providing less weight to rarer species.

Measures of species diversity are calculated for all species, and for native species only.

## 1.2 Tree basal area and density

Tree measurements include basal area and density. Basal area provides a measurement of area covered by the tree stems and is presented in units of m²/ha; density provides an estimate of the number of stems in a hectare. Both basal area and density are calculated by species, which in turn are totaled. Calculations are made for plots, and then the means and standard deviations are calculated for the plots within the ecological site. Tree species density data is also grouped according to size classes to provide a representation of forest structure. Basal area calculations are made for both living stems and standing dead stems (snags).

Sapling and seedling density are tallied by species and size class, and presented in units of stems per hectare.

Mean canopy closure with standard deviation are calculated for each ecological site. First, each canopy closure measurement is divided by 0.96. A mean is calculated for the 4 measurements taken at each point. Then the mean canopy closure is calculated for each plot. Finally, mean canopy closure and standard deviation are calculated for each ecological site.

Tree canopy cover is calculated by totaling the percent canopy cover of the transects for each plot, then calculating the mean and standard deviation for the ecological site.

## 1.3 Soil stability and hydrologic function

Soil stability and hydrologic function are monitored in 3 ways: through gap data collected in line intercept transects, soil aggregate stability tests, and percent cover of soil surface features in the quadrats.

Basal and canopy gap data are presented in 5 ways: (1) the percentage of the transect in gaps (not covered by plant bases or canopy), (2) the percentage of the transect in bases or canopy, (3) the median gap size, (4) the number of gaps per transect, and (5) the frequency of gaps in various size classes.

The soil aggregate stability test provides an index of the degree of soil structural development and its resistance to erosion. The index ranges from 1 to 6. Mean and standard deviation of soil aggregate stability are calculated for each plot, and are calculated separately for samples collected under vegetative cover and for those with no cover.

Cover of soil surface features, including bare ground, duff and litter, various types of biological soil crusts, various size classes of rock, and plant bases, are collected in the 1 m² quadrats. The mean and standard deviation for each soil surface feature are calculated for the cover class midpoints, in the same manner as the calculation of species cover and functional groups.

## 2 Preparation of annual summary reports

Reports are generated for each park unit for each year that monitoring occurs. In park units where multiple ecological sites are monitored, the data are summarized in one report. The primary objectives of these reports are to 1) summarize annual data, and document monitoring activities for the year, 2) describe the current conditions of the resources, and 3) provide this information to park managers in a timely manner to increase data utility and improve communication within and among network park units. Where appropriate, the current year's data are compared with selected data from previous years.

Annual reports consist of the following sections (see appendix F for an example annual report):

*1 Introduction*

This section provides background, purposes, and objectives of the integrated upland monitoring project, including park- or site-specific objectives where appropriate. This section also contains site descriptions, management concerns, and new and ongoing park management activities with the potential to impact vegetation and soil resources.

*2 Methods*

This section provides a summary of monitoring activities that have occurred at the ecological site during the current year. This summary should include sampling locations, sampling dates, the type of data collected, and methods that were used. Methods are briefly summarized, with references to indicate where to find more detailed descriptions. A brief description of data analysis methodology is included.

*3 Results*

This section provides a summary of all data collected in graphic, tabular and narrative form. When appropriate, selected data from previous years are included. For all data summary and analyses, the plot is the sample unit upon which all statistics are based.

*4 Discussion*

This section provides a description of current conditions and a comparison with the previous year's conditions. The narrative includes how this year's sampling effort fits within the context of sampling in previous years.

*5 Literature cited*

A literature cited section documents report references to outside material or sources of information.

## 3 Preparation of trend reports

Trend reports, based on comprehensive statistical analyses of long-term data, are prepared periodically. The main objectives of trend reports, as described in Thomas et al. (2006), are to (1) report patterns and trends in the condition of resources being monitored, (2) report characteristics of resources and correlations among related vital signs, (3) report the degree of change that can be detected by the current level of sampling, and (4) provide interpretation of monitoring data in a park context.

# Standard Operating Procedure #14: Revising the Protocol Narrative and SOPs

## Version 1.00

### Revision History Log

| Previous version number | Revision date | Author | Changes made | Section and paragraph | Reason | Approved by | New version number |
|---|---|---|---|---|---|---|---|
|  |  |  |  |  |  |  |  |
|  |  |  |  |  |  |  |  |
|  |  |  |  |  |  |  |  |
|  |  |  |  |  |  |  |  |
|  |  |  |  |  |  |  |  |
|  |  |  |  |  |  |  |  |
|  |  |  |  |  |  |  |  |
|  |  |  |  |  |  |  |  |

Only changes in this specific SOP will be logged here. Version numbers increase incrementally by hundredths (e.g., version 1.01, version 1.02) for minor changes. Major revisions should be designated with the next whole number (e.g., version 2.0, 3.0, 4.0). Record the previous version number, date of revision, author of the revision; identify paragraphs and pages where changes are made, who approved the revision, and the reason for making the changes along with the new version number.

This standard operating procedure (SOP) explains how to make and track changes to the *Integrated Upland Monitoring Protocol for the Southern Colorado Plateau Network* narrative and associated SOPs. Over time, the protocol narrative and SOPs may require modifications. The following procedures must be followed when making changes to ensure that previous data collection and processing procedures are clearly understood and accounted for when using and interpreting historical data sets. Similarly, clearly articulating new methods is critical to credible interpretation of data acquired after the implementation of changes. Personnel making changes must be familiar with this SOP to ensure that proper reviews are conducted, and that documentation standards are followed.

## 1 Modifications
Small changes or additions to existing methods will be reviewed in-house by SCPN staff. An outside review will be sought for major changes in methods.

## 2 Revision history
All changes must be documented, and updated protocol versions must be recorded in the Revision History Log that accompanies the protocol narrative and each SOP. Changes are recorded only in the protocol narrative or the SOP being modified. Version numbers increase incrementally by hundredths (e.g., version 1.01, version 1.02, etc.) for minor changes. Major revisions will be designated with the next whole number (e.g., version 2.0, 3.0, 4.0, etc.). Record the previous version number, date of revision, author of the revision; identify paragraphs and pages where changes are made, who approved the revision, and the reason for making the changes along with the new version number.

Changes to datasheets are documented in the Revision History Log of the SOPs associated with those datasheets. The SOP and current version number should be included in the datasheet header.

## 3 Narrative and SOP updates may occur independently
A change in one SOP will not necessarily necessitate changes in other SOPs or the narrative; a narrative update may not require SOP modifications. All narrative and SOP version changes must be noted in the Master Version Table

(MVT—see table 14-1), which is maintained in this SOP. Any time a narrative or an SOP version change occurs, a new Version Key (VK) number must be created and recorded in the MVT, along with the date of the change and the versions of the narrative and SOPs affected. The VK number increases by whole integers (e.g., 1, 2, 3, 4, 5). Updates to the MVT also must be provided to the SCPN data manager for inclusion in the MVT database. The VK number is essential for project information to be properly interpreted and analyzed. Protocol narrative changes are recorded in Table 14-2. The protocol narrative, SOPs, and data should not be distributed independently of this table.

## 4 New versions

New versions of the Protocol Narrative and SOPs must be posted on the SCPN web page. Previous versions of the protocol narrative and SOPs must be archived in the appropriate library.

**Table 14-1. Master Version Table,** *Integrated Upland Monitoring Protocol for the Southern Colorado Plateau Network*

| Version key # | Revision date | Narrative | SOP #1 | SOP #2 | SOP #3 | SOP #4 | SOP #5 | SOP #6 | SOP #7 | SOP #8 | SOP #9 | SOP #10 | SOP #11 | SOP #12 | SOP #13 | SOP #14 |
|---|---|---|---|---|---|---|---|---|---|---|---|---|---|---|---|---|
| | | | | | | | | | | | | | | | | |
| | | | | | | | | | | | | | | | | |
| | | | | | | | | | | | | | | | | |
| | | | | | | | | | | | | | | | | |
| | | | | | | | | | | | | | | | | |
| | | | | | | | | | | | | | | | | |
| | | | | | | | | | | | | | | | | |
| | | | | | | | | | | | | | | | | |

**Table 14-2. Revision History Log: Protocol narrative**
**Version 1.00**

| Previous version # | Revision date | Author | Changes made | Section and paragraph | Reason | Approved by | New version # |
|---|---|---|---|---|---|---|---|
| | | | | | | | |
| | | | | | | | |
| | | | | | | | |
| | | | | | | | |
| | | | | | | | |
| | | | | | | | |
| | | | | | | | |

Only changes in the narrative will be logged here. Version numbers increase incrementally by hundredths (e.g., version 1.01, version 1.02) for minor changes. Major revisions should be designated with the next whole number (e.g., version 2.0, 3.0, 4.0). Record the previous version number, date of revision, author of the revision; identify paragraphs and pages where changes are made, who approved the revision, and the reason for making the changes along with the new version number.

# Appendix A. Sampling Frames

## 1 Introduction

The sampling frame is the area from which we randomly select our sites, and hence the area to which statistical inferences can be made. Developing the final sampling frames for the integrated upland monitoring project involves a series of steps. These steps are outlined in detail in subsequent sections, organized by park and ecological site. The major steps, however, remain the same across the SCPN integrated upland monitoring project and are described here in this *Introduction* section.

### 1.1 Step 1—Develop the final sampling frame
#### 1.1.1 Determine the management priorities for the park

SCPN and park staff discuss the park's management priorities through meetings, teleconferences, and/or emails, depending on the size of the park and complexity of its ecosystems. Science advisors may participate in the discussion, but ultimately the park staff define the priorities. This generally involves identification of ecosystems, or specific management areas of concern. SCPN staff then identify the corresponding Natural Resource Conservation Service (NRCS) ecological sites, or NRCS soil map units. Finally, park staff determine which ecological site corresponds most closely with their management concerns.

Ecological sites are identified by name and by an 11 digit code. In this document we generally use the ecological site name, with a reference to the ecological site code on first usage, for example, "Sandy Loam Upland ecological site (R037XA030NM)".

The standards for assigning ecological site names vary. The standard used in Utah provides a good example of the ecological site names found in the SCPN park units (fig. A-1).

## Utah Ecological Site Naming Conventions

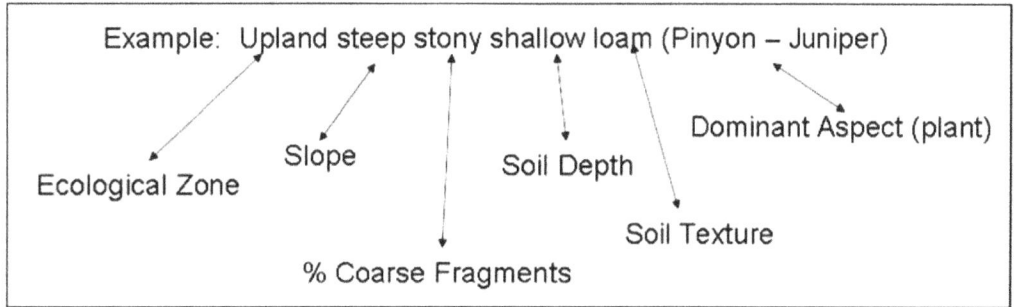

Figure A-1. Example of the ecological site naming convention used in Utah soil surveys. Precipitation zone may also be expressed at the end of the site name (e.g., 12–18" p.z.). Source: United States Department of Agriculture (2012).

Ecological site codes are assigned as follows (from Natural Resource Conservation Service [NRCS] 2011):

> Each ecological site in the ESIS (Ecological Site Information System) repository is identified with an eleven (11) digit number. The first digit identifies the land type (R for rangeland, F for forest land, and G for Forage Suitability Group). The next 4 digits identify the MLRA [Major Land Resource Areas] number. The sixth digit is a single digit letter (default is Y) that designates the Land Resource Unit (LRU). The next 3 digits are used to uniquely identify that specific site. The final part of the ID is the two-digit letter state postal code.

Ecological sites are not explicitly mapped in NRCS soil surveys. Instead, ecological sites are associated with specific map unit components, which in turn are associated with "map units"—the finest spatially defined features. Each map unit may be composed of multiple map unit components, and the soil survey includes an estimate of the proportion of each component (and therefore ecological site) within a map unit (fig. A-2). Typically, only those map units composed of ≥80% of a target ecological site are selected for monitoring.

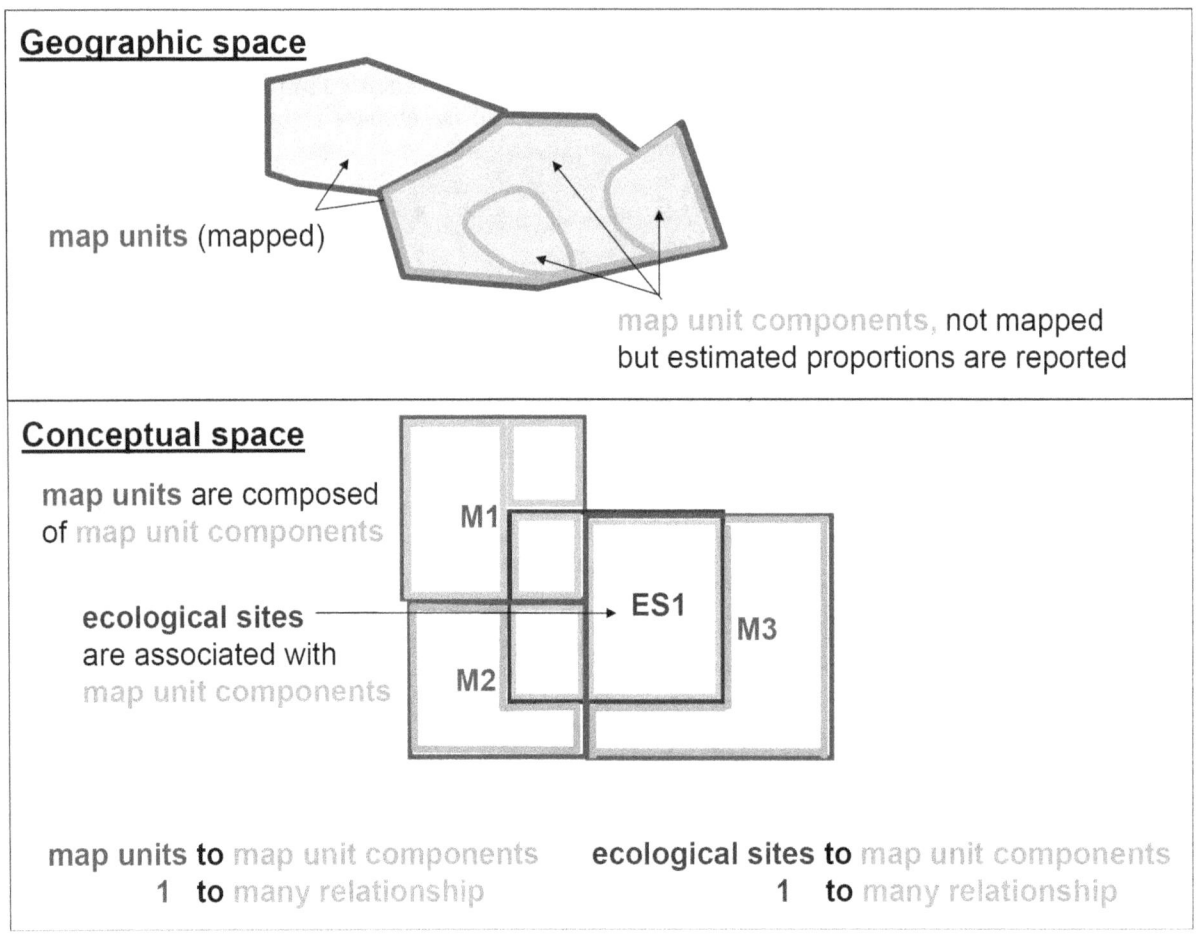

Figure A-2. Visualization in geographic space (top) and conceptual space (bottom) of the complex relationship between soil map units, soil map unit components, and ecological sites

### 1.1.2 Modify the sampling frame

Once agreement on target ecological sites and target map units is reached, SCPN staff work to refine the initial sampling frame to create a realistic GIS representation of the area to be sampled. Areas not suitable for monitoring are excluded from the ecological site final sampling frame. There are 3 general categories of exclusion:

- **Areas not within the target ecological sites.** These include areas near some utility lines, developed areas, archaeological ruins, and on or near roads. A buffer is applied to these features both to ensure that no part of the plot falls within the feature, and in some cases, additional buffer distance is added if it seems likely that the disturbance from the feature would affect a larger area (table A-1). In some cases, where good spatial data are not available, field visits are required to identify sites to be rejected.

- **Areas where site conditions differ substantially from the norm.** These areas are excluded to reduce statistical sample "noise" and make it easier to detect trends. Park resource managers play a large role in deciding what areas should be excluded, and exclusions are generally based on natural or human disturbances, such as wildland fires or mechanical thinning treatments. Where available, burn severity maps are used to identify areas to exclude, but in some cases, entire burns may be excluded (or retained), based on advice from park resource managers. Removal because of thinning or wildland fires is limited to forested and pinyon-juniper woodland ecological sites.

- **Areas excluded due to practical sampling considerations.** Steep slopes and areas that are difficult to access are excluded based on practical considerations. Areas on steep slopes may be rejected because of both safety concerns and concerns of increased erosion due to trampling from repeated site visits. Slope filters vary, depending on vegetation type. In more heavily vegetated areas, such as in mixed conifer forest, areas with less than 30% slope may be retained; while in pinyon-juniper, shrubland, and grasslands site types, areas with less than 20% slopes may be retained. Access is generally considered impractical if it requires more than a 2 hour hike, one-way. In cases where some of the frame is not accessible, a cost-distance analysis that estimates travel times based on trail presence and steepness of slope should be applied. Because of these considerations, SCPN is currently not sampling areas with difficult access or steep slopes. If time and funding become available, areas with difficult access could be added into the sampling effort; however, it is unlikely that areas with steep slopes will ever be included in the sampling effort.

**Table A-1. Steps used to modify sampling frames for the SCPN integrated upland monitoring project**

| Removal condition | Typical removal buffer distance measured from plot center | Specific criteria | Affected parks |
|---|---|---|---|
| Ecological site boundary | 50 m | | all |
| Roads or other infrastructure (developed areas, ruins, buildings, structures) | 200 m for interstate highways, 100 m for all other features | | all |
| Steep slopes | 50 m (40 m at Wupatki National Monument) | removed if >20% in woodlands, shrublands and grasslands, and >30% in forested ecological sites | all |
| Fires (forest and pinyon-juniper ecological sites only) | 100 m | removed moderate to high severity categories, in consultation with park staff | Grand Canyon National Park, Mesa Verde National Park |
| Fuels treatments | 50 m | variable by park and treatment plan | Bandelier National Monument, Grand Canyon National Park, Mesa Verde National Park |
| Research plots | 50 m | consultation with park staff | Bandelier National Monument, Mesa Verde National Park |
| Accessibility | retain areas within approximately 2 hours one-way walking distance | hiking times estimated using cost-distance analysis that favored travel on trails and shallow slopes | Bandelier National Monument |

## 1.1.3 Determine the plot center

Finally, we identify sampling locations by the plot center. Since the plot itself measures 71 × 71 m, the diagonal distance from the plot center to the plot corner is approximately 50 m. Consequently, target ecological sites must extend at least 50 m outward from any potential plot center. To accomplish this, a 50 m negative (inward) buffer was applied to the ecological site edge to ensure that the entire plot falls within the ecological site. One effect of buffering the ecological site edge inward is that areas too narrow to accommodate a plot are removed. Similarly, if a feature such as a road is excluded, a 50 m buffer is added to the exclusion to ensure that no part of a sampling plot can fall within the excluded area (fig. A-3).

After all filters are applied, plot centers are chosen (see below) and the remaining area should be buffered outward by 50 meters because of the 50 meter distance the plot extends from center to edge. This results in a geodataset that covers the area that has the potential to be sampled (fig. A-3).

Figure A-3. Buffer creation. The plot size (71 × 71 m) affects delineation of the area within which plot centroids can be chosen. Two types of buffer are shown. The plot centroid buffer is the minimum distance between plot center and removal condition. The effective plot buffer is the minimum distance between plot edge and removal condition. For example, to achieve a 50 meter buffer of any part of a plot away from roads, a buffer of 100 m is applied (panel 2) so that if a plot center lands on the edge (panel 3), then the entire plot still falls within the target area (panel 4). The area of inference (also called the final sampling frame) is the area which has the potential to be sampled, and is shown in Panel 4 by the combination of the darker shaded polygon plus the 50 meter lightly shaded buffer.

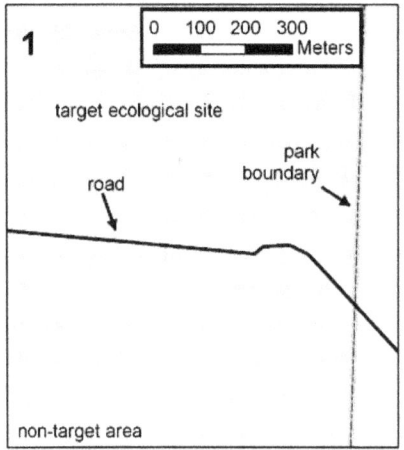
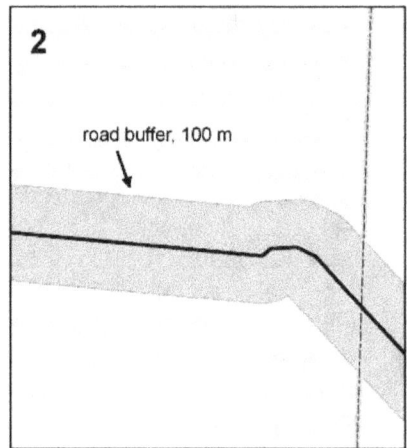
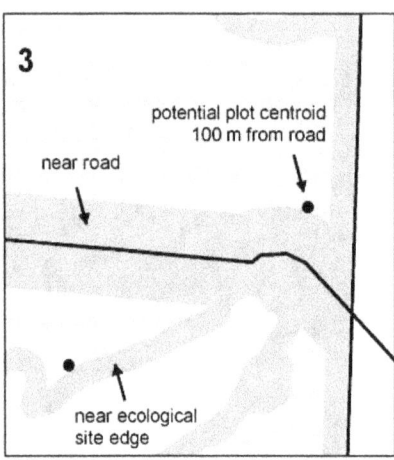
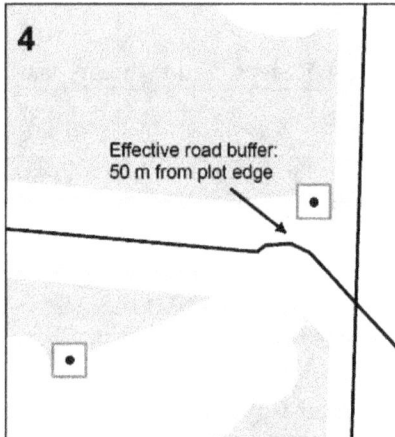

## 1.2 Step 2—Select the sampling site

SCPN is using a Generalized Random-Tessellation Stratified (GRTS) design (Stevens and Olsen 2004) to provide spatial balance in site selection. This design also allows for rejection of sites, establishment of additional sites, and weighting of selection areas based on user-selected criteria (e.g., accessibility).

For each ecological site, a set of spatially distributed sampling points are created using a script incorporating the GRTS design. The script is run using the R statistical computing software (http://www.r-project.org/) and the P.survey and P.design modules, which can be selected and installed from within the R program. For upland monitoring sites, the script uses the area-based option (polygons) and gives all areas equal probability of selection. Spatial balance is maintained by considering sites in a sequential order; if a site is rejected, the next site in sequential order is used.

## 1.3 Step 3—Determine rejection criteria and review sites

Park staff typically review the locations of the GRTS points provided in the initial research application and reject sites near sensitive areas (usually archaeological sites). Some parks require clearing the sites with an archaeologist. In addition, prior to plot establishment, the field crew conducts an ecological site assessment of topography (slope), soils, vegetation and disturbance to ensure it is the appropriate ecological site and is suitable for monitoring. Sites are accepted if they contain at least 80% of the target ecological site, have less than 20–30% slope (depending on whether the site is forested or dryland), do not contain significant disturbances, and are at least 200 m away from existing plot centers. Sites that do not meet these criteria are rejected. Documenting site rejection rates associated with archaeological clearance or site assessment is important because it is usually not included in the spatial representation of the final sampling frame.

## 2 Aztec Ruins National Monument sampling frame
### 2.1 Monitoring priorities
Due to the small size of Aztec Ruins National Monument, there was essentially only one possibility for integrated upland monitoring: the Limy ecological site (R037XA003NM). Target soil lineage came from the NRCS Soils Survey Geographic (SSURGO) Database spatial dataset for *San Juan County, New Mexico, Eastern Part* soil survey area (NRCS 2007).

### 2.2 Limy
#### 2.2.1 Sampling frame
Limy was the target ecological site; however, ecological sites are not explicitly mapped in soil surveys. Instead, "map units" are the finest spatially defined units. In general, map units having a high percentage of the target ecological site are selected to be part of the initial sampling frame. Two map units containing the target ecological site were selected. A lower component percent threshold was used for the Limy ecological site because the largest soil area within Aztec (map unit HA, fig. A-4) was estimated to include only 30% of the target ecological site. Excluding the HA map unit because of its low ecological site content would have resulted in a sampling frame that covered less than half of the estimated area of the ecological site occurring within the monument (table A-2).

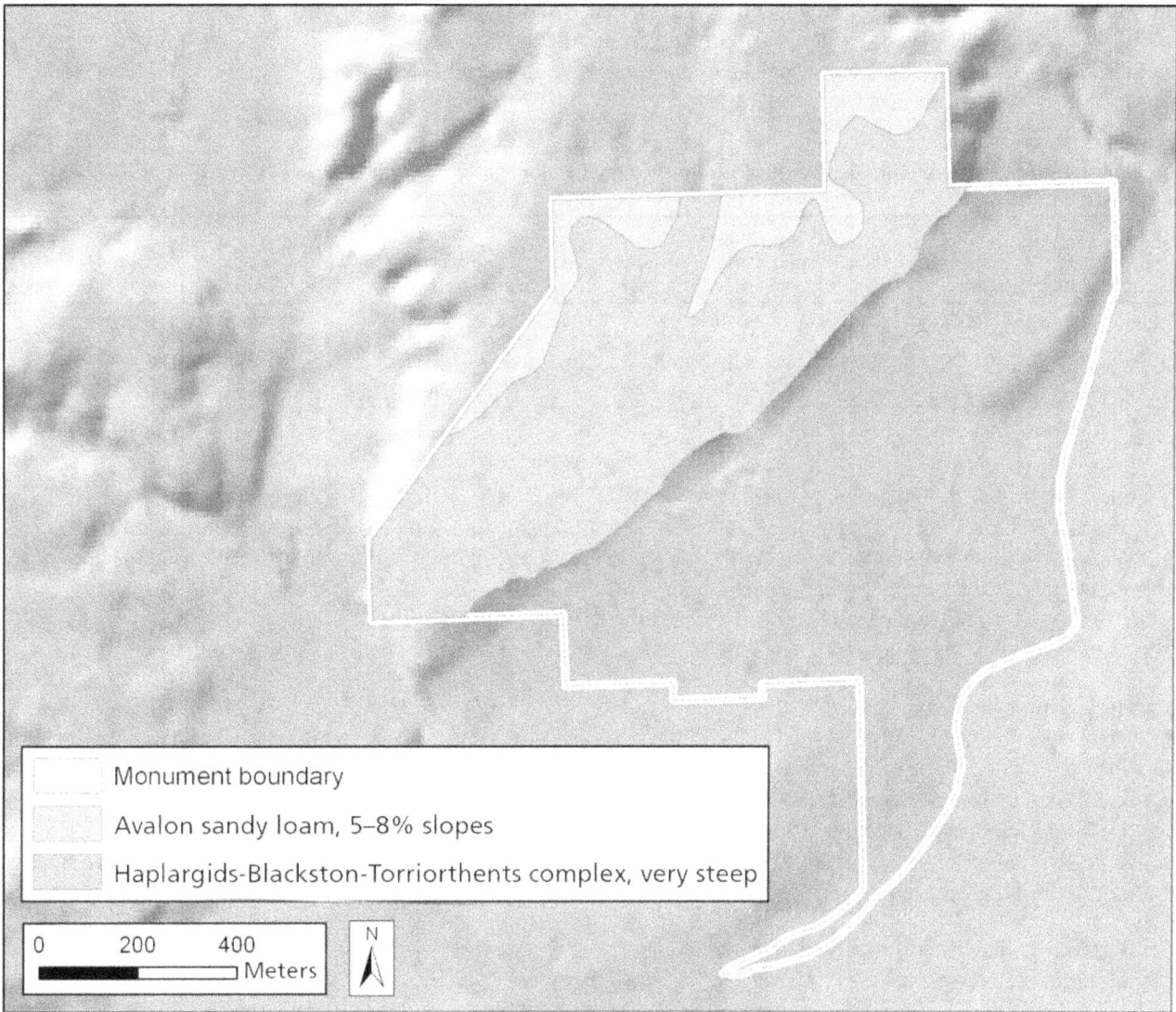

Figure A-4. Extent of the target soil map units for the Limy ecological site in Aztec Ruins National Monument

### 2.2.2 Field reconnaissance

Due to the small size of the ecological site, no reconnaissance was conducted prior to the installation of the plots.

### 2.2.3 Adjustments to sampling frame

Several spatial processing (GIS) steps were conducted to ensure the final sampling frame contained a realistic target population. Target soil lineage came from the NRCS SSURGO soils geodataset for the *San Juan County NM, Eastern Part* soil survey area NM618 (NRCS 2007). Individual target map unit polygons were selected from the NRCS soils shapefile and then merged.

**Table A-2. Target soil map units for the Limy ecological site in Aztec Ruins National Monument**

| Map unit name | Map unit symbol | Percent of map unit associated with the target ecological site |
|---|---|---|
| Avalon sandy loam, 5–8% slopes | Ax | 95 |
| Haplargids-Blackston-Torriorthents complex, very steep | HA | 30 |

Several additional buffering and erasing steps followed (table A-3), which resulted in the removal of large portions of the initial sampling frame (fig. A-5). Because the plot size is 71 × 71 m, the diagonal distance from the plot center to the plot edge (or corner) is approximately 50 m. Consequently, when a feature was excluded, a 50 m buffer was added to the exclusion to ensure that no part of a sampling plot would fall within the excluded area. This 50 m buffer was also applied as a negative buffer to the ecological site edge to ensure that the entire plot fell within the ecological site. One effect of buffering the ecological site edge is that areas too narrow to accommodate a plot were removed. Additionally, other filters were applied that removed the following: 1) areas that are not actually within the target ecological site (e.g., roads, developed areas, buildings), 2) steep slopes where sampling was impractical because of erosion and safety concerns.

**Table A-3. Buffer distances for areas removed from the Limy ecological site sampling frame in Aztec Ruins National Monument**

| Removal condition | Plot centroid buffer (minimum distance between plot center and removal condition) | Effective buffer (minimum distance between plot edge and removal condition) | Removal category |
|---|---|---|---|
| Ecological site or park boundary | 50 m | 0 m | buffer necessary to fit entire plot |
| Roads | 50 m | 0 m | non-target area |
| Slope: removed if >20% | 50 m | 0 m | sampling impractical |

### 2.2.4 Sampling sites

A set of spatially distributed sampling points was created using the GRTS design. A script incorporating the GRTS design was developed and run using the R statistical computing software (http://www.r-project.org/) and the P.survey and P.design modules, which can be selected and installed from within the R program. The script used the area-based option (polygons) and gave all potential sites an equal probability of selection. An advantage of the GRTS design is that is allows for rejection of sampling points (if found to be non-target or inaccessible, etc.). Spatial balance is maintained by following a sequential ordering of sites; if a site is rejected, the next site in sequential order is used.

### 2.2.5 Rejection criteria

Park staff reviewed the locations of the GRTS points provided in the initial research application and rejected 2 sites that were co-located with archaeology sites. Prior to each plot's establishment, the field crew conducted an ecological site assessment to evaluate topography (slope), soils, vegetation, and disturbance to ensure that the site was the target ecological site. We accepted sampling sites if they contained at least 80% of the target ecological site, were on slopes <20%, and did not contain significant disturbances. Sites not meeting these criteria were rejected. Due to the small spatial extent of the final sampling frame, we relaxed the criteria of plots needing to be 200 m apart from each other.

In 2008, 6 plots were established. Sites were visited and were accepted or rejected in sequential order with respect to GRTS point numbering. Two sites were rejected because they were co-located with archaeological sites. Six sites were rejected because they had ravines running through the plots, which were considered a different ecological site. One site was rejected because it overlapped with an existing plot.

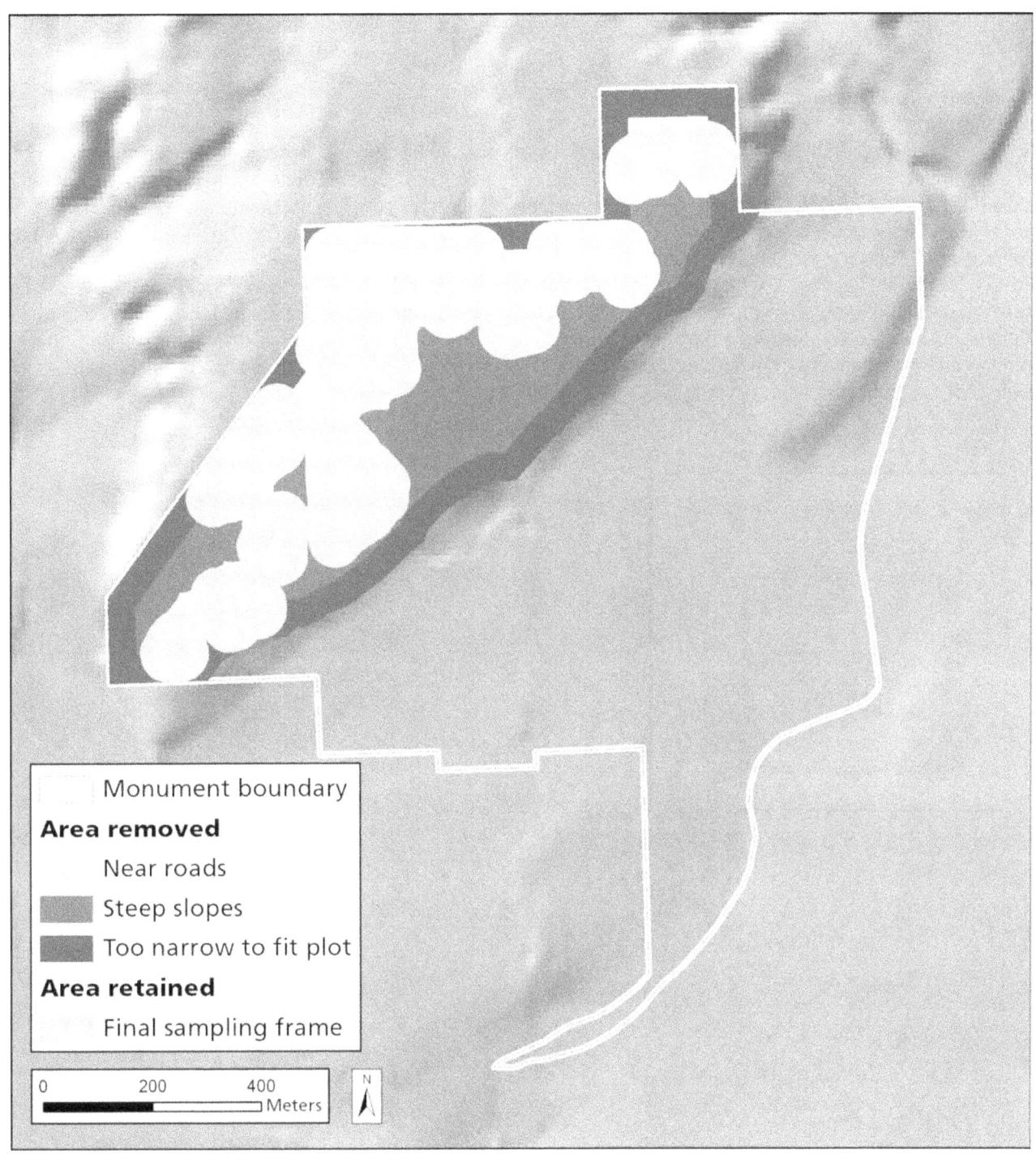

Figure A-5. Limy ecological site targeted for integrated upland monitoring in Aztec Ruins National Monument, showing areas removed during spatial processing to derive the final sampling frame and resulting area of inference

## 3 Bandelier National Monument sampling frame
### 3.1 Monitoring priorities
In October 2006, SCPN and Bandelier National Monument (BAND) natural resources staff met to discuss park priorities for upland monitoring. Three ecosystems were considered: mesa top pinyon-juniper woodland, mixed conifer forest and montane meadows. The mesa top pinyon-juniper ecosystem was determined to be the top priority as this ecosystem has not been well studied. Moreover, the park was planning to implement a landscape–scale

restoration of these woodlands, entailing the reduction of juniper density through mechanical thinning. The mixed conifer forest was considered the second priority.

## 3.2 Mesa Top Pinyon-Juniper

### 3.2.1 Sampling frame

Two recent soil surveys had been conducted at BAND by the Natural Resource Conservation Service prior to the sampling frame development: a high-resolution soil survey covering only the area of the monument (Hibner 2000), and a standard Soils Survey Geographic (SSURGO) Database soil survey covering the monument as well as large areas of Sandoval County (NRCS 2005c). Ecological sites for pinyon-juniper woodland were not initially assigned as a part of either soil survey. Although ecological sites were later assigned to the coarser SSURGO survey, this occurred after SCPN monitoring began. With this limitation, we chose to work with the higher resolution, monument-specific survey and created our initial sampling frame by first identifying soil map units that contained the target vegetation. With the encouragement of park staff, we chose a liberal interpretation of the target area, combining soil units that were considerably different from one another, to define for our own purposes, the "Mesa Top Pinyon-Juniper" target ecosystem. Six map units were selected (fig. A-6 and table A-4).

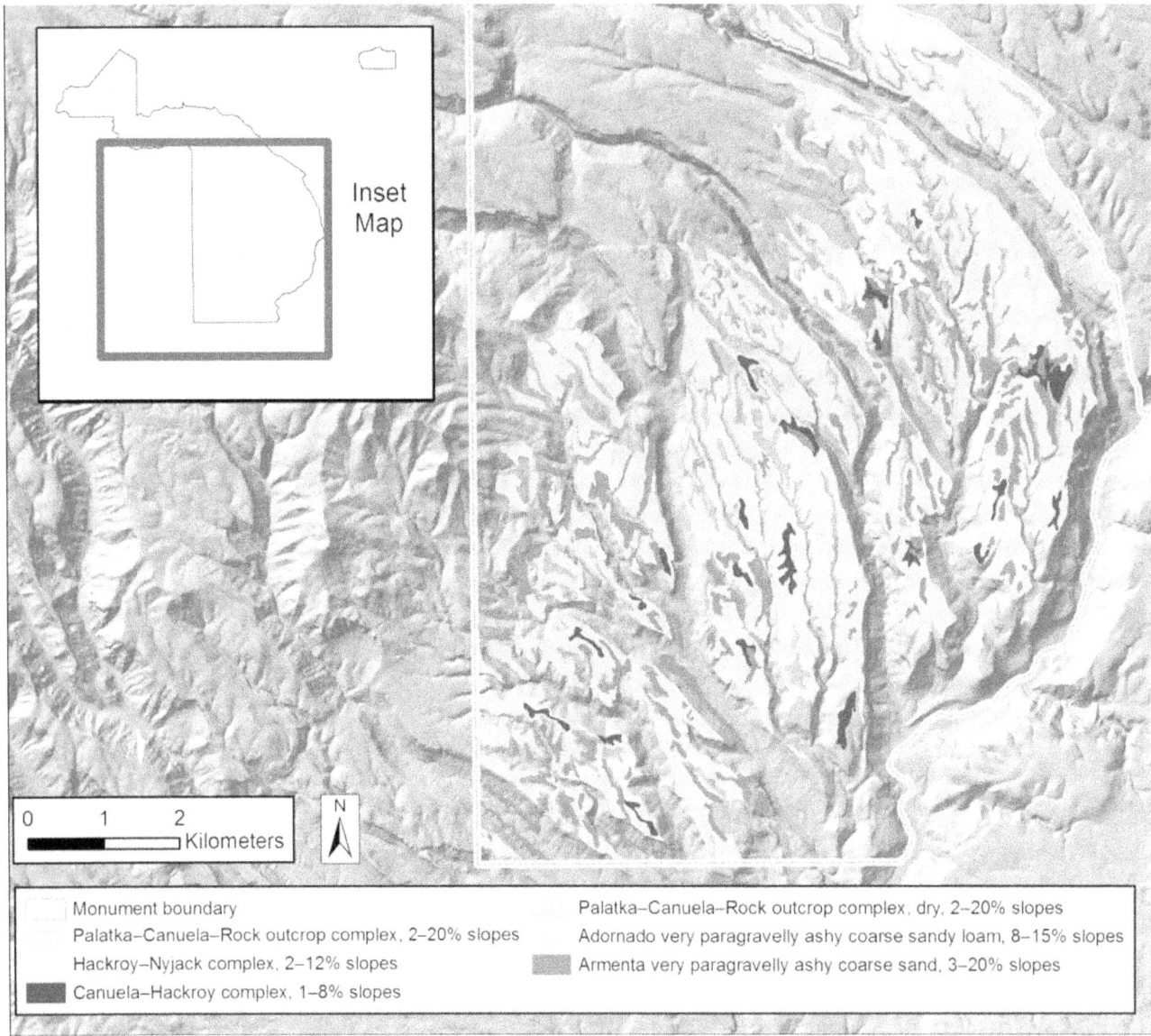

Figure A-6. Extent of the target soil map unit for the Mesa Top Pinyon-Juniper target ecosystem in Bandelier National Monument

The area of inference from the final sampling frame was later checked against the more recent assignment of ecological sites to the SSURGO soil survey for the area (NRCS 2008), and these soil units are predominantly associated with the Pinyon-Juniper/Skunkbush Sumac Shallow Sandy ecological site (NRCS ID F036XB133NM).

### 3.2.2 Field reconnaissance

During the spring of 2007, SCPN staff visited a number of randomly generated points throughout the proposed sampling frame. High variation in the vegetation and soils was noted. For example, with respect to variation in the vegetation, some areas were dominated by annual forbs such as *Verbascum thapsus*, other areas were dominated by *Bouteloua gracilis*, and one area was dominated by *Erigeron flagellaris*.

### 3.2.3 Adjustments to sampling frame

Several spatial processing (GIS) steps were conducted to ensure the final sampling frame contained a realistic target population for sampling. Target soil lineage came from the NRCS *Special Project Soil Survey of Bandelier National Monument* (Hibner 2000). Individual polygons of the target map units were selected from the NRCS soils shapefile and then merged.

Several additional buffering and erasing steps followed (table A-5), which resulted in the removal of large portions of the initial sampling frame (fig. A-7). Because the plot size is 71 × 71 m, the diagonal distance from the plot center to the plot edge (or corner) is approximately 50 m. Consequently, when a feature was excluded, a 50 m buffer was added to the exclusion to ensure that no part of a sampling plot would fall within the excluded area. This 50 m buffer was also applied as a negative buffer to the target ecosystem edge to ensure that the entire plot fell within the target ecosystem. One effect of buffering the target ecosystem edge is that areas too narrow to accommodate a plot were removed. Additionally, other filters were applied that removed the following: 1) areas that were not actually within the target ecosystem (e.g., roads, developed areas, buildings), 2) areas where site conditions were expected to differ substantially from the norm (e.g., burned areas and areas treated for fuels reduction), thereby increasing ecological variation and making it more difficult to detect trends, and 3) areas where sampling was impractical because of distance, safety, or erosion concerns. These adjustments are discussed in more detail below. In some cases, an additional buffer distance was added if the disturbance from the feature was likely to affect a larger area (table A-5).

**Table A-4. Target soil map units for the Mesa Top Pinyon-Juniper ecosystem in Bandelier National Monument**

| Map unit name | Map unit symbol |
|---|---|
| Palatka-Canuela-Rock Outcrop complex, 2–20% slopes | 400 |
| Adornado very paragravelly ashy coarse sandy loam, 8–15% slopes | 408 |
| Hackroy-Nyjack complex, 2–12% slopes | 409 |
| Palatka-Canuela-Rock outcrop complex, dry, 2–20% slopes | 410 |
| Canuela-Hackroy complex, 1–8% slopes | 412 |
| Armenta very paragravelly ashy coarse sand, 3–20% slopes | 413 |

**Table A-5. Buffer distances for areas removed from the initial Mesa Top Pinyon-Juniper ecosystem sampling frame in Bandelier National Monument**

| Removal condition | Plot centroid buffer (minimum distance between plot center and removal condition) | Effective buffer (minimum distance between plot edge and removal condition) | Removal category |
|---|---|---|---|
| Ecological site or park boundary | 50 m | 0 m | buffer necessary to fit entire plot |
| Roads | 100 m | 50 m | non-target area |
| Slope: removed if >20% | 50 m | 0 m | sampling impractical |
| Mechanical treatment pilot site | 50 m | 0 m | area substantially different |
| Fire | 50 m | 0 m | area substantially different |
| Areas that required more than a 2 hour hike from a park road or Base Camp | N/A | N/A | sampling impractical |

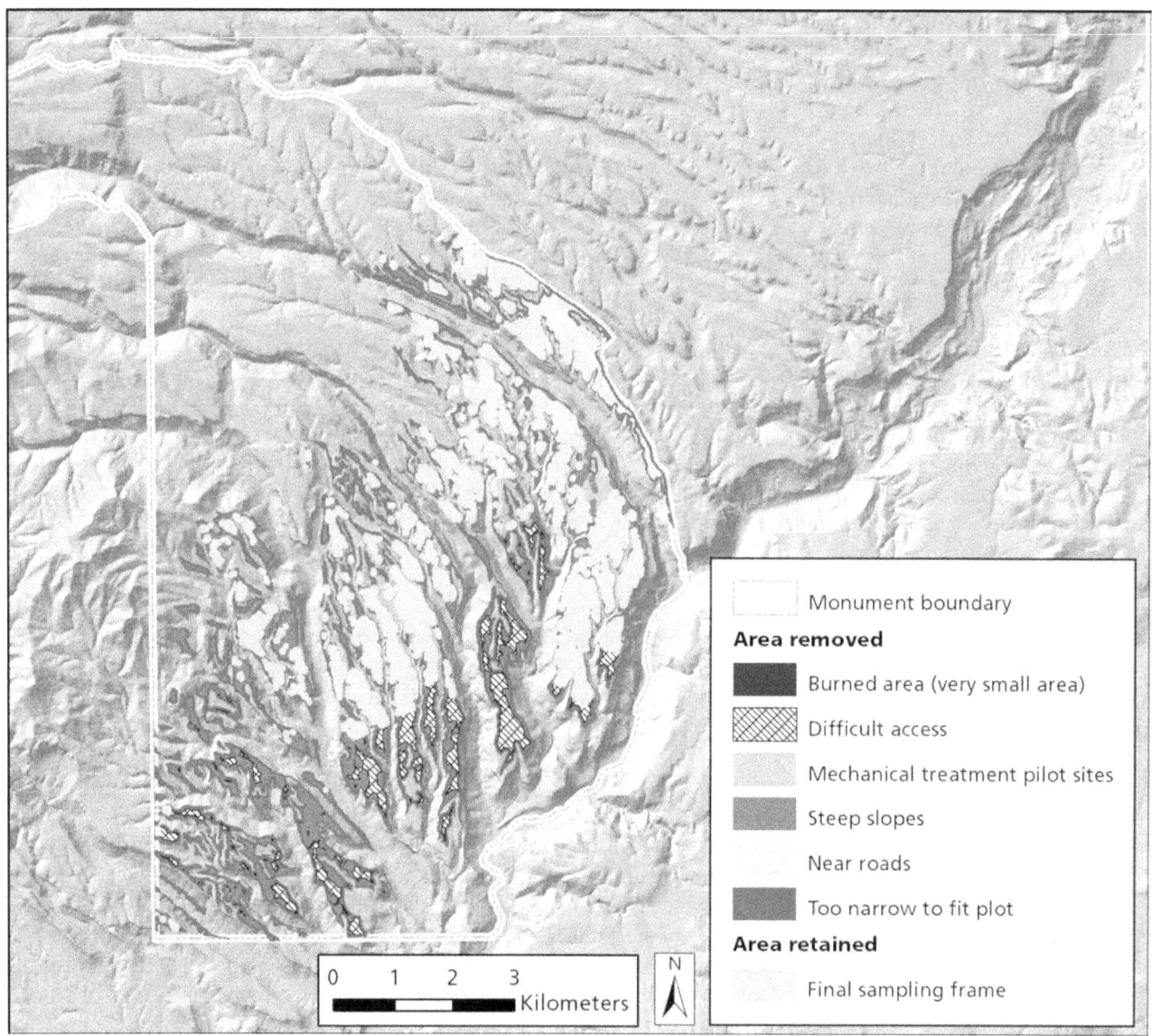

**Figure A-7. Mesa Top Pinyon-Juniper ecosystem targeted for integrated upland monitoring in Bandelier National Monument, showing areas removed during spatial processing to derive the final sampling frame and resulting area of inference**

Areas on or near roads were not considered to be part of the target ecosystem. Areas removed because of sampling considerations include all areas with slopes of ≥20%. Areas with steep slopes were removed based on concerns about safety and potential soil erosion caused by monitoring efforts. Areas that required more than 2 hours hiking time from a park road or from Base Camp were removed due to logistical reasons. An area that had been mechanically thinned in 1997 was removed because it was likely to be substantially different.

### 3.2.4 Sampling sites
A set of spatially distributed sampling points was created using the GRTS design. A script incorporating the GRTS design was developed and run using the R statistical computing software (http://www.r-project.org/) and the P.survey and P.design modules, which can be selected and installed from within the R program. The script used the area-based option (polygons) and gave all potential sites an equal probability of selection. An advantage of the GRTS design is that is allows for rejection of sampling points (if found to be non-target or inaccessible, etc.). Spatial balance is maintained by following a sequential ordering of sites; if a site is rejected, the next site in sequential order is used.

<u>3.2.5 Rejection criteria</u>
Park staff reviewed the locations of the GRTS points provided in the initial application and rejected no sites. Prior to each plot establishment, the field crew conducted an ecosystem assessment to evaluate topography (slope), soils, vegetation, and disturbance to ensure that the site was the target ecosystem. Sampling sites were accepted if they contained at least 80% of the target ecosystem (e.g., <20% combined of rock outcrop or ponderosa pine forest, or other components), were on slopes less than 20%, did not contain significant disturbances, and were not located within 200 m of the centroid of an existing plot. Sites that did not meet these criteria were rejected. Based on discussion with park staff, sites co-located with archaeological sites were accepted unless the vegetation had been visibly altered.

Between 2008 and 2010, 46 plots were established. Sites were visited and were accepted or rejected in sequential order with respect to GRTS point numbering. A total of 19 plots were rejected. Eight sites were rejected because they required more than 2 hours of hiking. Five sites were rejected because they were within 50 m of a hiking trail. One site was rejected because it was co-located with a large archaeological site. One site was rejected because it contained an elk exclosure. One site was rejected because it was within 200 m of an established plot. One site was rejected because it was in a ponderosa pine forest. Two sites were rejected because they had more than 20% rock outcrop (one of which also had more than a 20% slope).

# 4 Chaco Culture National Historical Park sampling frame
## *4.1 Monitoring priorities*
SCPN and Chaco Culture National Historical Park (CHCU) natural resources staff met in September 2006 to discuss park priorities for upland monitoring. NRCS ecological sites served as the basis for defining the initial sampling frame. Sandy Loam Upland and Clay Loam Terrace ecological sites were identified as potential sites for monitoring based on their relatively large size. The Sandy Loam Upland ecological site (R037XA030NM) was selected as the first priority due to its prominence in the park (fig. A-8). Clay Loam Terrace was identified as the second priority.

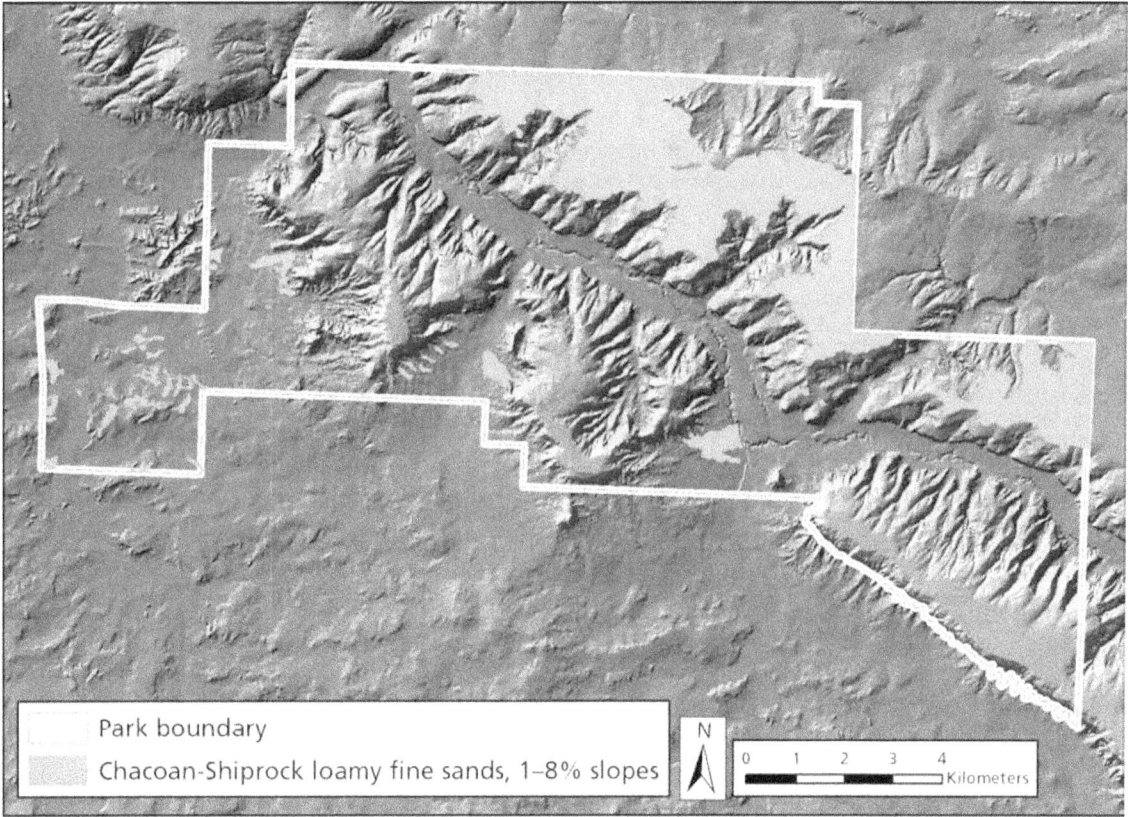

Figure A-8. Extent of the target soil map unit for the Sandy Loam Upland ecological site in Chaco Culture National Historical Park

## 4.2 Sandy Loam Upland
### 4.2.1 Sampling frame
Sandy Loam Upland is the target ecological site, but ecological sites are not explicitly mapped in NRCS soil surveys. Instead, "map units" are the finest spatially defined units. In CHCU, the Sandy Loam Upland ecological site occurred across 3 soil map units. In general, map units having a high percentage of the target ecological site are chosen to be part of the initial sampling frame. One map unit was selected because it was estimated to contain the target ecological site on 90% or more of its area (table A-6). Two map units were excluded from the initial frame because the percentage of the target ecological site was less than 50%. Target soil lineage is from the *National Park Service-Soil Survey Geographic (SSURGO) Database for Chaco Culture National Historical Park, New Mexico* (National Park Service 2006).

### 4.2.2 Field reconnaissance
A number of randomly generated points were visited in the Sandy Loam Upland ecological site in November 2006. At all sites visited, surface soil was textured by hand, dominant vegetation was recorded, and photos of the soil surface and the surrounding landscape were taken. Overall variation between the sites was quite low and the soil and vegetation characteristics matched those expected for the ecological site.

**Table A-6. Target map unit for the Sandy Loam Upland ecological site in Chaco Culture National Historical Park**

| Map unit name | Map unit symbol | Percent of map unit associated with the target ecological site |
|---|---|---|
| Chacoan-Shiprock loamy fine sands, 1–8% slopes | 6 | 90 |

### 4.2.3 Adjustments to the sampling frame
Several spatial processing (GIS) steps were conducted to adjust the initial sampling frame to contain a realistic target population for sampling. All polygons of the target soil map unit (#6) were selected from the NRCS soils shapefile. Several additional buffering and erasing steps followed (table A-7), which removed portions of the sampling frame (fig. A-9). Because the plot size is 71 × 71 m, the distance from the center of the plot to the plot edge (on a diagonal) is 50 m. Consequently, when a feature was excluded, a 50 m buffer was added to the exclusion to ensure that no part of a sampling plot would fall within the excluded area. This 50 m buffer was also applied to the ecological site edge to ensure that the entire plot fell within the ecological site. One effect of buffering the ecological site edge is that areas too narrow to accommodate a plot were removed. Additionally, other filters that were applied removed the following: 1) areas that are not actually within the target ecological site (e.g., roads), and 2) areas where sampling was impractical. Areas with steep slopes (i.e., slopes >20%) were removed because of concerns about the safety of field crews, and the potential to cause erosion from sampling efforts.

**Table A-7. Buffer distances for areas removed from the initial sampling frame in the Sandy Loam Upland ecological site in Chaco Culture National Historical Park**

| Removal condition | Plot centroid buffer (minimum distance between plot center and removal condition) | Effective buffer (minimum distance between plot edge and removal condition) | Removal category |
|---|---|---|---|
| Ecological site or park boundary | 50 m | 0 m | buffer necessary to fit entire plot |
| Roads | 100 m | 50 m | non-target area |
| Slope: removed if >20% | 50 m | 0 m | sampling impractical |

### 4.2.4 Sampling sites
A set of spatially distributed sampling points was created using the GRTS design. A script incorporating the GRTS design was run using the R statistical computing software (http://www.r-project.org/) and the P.survey and P.design modules, which can be selected and installed from within the R program. The script used the area-based option (polygons) and gave all areas equal probability of selection. The GRTS design allows for rejection of sampling points. Spatial balance is maintained by following a sequential ordering of sites; if a site is rejected, the next site in sequential order is used.

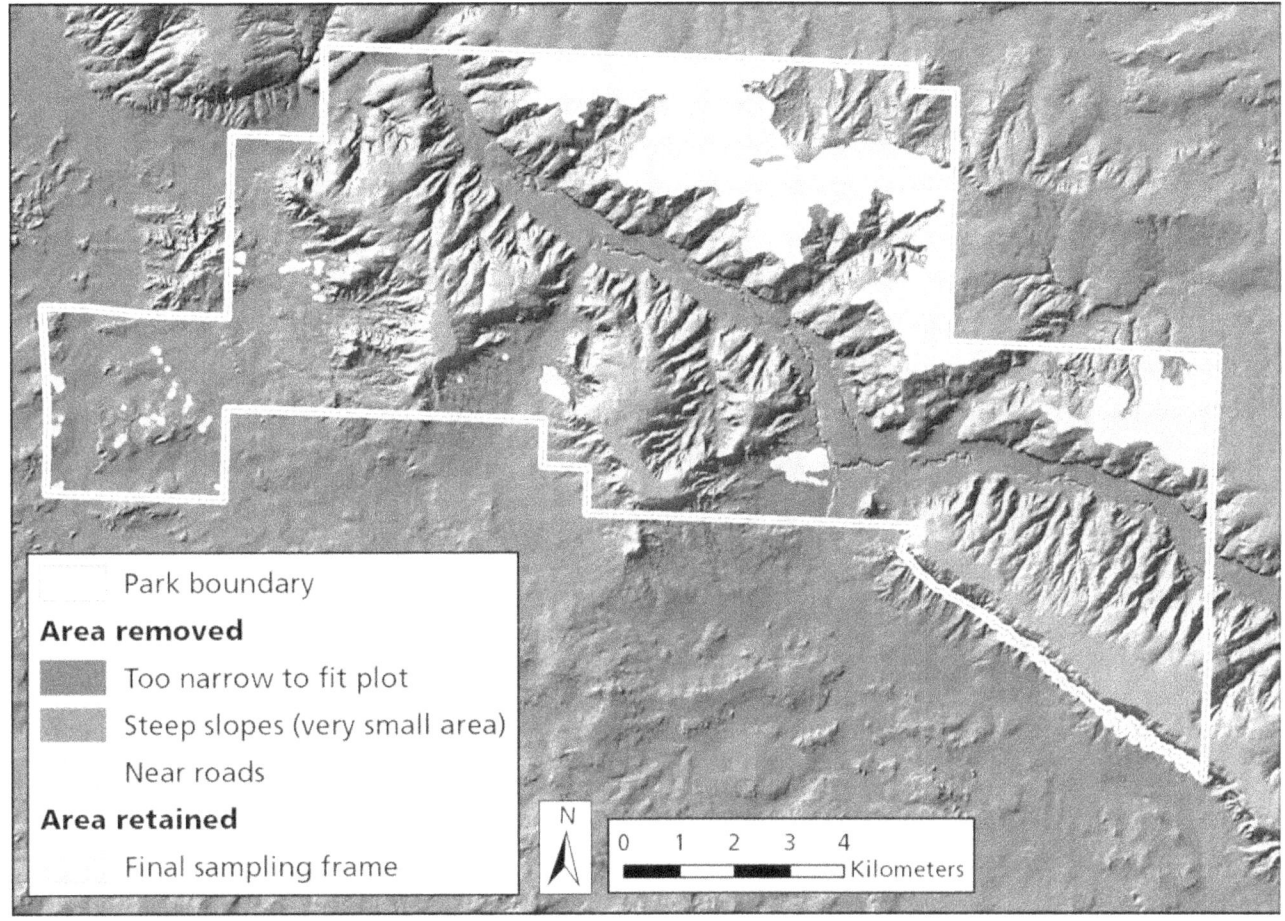

Figure A-9. Sandy Loam Upland ecological site targeted for integrated upland monitoring in Chaco Culture National Historical Park, showing areas removed during spatial processing to derive the final sampling frame and resulting area of inference

## 4.2.5 Rejection criteria

Park staff reviewed the locations of the GRTS points provided in the initial research permit application and but did not reject any sites. In 2011, an archaeologist did visit a number of the proposed sites, but did not reject any. He did verify that a site the crew had rejected in 2007 was co-located with a yet undocumented archaeological site. Prior to plot establishment, the field crew assessed sites for topography (slope), soils, vegetation, and disturbance to ensure that each site was the appropriate ecological site. Sites were accepted if they contained at least 80% of the target ecological site, had less than 20% slope, did not contain significant disturbances and were not located within 200 m of the centroid of an existing plot. Sites that did not meet these criteria were rejected.

Between 2007 and 2011, 30 plots were established. Sites were visited and accepted or rejected in sequential order with respect to GRTS point numbering. Two sites were rejected because they contained, or were in close proximity to archaeological sites as identified by the crew. One site was rejected because it contained a major disturbance—a road associated with a powerline. One site was rejected because it fell within the small section of the ecological site in the western portion of the park. Access to that section was poor and the park natural resources manager indicated that the vegetation in that unit differed substantially from the rest of the ecological site.

## 5 El Malpais National Monument sampling frame

The sampling frame for this park unit has not been developed.

## 6 El Morro National Monument sampling frame

The sampling frame for this park unit has not been developed.

# 7 Glen Canyon National Recreation Area sampling frame

The sampling frames for this park unit have not been developed.

# 8 Grand Canyon National Park sampling frames

## 8.1 Monitoring priorities

SCPN and Grand Canyon National Park (GRCA) natural resources staff met several times during 2006 to discuss park priorities for upland monitoring. Various park ecosystems were discussed, and 2 were ultimately ranked as highest priority for monitoring: mixed conifer forest on the North Rim, and pinyon-juniper woodland/savanna. Ecological site descriptions and associated map units were obtained from the NRCS *Soil Survey for Grand Canyon Area, Arizona, Parts of Coconino and Mohave Counties* (Natural Resource Conservation Service [NRCS] 2003).

For the mixed conifer forest, 2 ecological sites were considered: Loamy Hills, Cold (ABLA, PIEN) 25–33" p.z. F035XI903AZ and Loamy Hills (ABCO, PIPO, POTR5) 25–33" p.z. F035XI902AZ. In discussions with park staff concerning the drivers and natural variability of the mixed conifer forest, we concluded that topography, elevation, and aspect were more important than soils in determining variation in forest structure and composition. After reviewing the total spatial coverage of the soil map units associated with the target ecological sites on the North Rim, we agreed, for this effort, to combine them to form the initial target population. Thus, we agreed not to apply formal stratification by ecological site for this target, and to consider increasing the sample size to address the increase in natural variation that occurred because of the decision to combine the 2 ecological sites.

Discussions between SCPN and GRCA natural resources staff continued in 2009 to prioritize the pinyon-juniper woodland/savanna sites. The Limestone Upland (JUOS, PIED) 13–17" p.z.; F035XF619AZ ecological site was selected as the top priority. This site is found in 2 areas—one on the South Rim and one on the North Rim. The second priority was the Clay Loam Upland, Gravelly (PIED, JUOS) 13-17" p.z.; F035XF611AZ, particularly the portion of the ecological site that occurs on the Shivwits Plateau.

## 8.2 Mixed conifer forest

### 8.2.1 Sampling frame

In consultations with park staff, and using a forest type vegetation map for the park as a guideline, the initial sampling frame for the mixed conifer forest was composed of 4 soil map units (table A-8). These were identified in the soil survey of GRCA (NRCS 2003) and contained 80% or more of the Loamy Hills (ABCO, PIPO, POTR5) 25–33" p.z. and Loamy Hills, Cold (ABLA, PIEN) 25–33" p.z. ecological sites. Collectively, the spatial coverage of these 4 soil map units approximated the distribution of the mixed conifer forest (fig. A-10). A total of 6 map units were associated with the target ecological sites in GRCA; however, 2 of the 6 contained 50% or less of the target ecological sites and were excluded from the initial sampling frame. Target soil lineage was obtained from an updated NRCS SSURGO database for *Grand Canyon Area, Arizona, Parts of Coconino and Mohave Counties* (NRCS 2005b).

### 8.2.2 Field reconnaissance

In October 2006, SCPN staff conducted a short reconnaissance trip to examine the variability in mixed conifer forest composition, and determine upper and lower elevation limits. It was decided to include the spruce-fir forest (although not technically mixed conifer forest), because only small areas were pure spruce-fir. Scattered ponderosa pines were also present over larger areas. A lower elevation limit of 2500 meters was set to eliminate ponderosa pine forest that had no spruce or fir species. No upper limit was set.

### 8.2.3 Adjustments to sampling frame

Because of safety, logistical, and ecological concerns, we adjusted the spatial coverage of the sampling frame using GIS so that it contained a realistic target population for sampling. All polygons of the target soil map units were selected from the NRCS soils shapefile and then merged. Several additional erasing and buffering steps followed (table A-9), which removed portions of the initial sampling frame (fig. A-11). Because the plot size is 71 × 71 m, the distance from the center of the plot to the plot edge (on a diagonal) is approximately 50 m. Consequently, when a feature was excluded, a 50 m buffer was added to the exclusion so that no part of a sampling plot fell within the excluded area. This 50 m buffer was also applied to the ecological site edge to ensure that the entire plot fell within the ecological site; as a result, areas too narrow to accommodate a plot were removed.

Additional filters were applied to remove the following: (1) areas that were not actually within the target ecological site (e.g., roads, developed areas, buildings), (2) areas where site conditions were expected to differ substantially from the norm (e.g., burned areas and areas treated for fuels reduction), thus increasing ecological variation and making it more difficult to detect trends, and (3) areas where sampling was impractical. These adjustments are discussed in more detail below.

**Table A-8. Two ecological sites and their associated soil map units for the targeted mixed conifer forest in Grand Canyon National Park**

| Map unit name | Map unit symbol | Percent of map unit associated with the target ecological site |
|---|---|---|
| Ecological site: Loamy Hills, Cold (ABLA, PIEN) 25–33″ p.z. | | |
| Kaiparowits gravelly fine sandy loam 15–40% slope | 49 | 80 |
| Kanabownits-Kippers-Kaiparowits) complex, cool, 2–15% slope | 53 | 90 |
| Ecological site: Loamy Hills (ABCO, PIPO, POTR5) 25–33″ p.z. | | |
| Kanabownits fine sandy loam 15–40% slope | 51 | 80 |
| Kanabownits-Kippers-Kaiparowits complex, 2–15% slope | 52 | 95 |

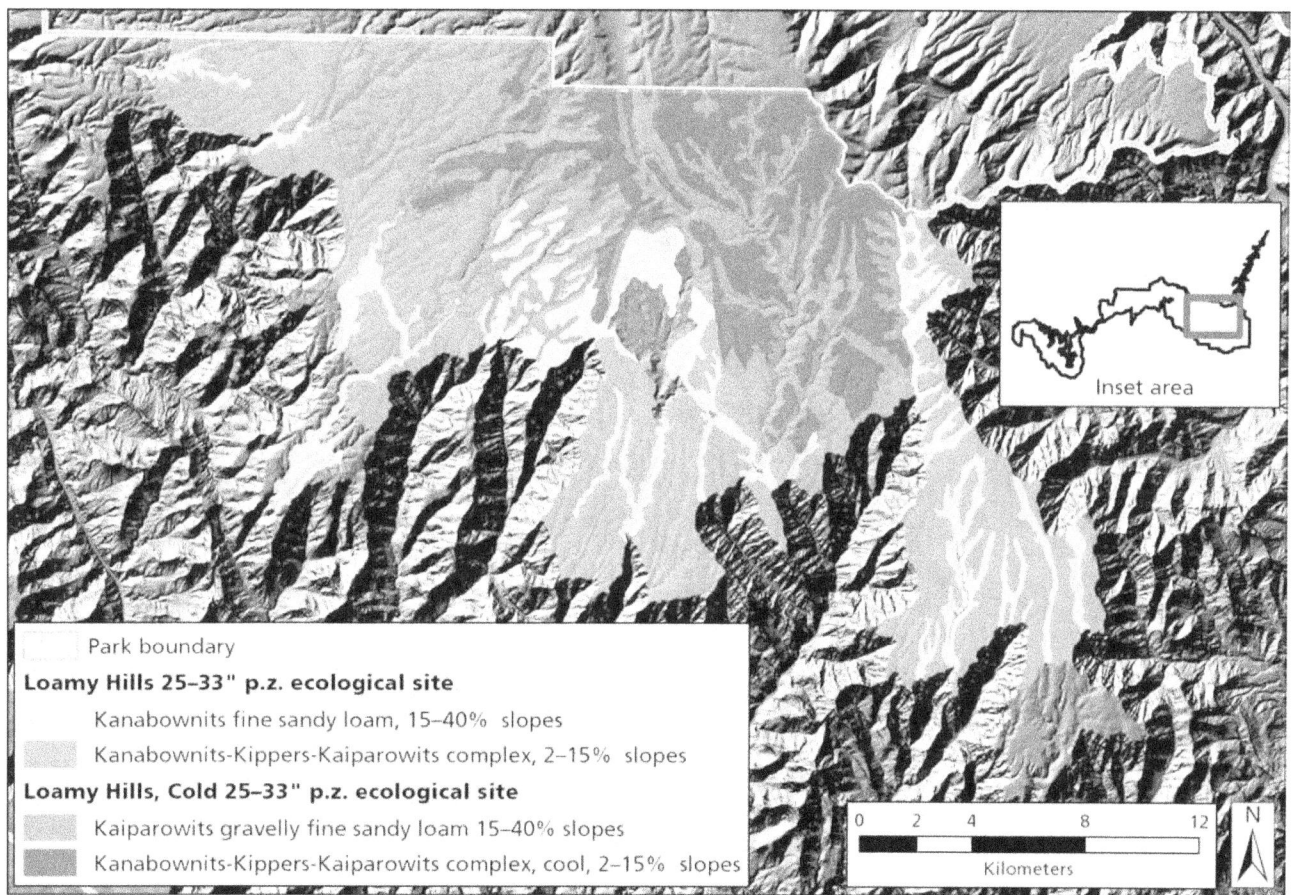

Park boundary

**Loamy Hills 25–33" p.z. ecological site**

Kanabownits fine sandy loam, 15–40% slopes

Kanabownits-Kippers-Kaiparowits complex, 2–15% slopes

**Loamy Hills, Cold 25–33" p.z. ecological site**

Kaiparowits gravelly fine sandy loam 15–40% slopes

Kanabownits-Kippers-Kaiparowits complex, cool, 2–15% slopes

Inset area

0  2  4  8  12
Kilometers

N

Figure A-10. Extent of the target soil map units for the Loamy Hills, Cold (ABLA, PIEN) 25–33″ p.z. and Loamy Hills (ABCO, PIPO, POTR5) 25–33″ p.z. ecological sites in Grand Canyon National Park

A lower elevation limit (2500 m) was applied to the initial sampling frame using a digital elevation model (DEM) to eliminate areas dominated by non-target forests (i.e., ponderosa pine forest). Sampling on steep slopes (>30%) was considered impractical because of the potential to cause erosion by sampling efforts and concerns about the safety of field crews. Areas of the initial sampling frame that were substantially different included areas burned by fires and sites that were or will be thinned (mechanically). These disturbances result in significant changes in vegetation structure and composition compared to undisturbed forests. Based on burn severity maps, and in consultation with park staff, a decision was made to remove moderately to severely burned areas from the sampling population.

**Table A-9. Buffer distances for areas removed from the initial mixed conifer forest sampling frame in Grand Canyon National Park**

| Removal condition | Plot centroid buffer (minimum distance between plot center and removal condition) | Effective buffer (minimum distance between plot edge and removal condition) | Removal category |
|---|---|---|---|
| Ecological site boundary | 50 m | 0 m | buffer necessary to fit entire plot |
| Roads, buildings or other infrastructure | 100 m | 50 m | non-target area |
| Slope: removed if >30% | 50 m | 0 m | sampling impractical |
| Elevation: below 2500 m | 50 m | 0 m | non-target area |
| Moderate to high severity burns | 50 m | 0 m | area substantially different |
| Mechanical treatments along boundary | 50 m | 0 m | area substantially different |

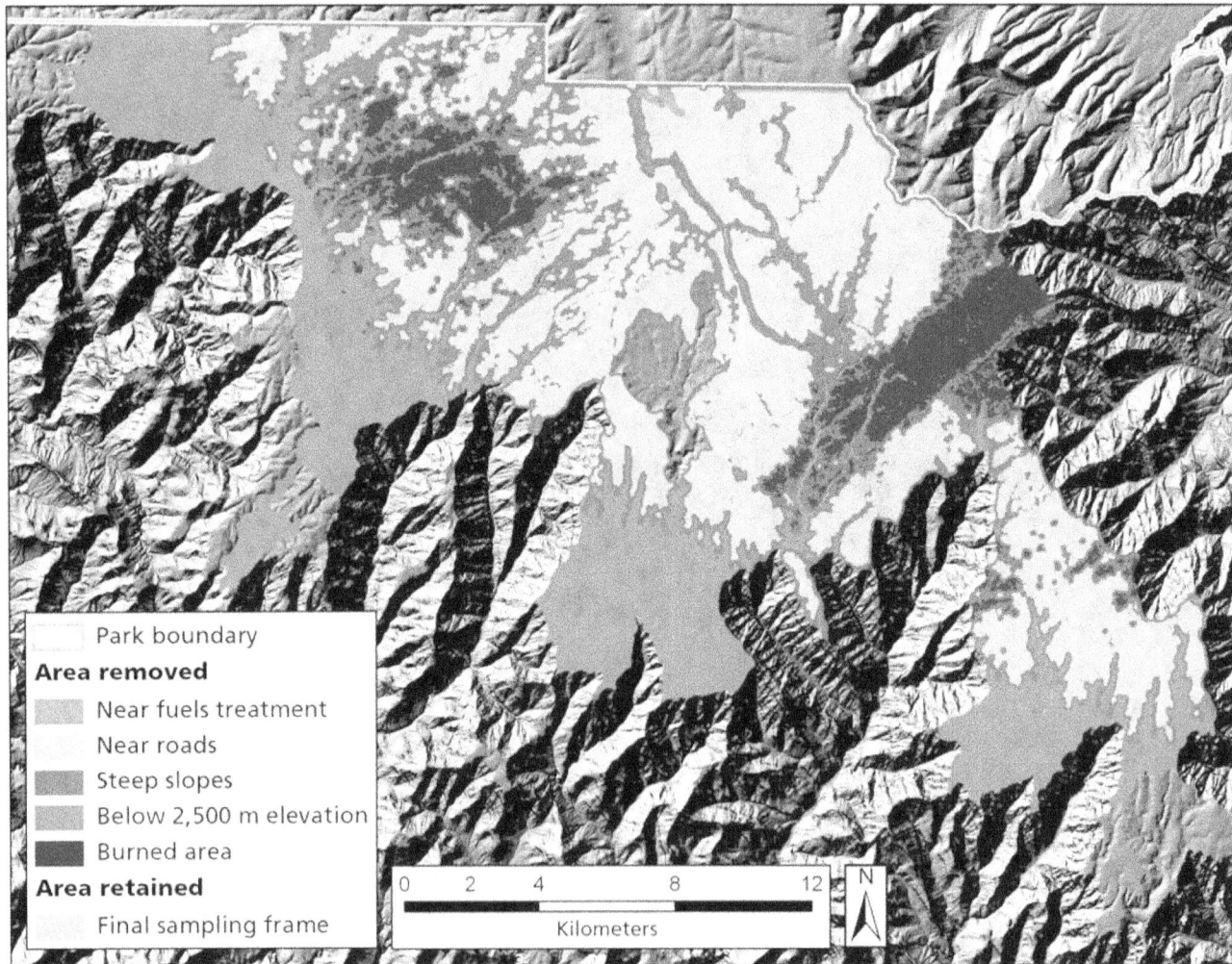

Figure A-11. Mixed conifer forest targeted for integrated upland monitoring in Grand Canyon National Park, showing areas removed during spatial processing to derive the final sampling frame and resulting area of inference

## 8.2.4 Sampling sites

A set of spatially distributed sampling points was created using the GRTS design. A script incorporating the GRTS design was run using the R statistical computing software (http://www.r-project.org/) and the P.survey and P.design modules, which can be selected and installed from within the R program. The script used the area-based option (polygons) and gave all areas equal probability of selection. The GRTS design allowed for rejection of sampling points. Spatial balance was maintained by following a sequential ordering of sites; if a site was rejected, the next site in sequential order was used.

## 8.2.5 Rejection criteria
Park staff reviewed the locations of the GRTS points provided in the research permit applications. Two points were rejected because they were co-located with archaeological sites according to GIS layers in the park where archaeological surveys had been conducted. All remaining sites were visited by an archaeologist to ensure that there were no archaeological sites in the potential plots. Prior to plot establishment, the field crew conducted an ecological site assessment of topography (slope), soils, vegetation and disturbance to ensure that each site was the appropriate ecological site. Sites were accepted if they contained at least 80% of the target ecological site, had less than 30% slope, contained the target vegetation, did not contain significant disturbances, and were not located within 200 m of the centroid of an existing plot. Sites that did not meet these criteria were rejected.

Between 2007 and 2011, 46 plots were established. Sites were visited and were accepted or rejected in sequential order with respect to GRTS point numbering. Four sites were rejected because the vegetation was ponderosa pine. (In 3 of these sites, there were other mixed conifer species, but these had been killed in a fire.) Five sites were rejected because they contained slopes that were greater than 30%. Five sites were rejected because they had experienced severe fire (more than half the basal area of the overstory trees had been killed by the fire). One site was within 50 m of a trail. One site was within 200 m of another plot. Two sites required hikes that were greater than 2 hours. As previously mentioned, 2 sites were co-located with archaeological sites.

## *8.3 Pinyon-Juniper Woodland*
### 8.3.1 Sampling frame
The initial sampling frame for the Pinyon-Juniper Woodland is based on the Limestone Upland (JUOS, PIED) 13–17" p.z (F035XF619AZ) ecological site. Target soil lineage came from the NRCS SSURGO database for *Grand Canyon Area, Arizona, Parts of Coconino and Mohave Counties* (NRCS 2005b), and the target map unit is shown in Table A-10.

### 8.3.2 Field reconnaissance
In fall, 2009, SCPN staff conducted a series of short reconnaissance trips to examine the variability in pinyon-juniper woodland composition. Areas on the North Rim in the Tuweep area

**Table A-10. Target map unit for the Limestone Upland (JUOS, PIED) 13-17" p.z. ecological site in Grand Canyon National Park**

| Map unit name | Map unit symbol | Percent of map unit associated with the target ecological site |
|---|---|---|
| Chunkmonk-Wodomont-Toqui families complex, 2–15% slopes | 23 | 75 |

had a very sparse understory, likely the result of grazing and fire history. It was decided to focus monitoring efforts on the accessible area around Pasture Wash and west of Hermit's Rest. This area consists of a single soil map unit, the Chunkmonk-Wodomont-Toqui families complex, 2–15% slopes (fig. A-12).

### 8.3.3 Adjustments to sampling frame
Because of safety, logistical, and ecological concerns, we adjusted the spatial coverage of the sampling frame using GIS technology so that it contained a realistic target population for sampling. Polygons of the target soil map units were selected from the NRCS soils shapefile and then merged. Three small polygons were unintentionally excluded during this step, but because of the small area covered by them (1.4% of the final sampling frame), it was not possible to account for this area by adding sampling points within them proportional to their area. Consequently, the area of inference does not extend to them.

Several additional erasing and buffering steps followed (table A-11), which removed portions of the initial sampling frame (fig. A-13). Because the plot size is 71 × 71 m, the distance from the center of the plot to the plot edge (on a diagonal) is approximately 50 m. Consequently, when a feature was excluded, a 50 m buffer was added to the exclusion to ensure that no part of a sampling plot would fall within the excluded area. This 50 m buffer was also

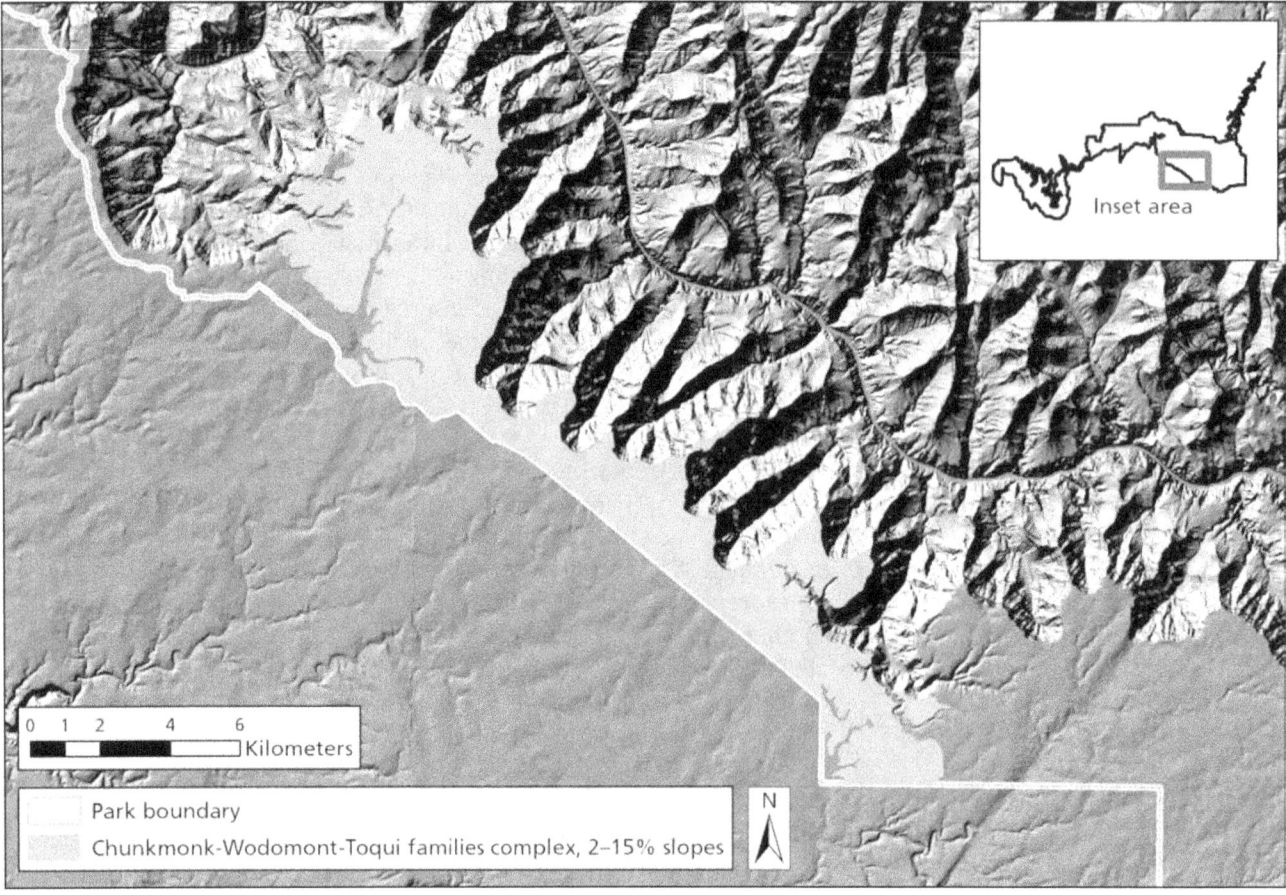

**Figure A-12. Extent of the target soil map unit for the Limestone Upland ecological site in Grand Canyon National Park**

applied to the ecological site edge to ensure that the entire plot fell within the ecological site. One effect of buffering the ecological site edge is that areas too narrow to accommodate a plot were removed.

Additionally, other filters were applied to remove the following: (1) areas that were not actually within the target ecological site (e.g., roads, developed areas, buildings), and (2) areas where sampling was impractical because of safety concerns and erosion concerns.

### 8.2.4 Sampling sites

A set of spatially distributed sampling points was created using the GRTS design. A script incorporating the GRTS design was run using the R statistical computing software (http://www.r-project.org/) and the P.survey and P.design modules, which can be selected and installed from within the R program. The script used the area-based option

**Table A-11. Buffer distances for areas removed from the initial pinyon-juniper woodlands sampling frame in Grand Canyon National Park**

| Removal condition | Plot centroid buffer (minimum distance between plot center and removal condition) | Effective buffer (minimum distance between plot edge and removal condition) | Removal category |
|---|---|---|---|
| Ecological site boundary | 50 m | 0 m | buffer necessary to fit entire plot |
| Roads, buildings or other infra-structure | 100 m | 50 m | non-target area |
| Slope: removed if >20% | 50 m | 0 m | sampling impractical |

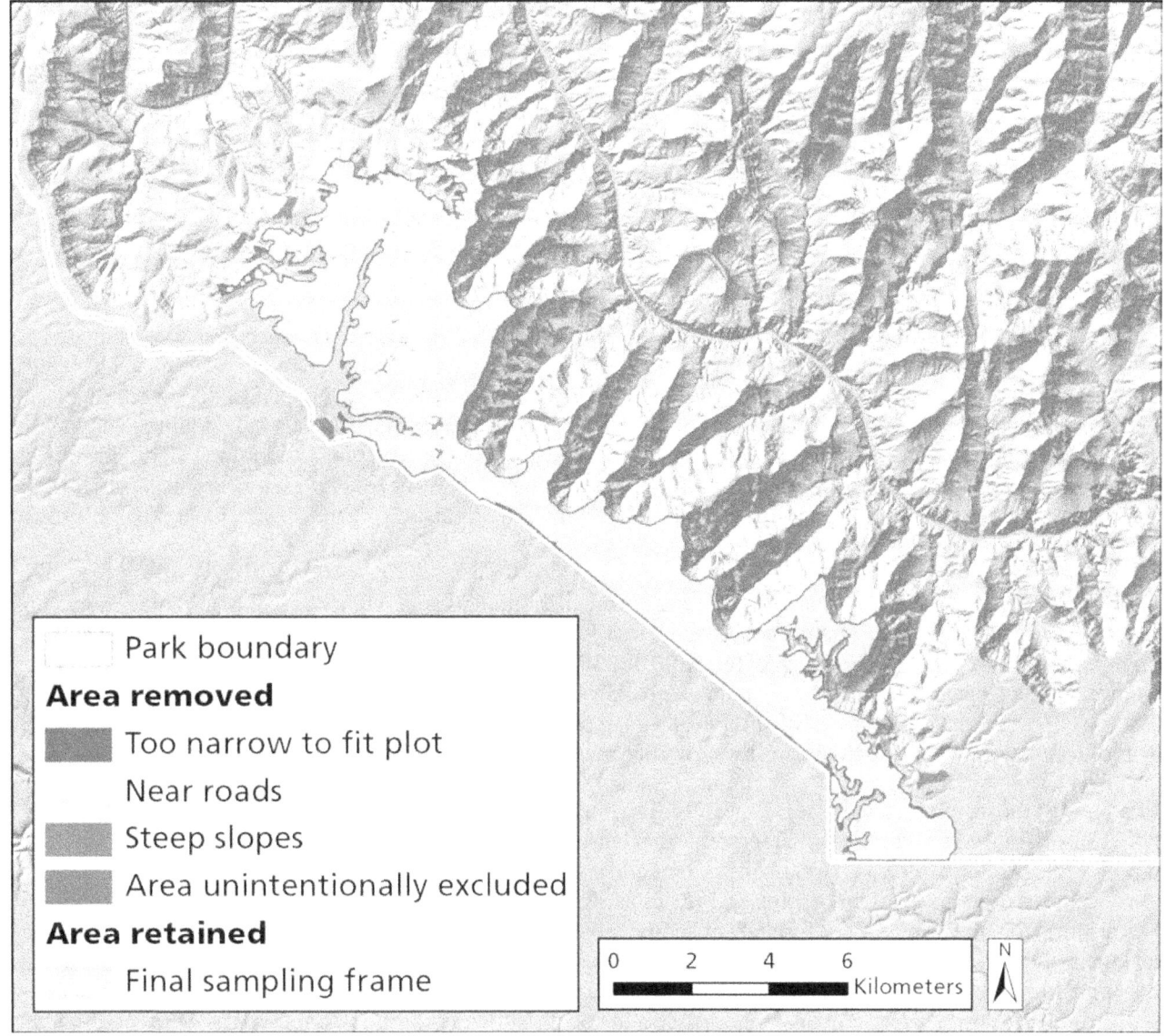

**Figure A-13. Pinyon-juniper woodland forest targeted for integrated upland monitoring in Grand Canyon National Park, showing areas removed during spatial processing to derive the final sampling frame and resulting area of inference**

(polygons) and gave all areas equal probability of selection. The GRTS design allowed for rejection of sampling points. Spatial balance was maintained by following a sequential ordering of sites; if a site was rejected, the next site in sequential order was used.

## 8.2.5 Rejection criteria
Park staff reviewed the locations of the GRTS points provided in the initial research application. Consultation with the Havasupai tribe was initiated through GRCA, although efforts to have tribal members visit the sites in the field were not successful. An archaeologist visited the first 37 sites. Ten sites were rejected because they contained archaeological sites, 2 sites contained historic fences, and 2 sites were on the wrong ecological site. Prior to plot establishment, the field crew conducted an ecological site assessment of topography (slope), soils, vegetation and disturbance to ensure that each site was the appropriate ecological site. Sites were accepted if they contained at least 80% of the target ecological site, had less than 20% slope, contained the target vegetation, did not contain significant disturbances and were not located within 200 m of the centroid of an existing plot. Sites that did not meet these criteria were rejected.

In 2010, 10 plots were established. Sites were visited and accepted or rejected in sequential order with respect to GRTS point numbering.

# 9 Mesa Verde National Park sampling frame
## 9.1 Monitoring priorities
In May 2006, SCPN and Mesa Verde National Park (MEVE) natural resources staff met to discuss park priorities for upland monitoring. MEVE has 2 dominant upland ecosystems—pinyon-juniper woodland and mountain shrub. The mountain shrub community, while interesting, is considered by park staff and researchers to be very resilient and unlikely to undergo change in response to changing environmental conditions. Therefore, it was designated as low priority for network monitoring. The pinyon-juniper ecosystem, however, was considered a high priority.

Within MEVE, dense, old-growth pinyon-juniper woodland (*Pinus edulis* and *Juniperus osteosperma*) is estimated to be from 400 to 500 years old. This system is thought to be very dynamic. A combination of 20 wet years in the 1980's and 90's, followed by a continuing drought, has resulted in increased stand replacing fire frequency, which seems to be unprecedented for this ecosystem based on stand age structure (Floyd-Hanna et al. 2004). In addition, pinyon-juniper in other areas of the Colorado Plateau has experienced die-off of pinyon pine in addition to large-scale changes in the geographic range of the this plant community (Allen and Breshears 1998, Breshears et al. 2005). These factors indicated the need for baseline data in undisturbed pinyon-juniper, making the pinyon-juniper woodlands the top priority for SCPN upland monitoring.

NRCS ecological sites serve as the basis for defining the initial sampling frame. There are 3 pinyon-juniper dominated ecological sites within the park boundaries: Loamy Mesa Top Pinyon-Juniper, Shallow Loamy Mesa Top Pinyon-Juniper, and Pinyon-Juniper. The purity of the ecological sites varies by soil map unit (i.e., map units can contain complexes of ecological sites). In order to reduce ecological variation, SCPN identified map units composed of at least 80% of target pinyon-juniper ecological sites. A map of these ecological sites, along with a map depicting the areas of recent fires, was provided during the May 2006 meeting.

All present at the meeting agreed that Loamy Mesa Top Pinyon-Juniper (R036XY142CO) was the top priority for monitoring because this ecological site represents the dense old-growth stands unique to the park. The Pinyon-Juniper ecological site occurs in the canyon bottoms and associated benches and side slopes. This ecological site was selected as the second priority ecological site, primarily because it occupies a different landscape position and is thus distinct from the Loamy Mesa Top Pinyon-Juniper ecological site. In fall of 2006, SCPN staff conducted a brief reconnaissance visit to examine the feasibility of monitoring this site. The conclusions from this visit were that access was difficult, and that the site had limited spatial extent; we would only be able to install a small number of plots. The Shallow Loamy Mesa Top Pinyon-Juniper site occurs on the shoulders and side slopes of the mesas between the mesa tops and the escarpments, directly adjacent to the Loamy Mesa Top Pinyon-Juniper ecological site. Discussions between SCPN and park staff continued, and in 2012, the Shallow Loamy Mesa Top Pinyon-Juniper site was chosen as the second ecological site for monitoring.

Park staff were also interested, but did not prioritize, 3 other ecosystems: burned mesa top pinyon-juniper woodland, Mancos Shale sparse shrublands, and Douglas fir woodlands. The burned pinyon-juniper woodland has been invaded by many nonnative species, and its successional trajectory is unknown. The Mancos Shale shrublands contain a number of rare plant species and species of concern. The Douglas fir woodlands occur in cool microclimates, and are likely to be impacted by climate change.

## 9.2 Loamy Mesa Top Pinyon-Juniper
### 9.2.1 Sampling frame
Loamy Mesa Top Pinyon-Juniper was the target ecological site; however, ecological sites are not explicitly mapped in soil surveys. Instead, "map units" are the finest spatially defined units. In general, map units containing a high percentage of the target ecological site are selected to be part of the initial sampling frame. Three map units were selected because each map unit was estimated to contain the target ecological site on 80% or more of its area (fig. A-14 and table A-12).

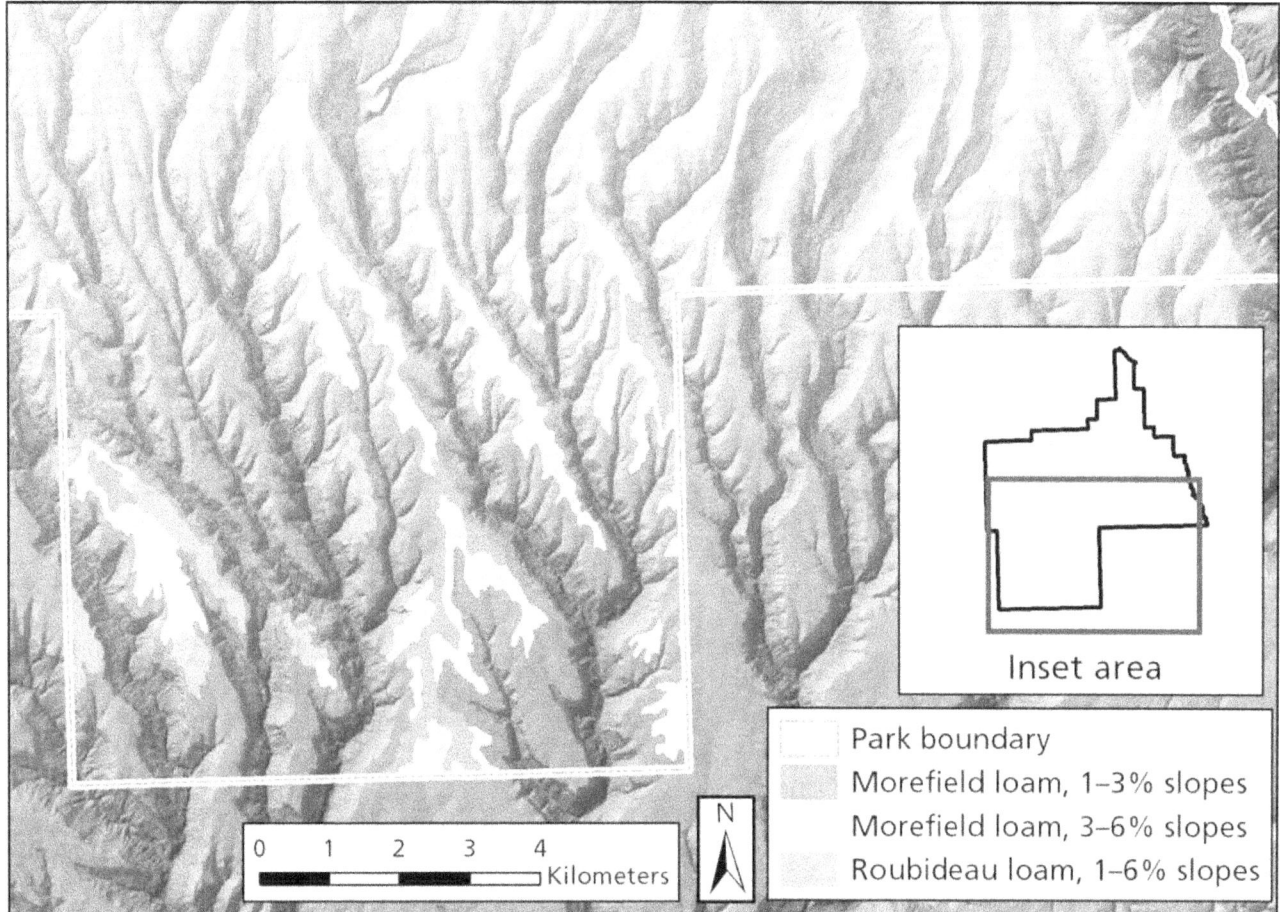

Figure A-14. Extent of the target soil map units for the Loamy Mesa Top Pinyon-Juniper ecological site in Mesa Verde National Park

## 9.2.2 Field reconnaissance

Seventy-five randomly generated points were visited in the Loamy Mesa Top Pinyon-Juniper ecological site during the summer of 2006. At each site, the texture of the surface soil was determined by hand, dominant vegetation was recorded, and photos of the soil surface and the surrounding landscape were taken. Overall variation between the sites was quite low, and the soil and vegetation characteristics matched those expected for the ecological site. Two areas were identified for exclusion from the final sampling frame as a result of this reconnaissance: a small northern area with considerably different understory vegetation due wetter and cooler conditions, and a small area near the developed Spruce Tree House area on Chapin Mesa, which had been cleared as a firebreak.

**Table A-12. Target soil map units for the Loamy Mesa Top Pinyon-Juniper ecological site in Mesa Verde National Park**

| Map unit name | Map unit symbol | Percent of map unit associated with the target ecological site |
|---|---|---|
| Roubideau loam, 1–6% slopes | 111 | 80 |
| Morefield loam, 1–3% slopes | 76 | 90 |
| Morefield loam, 3–6% slopes | 77 | 90 |

## 9.2.3 Adjustments to sampling frame

Several spatial processing (GIS) steps were conducted to ensure the final sampling frame contained a realistic target population for sampling. Target soil lineage came from the NRCS Soils Survey Geographic (SSURGO) Database for *Cortez Area, Colorado, Parts of Dolores and Montezuma Counties* (NRCS 2004). Individual polygons of the target map units were selected from the NRCS soils shapefile and then merged.

Several additional buffering and erasing steps followed (table A-13), which resulted in the removal of large portions of the initial sampling frame (fig. A-15). Because the plot size is 71 × 71 m, the diagonal distance from the plot center to the plot edge (or corner) is approximately 50 m. Consequently, when a feature was excluded, a 50 m buffer was added to the exclusion to ensure that no part of a sampling plot would fall within the excluded area. This 50 m buffer was also applied as a negative buffer to the ecological site edge to ensure that the entire plot fell within the ecological site. One effect of buffering the ecological site edge is that areas too narrow to accommodate a plot were removed. Additional filters were applied that removed the following: 1) areas that are not actually within the target ecological site (e.g., roads, developed areas, buildings), 2) areas where site conditions were expected to differ substantially from the norm (e.g., burned areas and areas treated for fuels reduction), thereby increasing ecological variation and making it more difficult to detect trends, and 3) areas where sampling was impractical because of distance or safety concerns. These adjustments are discussed in more detail below. In some cases, an additional buffer distance was added if the disturbance from the feature was likely to affect a larger area (table A-13).

**Table A-13. Buffer distances for areas removed from the initial Loamy Mesa Top Pinyon-Juniper ecological site sampling frame in Mesa Verde National Park**

| Removal condition | Plot centroid buffer (minimum distance between plot center and removal condition) | Effective buffer (minimum distance between plot edge and removal condition) | Removal category |
|---|---|---|---|
| Ecological site or park boundary | 50 m | 0 m | buffer necessary to fit entire plot |
| Roads | 100 m | 50 m | non-target area |
| Slope: removed if >20% | 50 m | 0 m | sampling impractical |
| Burned areas | 100 m | 50 m | area substantially different |
| Fuels treatments | 50 m | 0 m | area substantially different |
| Arthropod research plots | 80 m | 30 m | sampling impractical |

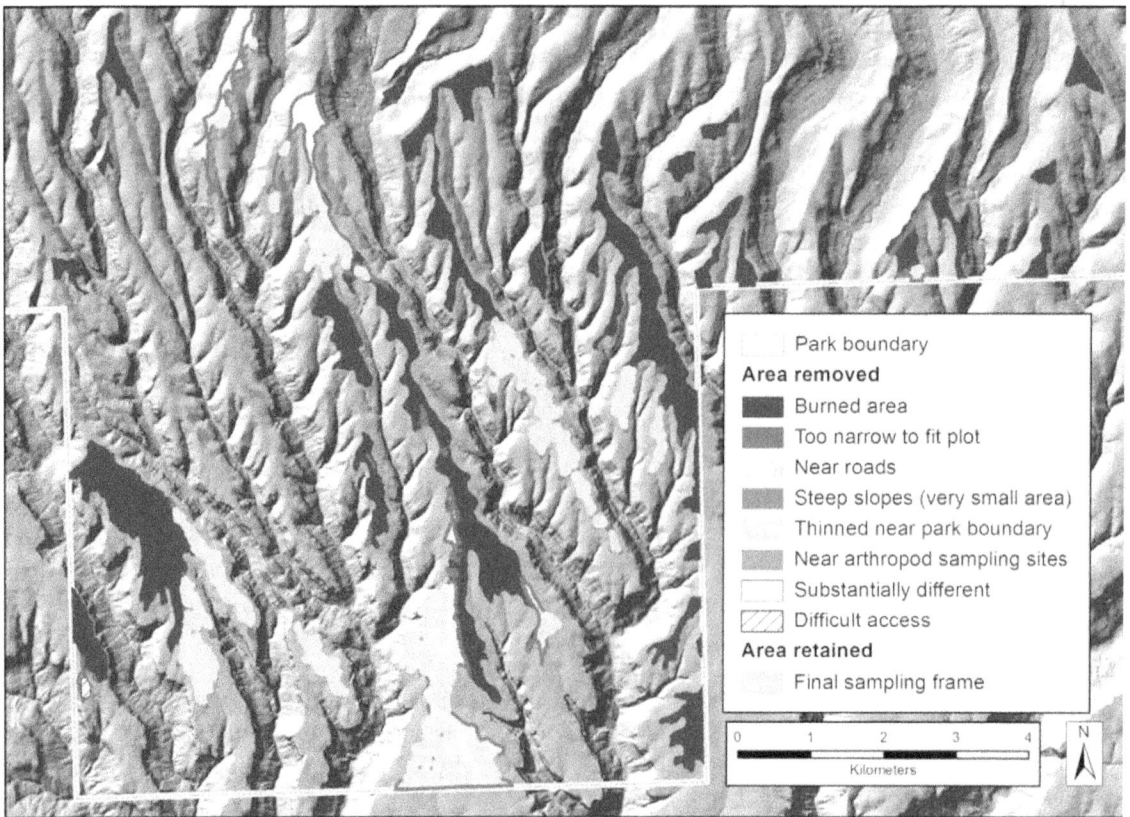

**Figure A-15. Loamy Mesa Top Pinyon-Juniper ecological site targeted for integrated upland monitoring in Mesa Verde National Park, showing areas removed during spatial processing to derive the final sampling frame and resulting area of inference**

Areas on or near roads and around developed areas were not part of the target ecological site. Areas removed because they were substantially different from the target population included burned areas and areas where fuels thinning treatments occurred (e.g., near park boundaries and near Spruce Tree House). Under the advice of park resource managers, all burned areas (using records going back to the 1930s) were excluded because of the severe and long-lasting effects of these burns in the pinyon-juniper woodlands. In addition, some small areas were removed in the northern part of the park, based on field visits that identified those areas as being substantially different from the majority of the ecological site (see *9.2.2 Field reconnaissance*).

Areas removed because of sampling considerations included one very small area with very difficult access in the southwest part of the park on Wildhorse Mesa, monitoring plots for the SCPN ground-dwelling arthropod study, and all areas with slopes of ≥20%. Areas with steep slopes were removed based on the potential for soil erosion caused by monitoring efforts and concerns about safety.

### 9.2.4 Sampling sites
A set of spatially distributed sampling points was created using the GRTS design. A script incorporating the GRTS design was developed and run using the R statistical computing software (http://www.r-project.org/) and the P.survey and P.design modules, which can be selected and installed from within the R program. The script used the area-based option (polygons) and gave all potential sites an equal probability of selection. An advantage of the GRTS design is that is allows for rejection of sampling points (if found to be non-target or inaccessible, etc.). Spatial balance is maintained by following a sequential ordering of sites; if a site is rejected, the next site in sequential order is used.

### 9.2.5 Rejection criteria
Park staff reviewed GRTS point locations provided in the initial application and rejected sites that were co-located with archaeology sites in the park's spatial records. Due to poor spatial resolution for some of the archaeological data, these rejected sites were visited in 2010 by an archaeologist. Many of the sites that had been previously rejected for archaeological concerns were accepted as suitable for monitoring. Prior to each plot's establishment, the field crew conducted an ecological site assessment to evaluate topography (slope), soils, vegetation, and disturbance to ensure that the site was the target ecological site. Sampling sites were accepted if they contained at least 80% of the target ecological site, were on slopes less than 20%, did not contain significant disturbances, and were not located within 200 m of the centroid of an existing plot. Sites not meeting these criteria were rejected.

Between 2007 and 2011, 30 plots were established. Sites were visited and were accepted or rejected in sequential order with respect to GRTS point numbering. Eleven sites were rejected because they were not in the target ecological site: 6 were in the Shallow Loam ecological site and 5 were in an area of the northern portion of the ecological site that was determined to be substantially different from the remainder of the target site. Seventeen sites were rejected because they were located within 200 m of existing plots. Two sites were rejected because they contained archaeological sites. Two sites were rejected because they were within 50 m of a road. For 2 of the rejected sites, there were no records for why the site was rejected.

## 10 Petrified Forest National Park sampling frames
### 10.1 Monitoring priorities
SCPN and Petrified Forest National Park (PEFO) natural resources staff met several times between August and October 2006 to discuss park priorities for upland monitoring.

NRCS ecological sites serve as the basis for defining the initial sampling frame. Because of their co-occurrence with large areas of grasslands and shrublands within PEFO (fig. A-16), 3 ecological sites were identified as priorities for upland monitoring: Sandy Loam Upland (10-14"p.z.; RO35XA117AZ), Loamy Upland (10-14" p.z.; RO35XA113AZ), and Clayey Fan (6-10" p.z.; R035XB239AZ).

The Petrified Forest Expansion Act of 2004 expanded the existing park boundary, more than doubling the park's size. The expansion lands are characterized by a checkerboard of private, state and Bureau of Land Management (BLM) land. The expansion lands were not considered for upland monitoring due to servicewide I&M guidance for not monitoring newly acquired lands.

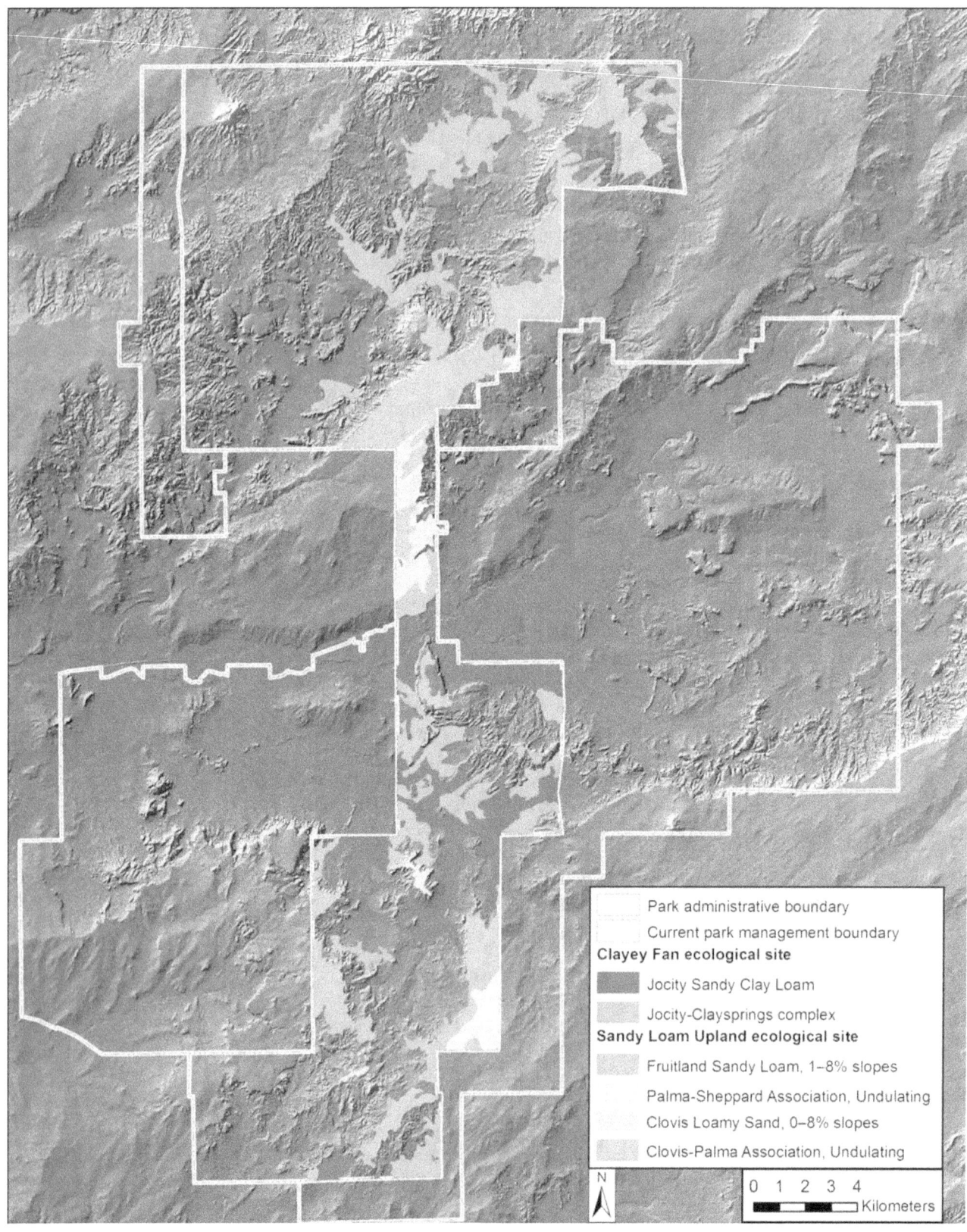

**Figure A-16. Extent of the target soil map units for the Clayey Fan and Sandy Loam Upland ecological sites in Petrified Forest National Park. The Sandy Loam Upland ecological site was initially composed of both the Sandy Loam Upland and Loamy Upland ecological sites, however these were later combined by the NRCS, as described in the text.**

We developed sampling frames for all 3 ecological sites. Sampling sites were identified using the GRTS design (see below), and in 2007, we established 10 plots in each of the sites. That year NRCS published an updated survey that merged the Sandy Loam Upland and Loamy Upland ecological sites into a single ecological site, designated Sandy Loam Upland. This change likely took place due to the fine-scale mosaic pattern the 2 ecological sites display in the field and their similarity in soils and vegetation. As a result of this change, in 2008 we merged the Sandy Loam Upland and Loamy Upland ecological sites.

## 10.2 Sandy Loam Upland and Loamy Upland

### 10.2.1 Sampling frame

Sampling frames for the Sandy Loam Upland and Loamy Upland ecological sites were developed independently in 2007 based on the way those 2 ecological sites were defined and mapped in 2006. These sampling frames were merged in 2008 to become the final Sandy Loam Upland sampling frame.

Ecological sites are not explicitly mapped in NRCS Soils Survey Geographic (SSURGO) Database spatial layers. Instead, "map units" are the finest spatially defined units. In general, map units having a high percentage of the target ecological site were selected to be part of the initial sampling frame. The original Sandy Loam Upland ecological site occurred in 3 soil map units within the park management boundary (table A-14). One of the map units contained only 30% of the target ecological site, but the remaining area was composed of the Loamy Upland ecological site. These 3 map units represented the initial sampling frame. Target soil lineage came from the NRCS SSURGO soils shapefile for the *Apache County, Arizona, Central Part* soil survey area (NRCS 2002). The Loamy Upland ecological site occurred in 2 soil map units within the park management boundary (table A-15). Each of the map units is estimated to contain 65% or greater of a target ecological site. These 2 map units represented the initial sampling frame. Target soil lineage came from the NRCS SSURGO soils shapefile for the *Apache County, Arizona, Central Part* soil survey area (NRCS 2002).

### 10.2.2 Field reconnaissance

A number of randomly generated points were visited in the original Sandy Loam Upland and Loamy Upland ecological sites in the fall of 2006. At all sites visited, surface soil was textured by hand, dominant vegetation was recorded, and photos of the soil surface and surrounding landscape were taken. Overall variation between the sites was quite low and the soil and vegetation characteristics matched those expected for these ecological sites. Moreover, the 2 ecological sites were similar to each other (and were paired with each other in one map unit). The primary difference between the 2 ecological sites is the lack of a Bt horizon in the Sandy Loam Upland soils.

**Table A-14. Target soil map units for the original Sandy Loam Upland ecological site in Petrified Forest National Park**

| Map unit name | Map unit symbol | Percent of map unit associated with the target ecological site |
|---|---|---|
| Clovis-Palma Association, Undulating | CTB | 30[a] |
| Fruitland Sandy Loam, 1–8% slopes | FRB | 79 |
| Palma-Sheppard Association, Undulating | PSB | 50 |

[a]After the Sandy Loam Upland and the Loamy Upland ecological sites were merged, this map unit contained 95% of the resulting target site.

**Table A-15. Target soil map units for the Loamy Upland ecological site in Petrified Forest National Park**

| Map unit name | Map unit symbol | Percent of map unit associated with the target ecological site |
|---|---|---|
| Clovis Loamy Sand, 0–8% slopes | CLB | 100 |
| Clovis-Palma Association, Undulating | CTB | 65[a] |

[a]After the Sandy Loam Upland and the Loamy Upland ecological sites were merged, this map unit contained 95% of the resulting target site.

### 10.2.3 Adjustments to sampling frame

Each sampling frame was adjusted by several spatial processing (GIS) steps to result in a realistic target population for sampling. All polygons of the target map units were selected from the NRCS soils shapefile and then merged. Several additional buffering and erasing steps followed (table A-16), which resulted in removal of large portions of the initial sampling frame from being selected as a plot centroid. First, a general negative 50 m (interior) buffer was applied to ensure that the entire plot would fall within the target soil ecological site. Next, filters were applied to remove (1) areas that were not actually within the target ecological site (e.g., roads, buildings, developed areas), and (2) areas where sampling was impractical because of safety concerns.

**Table A-16. Buffer distances for areas removed from the initial sampling frames for target ecological sites in Petrified Forest National Park**

| Removal condition | Plot centroid buffer (minimum distance between plot center and removal condition) | Effective buffer (minimum distance between plot edge and removal condition) | Removal category |
|---|---|---|---|
| Ecological site boundary | 50 m | 0 m | buffer necessary to fit entire plot |
| Roads, buildings or other infra-structure | 200 m for the interstate, 100 m for all other features | 150 m for the interstate, 50 m for all other features | non-target area |
| Slope: removed if >20% | 50 m | 0 m | sampling impractical |

Areas that were not a part of the target ecological site included buildings, other developed areas, or areas on or near roads. A buffer was applied to these features to ensure that no part of the plot fell within the feature, and in some cases, an additional buffer distance was added if the disturbance from the feature was likely to affect a larger area. A few additional small areas were removed in the northern part of the park based on field visits that identified those areas as being substantially different from the majority of the ecological site.

Areas with steep slopes were removed based on the potential for soil erosion caused by monitoring efforts and concerns about safety. Areas were retained if their slope was less than 20%.

### 10.2.4 Sampling sites
For each of the original 2 sampling frames, a set of spatially distributed sampling points was created using the GRTS design. A script incorporating the GRTS design was run using the R statistical computing software (http://www.r-project.org/) and the P.survey and P.design modules, which can be selected and installed from within the R program. The script used the area-based option (polygons) and gave all areas equal probability of selection. The GRTS design allows for rejection of sampling points. Spatial balance is maintained by following a sequential ordering of sites; if a site is rejected, the next site in sequential order is used. The map unit that contained both the Sandy Loam Upland and Loamy Upland ecological sites contained both sets of GRTS points. Final point selection and rejection after the 2 sites were merged are described in section 10.3.

## 10.3 Sandy Loam Upland final sampling frame
In 2008, the original sampling frames for the Sandy Loam Upland and the Loamy Upland sites were spatially merged to create the final sampling frame for the Sandy Loam Upland ecological site (fig. A-17). The merging of the sampling frames for the 2 ecological sites was a fairly simple additive process. The 2 separate areas had roughly equal estimated areal extents: of the original Loamy Upland and Sandy Loam Upland sites, 48.5% of the summed area was estimated to be Sandy Loam Upland and 51.5% was estimated to be Loamy Upland. As a result, we were able to use both sets of GRTS points with equal weighting.

### 10.3.1 Rejection criteria
Park staff reviewed the locations of the GRTS point provided in the research permit application and had the opportunity to reject sites that were co-located with archaeology sites or other sensitive resources. Prior to plot establishment, the field crew conducted an ecological site assessment of topography (slope), soils, vegetation and disturbance to ensure that the site was the appropriate ecological site. Sites were accepted if they contained at least 80% of the target ecological site, had less than a 20% slope, and did not contain significant disturbances. Sites that did not meet these criteria were rejected.

In 2007, 10 plots were established in each of the original ecological sites. Sites for potential plots were visited and accepted or rejected in sequential order with respect to GRTS point numbering. A large number of sites were rejected because they were composed of a combination of the Sandy Loam Upland and Loamy Upland ecological sites (between 20% and 80% of each). In 2010, 10 more plots were to be established for a total number of 30 plots. The plots that were rejected in 2007 because they contained a combination of the original 2 ecological sites were revisited, and plots were established if they met all other criteria for acceptance. Because there were more than 10 plots that

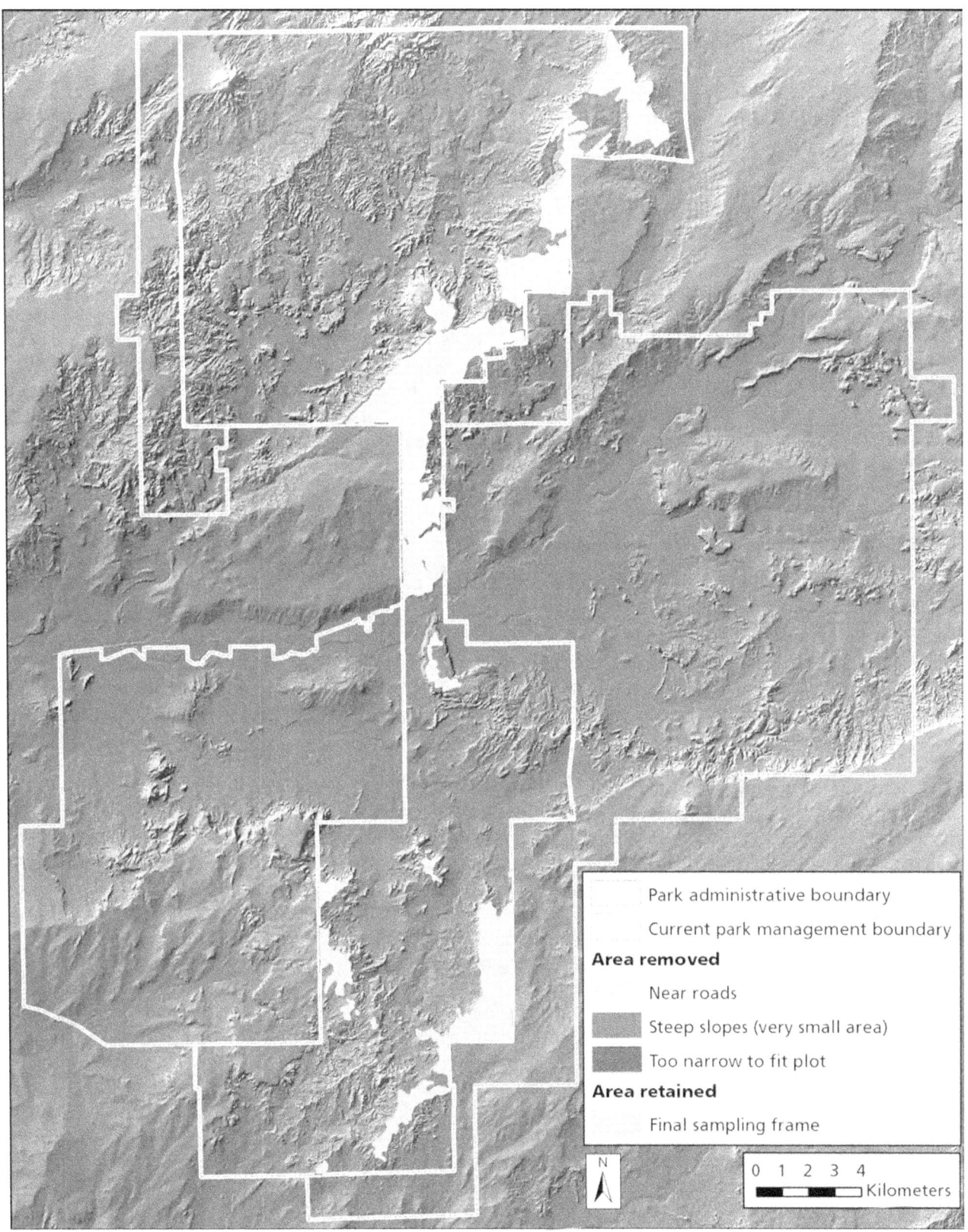

**Legend:**

Park administrative boundary

Current park management boundary

**Area removed**

Near roads

Steep slopes (very small area)

Too narrow to fit plot

**Area retained**

Final sampling frame

N

0 1 2 3 4 Kilometers

Figure A-17. Sandy Loam Upland ecological site targeted for integrated upland monitoring in Petrified Forest National Park, showing areas removed during spatial processing to derive the final sampling frame and resulting area of inference

were rejected on this account, there were 3 plots of the highest GRTS numbers that exceeded the 30 acceptable points. These 3 plots were thereby "decommissioned."

Of all of the sites that were examined for the establishment of 30 plots in 2010, 3 sites were rejected because they were co-located with archaeological sites. One site was rejected because it was located close to a road. One site was rejected because it was a different ecological site (Claysprings). One site was rejected because it was located within 200 m of another plot. Of these rejected 6 sites, 3 occurred in the original Sandy Loam Upland ecological site, and 3 occurred on the Loamy Upland ecological site. Therefore, the 30 plots established within the final sampling frame were balanced evenly between the original 2 sampling frames.

## 10.4 Clayey Fan
### 10.4.1 Sampling frame
Clayey Fan is a target ecological site, but ecological sites are not explicitly mapped in NRCS SSURGO soils geospatial layers. Instead, "map units" are the finest spatially defined units. In general, map units having a high percentage of the target ecological site are selected to be part of the initial sampling frame. In this case, the Clayey Fan ecological site occurs in 2 soil map units within the park management boundary. Each of the 2 map units is estimated to contain 85% or greater of a target ecological site (table A-17). These 2 map units represented the initial sampling frame. Target soil lineage came from the NRCS SSURGO soils shapefile for the *Apache County, Arizona, Central Part* soil survey area (NRCS 2002).

**Table A-17. Target soil map units for the Clayey Fan ecological site in Petrified Forest National Park**

| Map unit name | Map unit symbol | Percent of map unit associated with the target ecological site |
|---|---|---|
| Jocity Sandy Clay Loam | JR | 100 |
| Jocity-Claysprings complex | JS | 85 |

### 10.4.2 Field reconnaissance
A number of randomly generated points were visited in the Clayey Fan ecological site during the fall of 2006. At all sites visited, surface soil was textured by hand, dominant vegetation was recorded, and photos of the soil surface and the surrounding landscape were taken. Overall variation between the sites was quite low and the soil and vegetation characteristics matched those expected for the ecological site.

### 10.4.3 Adjustments to sampling frame
Several spatial processing (GIS) steps were conducted to adjust the sampling frame to contain a realistic target population for sampling. All polygons of the target map units were selected from the NRCS soils shapefile and then merged. Several additional buffering and erasing steps followed (table A-16), which resulted in removal of portions of the initial sampling frame (fig. A-18). First, a general negative 50 m (interior) buffer was applied to ensure that the entire plot would fall within the target soil ecological site. Next, filters were applied to remove (1) areas that were not actually within the target ecological site (e.g., roads, developed areas, buildings), (2) areas where sampling was impractical because of safety or trampling/erosion concerns, and (3) areas that were substantially different.

Areas that were not a part of the target ecological site included areas on or near roads, developed areas, or other infrastructure. A buffer was applied to these features to ensure that no part of the plot fell within the feature, and in some cases, an additional buffer distance was added if the disturbance from the feature was likely to affect a larger area (table A-16). A few additional small areas were removed in the northern part of the park based on field visits that identified those areas as being substantially different from the majority of the ecological site.

Areas with steep slopes were removed based on concerns about safety and potential soil erosion caused by monitoring efforts. Areas were retained if their slope was less than 20%.

### 10.4.4 Sampling sites
A set of spatially distributed sampling points was created using the GRTS design. A script incorporating the GRTS design was run using the R statistical computing software (http://www.r-project.org/) and the P.survey and P.design modules, which can be selected and installed from within the R program. The script used the area-based option

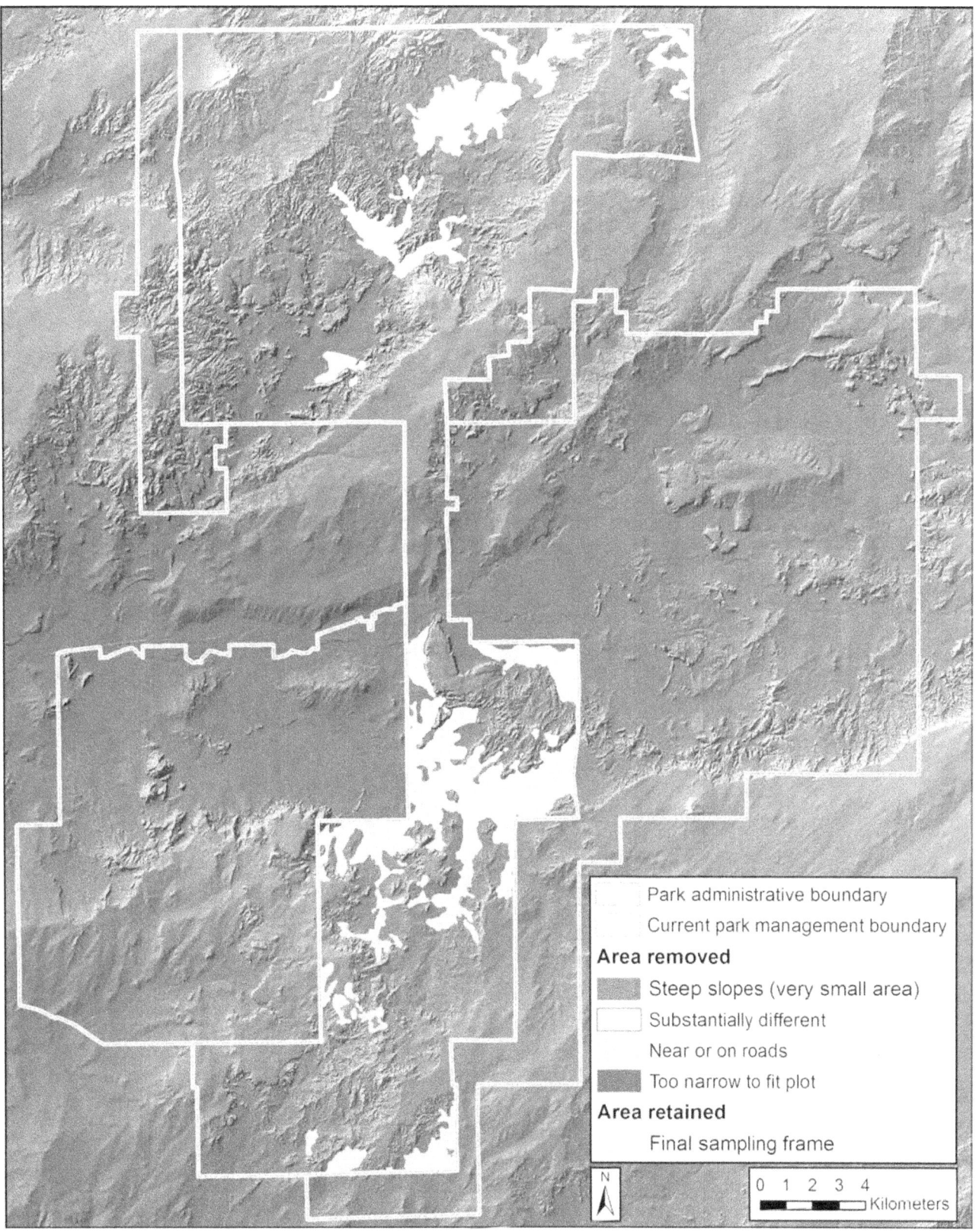

**Park administrative boundary**

Current park management boundary

**Area removed**

Steep slopes (very small area)

Substantially different

Near or on roads

Too narrow to fit plot

**Area retained**

Final sampling frame

N

0 1 2 3 4 Kilometers

Figure A-18. Clayey Fan ecological site targeted for integrated upland monitoring in Petrified Forest National Park, showing areas removed during spatial processing to derive the final sampling frame and resulting area of inference (polygons) and gave all areas equal probability of selection. The GRTS design allows for rejection of sampling points. Spatial balance is maintained by following a sequential ordering of sites; if a site is rejected, the next site in sequential order is used.

### 10.4.5 Rejection criteria
Park staff reviewed the locations of the GRTS points provided in the initial research application and rejected sites that were co-located with archaeology sites. Prior to plot establishment, the field crew conducted an ecological site assessment of topography (slope), soils, vegetation and disturbance to ensure that the site was the appropriate ecological site. Sites were accepted if the contained at least 80% of the target ecological site, had less than 20% slope, did not contain significant disturbances, and were not located within 200 m of the centroid of an existing plot. Sites that did not meet these criteria were rejected.

In 2007 and 2010, 30 plots were established. Sites were visited sequentially with respect to GRTS point numbers. Fifty-seven sites were rejected because more than 20% of the site was comprised of other ecological sites. Two sites were rejected because they required more than a 2 hour hike.

## 11 Petroglyph National Monument sampling frame
### 11.1 Monitoring priorities
At Petroglyph National Monument there was one logical choice for an ecological site for integrated upland monitoring: the "Malpais 8–10 inches" ecological site (R042XA056NM). This site encompassed the majority of the mesa top within the boundaries of the monument, hence occupying a large area of the monument (fig. A-19). Target soil lineage came from the NRCS Soils Survey Geographic (SSURGO) Database soils geodataset for *Bernalillo County and Parts of Sandoval and Valencia Counties, New Mexico* (NRCS 2005a).

**Figure A-19. Extent of the target soil map unit for the Malpais ecological site in Petroglyph National Monument**

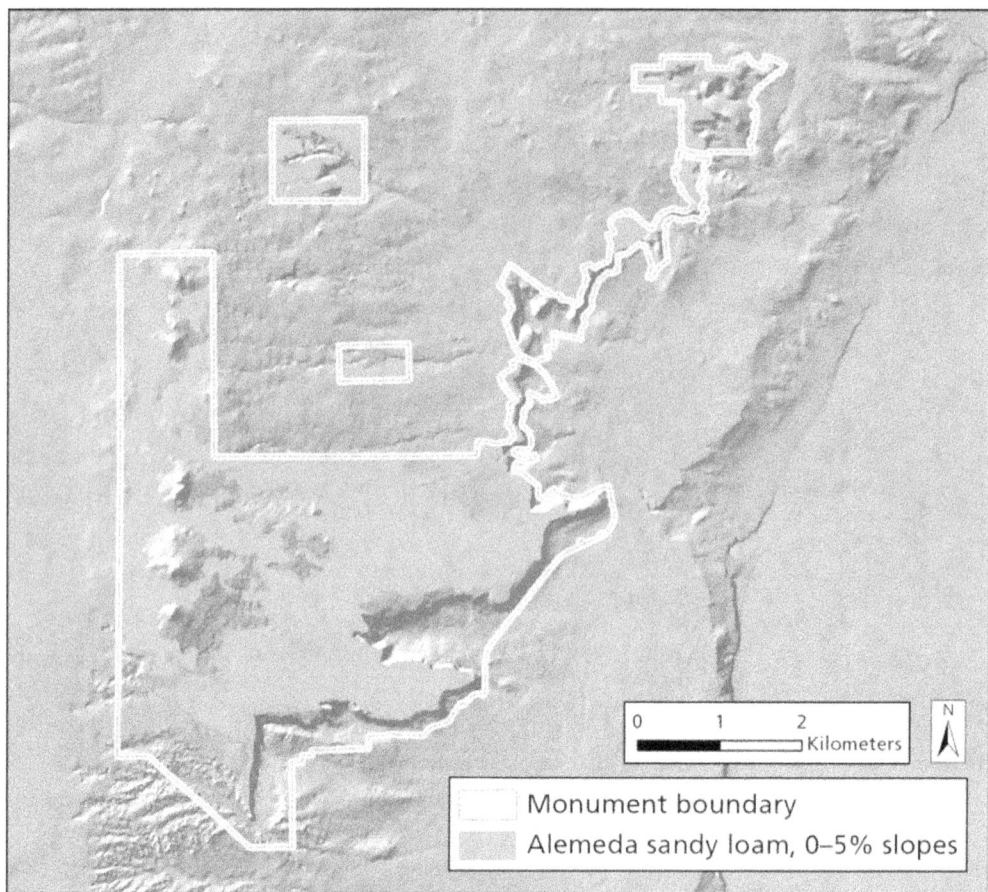

## 11.2 Malpais

### 11.2.1 Sampling frame
Malpais was the target ecological site; however, ecological sites are not explicitly mapped in soil surveys. Instead, "map units" are the finest spatially defined units. In general, map units having a high percentage of the target ecological site are selected to be part of the initial sampling frame. One map unit was selected because it was estimated to contain the target ecological site on 70% or more of its area (table A-18).

### 11.2.2 Field reconnaissance
No reconnaissance was conducted prior to the installation of the plots.

### 11.2.3 Adjustments to sampling frame
Several spatial processing (GIS) steps were conducted to ensure the final sampling frame contained a realistic target population for sampling. Target soil lineage came from the NRCS SSURGO soils geodataset for the *Bernalillo County and Parts of Sandoval and Valencia Counties, New Mexico* soil survey area (NRCS 2005a). Individual polygons of the target map units were selected from the NRCS soils shapefile and then merged. Through discussions with park staff, it was decided that long term monitoring plots would only be placed within the Atrisco management unit.

Several additional buffering and erasing steps followed (table A-19), which resulted in the removal of large portions of the initial sampling frame (fig. A-20). Because the plot size is 71 × 71 m, the diagonal distance from the plot center to the plot edge (or corner) is approximately 50 m. Consequently, when a feature was excluded, a 50 m buffer was added to the exclusion to ensure that no part of a sampling plot would fall within the excluded area. This 50 m buffer was also applied as a negative buffer to the ecological site edge to ensure that the entire plot fell within the ecological site. One effect of buffering the ecological site edge is that areas too narrow to accommodate a plot were removed. Additionally, other filters were applied that removed the following: 1) areas that were not actually within the target ecological site 2) areas where site conditions were expected to differ substantially from the norm, thereby increasing ecological variation and making it more difficult to detect trends, and 3) areas where sampling was impractical because of erosion, and safety concerns. In some cases, an additional buffer distance was added if the disturbance from the feature was likely to affect a larger area (table A-19).

Areas on or near roads were not considered to be part of the target ecological site. Areas with steep slopes were removed based on concerns about safety and potential soil erosion caused by monitoring efforts. Areas associated with past off-road vehicle use and with overhead utility line rights-of-way were considered substantially different.

### 11.2.4 Sampling sites
A set of spatially distributed sampling points was created using the GRTS design. A script incorporating the GRTS design was developed and run using the R statistical computing software (http://www.r-project.org/) and the P.survey

**Table A-18. Target soil map unit for the Malpais ecological site in Petroglyph National Monument**

| Map unit name | Map unit symbol | Percent of map unit associated with the target ecological site |
|---|---|---|
| Alemeda sandy loam, 0–5% slopes | AmB | 70 |

**Table A-19. Buffer distances for areas removed from the initial Malpais ecological site sampling frame in Petroglyph National Monument**

| Removal condition | Plot centroid buffer (minimum distance between plot center and removal condition) | Effective buffer (minimum distance between plot edge and removal condition) | Removal category |
|---|---|---|---|
| Ecological site or park boundary | 50 m | 0 m | buffer necessary to fit entire plot |
| Roads | 100 m | 50 m | non-target area |
| Slope: removed if >20% | 50 m | 0 m | sampling impractical |
| Area formerly used for off-road vehicle recreation | 100 m | 50 m | area substantially different |
| Right-of-way associated with power line | 50 m | 0 m | area substantially different |

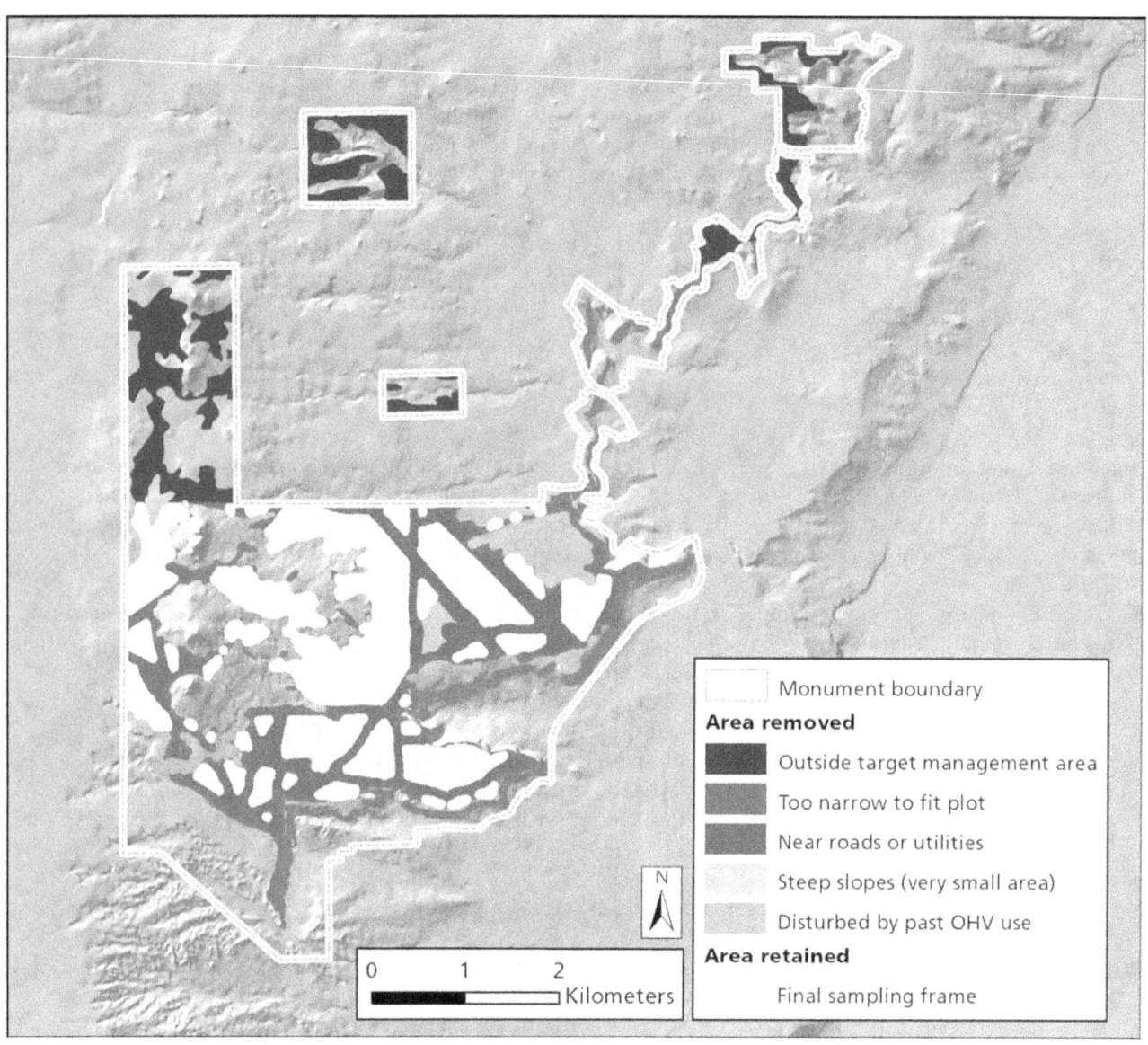

**Figure A-20. Malpais ecological site targeted for integrated upland monitoring in Petroglyph National Monument, showing areas removed during spatial processing to derive the final sampling frame and resulting area of inference**

and P.design modules, which can be selected and installed from within the R program. The script used the area-based option (polygons) and gave all potential sites an equal probability of selection. An advantage of the GRTS design is that is allows for rejection of sampling points (if found to be non-target or inaccessible, etc.). Spatial balance is maintained by following a sequential ordering of sites; if a site is rejected, the next site in sequential order is used.

## 11.2.5 Rejection criteria

Park staff reviewed the locations of the GRTS points provided in the initial application. No sites were rejected by park staff. Prior to each plot's establishment, the field crew conducted an ecological site assessment to evaluate topography (slope), soils, vegetation, and disturbance to ensure that the site was the target ecological site. Sampling sites were accepted if they contained at least 80% of the target ecological site, were on slopes less than 20%, did not contain significant disturbances, and were not located within 200 m of the centroid of an existing plot. Sites that did not meet these criteria were rejected.

In 2008, 6 plots were established. Sites were visited to determine acceptance or rejection in sequential order with respect to GRTS point numbering. No sites were rejected.

## 12 Walnut Canyon National Monument sampling frame
The sampling frame for this park unit has not been developed.

## 13 Wupatki National Monument sampling frames
### 13.1 Monitoring priorities
SCPN and Wupatki National Monument (WUPA) natural resources staff met during May 2006 to discuss park priorities for upland monitoring. NRCS ecological sites served as the basis for defining the initial sampling frame. Because of their predominance within WUPA, 3 ecological sites were considered: Limy Upland (6–10" p.z.) (R035XB208AZ), Shallow Loamy (10–14" p.z.) and Sandstone Upland (6–10" p.z.) (R035XB215AZ). We agreed that the Limy Upland and Sandstone Upland (6–10" p.z.) ecological sites were the highest priority for monitoring (fig. A-21), because these ecological sites occurred in different areas of the park and varied ecologically. The Shallow Loamy ecological site was considered a slightly lower priority because it was transitional, both geographically and ecologically, to the other ecological sites.

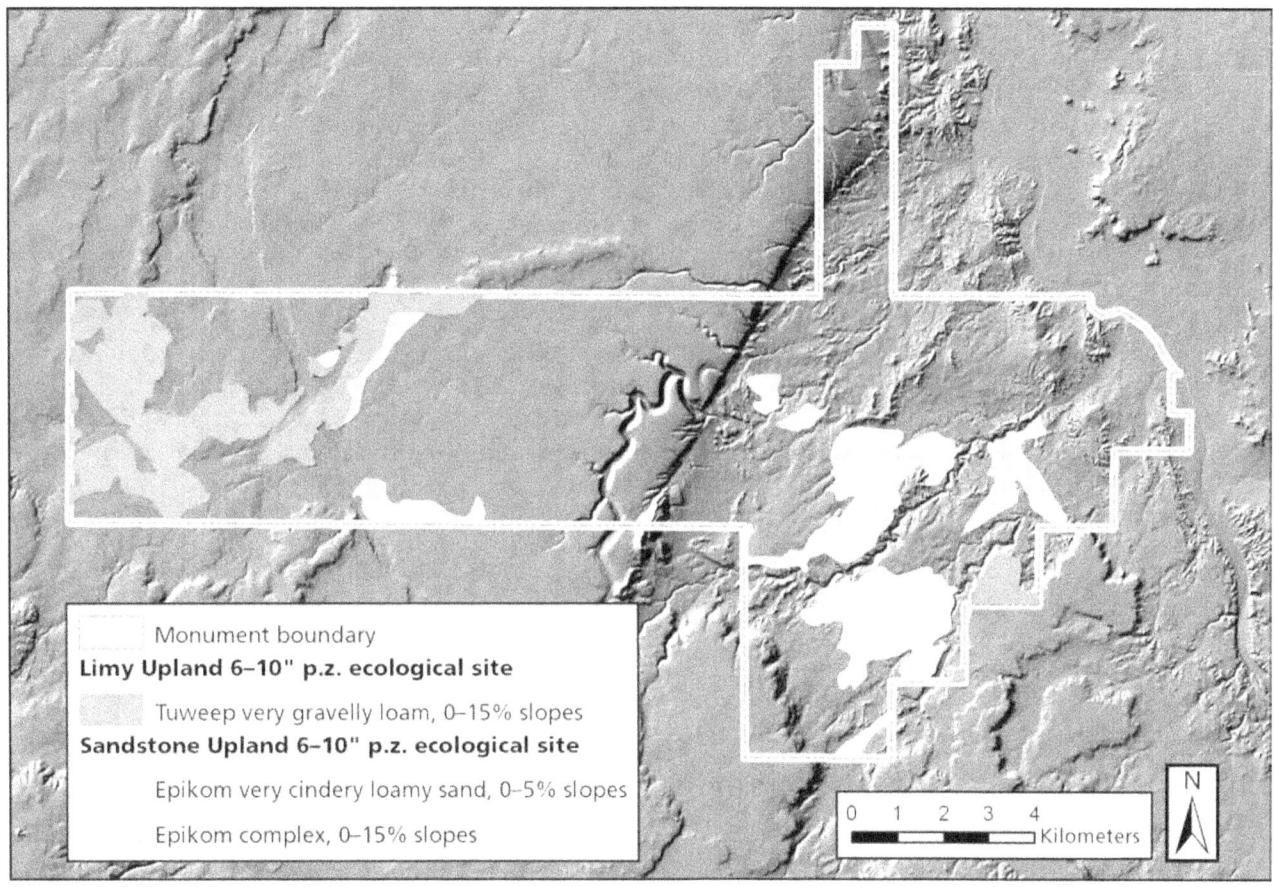

Figure A-21. Extent of the target soil map units for the Limy Upland (6–10" p.z.) and Sandstone Upland (6–10" p.z.) ecological sites in Wupatki National Monument

### 13.2 Limy Upland (6–10" p.z.)
#### 13.2.1 Sampling frame
Limy Upland (6–10" p.z.) is a target ecological site, but ecological sites are not explicitly mapped in NRCS Soils Survey Geographic (SSURGO) Database geospatial layers. Instead, "map units" are the finest spatially defined units. In general, map units having a high percentage of the target ecological site are selected to be part of the initial sampling frame. In this case, the Limy Upland (6–10" p.z.) ecological site occurs in one soil map unit within the park. That soil unit is estimated to be composed of 100% Limy Upland (6–10" p.z.) ecological site and represented the initial sampling frame (table A-20). Target soil lineage came from the NRCS SSURGO soils geodataset for *Coconino County Area, Arizona, Central Part* soil survey area (NRCS 2006).

### 13.2.2 Field reconnaissance

A number of randomly generated points were visited in the Limy Upland (6–10" p.z.) ecological site during the fall of 2006. At all sites visited, surface soil was textured by hand, dominant vegetation was recorded, and photos of the soil surface and the surrounding landscape were taken. Overall variation between the sites was quite low and the soil and vegetation characteristics matched those expected for the ecological site.

**Table A-20. Target map unit for the Limy Upland (6–10" p.z.) ecological site in Wupatki National Monument**

| Map unit name | Map unit symbol | Percent of map unit associated with the target ecological site |
|---|---|---|
| Tuweep very gravelly loam, 0–15% slopes | 56 | 100 |

### 13.2.3 Adjustments to sampling frame

Several spatial processing (GIS) steps were conducted to adjust the sampling frame to contain a realistic target population for sampling. All polygons of the target map unit were selected from the NRCS soils shapefile. Several additional buffering and erasing steps followed (table A-21), which removed portions of the sampling frame (fig. A-22). Because the plot size is 71 × 71 m, the distance from the center of the plot to the plot edge (on a diagonal) is approximately 50 meters. Consequently, when a feature was excluded, a 50 m buffer was added to the exclusion to ensure that no part of a sampling plot would fall within the excluded area. This 50 m buffer was also applied as a negative buffer to the ecological site edge to ensure that the entire plot fell within the ecological site. One effect of buffering the ecological site edge is that areas too narrow to accommodate a plot were removed. Additionally, filters were applied to remove areas that were not actually within the target ecological site (e.g., roads, developed areas, buildings). A buffer was applied to these features to ensure that no part of the plot fell within the feature.

### 13.2.4 Sampling sites

A set of spatially distributed sampling points was created using the Generalized Random-Tessellation Stratified (GRTS) design. A script incorporating the GRTS design was run using the R statistical computing software (http://www.r-project.org/) and the P.survey and P.design modules, which can be selected and installed from within the R program. The script used the area-based option (polygons) and gave all areas equal probability of selection. The GRTS design allows for rejection of sampling points. Spatial balance is maintained by following a sequential ordering of sites; if a site is rejected, the next site in sequential order is used.

### 13.2.5 Rejection criteria

Park staff reviewed the locations of the GRTS points provided in the initial research application. A park archaeologist visited each of the sites and rejected those that were co-located with archaeology sites. Prior to plot establishment, the field crew conducted an ecological site assessment of topography (slope), soils, vegetation and disturbance to ensure that each site was the appropriate ecological site. Sites were accepted if they contained at least 80% of the target ecological site, had less than 20% slope, did not contain significant disturbances, and were not located within 200 m of an existing plot. Sites that did not meet these criteria were rejected.

In 2007 and 2010, 30 plots were established in the Limy Upland (6–10" p.z.) ecological site. Sites were visited sequentially by GRTS point number. Five sites were rejected because they contained or were near archaeological sites. One site was not in the target ecological site. Two sites were located less than 200 m from an existing plot.

**Table A-21. Buffer distances for areas removed from the initial sampling frames for both ecological sites in Wupatki National Monument**

| Removal condition | Plot centroid buffer (minimum distance between plot center and removal condition) | Effective buffer (minimum distance between plot edge and removal condition) | Removal category |
|---|---|---|---|
| Ecological site or park boundary | 50 m | 0 m | buffer necessary to fit entire plot |
| Roads, ruins, buildings or other infrastructure | 100 m | 50 m | non-target area |
| Slope: removed if >20% | 40 m | 0 | sampling impractical |

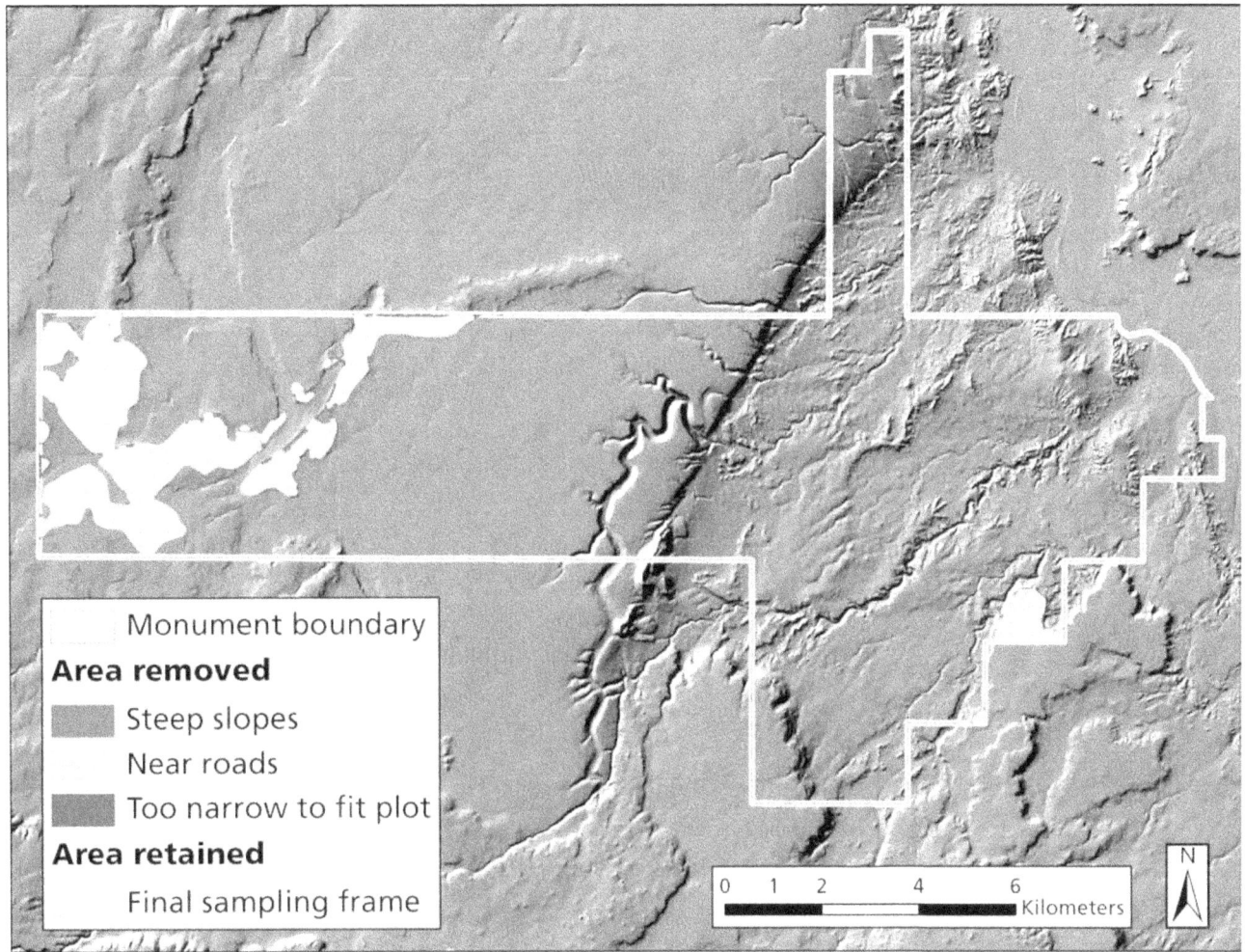

Figure A-22. Limy Upland (6–10" p.z.) ecological site targeted for integrated upland monitoring in Wupatki National Monument, showing areas removed during spatial processing to derive the final sampling frame and resulting area of inference

## 13.3 Sandstone Upland (6–10" p.z.)

### 13.3.1 Sampling frame

Sandstone Upland (6–10" p.z.) is a target ecological site, but ecological sites are not explicitly mapped in NRCS SSURGO soils geospatial layers. Instead, "map units" are the finest spatially defined units. In this case, the Sandstone Upland (6–10" p.z.) ecological site is part of 3 soil map units occurring in the park. In general, map units having a high percentage of the target ecological site were selected to be part of the initial sampling frame. In this case, 2 map units were selected to represent the initial sampling frame because they were estimated to have the target ecological site covering greater than or equal to 90% of their area (table A-22). Target soil lineage came from the NRCS SSURGO soils geodataset for *Coconino County Area, Arizona, Central Part* soil survey area (2006).

### 13.3.2 Field reconnaissance

A number of randomly generated points were visited in the Sandstone Upland (6–10" p.z.) ecological site during the fall of 2006. At all sites visited, surface soil was textured by hand, dominant vegetation was recorded, and photos of the soil surface and the surrounding landscape were taken. There was large variation in the soils and vegetation among the sites, particularly in cover and depth of cinders, and cover of grass.

### 13.3.3 Adjustments to sampling frame

Several spatial processing (GIS) steps were conducted to adjust the sampling frame to contain a realistic target population for sampling. All polygons of the target map units were selected from the NRCS soils shapefile and then merged. Several additional buffering and erasing steps followed (table A-21), which removed portions of the initial sampling frame (fig. A-23). Because the plot size is 71 × 71 m, the distance from the center of the plot to the plot edge (on a diagonal) is 50 meters. Consequently, when a feature was excluded, a 50 m buffer was added to the exclusion to ensure that no part of a sampling plot would fall within the excluded area. This 50 m buffer was also applied as a negative buffer to the ecological site edge to ensure that the entire plot fell within the ecological site. One effect of buffering the ecological site edge is that areas too narrow to accommodate a plot were removed. Additionally, filters were applied to remove areas that were not actually within the target ecological site (e.g., roads, developed areas, buildings). A buffer was applied to these features to ensure that no part of the plot fell within the feature.

**Table A-22. Target map units for the Sandstone Upland (6–10″ p.z.) ecological site in Wupatki National Monument**

| Map unit name | Map unit symbol | Percent of map unit associated with the target ecological site |
|---|---|---|
| Epikom very cindery loamy sand, 0–5% slopes | 17 | 100 |
| Epikom complex, 0–15 % slopes | 18 | 90 |

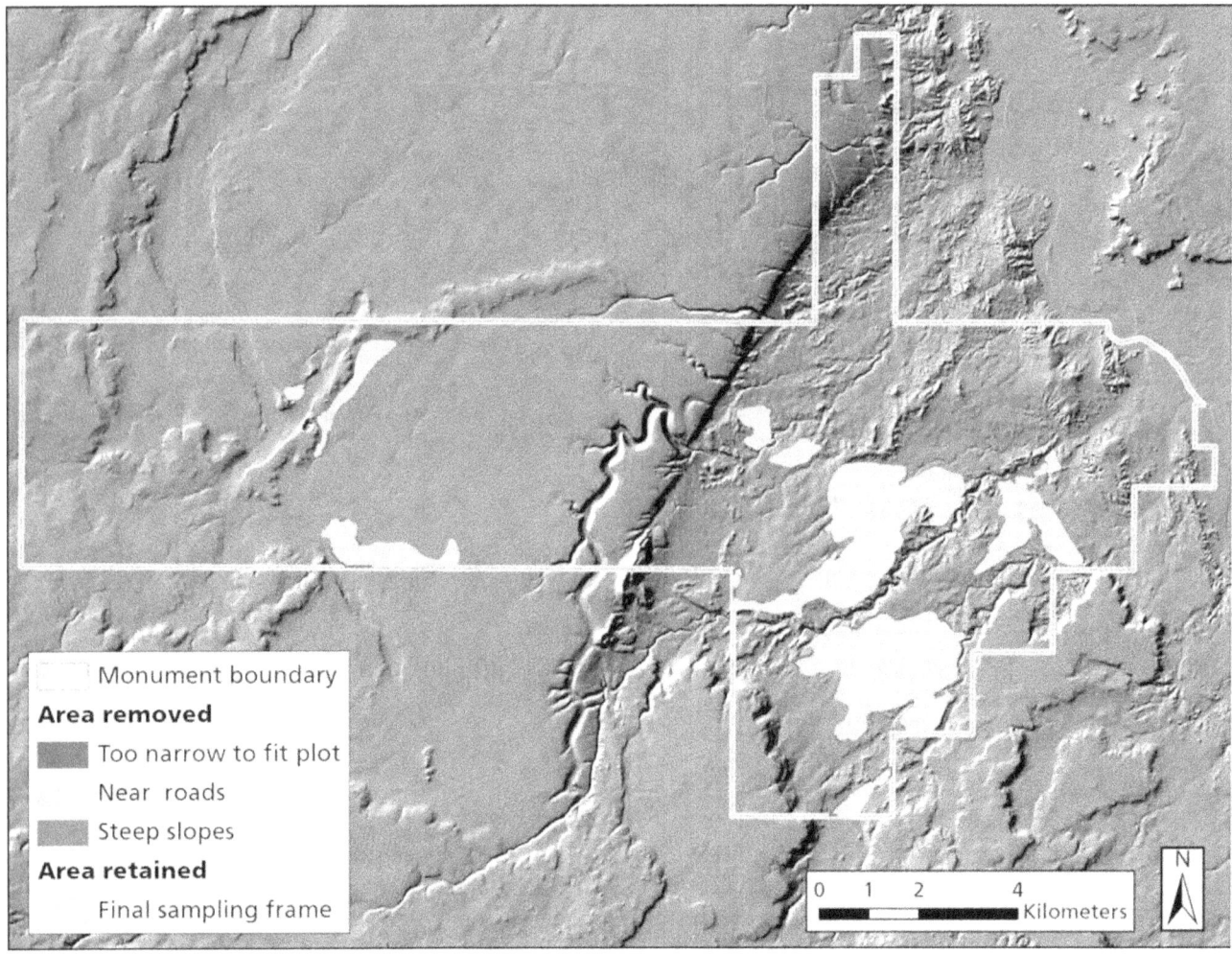

Figure A-23. Sandstone Upland (6–10″ p.z.) ecological site targeted for integrated upland monitoring in Wupatki National Monument, showing areas removed during spatial processing to derive the final sampling frame and resulting area of inference

## 13.3.4 Sampling sites

A set of spatially distributed sampling points was created using the GRTS design. A script incorporating the GRTS design was run using the R statistical computing software (http://www.r-project.org/) and the P.survey and P.design modules, which can be selected and installed from within the R program. The script used the area-based option (polygons) and gave all areas equal probability of selection. The GRTS design allows for rejection of sampling points. Spatial balance is maintained by following a sequential ordering of sites; if a site is rejected, the next site in sequential order is used.

## 13.3.5 Rejection criteria

Park staff reviewed the locations of the GRTS point provided in the initial research application. A park archaeologist visited each site and rejected those that were co-located with archaeology sites. Prior to plot establishment, the field crew conducted an ecological site assessment of topography (slope), soils, vegetation and disturbance to ensure that each site was the appropriate ecological site. Sites were accepted if they contained at least 80% of the target ecological site, had less than 20% slope, did not contain significant disturbances, and were not located within 200 m of the centroid of an existing plot. Sites that did not meet these criteria were rejected.

In 2007 and 2010, 30 plots were established. Sites were visited and accepted or rejected in sequential order with respect to GRTS point numbering. Four sites were rejected because they did not occur on the target ecological site. (One of these sites also had a human disturbance—construction debris). Three sites were located within 200 m of an existing plot. One site was co-located with an archaeological site. One plot was located within 50 m of a road.

## 14 Literature cited

Allen, C. D. and D. D. Breshears. 1998. Drought-induced shift of a forest-woodland ecotone: Rapid landscape response to climate variation. Proc Natl Acad Sci USA 95:14839–14842.

Breshears, D. D., N. S. Cobb, P. M. Rich, K. P. Price, C. D. Allen, R. G. Balice, W. H. Romme, J. H. Kastens, M. L. Floyd, J. Belnap, J. J. Anderson, O. B. Myers, C. W. Meyer. 2005. Regional vegetation die-off in response to global-change-type drought: Proc Natl Acad Sci USA, 102:15144–15148.

Floyd-Hanna, L., D. D. Hanna, W. H. Romme. 2004. Historical and recent fire regimes in Piñon-Juniper Woodlands on Mesa Verde, Colorado, USA. Forest Ecology and Management. 198:269–289.

Hibner, C. D. 2000. Special project soil survey of Bandelier National Monument: Parts of Los Alamos, Sandoval, and Santa Fe Counties, New Mexico. United States Department of Agriculture, Natural Resource Conservation Service [NRCS], in cooperation with United States Department of the Interior, National Park Service and the New Mexico Agricultural Experiment Station. Interim copy—subject to change.

National Park Service. 2006. Soil Survey Geographic (SSURGO) Database for Chaco Culture National Historical Park, New Mexico. National Park Service, Geologic Resources Division, Soil Inventory and Monitoring Program. An updated version is available online at https://irma.nps.gov/App/Reference/Profile/1048840. Accessed [11/06/2006].

Natural Resources Conservation Service [NRCS], United States Department of Agriculture. 2002. Soil Survey Geographic (SSURGO) Database for Apache County, Arizona, Central Part (AZ635). Available online at http://soildatamart.nrcs.usda.gov. Accessed [02/22/2005].

Natural Resources Conservation Service [NRCS], United States Department of Agriculture. 2003. Soil Survey for Grand Canyon Area, Arizona, Parts of Coconino and Mohave Counties (AZ701). An updated version of the data contained in this report is available online at http://soildatamart.nrcs.usda.gov.

Natural Resources Conservation Service [NRCS], United States Department of Agriculture. 2004. Soil Survey Geographic (SSURGO) Database for Cortez Area, Colorado, Parts of Dolores and Montezuma Counties (CO671). An updated version is available online at http://soildatamart.nrcs.usda.gov. Accessed [03/09/2005].

Natural Resources Conservation Service [NRCS], United States Department of Agriculture. 2005a. Soil Survey Geographic (SSURGO) Database for Bernalillo County and Parts of Sandoval and Valencia Counties, New Mexico (NM600). Available online at http://soildatamart.nrcs.usda.gov. Accessed [10/28/2005].

Natural Resources Conservation Service [NRCS], United States Department of Agriculture. 2005b. Soil Survey Geographic (SSURGO) Database for Grand Canyon Area, Arizona, Parts of Coconino and Mohave Counties (AZ701). An updated version is available online at http://soildatamart.nrcs.usda.gov. Accessed [03/09/2005].

Natural Resources Conservation Service [NRCS], United States Department of Agriculture. 2005c. Soil Survey Geographic (SSURGO) Database for Sandoval County Area, New Mexico, Parts of Los Alamos, Sandoval and Rio Arriba Counties (NM656). An updated version is available online at http://soildatamart.nrcs.usda.gov. Accessed [02/24/2005].

Natural Resources Conservation Service [NRCS], United States Department of Agriculture. 2006. Soil Survey Geographic (SSURGO) Database for Coconino County Area, Arizona, Central Part (AZ631). Available online at http://soildatamart.nrcs.usda.gov. Accessed [05/25/2006].

Natural Resources Conservation Service [NRCS], United States Department of Agriculture. 2007. Soil Survey Geographic (SSURGO) Database for San Juan County New Mexico, Eastern Part (NM 618). Updated version available online at http://soildatamart.nrcs.usda.gov. Accessed [04/22/2008].

Natural Resources Conservation Service [NRCS], United States Department of Agriculture. 2008. Soil Survey Geographic (SSURGO) Database for Sandoval County Area, New Mexico, Parts of Los Alamos, Sandoval and Rio Arriba Counties (NM656). Available online at http://soildatamart.nrcs.usda.gov. Accessed [05/09/2012].

Natural Resources Conservation Service [NRCS], United States Department of Agriculture. 2011. Ecological Site Information System (ESIS) Database ESD User Guide. Available online at http://esis.sc.egov.usda.gov/Welcome/Files/ESIS%20User%20Guide.doc. Accessed [05/29/2012].

Stevens, D. L. and A. R. Olsen. 2004. Spatially balanced sampling of natural resources. Journal of the American Statistical Association 99:262–278.

United States Department of Agriculture, 2012. Utah Ecological Site Naming Conventions. Unpublished report. Available online at ftp://ftp-fc.sc.egov.usda.gov/UT/Range/Utah_Ecological_Site_Naming_Conventions.pdf.

# Appendix B. Yearly Project List

**Table B-1. This table identifies each task by project stage, indicates who is responsible, and establishes the timing for its execution. Protocol sections and SOPs are referred to as appropriate.**

| Stage | Task description | Responsibility | Timing |
|---|---|---|---|
| Preparation | Initiate announcements for seasonal technician positions; begin hiring. | project manager | Jan |
| | Determine field season objectives and general schedule. | project manager, botanist | Feb |
| | Notify data manager and GIS specialist of needs for the coming season (maps, GPS support, etc.). | project manager | Feb |
| | Submit/renew research permit applications. | project manager | Mar–Apr |
| | Order equipment and supplies. | botanist | Mar–Apr |
| | Develop detailed field schedule; make logistic arrangements, including housing and transportation. | project manager, botanist | Mar–Apr |
| | Generate revisit reports, to include plot establishment sheets, data summaries and species list. | project manager, botanist | Apr |
| | Generate ecological site folders, including ecological site descriptions, soil descriptions, park and ecological site species lists, copies of the research permits and other permits, revisit reports, plot coordinates, field maps, aerial photographs, and access information. | project manager, botanist | Apr |
| | Initiate computer access and key requests. | | May |
| | Ensure that project workspace is ready for use and implement working database copy. | data manager | May |
| | Train field crew in sampling methods. | project manager, botanist | Jun |
| | Notify park contacts of schedule/itinerary; obtain backcountry permits. | project manager, botanist | at least 1 month prior to sampling trip |
| | Update and load background maps and target coordinates into GPS units. | GIS specialist | prior to sampling trip |
| Data collection | Perform any necessary ecological site reconnaissance or plot establishment tasks. | project manager, botanist, crew | Mar–Nov |
| | Perform sampling. | crew | May–Oct |
| | Review data forms after each plot. | crew | daily |
| | Check in with park contacts and project manager. | | after each field trip |
| | De-brief crew on operations, field methods, gear needs, etc. | crew leader | after each field trip |
| | Download and process GPS data. | GIS specialist | after each field trip |
| | Download and organize digital images. | crew | Nov |
| | Scan datasheets. | crew | Nov |
| | Write trip report. | botanist, project manager | after each sampling trip |
| Data entry, verification & validation | Enter data into database. | crew | throughout and following field season (complete by Nov) |
| | Field data verification. | crew | Nov |

**Table B-1 (*continued*)**

| Stage | Task description | Responsibility | Timing |
|---|---|---|---|
| Data entry, verification & validation (*cont'd*) | Merge and export GPS data. Upload processed and verified GPS data to database. | GIS specialist, data manager | Jan |
| | Field data validation (tabular and spatial). | project manager, data manager | Nov–Dec |
| Data management | Upload working data into master project database. | data manager | Jan |
| | Create/update project metadata records. | data manager, project manager | Jan |
| | Re-scan datasheets if original datasheets have been annotated during data validation. | data manager assistant | Feb |
| | Export automated summary queries and reports from database. | data manager | Feb–Mar |
| | Certify database. | data manager | Feb–Mar |
| Data summary & reporting | Generate report-quality map output for reports. | GIS specialist | Feb–Mar |
| | Prepare draft annual reports; complete internal review. | project manager, program manager | Feb–Mar |
| | Prepare and submit IARs. | project manager | Jan–Mar |
| Posting & distribution | Post annual reports to website and distribute to parks. | data manager and project manager | Apr |
| | Submit metadata to NPS IRMA. | data manager, project manager | Apr |
| | Create and update bibliographic and species records in NPS IRMA. | data manager | upon receipt |
| Archival & collections | Archive all digital and hardcopy products. | project manager, data manager | ongoing |
| | Mount herbarium specimens. | botanist | Dec–Apr |
| | Notify parks of new species. Work with park curators to manage voucher collections. | botanist, data manager | ongoing |
| Season close-out | Identify unknown species and update database. | botanist | Nov–Mar |
| | Inventory equipment. | crew | Nov |
| | Organize season photos. | crew | Nov |
| | Meet to discuss recent field season and any needed changes to protocols, database, or analysis and reporting procedures. | project manager, botanist | Nov |
| | Generate report based on field season highlighting successes and necessary improvements. | project manager | Nov |
| | Update SOPs and datasheets with any changes/corrections. | project manager, botanist | Mar |

# Appendix C. Commonly Used Landforms for Integrated Upland Monitoring

The following definitions are derived from Schoeneberger and Wysocki (2008). The full reference is available at the end of this appendix.

**alluvial fan**. A low, outspread mass of loose materials and/or rock material, commonly with gentle slopes, shaped like an open fan or a segment of a cone, deposited by a stream (best expressed in semiarid regions) at the place where it issues from a narrow mountain or upland valley; or where a tributary stream is near or at its junction with the main stream. It is steepest near its apex which points upstream and slopes gently and convexly outward (downstream) with a gradual decrease in gradient.

**arroyo**. The channel of a flat-floored, ephemeral stream, commonly with very steep to vertical banks cut in unconsolidated material; sometimes called a wash. It is usually dry but can be transformed into a temporary watercourse or short-lived torrent after heavy rain within the watershed.

**badlands**. A landscape which is intricately dissected and characterized by a very fine drainage network with high drainage densities and short, steep slopes with narrow interfluves. Badlands develop on surfaces with little or no vegetative cover, overlying unconsolidated or poorly cemented materials (clays, silts, or in some cases sandstones) sometimes with soluble minerals such as gypsum or halite.

**butte**. An isolated, generally flat-topped hill or mountain with relatively steep slopes and talus or precipitous cliffs and characterized by summit width that is less than the height of bounding escarpments, commonly topped by a caprock of resistant material and representing an erosion remnant carved from flat-lying rocks. Compare: mesa, plateau, cuesta.

**canyon**. A long, deep, narrow, very steep-sided valley cut primarily in bedrock with high and precipitous walls in an area of high local relief (e.g., mountain or high plateau terrain), often with a perennial stream at the bottom; similar to but larger than a gorge.

**canyon bench**. One of a series of relatively narrow, flat landforms occurring along a canyon wall and caused by differential erosion of alternating strong and weak horizontal strata; a type of structural bench.

**cuesta**. An asymmetric ridge capped by resistant rock layers of slight to moderate dip, commonly less than 10° (approximately <15 percent); a homocline type produced by differential erosion of interbedded resistant and weak rocks. A cuesta has a long, gentle slope on one side (dip slope), that roughly parallels the inclined beds, and on the opposite side has a relatively short, steep or cliff-like slope (scarp slope) that cuts the tilted rocks.

**dip**. A geomorphic component (characteristic piece) of flat plains (e.g., lake plain, low coastal plain, low-relief till plain) consisting of a shallow and typically closed depression that tends to be an area of focused groundwater recharge but not a permanent water body and that lies slightly lower and is wetter than the adjacent talf, and favors the accumulation of fine sediments and organic materials.

**dip slope**. A slope of the land surface, roughly determined by and approximately conforming to the dip of underlying bedded rocks; (i.e., the long, gently inclined surface of a cuesta).

**dunc**. A low mound, ridge, bank or hill of loose, windblown, subaerially deposited granular material (generally sand), either barren and capable of movement from place to place, or covered and stabilized with vegetation, but retaining its characteristic shape.

**escarpment**. A relatively continuous and steep slope or cliff produced by erosion or faulting and that topographically interrupts or breaks the general continuity of more gently sloping land surfaces.

**flood plain**. The nearly level plain that borders a stream and is subject to inundation under flood-stage conditions unless protected artificially. It is usually a constructional landform built of sediment deposited during overflow and lateral migration of the streams.

**interfluve**. A landform composed of the relatively undissected upland or ridge between two adjacent valleys containing streams flowing in the same general direction. An elevated area between two drainageways that sheds water to those drainageways.

**kipuka**. A low "island" of land surrounded by a younger (more recent) lava flow.

**knob**. A peak or other projection from the top of a hill or mountain. Also, a boulder or group of boulders or an area of resistant rocks protruding from the side of a hill or mountain.

**mesa**. A broad, nearly flat-topped, and usually isolated landmass bounded by steep slopes or precipitous cliff and capped by layers of resistant, nearly horizontal, rocky summit width greater than the height of bounding escarpments. Also used to designate broad structural benches and alluvial terraces that occupy intermediate levels in stepped sequences of platforms bordering canyons and valleys.

**plain**. A general term referring to any flat, lowland area, large or small, at a low elevation. Specifically, any extensive region of comparatively smooth and level gently undulating land. A plain has few or no prominent hills or valleys but sometimes has considerable slope, and usually occurs at low elevation relative to surrounding areas. Where dissected, remnants of a plain can form the local uplands. A plain may be forested or bare of trees and may be formed by deposition or erosion.

**plateau**. A comparatively flat area of great extent and elevation; specifically an extensive land region considerably elevated (more than 100 meters) above adjacent lower-lying terrain, and is commonly limited on at least one side by an abrupt descent, has a flat or nearly level surface. A comparatively large part of a plateau surface is near summit level. Compare: hill, foothill, mountain, mesa, plain.

**ridge**. A long, narrow elevation of the land surface, usually sharp crested with steep sides and forming an extended upland between valleys.

**sand sheet**. A large, irregularly shaped, commonly thin, surficial mantle of eolian sand, lacking the discernible slip faces that are common on dunes.

**scarp**. An escarpment, cliff, or steep slope of some extent along the margin of a plateau, mesa, terrace, or structural bench. A scarp may be of any height.

**side slope**. A geomorphic component of hills consisting of a laterally planar area of a hillside, resulting in predominantly parallel overland water flow (e.g., sheet wash); contour lines generally form straight lines. Side slopes are dominated by colluvium and slope wash sediments.

**structural bench**. A platform-like, nearly level to gently inclined erosional surface developed on resistant strata in areas where valleys are cut in alternating strong and weak layers with an essentially horizontal attitude. Structural benches are bedrock controlled, and in contrast to stream terraces, have no geomorphic implication of former, partial erosion cycles and base-level controls, nor do they represent a stage of flood-plain development following an episode of valley trenching.

**swale**.  A shallow, open depression in unconsolidated materials which lacks a defined channel but can funnel over-land or subsurface flow into a drainageway. Soils in swales tend to be moister and thicker (cumulic) compared to surrounding soils.

**terrace**.  A step-like surface bordering a valley floor or shoreline, that represents the former position of a flood plain, or lake or sea shore. The term is usually applied to both the relatively flat summit surface (tread), cut or built by stream or wave action, and the steeper descending slope (scarp, riser), graded to a lower base level of erosion.

**valley**.  An elongate, relatively large, externally drained depression of the Earth's surface that is primarily developed by stream erosion or glacial activity.

**wash** (dry wash).  The broad, flat-floored channel of an ephemeral stream, commonly with very steep to vertical banks cut in alluvium. Note: When channels reach intersect zones of ground-water discharge they are more properly classed as "intermittent stream" channels.

# Reference

Schoeneberger, P. J. and Wysocki, D. A. (editors). 2008. Geomorphic Description System, version 4.1. Natural Resources Conservation Service, National Soil Survey Center, Lincoln, Nebraska.

# Appendix D. Instructions for Using the MobileMapper6 GPS Unit

## 1 Locating a GRTS point

The file named, <park name>_nav.shp, must be correctly loaded into the GPS unit by the data manager, to begin. Then, follow these instructions to locate your initial GRTS destination point when establishing a transect:

1. Turn on unit (push and hold the power button on the side of the unit and release after 5 seconds).

2. Facing south, hold the unit at a 45 degree tilt—top away from you—at a comfortable height and distance from your body. Wait about 45–60 seconds for the unit to fix satellites.

3. Tap the **MobileMapper Field** icon. Select **Menu > Status**. If no satellites are fixed, close this window (upper right hand **X**) and wait another 45–60 seconds. When your reception is good, you are ready to locate your destination point.

4. Return to **Menu > Job > Open** and select the folder with the appropriate park code and select and open the layer with the name for your transect destination, e.g., "BAND_job". In **Menu > Layers**, select the layer and then select **OK** in the upper right corner.

5. In the open **Job** window, you should see a black arrowhead and multiple points marked by an "X".

6. Return to **Menu** and select **Go To**. Ensure that the correct destination file is in the **Go to** dialog box and select the destination GRTS point from the list under **LABEL**, and press **OK**.

7. Depending on your distance from the point, you can **ZOOM** - or + **ZOOM** until an arrowhead AND a red line connecting the arrowhead and your destination point clearly appear on the screen. Walk about 6–10 steps while observing the arrowhead. The arrowhead will turn and indicate the direction you are walking relative to your destination point. When the arrowhead points toward the red line and your destination point, you are headed in the right direction! When you are within a few meters of the destination coordinates, the GPS unit may lead you in a circle around the actual desired point. Return to **Menu > Status** and stand still for 60 seconds. This will report your averaged position coordinates and may be used to help refine your search if required.

## 2 Logging field locations

Follow these instructions to record GPS point positions for transect surveys:

1. If you are just now activating the GPS, power on and tap the **MobileMapper Field** icon. Go to **Menu > Job > Open** and select the folder and file named for this park. After ensuring that the unit is reading 6 or more satellites (using **Menu > Status**), make sure that the raw data recording check box is on (go to **Menu > Options > Recording** [tab at bottom of page] and select the box for the **Record Raw Data** field). This MUST BE turned on for post-processing back in the office! The unit should be collecting raw data for approximately 4–5 minutes before you log your first point at the transect, it should be placed—file still open and running—near the center point of the plot during plot setup, and it must continue recording for approximately 4–5 minutes after logging your final point at the site. You do not need to be holding the unit this entire time, but it must be receiving satellites. Also ensure that the **Units** (tab) shows "kilometers/meters" and the **Area** units are "square meters". Select **OK** in the upper right corner.

2. Go to **Menu > Options**, and, at the bottom of the page, scroll right and select the **Filter** tab. While a **Maximum PDOP** of 4 or less is best, you can increase the filter level to 6 or higher if you have heavy canopy cover. Select **OK**.

3. In **Menu**, open the existing job named for the current park. Return to the **Layers** list and ensure that the "<park name>_log.shp" layer is present and is "ON". If not, go to **Menu > Layers > Add > Select an Existing Layer** and navigate to the file in the **Template** folder.

4. To record and log a transect position, stand over the point with the GPS and face south. MobileMapper instructions recommend keeping the unit at a 45 degree tilt. In the lower left corner of the window, select **Log**. The next

window will present the layers in this job where you can record your points. Select the "<park name>_log.shp" file. At the bottom of the page, select the **Settings** tab. In the following window, the recording interval should be set to 60 seconds. The unit will begin recording your point location when you click **OK**. Hold still!

5.  After the required 60 seconds, another window will open permitting you to select each of the attribute fields where you enter or assign the requisite information. Selecting any of the attributes opens the appropriate dialog window. Most fields have drop down lists to choose from for your entry.

6.  After you have finished logging all desired points, remember to record for another 4–5 minutes and then close the unit by pushing and holding down the power button for 4–5 seconds.

# Appendix E. Integrated Upland Monitoring Protocol Database Documentation

## 1 Purpose
This appendix documents the Integrated Upland Monitoring Database for the SCPN. Microsoft Access is the primary software used to manage data.

## 2 Integrated upland database data model
The integrated upland database employs a front-end/back-end configuration. The front-end file (integrated_upland_FE_v1.0.mdb) contains the forms, queries, modules, macros, and reports, as well as a Back-End Linking Utility that allows the user to control the front-end/back-end file link. The back-end file (integrated_upland_BE_v1.0.mdb) contains the data tables. This front-end/back-end configuration allows for continual improvements to the user interface (i.e., the various forms and queries for getting data into and out of the database) without requiring duplication or modification of the underlying data tables. Figure E-1 shows the relationships among the primary tables in the database, and Tables E-1 through E-43 specifically document the tables. The database is based on the National Park Service Natural Resources Database Template (NRDT) Version 3.

## 3 Documentation of database tables
The following diagram shows the content and relationship of tables in the integrated upland database.

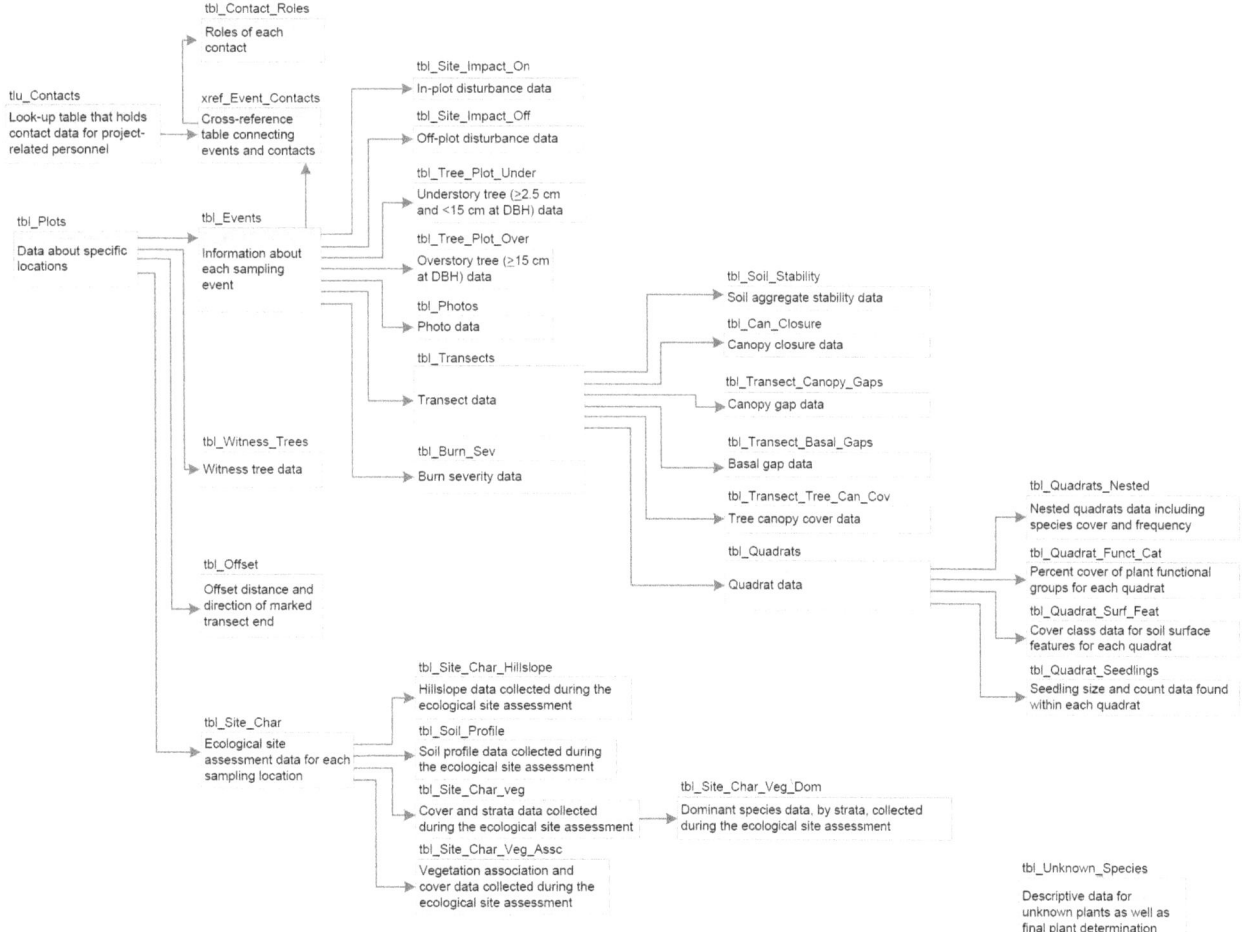

Figure E-1. Data structure of the integrated upland database

**Table E-1: *tbl_Plots*. Stores data about specific locations. There is one record for each plot.**

| Field name | Field type | Field description |
|---|---|---|
| Location_ID | ReplicationID | Primary key, plot identifier |
| Unit_Code | Text | 4-letter park code |
| Ecosite | Text | Ecological site—landscape division with specific physical characteristics that differs from other landscape divisions in its ability to produce distinctive types and amounts of vegetation, and in its response to management |
| Loc_Name | Text | Name of the plot |
| Updated_Date | Date/Time | Date of entry or last change |
| Loc_Notes | Memo | General notes on the location |
| GRTS_Point | Text | Generalized Random Tessellation Stratified sampling design point |
| Elevation | Double | Elevation (in meters) of plot centroid |
| UTMX_Centroid | Double | UTM Easting coordinate for plot centroid |
| UTMY_Centroid | Double | UTM Northing coordinate for plot centroid |
| Coord_Units | Text | Coordinate distance units |
| Coord_System | Text | Coordinate system |
| UTM_Zone | Text | UTM Zone---Either Zone 12 or Zone 13 |
| Datum | Text | Datum of mapping ellipsoid |
| Est_H_Error | Single | Estimated horizontal accuracy |
| Accuracy_Notes | Memo | Positional accuracy notes |
| Aspect | Integer | Mean plot aspect, facing downslope, in degrees |
| Azimuth_center | Integer | Transect azimuth, facing transect finish, in degrees |
| Directions | Memo | Directions to plot |
| Witness_Tree_Comments | Memo | Any comments about the witness trees |
| Comments | Memo | Overall plots establishment comments |

**Table E-2: *tbl_Events*. Stores information about each sampling event. There is one record for each sampling event.**

| Field name | Field type | Field description |
|---|---|---|
| Event_ID | ReplicationID | Primary key; sampling event identifier |
| Location_ID | ReplicationID | Foreign key; links to Location_ID in tbl_Plots |
| Protocol_Name | Text | The name of the protocol governing the event |
| Start_Date | Date/Time | Starting date for the event, in format MM/DD/YYYY |
| End_Date | Date/Time | Ending date for the event, in format MM/DD/YYYY |
| Photo_Start | Date/Time | Time transect photo collection was started |
| Tree_Plot_Start | Date/Time | Time overstory sampling started |
| Tree_Plot_End | Date/Time | Time overstory sampling ended |
| Can_Clos_Start | Date/Time | Time that canopy closure sampling started |
| Can_Clos_End | Date/Time | Time that canopy closure sampling ended |
| Can_Cov_Start | Date/Time | Time that tree canopy cover sampling started |
| Can_Cov_End | Date/Time | Time that tree canopy cover sampling ended |
| Notes | Memo | Any notes for this sampling event |
| Declination | Single | Declination of plot during this sampling event |
| No_Overstory | Yes/No | Checked if there are no overstory trees in plot |
| No_Understory | Yes/No | Checked if there are no saplings in plot |
| Data_Enterer | Text | Person who entered data |
| Data_Proofer | Text | Person who verified data |

**Table E-3: *tbl_Offset*. Holds data for when rebar marking a transect end is offset.**

| Field name | Field type | Field description |
|---|---|---|
| Location_ID | ReplicationID | Foreign key; links to Location_ID in tbl_Plots |
| Transect_Loc | Text | Location of transect that was offset (AS, BS, CS, AC, BC, CC, AF, BF, CF) |
| Offset | Single | Distance rebar is offset: (+) is towards center, (-) is away from center |

**Table E-4: *tbl_Site_Impact_On*. Contains information about in-plot disturbances.**

| Field name | Field type | Field description |
|---|---|---|
| Event_ID | ReplicationID | Foreign key; links to Event ID in tbl_Events |
| Disturbance_type_On | Text | In-plot disturbance type |
| Affected_area_size_On | Text | Size of affected area, in square meters |
| Centroid_distance | Text | Distance from plot centroid |
| Centroid_Direction | Text | Direction from plot centroid |
| Potential_Effects | Memo | Potential effect on erosional processes, fire behavior, vegetation, and soil |
| Comments_On | Memo | Additional comments about in-plot disturbance |

**Table E-5: *tbl_Site_Impact_Off*. Contains information about off-plot disturbances.**

| Field name | Field type | Field description |
|---|---|---|
| Event_ID | ReplicationID | Foreign key; links to Event ID in tbl_Events |
| Disturbance_type_Off | Text | Off-plot disturbance type |
| Affected_area_size_Off | Text | Size of area affected, in square meters |
| Plot_Distance | Text | Distance from plot |
| Plot _Direction | Text | Direction from plot |
| Potential_Effects | Memo | Potential effect on erosional processes, fire behavior, vegetation, and soil |
| Comments_Off | Memo | Additional comments about off-plot disturbance |

**Table E-6: *tbl_Tree_Plot_Under*. Holds understory tree (≥2.5 cm and <15 cm at DBH) data.**

| Field name | Field type | Field description |
|---|---|---|
| Event_ID | ReplicationID | Foreign key; links to Event ID in tbl_Events |
| Species_Name | Text | Latin name of tree |
| DBH_group | Text | Tree diameter groups: 2.5 to <5.0 cm, 5.0 to <10.0 cm, and 10.0 to <15.0 cm |
| Comments | Memo | Any notes about tree plot sampling group |
| Number_Stems | Integer | Number of stems in each DBH group |
| TSN | Long Integer | Taxonomic Serial Number – refer to tlu_Taxon for detailed taxonomic information |
| Unknown_ID | ReplicationID | Identification number for unknown species—refer to tbl_Unknown_Species |

**Table E-7: *tbl_Tree_Plot_Over*. Holds overstory tree (≥15 cm at DBH) data.**

| Field name | Field type | Field description |
|---|---|---|
| Event_ID | ReplicationID | Foreign key; links to Event ID in tbl_Events |
| ID_Number | Long Integer | Unique tree tag number (physically attached to tree) |

**Table E-7. (*continued*)**

| Field name | Field type | Field description |
|---|---|---|
| Species_Name | Text | Latin name of tree |
| DBH_DRC_1 | Single | Tree diameter taken at breast height or root crown (in centimeters). Record here if there is only one diameter measurement. |
| DBH_DRC_2 | Single | Additional tree diameter taken at breast height or root crown (in centimeters) if there is more than one stem |
| Status | Integer | Status of tree condition: 1 = live, 2 = standing dead, 3 = dead & down, 4 = dead but sprouting, 5 = cut, 6 = status unclear |
| Height | Single | Tree height in meters |
| CBH | Single | Crown base height in meters |
| Comments | Memo | Any notes about tree sampling |
| TSN | Long Integer | Taxonomic Serial Number—refer to tlu_Taxon for detailed taxonomic information |
| Unknown_ID | ReplicationID | Identification number for unknown species—refer to tbl_Unknown_Species |

**Table E-8: *tbl_Photos*. Holds photo data.**

| Field name | Field type | Field description |
|---|---|---|
| Event_ID | ReplicationID | Foreign key; links to Event ID in tbl_Events |
| AS_Photo# | Text | Number for the photo taken at the start of Transect A |
| AF_Photo# | Text | Number for the photo taken at the finish of Transect A |
| BS_Photo# | Text | Number for the photo taken at the start of Transect B |
| BF_Photo# | Text | Number for the photo taken at the finish of Transect B |
| CS_Photo# | Text | Number for the photo taken at the start of Transect C |
| CF_Photo# | Text | Number for the photo taken at the finish of Transect C |
| AS_Location | Text | Location where photo was taken for start of Transect A |
| AF_Location | Text | Location where photo was taken for finish of Transect A |
| BS_Location | Text | Location where photo was taken for start of Transect B |
| BF_Location | Text | Location where photo was taken for finish of Transect B |
| CS_Location | Text | Location where photo was taken for start of Transect C |
| CF_Location | Text | Location where photo was taken for finish of Transect C |
| Notes | Memo | Any notes for photos taken during this sampling event |

**Table E-9: *tbl_Transects*. Holds transect data (there are typically 3 transects for each sampling event).**

| Field name | Field type | Field description |
|---|---|---|
| Transect_ID | ReplicationID | Transect table row identifier |
| Event_ID | ReplicationID | Foreign key; links to Event ID in tbl_Events |
| Transect_Letter | Text | Transect A, B, or C |
| Basal_Gap_Start | Date/Time | Time that basal gap sampling started |
| Basal_Gap_End | Date/Time | Time that basal gap sampling ended |
| Canopy_Gap_Start | Date/Time | Time that canopy gap sampling started |
| Canopy_Gap_End | Date/Time | Time that canopy gap sampling ended |
| Quad_Time_Start | Date/Time | Time that quadrat sampling started |
| Quad_Time_End | Date/Time | Time that quadrat sampling ended |
| Can_Clos_Comments | Memo | Any comments about canopy closure |
| Can_Cov_Comments | Memo | Any comments about tree canopy cover |
| Notes | Memo | Any notes about the transect sampling event |

**Table E-10:** *tbl_Soil_Stability*. **Holds soil aggregate stability data.**

| Field name | Field type | Field description |
|---|---|---|
| Transect_ID | ReplicationID | Foreign key; links to Transect_ID in tbl_Transects |
| Veg | Text | Dominant vegetation cover class: NC = no perennial canopy, G = perennial grass/ grass shrub mix, F = perennial forb, S = shrub/cactus/succulent |
| Position | Single | Position along transect where soil sample was taken |
| Rating | Integer | Stability class: ratings 1–6 (see protocol) – Ranges from "1 = 50% of structural integrity lost within 5 seconds of immersion in water" to " 6 = 75–100% of soil remains on the sieve after 5 dipping cycles" |
| Sample# | Text | The sample number (order) in which the samples were taken (1–6) |

**Table E-11:** *tbl_Can_Closure*. **Holds canopy closure data.**

| Field name | Field type | Field description |
|---|---|---|
| Transect_ID | ReplicationID | Links to Transect_ID in tbl_Transects |
| Position | Integer | Position along transect |
| Finish | Integer | Canopy closure measurement taken facing the end of the transect |
| Down | Integer | Canopy closure measurement taken facing downhill |
| Start | Integer | Canopy closure measurement taken facing the start of the transect |
| Up | Integer | Canopy closure measurement taken facing uphill |

**Table E-12:** *tbl_Transect_Canopy_Gaps*. **Holds canopy gap data collected on each transect.**

| Field name | Field type | Field description |
|---|---|---|
| Transect_ID | ReplicationID | Foreign key; links to Transect_ID in tbl_Transects |
| Type | Text | Segment class: G = gap, H = herbaceous, DH = dead herbaceous, S= shrub, DS = dead shrub, C= cactus/succulent, and DC = dead cactus/succulent |
| End | Integer | End position of segment in centimeters |
| Notes | Memo | Notes about canopy gaps by transects |
| Order | Long Integer | Order that record was recorded on the datasheet |

**Table E-13:** *tbl_Transect_Basal_Gaps*. **Holds basal gap data that are collected on each transect.**

| Field name | Field type | Field description |
|---|---|---|
| Transect_ID | ReplicationID | Foreign key; links to Transect_ID in tbl_Transects |
| Start | Integer | Start of segment in centimeters |
| End | Integer | End of segment in centimeters |
| Notes | Memo | Notes about basal gaps by transect |
| Order | Long Integer | Order that record was recorded on the datasheet |

**Table E-14:** *tbl_Transect_Tree_Can_Cov*. **Holds tree canopy cover data that are collected on each transect.**

| Field name | Field type | Field description |
|---|---|---|
| Iransect_ID | ReplicationID | Foreign key; links to Transect_ID in tbl_Transects |
| Start | Integer | Start of canopy intercept in centimeters |
| End | Integer | End of canopy intercept in centimeters |

**Table E-15: *tbl_Quadrats*. Holds quadrat data. There are 5 quadrats per transect.**

| Field name | Field type | Field description |
|---|---|---|
| Quadrat_ID | ReplicationID | Unique identifier for each quadrat |
| Transect_ID | ReplicationID | Foreign key; links to Transect_ID in tbl_Transects |
| Quadrat_number | Text | Quadrat position along transect – there are five quadrats per transect |
| No_Seedlings | Yes/No | Checked if there are no seedlings – this is an error checking field. If it is checked, then there should be no related data in tbl_quadrats_seedlings. |
| No_Quad_Spp | Yes/No | Checked if there are no species in the quadrat—this is an error checking field. If it is checked, then there should be no related data in tbl_quadrats_nested. |
| No_Func_Cat | Yes/No | Checked if there are no functional categories—this is an error checking field. If it is checked, then there should be no related data in tbl_quadrat_funct_cat. |

**Table E-16: *tbl_quadrats_nested*. Holds nested quadrats data including species cover and frequency.**

| Field name | Field type | Field description |
|---|---|---|
| Quadrat_ID | ReplicationID | Links to Quadrat_ID in tbl_quadrats |
| Species | Text | Latin name of plant species |
| Alias | Text | Alternate plant name—this field is used to group species. This field is generally used for reporting purposes. |
| Q1 | Yes/No | Quadrat size = 0.01 m² —This box is checked if the listed species occurs in this quadrat (because of nested design, if a species occurs in this quadrat, it occurs in Q2, Q3, Q4, and Q5) |
| Q2 | Yes/No | Quadrat size = 0.1 m² —This box is checked if the listed species occurs in this quadrat (because of nested design, if a species occurs in this quadrat, it occurs in Q3, Q4, and Q5) |
| Q3 | Yes/No | Quadrat size = 1.0 m² —This box is checked if the listed species occurs in this quadrat (because of nested design, if a species occurs in this quadrat, it occurs in Q4 and Q5) |
| Q4 | Yes/No | Quadrat size = 5.0 m² —This box is checked if the listed species occurs in this quadrat (because of nested design, if a species occurs in this quadrat, it occurs in Q5) |
| Q5 | Yes/No | Quadrat size = 10.0 m² —This box is checked if the listed species occurs in this quadrat |
| Cover_Value | Integer | Cover value for the 10 m² plot—cover classes: 1) <0.1%, 2) 0.1 to <0.5%, 3) 0.5 to <1%, 4) 1 to <2%, 5) 2 to <5%, 6) 5 to <10%, 7) 10 to <15%, 8) 15 to <25%, 9) 25 to <35%, 10) 35 to <50%, 11) 50 to <75%, 12) 75–100% |
| TSN | Long Integer | Taxonomic Serial Number—refer to tlu_Taxon for detailed taxonomic information |
| Unknown_ID | ReplicationID | Identifier given to plants that currently are not known (this can be linked to tbl_Unknown_Species) |
| Unk_Updated | Yes/No | Notes whether an unknown species has been updated |
| cover_only | Yes/No | This box is checked if there is no frequency data but there is cover data (because it provides cover but is not rooted in the quadrat) |
| Notes | Memo | Any notes for nested quadrat data |

**Table E-17: *tbl_quadrat_funct_cat*. Holds percent cover of plant functional groups for each quadrat.**

| Field name | Field type | Field description |
|---|---|---|
| Quadrat_ID | ReplicationID | Foreign key; links to Quadrat_ID in tbl_quadrats |
| Category | Text | Functional groups: Total foliar cover; Perennial grass/Graminoids; Shrub, Forbs; Annual grass; Cactus/Succulents; Standing dead herbaceous; and Standing dead woody |
| Cover_Class | Integer | Cover classes: 1) <0.1%, 2) 0.1 to <0.5%, 3) 0.5 to <1%, 4) 1 to <2%, 5) 2 to <5%, 6) 5 to <10%, 7) 10 to <15%, 8) 15 to <25%, 9) 25 to <35%, 10) 35 to <50%, 11) 50 to <75%, 12) 75–100% |

**Table E-18: *tbl_quadrat_surf_feat*. Holds cover class data for soil surface features for each quadrat.**

| Field name | Field type | Field description |
|---|---|---|
| Quadrat_ID | ReplicationID | Foreign key; links to Quadrat_ID in tbl_quadrats |
| Surface_features | Text | Features include: Live plant base, Dead herbaceous base; Dead woody base; Duff/Litter; Undifferentiated crust; Bare soil; Woody debris (>2.5cm diam); Fine gravel (0.2 to <2 cm); Coarse gravel (2 to <7.5 cm); Cobble (7.5 to <25 cm); Stone, boulder (≥25 cm); Cyanobacteria; Lichen; and Moss |
| Cover_Class | Integer | Cover classes: 1) <0.1%, 2) 0.1 to <0.5%, 3) 0.5 to <1%, 4) 1 to <2%, 5) 2 to <5%, 6) 5 to <10%, 7) 10 to <15%, 8) 15 to <25%, 9) 25 to <35%, 10) 35 to <50%, 11) 50 to <75%, 12) 75–100% |

**Table E-19: *tbl_quadrat_seedlings*. Holds seedling size and count data found within each quadrat.**

| Field name | Field type | Field description |
|---|---|---|
| Quadrat_ID | ReplicationID | Foreign key; links to Quadrat_ID in tbl_quadrats |
| Species | Text | Latin name of seedling |
| Size_Class | Integer | Size class of seedlings: 1) 0 to <15 cm height; 2) 15 to <137 cm height; 3) 0.1 to <2.5 cm DBH; 4) <0.5 cm DRC (*Juniperus* species only); 5) 0.5 to <2.5 cm DRC (*Juniperus* species only) |
| Count | Integer | Number of seedlings for each species and size class |
| TSN | Long Integer | Taxonomic Serial Number – refer to tlu_Taxon for detailed taxonomic information |
| Unknown_ID | ReplicationID | Identifier given to plants that currently are not known (this can be linked to tbl_Unknown_Species) |

**Table E-20: *tbl_burn_sev*. Holds plot burn severity data.**

| Field name | Field type | Field description |
|---|---|---|
| Burn_Sev_ID | ReplicationID | Primary key; record identifier |
| Event_ID | ReplicationID | Foreign key; links to Event_ID in tbl_Events |
| Fire_Name | Text | Name of fire |
| Fire_Date | Text | Date the fire occurred (month and year in format MM/YYYY) |
| Fire_Type | Text | Type of fire- wildfire or prescribed |
| Plot_No_Impact | Yes/No | Checked if plot was not impacted by fire |
| Canopy_Low | Integer | Cover class code for percent total plot area where tree canopy burn severity is low (0 to <25% scorched canopy). Categories are: 1) <1%, 2) 1 to <5%, 3) 5 to <10%, 4) 10 to <25%, 5) 25 to <50%, 6) 50 to <75%, and 7) 75–100%. |
| Canopy_Low_Med | Integer | Cover class code for percent total plot area where tree canopy burn severity is low-medium (25 to <75% scorched canopy and needle consumption). Categories are: 1) <1%, 2) 1 to <5%, 3) 5 to <10%, 4) 10 to <25%, 5) 25 to <50%, 6) 50 to <75%, and 7) 75–100%. |
| Canopy_Med_High | Integer | Cover class code for percent total plot area where tree canopy burn severity is medium-high (75 to <100% scorched canopy and needle consumption). Categories are: 1) <1%, 2) 1 to <5%, 3) 5 to <10%, 4) 10 to <25%, 5) 25 to <50%, 6) 50 to <75%, and 7) 75–100%. |
| Canopy_High | Integer | Cover class code for percent total plot area where tree canopy burn severity is high (100% complete consumption of needles). Categories are: 1) <1%, 2) 1 to <5%, 3) 5 to <10%, 4) 10 to <25%, 5) 25 to <50%, 6) 50 to <75%, and 7) 75–100%. |
| Canopy_Comments | Memo | Comments about tree canopy burn severity |
| Understory_Low | Integer | Cover class code for percent total plot area where understory/substrate burn severity is low (most foliage and twigs remain intact, small organic material on ground is scorched but not entirely consumed; mineral soil is rarely exposed). Categories are: 1) <1%, 2) 1 to <5%, 3) 5 to <10%, 4) 10 to <25%, 5) 25 to <50%, 6) 50 to <75%, and 7) 75–100%. |

**Table E-20. (*continued*)**

| Field name | Field type | Field description |
|---|---|---|
| Understory_Low_Med | Integer | Cover class code for percent total plot area where understory/substrate burn severity is low-medium (majority of shrub/herbaceous layer, woody debris is scorched to partially burned; most fine organic materials are partially burned; mineral soil is intermittently exposed). Categories are: 1) <1%, 2) 1 to <5%, 3) 5 to <10%, 4) 10 to <25%, 5) 25 to <50%, 6) 50 to <75%, and 7) 75–100%. |
| Understory_Med_High | Integer | Cover class code for percent total plot area where understory/substrate burn severity is medium-high (most woody debris <7.5cm diameter is entirely consumed; most organic matter is entirely consumed; mineral soil is exposed, but remains intact; possible vigorous vegetative regrowth may be evident). Categories are: 1) <1%, 2) 1 to <5%, 3) 5 to <10%, 4) 10 to <25%, 5) 25 to <50%, 6) 50 to <75%, and 7) 75–100%. |
| Understory_High | Integer | Cover class code for percent total plot area where understory/substrate burn severity is high (all woody debris is entirely consumed, with the exception of an occasional large log; all litter and duff are consumed, exposing bare mineral soil; substantial soil erosion may be evident). Categories are: 1) <1%, 2) 1 to <5%, 3) 5 to <10%, 4) 10 to <25%, 5) 25 to <50%, 6) 50 to <75%, and 7) 75–100%. |
| Understory_Comments | Memo | Comments about understory/substrate burn severity |
| Burn_Heterogeneity | Text | Low (uniformly affected by burn), Medium (2 or 3 discrete areas of differing severities), or High (patchy distribution of differing severities) |
| Burn_Het_Comments | Memo | Comments about burn heterogeneity |

**Table E-21: *tbl_Site_Char*. Holds ecological site assessment data for each sampling location.**

| Field name | Field type | Field description |
|---|---|---|
| Site_Char_ID | ReplicationID | Primary key for Site Characterization table |
| Location_ID | ReplicationID | Foreign key; links to Location_ID in tbl_Plots |
| Event_ID | ReplicationID | Foreign key; links to Event_ID in tbl_Events |
| Date_Surveyed | Text | Date that the ecological site assessment was performed. This may differ from the date the rest of the plot data are collected. |
| Landform | Text | Landforms commonly encountered on the Colorado Plateau include alluvial fans, cuestas, hillslopes, mesas, plateaus, sand sheets, and structural benches |
| Slope_complexity | Text | Simple or complex –the relative uniformity of the ground surface leading down slope and across the plot |
| Slope_shape_down | Text | Slope curvature (linear, concave, or convex) for downslope |
| Slope_shape_across | Text | Slope curvature (linear, concave, or convex) for across slope |
| Slope_mean | Single | Average of the slopes at start, center, and finish |
| Slope_Start | Integer | Percent slope at start |
| Slope_Center | Integer | Percent slope at center |
| Slope_Finish | Integer | Percent slope at finish |
| Aspect_Start | Integer | Aspect at start |
| Aspect_Center | Integer | Aspect at center |
| Aspect_Finish | Integer | Aspect at finish |
| Aspect_Mean | Single | Average of aspect at start, center, and finish |
| Soil_Depth | Text | Depth to bedrock or a root restricting layer is measured—categories are: Very shallow (<25 cm), shallow (25 to <50 cm), Moderately deep (50 to <100 cm), Deep to very deep (≥100 cm) |
| Soil_target_match | Text | Enter Yes if the most dominant component matches the target component; if the soil component does not match the target ecological site, or if non-target components are dominant, enter "No" |

**Table E-21.** *(continued)*

| Field name | Field type | Field description |
|---|---|---|
| Prob_soil_comp | Text | Probable soil composition based on Natural Resources Conservation Service soil classifications |
| Soil_assessment_comments | Memo | Comments about soil assessment |
| Veg_target_match | Text | Enter Yes if observed vegetation is within the range of potential dynamics (natural and anthropogenic) for this ecological site |
| Phy_Class_Dominant | Text | Dominant physionomic class |
| Veg_assessment_comments | Memo | Comments about the vegetation assessment |
| Ecosite_Target_Match | Text | Yes or No; data sheet is compared with the characteristics of the target ecological site on the ecological site table to determine if observed soil and landscape characteristics reasonably match those associated with the target soil component and ecological site |
| Ecosite_Comments | Memo | Comments about the overall ecological site |
| Ecological_site_primary | Text | An estimate of the plot area (%) comprised of this site type – "Unknown" is written if unable to determine the ecological site from known information |
| Ecological_site_primary_area | Integer | Percent area for primary ecological site |
| Ecological_site_other | Text | For plots with more than one ecological site type, indicate the second-most common and the percent area |
| Ecological_site_other_area | Integer | Percent area for other ecological site |
| Site_selection | Text | Accepted or rejected – Plots will be rejected if they do not match the target ecological site, or if >30% of the total transect length crosses into another ecological site or an impermeable obstruction or cliff |
| Site_selection_comments | Memo | Comments about the site selection |

**Table E-22:** *tbl_Site_Char_Hillslope*. Holds hillslope data collected during the ecological site assessment. More than one type of hillslope can be selected per plot.

| Field name | Field type | Field description |
|---|---|---|
| Site_Char_ID | ReplicationID | Foreign key; links to Site_Char_ID in tbl_Site_Char |
| Hillslope | Text | Hillslope position for the plot. Categories include: summit, shoulder, backslope, footslope, toeslope, and NA. |

**Table E-23:** *tbl_soil_profile*. Holds soil profile data collected during the ecological site assessment.

| Field name | Field type | Field description |
|---|---|---|
| Site_Char_ID | ReplicationID | Foreign key; links to Site_Char_ID in tbl_Site_Char |
| Depth | Text | Depth category |
| Texture | Text | Soil texture description |
| Rock_fragments | Text | Rock fragment quantity and size |
| Color | Text | Soil color |
| Effervescence | Text | Soil effervescence categories include: None, Very slight, Slight, Strong, and Violent |

**Table E-24: *tbl_Site_Char_veg*. Holds cover and strata data collected during the ecological site assessment.**

| Field name | Field type | Field description |
| --- | --- | --- |
| Site_Char_ID | ReplicationID | Foreign key; links to Site_Char_ID in tbl_Site_Char |
| Stratum | Text | Vegetation stratum categories include Tree, Shrub, and Herbaceous |
| Cover_Class | Integer | Cover class of each strata. Categories are: 1) <1%, 2) 1 to <5%, 3) 5 to <10%, 4) 10 to <25%, 5) 25 to <50%, 6) 50 to <75%, and 7) 75–100%. |
| Dom_Spp_ID | Long Integer | Site characterization vegetation identifier |

**Table E-25: *tbl_Site_Char_Veg_Dom*. Holds dominant species data, by strata, collected during the ecological site assessment. There can be multiple dominant species per strata.**

| Field name | Field type | Field description |
| --- | --- | --- |
| Dom_Spp_ID | Long Integer | Foreign key; links to Dom_Spp _ID in tbl_Site_Char_Veg |
| Species | Text | Latin name of plant within each strata |
| TSN | Long Integer | Taxonomic Serial Number – refer to tlu_Taxon for detailed taxonomic information |
| Unknown_ID | Replication_ID | Identification number for unknown species—refer to tbl_Unknown_Species |

**Table E-26: *tbl_Site_Char_Veg_Assc*. Holds vegetation association and cover data collected during the ecological site assessment.**

| Field name | Field type | Field description |
| --- | --- | --- |
| Site_Char_ID | ReplicationID | Foreign key; links to Site_Char_ID in tbl_Site_Char |
| Veg_Assc | Text | Vegetation association |
| Cover | Integer | Cover class of each association. Categories are: 1) <1%, 2) 1 to <5%, 3) 5 to <10%, 4) 10 to <25%, 5) 25 to <50%, 6) 50 to <75%, and 7) 75–100%. |

**Table E-27: *xref_Event_Contacts*. Cross-reference table connecting events and contacts.**

| Field name | Field type | Field description |
| --- | --- | --- |
| Event_ID | ReplicationID | Foreign key; links to Event ID in tbl_Events |
| Contact_ID | ReplicationID | Foreign key; links to Contact_ID in tlu_Contacts |
| Role_ID | ReplicationID | Primary key for xref_Event_Contacts table |

**Table E-28: *tbl_Contact_Roles*. Lists the roles of each contact.**

| Field name | Field type | Field description |
| --- | --- | --- |
| Role_ID | ReplicationID | Foreign key; links to Role_ID in xref_Event_Contacts |
| Role | Text | The role the contact played during this sampling event |

**Table E-29: *tlu_Contacts*. Look-up table that holds contact data for project-related personnel.**

| Field name | Field type | Field description |
| --- | --- | --- |
| Contact_ID | ReplicationID | Primary key for tlu_Contacts |
| Last_Name | Text | Last name of individual |
| First_Name | Text | First name of individual |
| Middle_Init | Text | Middle initial of individual |
| Organization | Text | Organization or employer |
| Position_Title | Text | Individual's title or position |

**Table E-29. (*continued*)**

| Field name | Field type | Field description |
| --- | --- | --- |
| Address_Type | Text | Address type: mailing, physical, or both |
| Address | Text | Street address |
| Address2 | Text | Address line 2, suit, apartment number |
| City | Text | City or town |
| State_Code | Text | State or province |
| Zip_Code | Text | Postal zip code |
| Country | Text | Country |
| Email_Address | Text | E-mail address |
| Work_Phone | Text | Work phone number |
| Work_Extension | Text | Extension for work phone number |
| Contact_Notes | Memo | Any notes about contact |
| Active | Yes/No | Check if the contact is for the current year |

**Table E-30: *tbl_Witness_Trees*. Holds witness tree data.**

| Field name | Field type | Field description |
| --- | --- | --- |
| Location_ID | ReplicationID | Foreign key; links to Location_ID in tbl_Plots |
| Start_Finish | Text | Transect letter plus start/finish—either AS, AF, BS, BF, CS, or CF |
| Tree_ID | Integer | Identification number of witness tree |
| Distance | Single | Distance from transect end to witness tree |
| Azimuth | Integer | Direction of witness tree from transect |
| Species | Text | Latin name of witness tree |

**Table E-31: *tlu_Taxon*. Look-up table for taxonomic information about plants.**

| Field name | Field type | Field description |
| --- | --- | --- |
| FullLatinName | Text | Latin name of plant |
| FamilyName | Text | Taxonomic family to which the species belongs |
| TSN | Long Integer | Taxonomic Serial Number – unique taxon identifier assigned by Integrated Taxonomic Information System (ITIS) |
| LocalAcceptedTSN | Long Integer | Locally accepted Taxonomic Serial Number – unique taxon identifier assigned by ITIS |
| Exotic | Yes/No | Checked if species is exotic |
| GrowthHabit | Text | Growth habit for species |
| New_Entry | Yes/No | Tracks entry of new taxonomic records |

**Table E-32: *tbl_Db_Revisions*. Holds database revision history data.**

| Field name | Field type | Field description |
| --- | --- | --- |
| Revision_ID | Text | Database revision (version) number or code |
| Revision_Contact_ID | ReplicationID | Foreign key; link to tlu_Contacts |
| Revision_Date | Date/Time | Database revision date |
| Revision_Reason | Memo | Reason for the database revision |
| Revision_Desc | Memo | Revision description |

**Table E-33: *tbl_Field_Errors*. Stores the total number of errors per field. Data stored is temporary and is deleted after each calculation of total of field errors.**

| Field name | Field type | Field description |
|---|---|---|
| Field | Text | Field in table that was corrected for errors |
| Total_Errors | Integer | Total number of errors made in the field |

**Table E-34: *tbl_Proof*. Table that tracks which plots were verified, as well as the date and person who verified the data.**

| Field name | Field type | Field description |
|---|---|---|
| Start_Date | Date/Time | Sampling event date, in format MM/DD/YYYY |
| Event_ID | ReplicationID | Event record identifier |
| Unit_Code | Text | 4-letter unit code of park |
| Loc_Name | Text | Name of plot |
| Proofed | Text | Indicates whether or not record was proofed |
| Proof_Count | Integer | The number of times the record was proofed |
| Corrected | Yes/No | Indicates if record was corrected for errors |
| Proof_Date | Date/Time | Date record was proofed |
| Proof_Reader | Text | Person who proofed the record |

**Table E-35: *tbl_Proof_Tracking*. Tracks error corrections. Used to populate tbl_Field_Data and generate reports.**

| Field name | Field type | Field description |
|---|---|---|
| Event_Date | Text | Sampling event date, in format MM/DD/YYYY |
| Field | Text | Field in table that was corrected for errors |
| Proof_Date | Date/Time | Date the record was proofed |
| Was | Memo | Describes what the corrected field originally contained |
| Changed_To | Memo | Describes what the corrected field was changed to |
| Park | Text | Park where the event took place |
| Plot | Text | Plot identifier for the event |

**Table E-36: *tbl_Unknown_Species*. Holds descriptive data for unknown plants as well as final plant determination.**

| Field name | Field type | Field description |
|---|---|---|
| Unknown_ID | ReplicationID | Unique record identifier for unknown species |
| UnknownIDCode | Text | Plant code assigned during field work |
| Family | Text | Taxonomic family to which the species belongs |
| Genus | Text | Taxonomic genus to which the species belongs |
| Species | Text | Latin species name |
| Photo_Number | Text | Photo identification number |
| Life_Form | Text | Plant type: herb, graminoid, subshrub, shrub, tree, vine, cactus, aquatic |
| Salient_Features | Memo | Salient features of plant |
| Collected | Yes/No | Checked if plant was collected |
| Growing_With | Memo | Other plants specimen was growing with |
| Habitat_Desc | Memo | Habitat description |

**Table E-36.** *(continued)*

| Field name | Field type | Field description |
|---|---|---|
| Determination | Text | Confirmed species name |
| TSN | Long Integer | Taxonomic Serial Number – refer to tlu_Taxon for detailed taxonomic information |
| Determined_By | Text | Who determined the plant taxon |
| Determination_Date | Text | Date the plant was determined, in format YYYYMMDD |
| UTM E | Double | UTM Easting for collection location |
| UTM N | Double | UTM Northing for collection location |

**Table E-37:** *tlu_Cover.* **Look-up table of cover classes and codes used in nested quadrats.**

| Field name | Field type | Field description |
|---|---|---|
| Code_07 | Integer | Cover class codes used in 2007 |
| Range_07 | Text | Percent cover ranges used in 2007 |
| Midpoint | Single | Midpoint of class ranges |
| Code_08 | Integer | Cover class codes used in all years except 2007 |
| Range_08 | Text | Percent cover ranges used in all years except 2007 |

**Table E-38:** *tlu_Parks.* **Look-up table of SCPN parks.**

| Field name | Field type | Field description |
|---|---|---|
| Unit_Code | Text | 4-letter park code |
| Park | Text | Park name |

**Table E-39:** *tlu_Dom_Phys.* **Look-up table of dominant physiognomic types.**

| Field name | Field type | Field description |
|---|---|---|
| Type | Text | Dominant physiognomic type |
| Canopy_Cov_Type | Text | Canopy cover and type |
| Canopy_Ht | Text | Canopy height |

**Table E-40:** *tlu_quadrat_funct_cat.* **Look-up table of quadrat functional categories.**

| Field name | Field type | Field description |
|---|---|---|
| Functional_Cat | Text | Functional categories |
| Order | Integer | Used to order functional categories on data entry forms |

**Table E-41:** *tlu_quadrat_surf_feat.* **Look-up table of quadrat surface features.**

| Field name | Field type | Field description |
|---|---|---|
| Surface_Features | Text | Surface features |
| Order | Integer | Used to order surface features on data entry forms |
| Size | Text | Size ranges of surface features |

**Table E-42: *tlu_Roles*. Look-up table of personnel roles.**

| Field name | Field type | Field description |
|---|---|---|
| Role | Text | Personnel roles or duties |

**Table E-43 *tlu_witness_trees*. Look-up table of witness trees.**

| Field name | Field type | Field description |
|---|---|---|
| Transect | Text | Transect letter |
| Witness_tree | Text | Witness tree location |

# Appendix F. Example Annual Data Summary Report

Integrated Upland Vegetation and Soils Monitoring for Mesa Verde National Park: 2009 Summary Report

National Park Service
U.S. Department of the Interior

Natural Resource Program Center

# Integrated Upland Vegetation and Soils Monitoring for Mesa Verde National Park

*2009 Summary Report*

Natural Resource Data Series NPS/SCPN/NRDS—2011/172

ON THE COVER
Loamy Mesa Top Pinyon-Juniper ecological site at Mesa Verde National Park
Photograph by: Jim DeCoster

# Integrated Upland Vegetation and Soils Monitoring for Mesa Verde National Park

*2009 Summary Report*

Natural Resource Data Series NPS/SCPN/NRDS—2011/172

James K. DeCoster
Megan C. Swan

National Park Service
Southern Colorado Plateau Network
Northern Arizona University
P.O. Box 5765
Flagstaff, AZ 86011-5765

June 2011

U.S. Department of the Interior
National Park Service
Natural Resource Program Center
Fort Collins, Colorado

Funding for the SCPN upland field crew was provided to Northern Arizona University by the National Park Service through Colorado Plateau CESU Agreement H1200040002 (Tasks NAU-285/289).

This report is available from the Southern Colorado Plateau Network website (http://science.nature.nps.gov/im/units/scpn/) and the Natural Resource Publications Management website (http://www.nature.nps.gov/publications/nrpm/).

The corresponding author and project manager for this project is Jim DeCoster (jim_decoster@nps.gov). Megan Swan is the botanist and crew leader for the project. Other contributions were made by the SCPN staff. The 2009 field crew consisted of Teresa DeKoker, Lara Dickson, Hillary Hudson, and Steve Till.

Please cite this publication as:

DeCoster, J. K., and M. C. Swan. 2011. Integrated upland vegetation and soils monitoring for Mesa Verde National Park: 2009 summary report. Natural Resource Data Series NPS/SCPN/NRDS—2011/172. National Park Service, Fort Collins, Colorado.

NPS 307/107811, June 2011

# Introduction and Background

The National Park Service Inventory and Monitoring (I&M) Program was designed to determine the status and monitor the conditions of park natural resources, providing park managers with a strong scientific foundation that informs resource management decisions. The Southern Colorado Plateau Network (SCPN) is monitoring vegetation and soils as overall indicators of upland ecosystem integrity (Thomas et al. 2006).

SCPN and park staff selected the Loamy Mesa Top Pinyon-Juniper ecological site for long-term monitoring of upland vegetation and soils at Mesa Verde National Park (MEVE). An ecological site is a landscape division with characteristic soils, hydrology, plant communities, and disturbance regimes and responses, and its classification is based on soil survey data (Butler et al. 2003). The Loamy Mesa Top Pinyon-Juniper woodland is a unique ecosystem containing old-growth pinyon-juniper woodland. It faces numerous threats, including changing fire regimes, climate change, and invasion by nonnative species.

In 2007 the Integrated Upland Monitoring program of SCPN began monitoring upland sites at MEVE with the installation of 10 plots in the Loamy Mesa Top Pinyon-Juniper ecological site. We have sampled the quadrats and gap intercept transects annually for three years to determine the range of temporal variability for key metrics. In this report, we document monitoring activities in the 2009 field season and compare these data with the data collected in 2007 and 2008.

# Methods

## Sampling frame

We derived the sampling frame from the map of the Loamy Mesa Top Pinyon-Juniper ecological site, which was developed by the US Natural Resources Conservation Service (See Appendix A of De-Coster et al., in review). The sampling frame is the area from which we randomly select our sites, and hence the area to which statistical inferences can be made. To create the sampling frame, we modified the map of the ecological site using Geographical Information System (GIS) technology. These modifications were necessary to avoid areas that were

- outside of the target ecological site (roads, buildings and other infrastructure)

- expected to differ substantially from the norm, such as burned areas and mechanically treated areas, because these areas would have increased ecological variation and made it more difficult to detect trends

- potentially at risk for erosion as a result of sampling (slopes ≥20%)

- containing arthropod monitoring sites (fig. 1).

We generated a set of spatially distributed sampling points using the Generalized Random Tessellation Stratified (GRTS) design (Stevens and Olsen 2004). Park staff reviewed the sampling points and rejected those points that landed too close to archaeological sites and other sensitive resources. Before establishing a plot, the Integrated Upland crew conducted an ecological site assessment for each sampling point and rejected sites that did not fall within the ecological site, had a slope greater than 20%, or contained a major disturbance. Twelve points were rejected. Park staff rejected 9 points that were determined to be too close to archaeological sites. The Integrated Upland crew rejected one point that was located in the Shallow Loamy Mesa Top Pinyon-Juniper ecological site and two

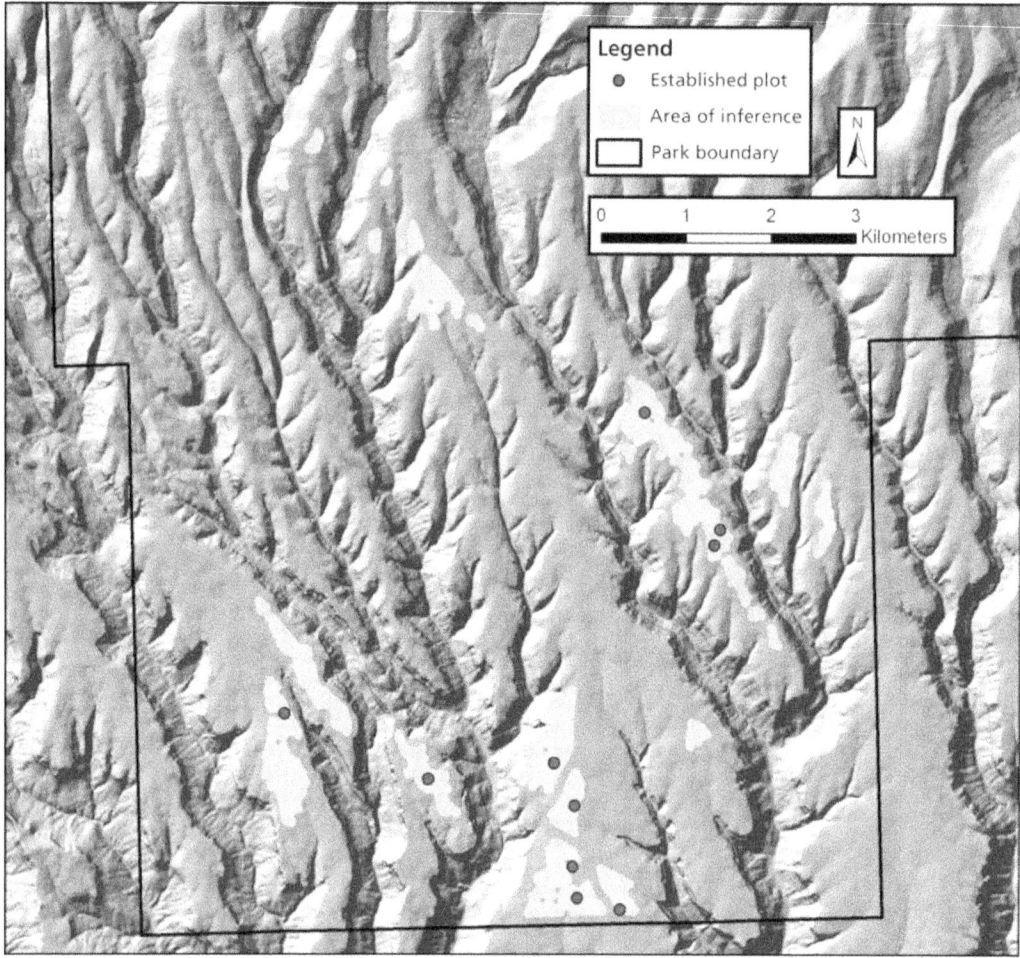

**Figure 1**. Sampling frame of the Loamy Mesa Top Pinyon-Juniper ecological site showing 10 plots sampled in 2007, 2008, and 2009

points located on the far north side of the ecological site that were distinctly different from the rest of the ecological site.

## Field methods

In 2009, the SCPN Upland Monitoring crew sampled the same 10 plots that were established at MEVE in 2007. The plots were 0.50 ha in size, measuring 71 × 71 m. Shrub and herbaceous data and soil data were collected on three 50 m transects, spaced 25 m apart, within each plot. Overstory tree and sapling data were collected in subplots located between two of the transects. In all three years the crew collected the data from the plots in early August. Field methodology is provided in detail in the SCPN Integrated Upland Protocol (DeCoster et al., in review).

### Shrub and herbaceous vegetation

The crew sampled shrub and herbaceous vegetation within five sets of nested quadrats at 10 m intervals along each transect. The largest quadrat size was 10 m² (2 × 5 m), with four smaller quadrats nested inside (0.01 m², 0.1 m², 1 m², 5 m²). For each nested sub-quadrat we recorded the presence of individual vascular species. For each 10 m² quadrat we estimated percent cover for herbaceous and shrub species and recorded it as one of 12 cover classes (e.g. 2%–5%, 5%–10%, etc.). We also estimated the percent cover for functional groups (e.g. perennial grasses, forbs, shrubs) in the 10 m² quadrats and recorded the cover class for each.

## Overstory trees and saplings

We measured and mapped trees in 2007, but did not remeasure them in 2008 or 2009. However, we did assess tree canopy in 2008 and 2009. In 2008 we measured tree canopy closure with a hemispherical densiometer at five points along each transect; in 2009 a different aspect of tree canopy, canopy cover, was measured using the line intercept method along the transects.

## Soil stability and hydrologic function

The crew estimated the percent cover of soil surface features in the 1 m² quadrats in conjunction with shrub and herbaceous data and recorded the cover in one of 12 cover classes. A soil aggregate stability test was conducted in 2007, using 18 soil samples collected along the transects. This procedure was not repeated in 2008 or 2009.

## Data summary

The sample unit for summary and analysis is the plot; hence, we summarized data at the level of the plot. In order to calculate summary statistics for the ecological site, means and standard deviations were calculated from the plot means.

For herbaceous and shrub vegetation, cover was calculated for each species from the cover class midpoints, e.g. using 7.5% for cover class 5%–10%. The mean cover was calculated for each plot, and the mean and standard deviation (SD) were calculated for the ecological site from the plot means. Species frequency was calculated for quadrats (mean percentage of quadrats per plot where the species occurs) and for plots (percentage of plots where the species occurs). Mean cover and SD of functional groups and surface features were calculated in a similar fashion.

We calculated four diversity measures for herbaceous and shrub species (Magurran 1988), first for all species and then for native species only.

(1) Species richness (S) is the number of species at a given spatial scale, and it was calculated at the level of the plot and at the level of the ecological site.

(2) The Shannon Diversity Index (H′) provides a measure of species diversity that takes into account the relative abundance of each species:

$$- \sum_{i=1}^{n} p_i \ln p_i$$

where $p_i$ is the abundance of each species.

(3) Species evenness (E) is a measure of the degree to which all species are equal in abundance:

$$H′ / \ln(S)$$

(4) Beta diversity ($\beta_w$) is a measure of within-ecological site heterogeneity:

$$S_e / (S_p - 1)$$

where $S_e$ is the total number of species found in the ecological site, and $S_p$ is the mean number of species found per plot.

Canopy closure and canopy cover were calculated by first deriving for the mean for each plot, and then the mean and standard deviation were calculated for the entire ecological site.

We made five calculations for the basal gaps data: median basal gap size, percentage of transects comprised by gaps and plant bases, percentage of transects comprised by each size class, and total number of gaps. Mean and SD were calculated for each metric.

# Results

### Shrub and herbaceous vegetation

Perennial grasses dominated herbaceous/shrub vegetation of the Loamy Mesa Top Pinyon-Juniper ecological site at MEVE (table 1 and fig. 2) with less cover of shrubs, forbs, and cacti/succulents. Total live vegetative cover showed a large decrease in 2008, from 14.17% to 10.05%. This change, however, is largely due to slight changes in methods: in 2007, tree foliar cover (< 2 m in height) was included in the estimation of total live vegetative cover, but tree cover was not included in 2008. Also, standing dead woody cover in 2007 included trees (< 2 m) and shrubs, but in 2008 and 2009 standing dead woody cover included only shrubs. While there were some changes in the cover of the other functional groups, most of these changes were small, particularly in light of the large among-plot variability, as indicated by the large standard deviations.

**Table 1**. Mean foliar cover of functional groups for 2007, 2008, and 2009

| | Foliar cover (%) | | | | | |
| | 2007 | | 2008 | | 2009 | |
| Functional groups | Mean | (SD) | Mean | (SD) | Mean | (SD) |
|---|---|---|---|---|---|---|
| Total live foliar cover | 14.17 | (4.80) | 10.05 | (6.25) | 9.46 | (5.17) |
| Perennial grasses, graminoids | 4.67 | (3.12) | 4.01 | (2.38) | 4.40 | (2.73) |
| Annual grasses | <0.01 | (0.01) | <0.01 | (<.01) | <0.01 | (<0.01) |
| Forbs | 0.94 | (0.77) | 1.19 | (0.66) | 0.94 | (0.47) |
| Shrubs | 2.30 | (2.61) | 2.82 | (3.50) | 2.67 | (2.87) |
| Cacti, succulents | 1.29 | (0.10) | 1.17 | (0.86) | 1.26 | (1.03) |
| Understory trees (<2 m height) | 5.17 | (2.56) | n/a | n/a | n/a | n/a |
| Standing dead herbaceous | 2.28 | (1.45) | 1.34 | (0.82) | 0.99 | (0.54 |
| Standing dead woody | 2.10 | (1.02) | 2.16 | (2.18) | 1.36 | (1.165) |

*Note:* Understory tree cover was only measured in 2007, and was included in the total foliar cover.

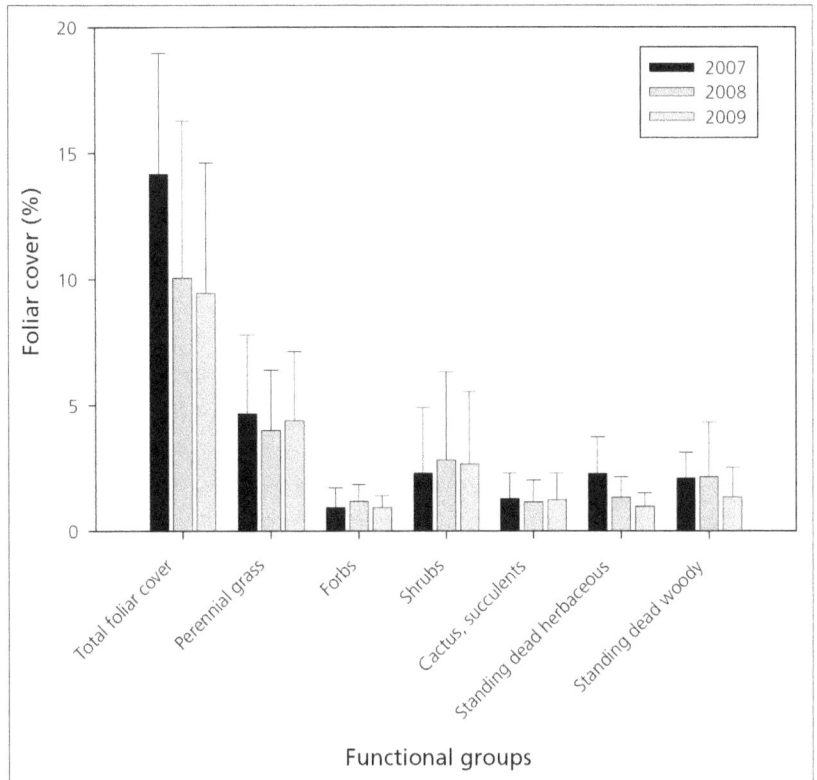

**Figure 2.** Mean cover of functional groups in 2007, 2008, and 2009. Note: means for total foliar and standing dead woody cover in 2007 include tree components. Error bars represent one standard deviation.

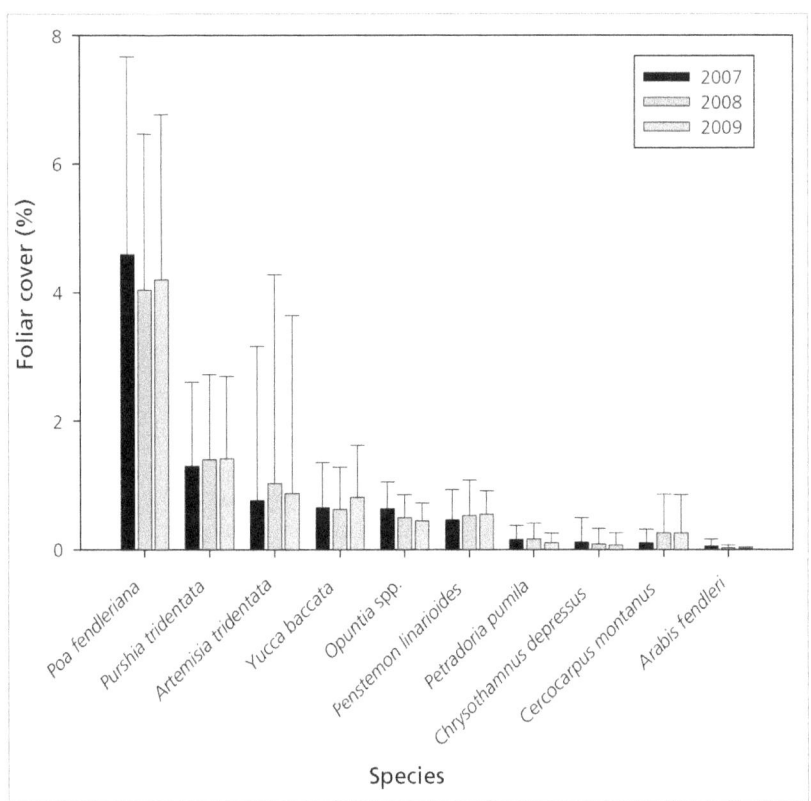

**Figure 3.** Mean foliar cover of the ten most abundant shrub and herbaceous species in 2007, 2008, and 2009. Error bars represent one standard deviation.

**Table 2**. Foliar cover and frequency of the fifteen most abundant vascular species and all nonnative species in 2007, 2008, and 2009

| Species | 2007 Mean cover (%) | SD | Quad freq | Plot freq | 2008 Mean cover (%) | SD | Quad freq | Plot freq | 2009 Mean cover (%) | SD | Quad freq | Plot freq |
|---|---|---|---|---|---|---|---|---|---|---|---|---|
| Poa fendleriana | 4.596 | 3.077 | 96.67 | 100 | 4.042 | 2.427 | 96.00 | 100 | 4.202 | 2.572 | 96.67 | 100 |
| Purshia tridentata | 1.297 | 1.306 | 48.00 | 90 | 1.398 | 1.326 | 50.67 | 90 | 1.412 | 1.287 | 46.67 | 90 |
| Artemisia tridentata | 0.760 | 2.404 | 10.00 | 10 | 1.028 | 3.252 | 10.00 | 10 | 0.875 | 2.767 | 10.00 | 10 |
| Yucca baccata | 0.651 | 0.703 | 32.00 | 80 | 0.628 | 0.654 | 32.67 | 70 | 0.813 | 0.809 | 30.00 | 70 |
| Opuntia spp. | 0.636 | 0.415 | 50.67 | 90 | 0.496 | 0.359 | 51.33 | 90 | 0.448 | 0.277 | 49.33 | 90 |
| Penstemon linarioides | 0.462 | 0.468 | 78.67 | 100 | 0.527 | 0.555 | 83.33 | 100 | 0.551 | 0.361 | 82.00 | 100 |
| Petradoria pumila | 0.158 | 0.217 | 14.67 | 50 | 0.165 | 0.246 | 16.67 | 50 | 0.108 | 0.150 | 18.67 | 50 |
| Chrysothamnus depressus | 0.119 | 0.375 | 8.67 | 30 | 0.087 | 0.242 | 11.33 | 40 | 0.067 | 0.196 | 10.00 | 40 |
| Cercocarpus montanus | 0.104 | 0.214 | 10.00 | 30 | 0.261 | 0.596 | 10.67 | 30 | 0.261 | 0.593 | 9.33 | 30 |
| Arabis fendleri | 0.054 | 0.109 | 20.67 | 90 | 0.026 | 0.043 | 16.67 | 70 | 0.015 | 0.026 | 10.67 | 60 |
| Phlox hoodii | 0.031 | 0.062 | 10.67 | 40 | 0.030 | 0.051 | 14.00 | 40 | 0.037 | 0.062 | 14.67 | 40 |
| Cordylanthus wrightii | 0.029 | 0.033 | 27.33 | 80 | 0.080 | 0.087 | 33.33 | 90 | 0.059 | 0.083 | 46.00 | 90 |
| Eriogonum racemosum | 0.028 | 0.037 | 20.00 | 80 | 0.053 | 0.059 | 22.00 | 80 | 0.036 | 0.049 | 22.00 | 80 |
| Gutierrezia sarothrae | 0.021 | 0.065 | 4.00 | 10 | 0.023 | 0.073 | 4.67 | 10 | 0.017 | 0.051 | 5.33 | 30 |
| Comandra umbellata | 0.020 | 0.05 | 10.00 | 30 | 0.033 | 0.083 | 10.00 | 30 | 0.032 | 0.072 | 8.67 | 20 |
| Descurainia sophia [a] | 0.008 | 0.016 | 10.67 | 40 | 0 | 0 | 0 | 0 | 0 | 0 | 0 | 0 |
| Bromus tectorum [a] | 0.007 | 0.011 | 6.67 | 50 | 0.001 | 0.002 | 2.00 | 20 | 0.001 | 0.002 | 2.00 | 30 |
| Ceratocephala testiculata [a] | 0.005 | 0.009 | 10.00 | 50 | 0 | 0 | 0 | 0 | 0.001 | 0.004 | 2.67 | 10 |
| Sisymbrium altissimum [a] | 0.002 | 0.005 | 3.33 | 10 | 0.002 | 0.006 | 4.67 | 20 | 0.005 | 0.012 | 6.67 | 20 |
| Carduus nutans [a] | 0.001 | 0.002 | 2.00 | 30 | 0.001 | 0.002 | 2.67 | 40 | 0 | 0 | 0 | 0 |
| Taraxacum officinale [a] | 0.001 | 0.001 | 1.33 | 20 | 0 | 0 | 0 | 0 | 0 | 0 | 0 | 0 |
| Erodium cicutarium [a] | <0.001 | 0.001 | 0.67 | 10 | 0 | 0 | 0 | 0 | 0 | 0 | 0 | 0 |
| Tragopogon dubius [a] | 0 | 0 | 0 | 0 | 0 | 0 | 0 | 0 | <0.001 | 0.001 | 0.67 | 10 |

Note: Species are arranged in descending order by their 2007 cover.

[a] Nonnative species.

The dominant grass was *Poa fendleriana* (muttongrass); the domninant shrubs were *Purshia tridentata* (antelope bitterbrush), *Chrysothamnus depressus* (longflower rabbitbrush) and *Cercocarpus montanus* (birchleaf mountain mahoghany); the dominant succulents were *Opuntia* spp. (prickly pear) and *Yucca baccata* (banana yucca); and the dominant forbs were *Penstemon linariodes* (toadflax penstemon) and *Petradoria pumila* (rock goldenrod). Like the functional groups, foliar cover of individual species differed among the three years, but most of these changes were quite small, especially considering the large standard deviations (table 2 and fig. 3). There was no overall pattern in cover changes among species; some species had their greatest cover in 2007, others had their greatest cover in 2008, and still others had their greatest cover in 2009.

Quadrat and plot frequencies did not change substantially between years, with a few exceptions: *Arabis fendleri* (Fendler rockcress) showed a gradual decrease in quadrat and plot frequency over the three years, and *Cordylanthus wrightii* (Wright bird's beak) showed an increase in quadrat and plot frequency over the three years. A number of species were not present in the plots in all three years. Some species were present in only one of the three years and are referred to here as unique species. Others were present in two of the three years. In 2007, there were nine unique species (not including the two unknowns), In 2008 there were two, and in 2009 there were five (See Appendix A).

In 2007, we found seven nonnative species in the plots. Only three of these species were found in 2008. Three nonnative species were also found in 2009, including one species not found previously: *Tragopogon dubius* (yellow salsify). Appendix A lists all species, along with common names, families, mean foliar covers, and plot frequencies by year.

Diversity indices varied among the three years (table 3). On the scale of the plot, species richness varied between 19.2 to 18.2 species per plot. Shannon diversity (which takes into account relative species abundance, and generally ranges between 1.5 and 3.5) ranged between 1.346 and 1.506, and evenness (the degree to which all species are of equal abundance, ranging from 0 to 1) ranged between 0.458 and 0.524 (Margalef 1972). On the scale of the ecological site, species richness ranged between 57 and 49 species, and beta diversity (a measure of within site heterogeneity, generally ranging between 1 and 5) ranged between 2.849 and 3.132 (McClune and Grace 2002). When these

**Table 3**. Species diversity metrics for all species and for native species only

| | 2007 | | 2008 | | 2009 | |
|---|---|---|---|---|---|---|
| | Mean | (SD) | Mean | (SD) | Mean | (SD) |
| **All species** | | | | | | |
| Plot | | | | | | |
| Plot richness | 19.2 | (5.1) | 18.2 | (4.2) | 18.4 | (5.0) |
| Shannon diversity | 1.346 | (0.347) | 1.506 | (0.264) | 1.443 | (0.238) |
| Evenness | 0.458 | (0.101) | 0.524 | (0.092) | 0.501 | (0.069) |
| Ecological site | | | | | | |
| Ecological site richness | 57 | | 49 | | 51 | |
| Beta diversity | | | | | | |
| **Native species** | | | | | | |
| Plot | | | | | | |
| Plot richness | 17.1 | (4.8) | 17.3 | (4.0) | 17.7 | (4.9) |
| Shannon diversity | 1.324 | (0.334) | 1.500 | (0.262) | 1.435 | (0.233) |
| Evenness | 0.469 | (0.101) | 0.531 | (0.093) | 0.505 | (0.073) |
| Ecological site | | | | | | |
| Ecological site richness | 50 | | 45 | | 47 | |
| Beta diversity | 3.106 | | 2.761 | | 2.814 | |

indices were recalculated using only native species, all indices were slightly lower, except evenness, which was higher.

## Trees

Tree diameters were not remeasured in 2008 or 2009, but tree canopy was assessed in both years. To help determine the best way to measure canopy we used a different methodology each year. In 2008 we measured canopy closure using a hemispherical densiometer. Mean canopy closure was 50.8% with a standard deviation of 15.6. In 2009, we measured canopy cover using the line intercept method, measuring the amount of canopy cover intersecting the three transects. Mean canopy cover was 37.4% with a standard deviation of 9.2%. Canopy closure refers to the proportion of the hemisphere of sky obscured by vegetation when viewed from a single point; canopy cover measures the proportion of the forest floor covered by the vertical projection of tree crowns (Jennings et al. 1999).

## Soil stability and hydrologic function

The crew monitored the amount of exposed soil in two ways: cover estimates of soil surface features in quadrats and measurements of basal gaps along transects. These measurements were undertaken in all three years. As expected, most changes in the surface features were relatively small (table 4 and fig. 4). However, three features—undifferentiated crust, bare soil and cyanobacteria—showed large variation among years: (table 4 and fig. 4). The basal gap data is difficult to interpret due to a change in protocol. In 2007 we did not include gaps < 20 cm in our measurement, hence the percentage of plant bases along the transect includes both plant bases and these small gaps (table 5 and fig. 5).

**Table 4**. Cover of soil surface features

| Surface feature | 2007 Mean (%) | (SD) | 2008 Mean (%) | (SD) | 2009 Mean (%) | (SD) |
|---|---|---|---|---|---|---|
| Live plant base | 3.02 | (1.81) | 3.34 | (1.62) | 3.22 | (1.68) |
| Dead woody base | 0.28 | (0.39) | 1.04 | (1.73) | 0.46 | (0.68) |
| Dead herbaceous base [a] | 0 | (0) | 0.75 | (0.44) | 0.53 | (0.31) |
| Bare soil | 0.84 | (0.74) | 1.14 | (1.08) | 5.43 | (4.66) |
| Duff and litter | 58.16 | (13.62) | 56.72 | (9.31) | 60.65 | (7.63) |
| Undifferentiated crust | 18.46 | (12.86) | 26.83 | (10.27) | 20.79 | (11.22) |
| Moss | 2.11 | (1.69) | 1.47 | (1.54) | 0.72 | (0.67) |
| Lichen | 0.15 | (0.26) | 0.14 | (0.19) | 0.16 | (0.24) |
| Cyanobacteria | 8.65 | (4.65) | 3.71 | (4.72) | 3.26 | (3.99) |
| Fine gravel (0.2–2 cm) | 0.01 | (0.01) | 0.02 | (0.03) | 0.01 | (0.03) |
| Coarse gravel (2–7.5 cm) | 0.06 | (0.10) | 0.06 | (0.11) | 0.07 | (0.09) |
| Cobble (7.5–25 cm) | 0.14 | (0.42) | 0.02 | (0.04) | 0.02 | (0.03) |
| Stone, bedrock (>25 cm) | 0 | (0) | 0 | (0) | 0.12 | (0.34) |
| Woody debris | 1.42 | (0.76) | 1.80 | (0.90) | 2.06 | (1.02) |

*Note*: The surface feature components do not add up to 100% because the calculations were made from cover class midpoints, and the estimations have observer error.

[a]Dead herbaceous base was not measured in 2007.

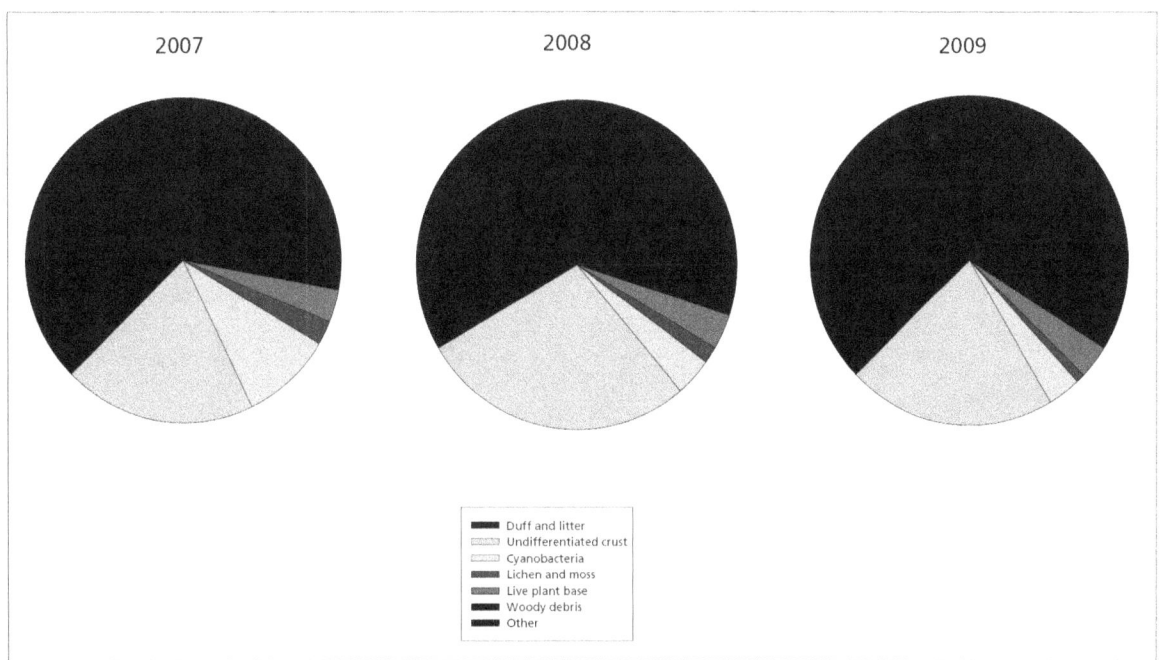

**Figure 4**. Mean cover of soil surface features in 2007, 2008, and 2009

**Table 5**. Number of basal gaps, median gap size, and percentage of transect in different gap size classes in 2007, 2008, and 2009

| Metric | 2007 Mean | (SD) | 2008 Mean | (SD) | 2009 Mean | (SD) |
|---|---|---|---|---|---|---|
| Number of gaps | 51.60 | (20.48) | 124.1 | (52.8) | 94.1 | (43.8) |
| Median gap size (cm) | 194.20 | (106.23) | 83.0 | (59.8) | 94.8 | (37.6) |
| Percent of transect in gaps 0–19 cm | n/a | n/a | 1.86 | (1.18) | 1.14 | (0.94) |
| Percent of transect in gaps 20–49 cm | 1.87 | (1.26) | 5.78 | (3.31) | 4.49 | (3.13) |
| Percent of transect in gaps 50–99 cm | 5.14 | (2.66) | 12.25 | (7.34) | 9.28 | (5.08) |
| Percent of transect in gaps ≥100 cm | 90.46 | (4.48) | 76.87 | (12.62) | 81.70 | (10.03) |
| Percent of transect in gaps | 97.46 | (1.43) | 96.75 | (1.62) | 96.61 | (1.75) |
| Percent of transect in plant bases | 2.54 | n/a | 3.25 | (1.62) | 3.39 | (1.76) |

*Note*: Gaps were measured slightly differently in 2007. Gaps <20 cm were not measured and are included with plant bases.

There is substantial among year variation in some of the metrics.

## Discussion

The data presented here indicate relatively small variation in the vegetation and surface features in the Loamy Mesa Top Pinyon-Juniper ecological site among the years 2007, 2008, and 2009. Variation in functional group cover and species cover and frequencies were minor, especially considering the

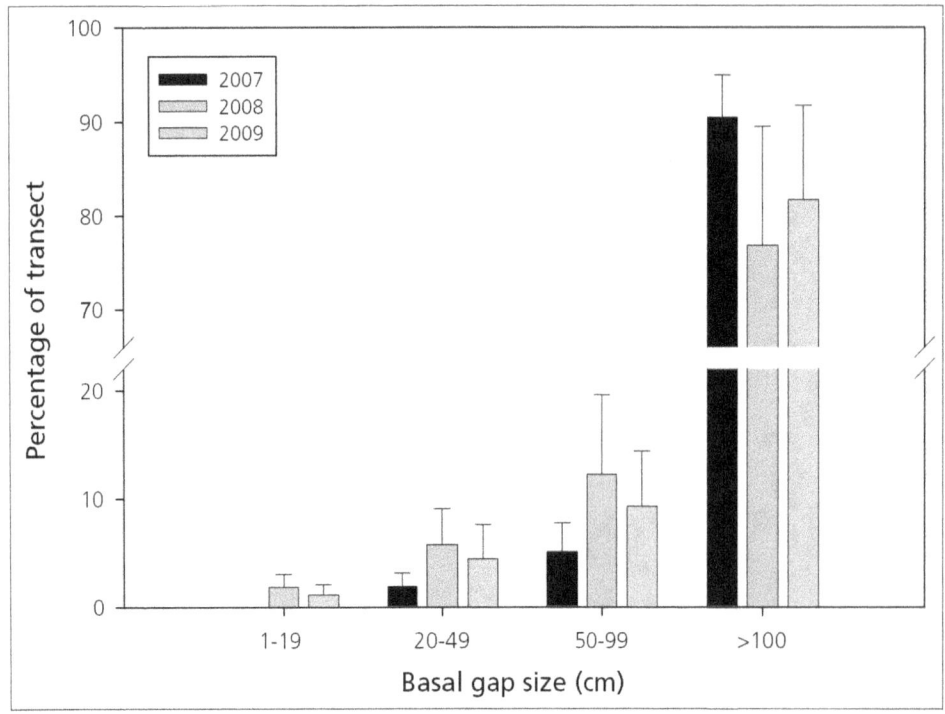

**Figure 5.** Percentage of transect in different gap sizes in 2007, 2008, and 2009. Note: In 2007 basal gaps <20 cm were not measured. Error bars represent one standard deviation.

high variability among plots. Similarly, the species diversity indices showed small among-year variation. The variation that did occur is, in part, attributable to variation in precipitation. 2008 had an extremely wet winter, and 2007 and 2008 had strong summer monsoons. 2009, on the other hand, was generally drier, rising above the long term precipitation average only slightly in April and June (fig. 6). The timing and the amount of precipitation differentially influences germination, growth, and flowering of species. Annual species and perennial forbs seem to be influenced the most by the climatic variation. Seven nonnative species were found in the plots in 2007, but three of these species were not found in 2008 and 2009. One new species was found in 2009. The large number of nonnative species in 2007 may have been a result of the large amount of precipitation. All but *Taraxacum officinale* and *Carduus nutans* were annuals.

Cover of soil surface features showed variation, particularly in undifferentiated crust, bare soil, and cyanobacteria. These variations may be attributable to how soil surface features appear in wet conditions versus dry conditions. When the ground surface is wet, cyanobacteria are much more visible, and undifferentiated crust becomes more difficult to distinguish from bare soil. In addition, physical crust is formed by raindrop impact and decreases with increasing time since the last rainfall. As a result of the particularly wet August in 2007, many of the plots were sampled during or shortly after precipitation events, which may have caused the crew to incorrectly estimate the cover of soil surface features.

We stress that the differences noted between years are not indicative of any trend, since trends cannot be determined with only three years of sampling. Nor should they be interpreted as being ecologically significant. Differences are due to ecological variability, such as annual climatic fluctuation or sampling errors inherent in the field sampling process. Cover estimation may vary among individuals (and crews), species may be mis-identified, slight differences between observers in applying sampling methods may go unnoticed, and the location of transects and quadrats vary slightly from

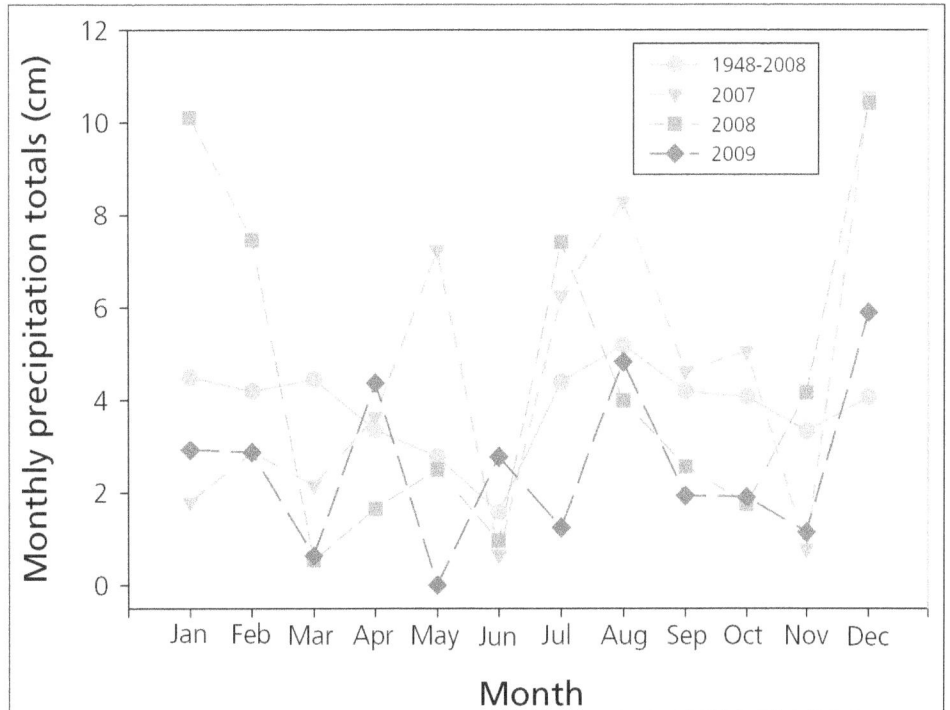

**Figure 6.**
Total monthly precipitation for 2007, 2008, and 2009 with the mean monthly totals for 1948 through 2009 (WRCC 2010)

year to year. We strive to minimize these errors by ensuring that transect lines are as straight as possible, quadrats are placed correctly, and field crews are thoroughly trained on methods and species identification and remain calibrated on cover estimation.

We plan to conduct power analysis using the three years of data, which will help determine the total number of plots necessary to detect change in the key metrics. A temporal sampling design will then be implemented, with the installation of additional plots in subsequent years. Each year's data will be compared to the previously collected data to analyze changes through time in vegetation composition and structure and in soil stability and hydrologic function. Trend analyses will be conducted once sufficient data have been collected.

## Literature Cited

Butler, L. D., J. B. Cooper, R. H. Johnson, A. J. Norman, G. L. Peacock, P. L. Shaver, and K. E. Spaeth. 2003. National range and pasture handbook. United States Department of Agriculture, National Resources Conservation Service, Grazing Lands Technology Institute, Fort Worth, TX.

DeCoster, J. K., C. L. Lauver, M. E. Miller, J. R. Norris, A. E. C. Snyder, M. C. Swan, L. P. Thomas, and D. L. Witwicki. Integrated upland monitoring protocol for the Southern Colorado Plateau Network. Natural Resource Technical Report, National Park Service, Fort Collins, CO, in review.

Jennings, S. B., N. D. Brown, and D. Sheil. 1999. Assessing forest canopies and understorey illumination: canopy closure, canopy cover and other measures. Forestry 72(1): 59–73.

Magurran, A. E. 1988. Ecological diversity and its measurement. Princeton University Press, Princeton, NJ.

Margalef, R. 1972. Homage to Evelyn Hutchinson, or why there is an upper limit to diversity. Transactions of the Connecticut Academy of Arts and Sciences 44: 211–35.

McCune, B. and J. B. Grace. 2002. Analysis of ecological communities. MJM Software Design.

Stevens, D. L. and A. R. Olsen. 2004. Spatially balanced sampling of natural resources. Journal of the American Statistical Association 99: 262–278.

Thomas, L. P., M. N. Hendrie (editor), C. L. Lauver, S. A. Monroe, N. J. Tancreto, S. L. Garman, and M. E. Miller. 2006. Vital signs monitoring plan for the Southern Colorado Plateau Network. Natural Resource Report NPS/SCPN/NRR-2006/002. National Park Service, Fort Collins, CO.

Western Regional Climate Center (WRCC). 2010. Monthly total precipitation for Mesa Verde National Park, CO. WRCC, Reno, NV. Available at http://www.wrcc.dri.edu/cgi-bin/cliMAIN.pl?co5531 (accessed 12 May 2010).

# Appendix A

Complete species list for the Loamy Mesa Top Pinyon-Juniper ecological site with mean foliar cover and frequency for species in 2007, 2008, and 2009

| | | | 2007 | | 2008 | | 2009 | |
|---|---|---|---|---|---|---|---|---|
| Species | Common name | Family | Foliar cover (%) | Plot fre-quency (%) | Foliar cover (%) | Plot fre-quency (%) | Foliar cover (%) | Plot fre-quency (%) |
| *Achnatherum hymenoides* | Indian ricegrass | Poaceae | 0.009 | 10 | 0.017 | 20 | 0.016 | 20 |
| *Amelanchier utahensis* | Utah serviceberry | Rosaceae | 0.002 | 10 | 0.002 | 10 | 0.025 | 20 |
| *Androsace septentrionalis* | pygmy rock jasmine | Primulaceae | <0.001 | 10 | 0 | 0 | 0 | 0 |
| *Antennaria parvifolia* | small leaf pussytoes | Asteraceae | <0.001 | 0 | <0.001 | 0 | <0.001 | 10 |
| *Antennaria rosea* | rosy pussytoes | Asteraceae | <0.001 | 10 | <0.001 | 10 | 0.000 | 0 |
| *Arabis fendleri* | Fendler's rockcress | Brassicaceae | 0.054 | 90 | 0.026 | 70 | 0.015 | 60 |
| *Arabis holboellii* | Holboell's rockcress | Brassicaceae | <0.001 | 10 | <0.001 | 10 | 0 | 0 |
| *Artemisia tridentata* | basin big sagebrush | Asteraceae | 0.760 | 10 | 1.028 | 10 | 0.875 | 10 |
| *Astragalus* | milkvetch | Fabaceae | 0.008 | 50 | 0.044 | 70 | 0.030 | 70 |
| *Astragalus pattersonii* | Patterson's milkvetch | Fabaceae | 0 | 0 | 0 | 0 | 0.010 | 20 |
| *Bromus tectorum* [a] | cheatgrass | Poaceae | 0.007 | 50 | 0.001 | 20 | 0.001 | 30 |
| *Calochortus flexuosus* | winding mariposa lily | Liliaceae | 0 | 0 | 0 | 0 | 0.002 | 10 |
| *Carduus nutans* [a] | nodding thistle | Asteraceae | 0.001 | 30 | 0.001 | 40 | 0.000 | 0 |
| *Carex rossii* | Ross' sedge | Cyperaceae | 0 | 0 | 0 | 0 | <0.001 | 10 |
| *Ceratocephala testiculata* [a] | curveseed butterwort | Ranunculaceae | 0.005 | 40 | 0 | 0 | 0.001 | 10 |
| *Cercocarpus montanus* | birchleaf mountain mahogany | Rosaceae | 0.104 | 30 | 0.261 | 30 | 0.261 | 30 |
| *Chenopodium album* | lambsquarters | Chenopodiaceae | 0.004 | 50 | 0.002 | 40 | 0.001 | 30 |
| *Chenopodium leptophyllum* | narrowleaf goosefoot | Chenopodiaceae | 0 | 0 | 0.001 | 10 | 0.001 | 20 |
| *Chrysothamnus depressus* | longflower rabbitbrush | Asteraceae | 0.119 | 30 | 0.087 | 40 | 0.067 | 40 |
| *Comandra umbellata* | bastard toadflax | Santalaceae | 0.020 | 30 | 0.033 | 30 | 0.032 | 20 |
| *Cordylanthus wrightii* | Wright's bird's beak | Scrophulariaceae | 0.029 | 80 | 0.080 | 90 | 0.059 | 90 |
| *Cryptantha* sp. | cryptantha | Boraginaceae | 0 | 0 | 0 | 0 | <0.001 | 10 |
| *Dalea* sp. | prairie clover | Fabaceace | 0.001 | 10 | 0 | 0 | 0 | 0 |
| *Delphinium* sp. | larkspur | Ranunculaceae | 0 | 0 | 0 | 0 | <0.001 | 10 |

# Appendix A continued.

| Species | Common name | Family | 2007 Foliar cover (%) | 2007 Plot frequency (%) | 2008 Foliar cover (%) | 2008 Plot frequency (%) | 2009 Foliar cover (%) | 2009 Plot frequency (%) |
|---|---|---|---|---|---|---|---|---|
| *Descurainia sophia* [a] | herb sophia | Brassicaceae | 0.008 | 40 | 0 | 0 | 0 | 0 |
| *Draba reptans* | Carolina draba | Brassicaceae | 0.017 | 60 | 0 | 0 | <0.001 | 10 |
| *Echinocereus sp.* | hedgehog cactus | Cactaceae | 0.000 | 10 | 0 | 0 | 0 | 0 |
| *Elymus elymoides* | squirreltail | Poaceae | 0.019 | 40 | 0.022 | 40 | 0.011 | 50 |
| *Erigeron divergens* | spreading fleabane | Asteraceae | 0.006 | 10 | 0.011 | 20 | 0.002 | 30 |
| *Eriogonum racemosum* | redroot buckwheat | Polygonaceae | 0.028 | 80 | 0.053 | 80 | 0.036 | 80 |
| *Eriogonum umbellatum* | sulphur-flowered buckwheat | Polygonaceae | 0.002 | 30 | 0.007 | 30 | 0.007 | 20 |
| *Erodium cicutarium* [a] | stork's bill | Geraniaceae | <0.001 | 10 | 0 | 0 | 0 | 0 |
| *Escobaria vivipara* | spinystar | Cactaceae | <0.001 | 10 | <0.001 | 10 | <0.001 | 10 |
| *Gutierrezia sarothrae* | broom snakeweed | Asteraceae | 0.021 | 10 | 0.023 | 10 | 0.017 | 30 |
| *Hesperostipa comata* | needle and thread | Poaceae | 0 | 0 | 0.013 | 10 | 0.098 | 10 |
| *Heterotheca villosa* | hairy false goldenaster | Asteraceae | 0.001 | 20 | 0.002 | 10 | 0.002 | 10 |
| *Ipomopsis aggregata* | scarlet gilia | Polemoniaceae | <0.001 | 10 | 0 | 0 | 0 | 0 |
| *Iris missouriensis* | western blue flag | Iridaceae | 0 | 0 | <0.001 | 10 | 0 | 0 |
| *Koeleria macrantha* | prairie junegrass | Poaceae | 0.013 | 30 | 0.035 | 40 | 0.008 | 20 |
| *Lappula occidentalis* | flatspine stickseed | Boraginaceae | 0.001 | 10 | 0 | 0 | 0 | 0 |
| *Lepidium montanum* | mountain pepperweed | Brassicaceae | 0.001 | 10 | 0 | 0 | 0 | 0 |
| *Lesquerella rectipes* | straight bladderpod | Brassicaceae | 0.004 | 10 | 0.011 | 20 | 0.005 | 30 |
| *Lupinus ammophilus* | sand lupine | Fabaceae | 0.002 | 40 | 0.165 | 70 | 0.032 | 80 |
| *Lupinus argenteus* | silvery lupine | Fabaceae | <0.001 | 10 | 0.006 | 40 | <0.001 | 10 |
| *Machaeranthera canescens* | hoary tansyaster | Asteraceae | 0.009 | 60 | 0.020 | 70 | 0.007 | 80 |
| *Opuntia spp.* | prickly pear | Cactaceae | 0.636 | 90 | 0.496 | 90 | 0.448 | 90 |
| *Packera multilobata* | lobeleaf groundsel | Asteraceae | <0.001 | 10 | <0.001 | 10 | <0.001 | 10 |
| *Pedicularis centranthera* | dwarf lousewort | Scrophulariaceae | 0.001 | 20 | 0.024 | 30 | 0.043 | 40 |
| *Penstemon barbatus* | beardlip penstemon | Scrophulariaceae | 0.017 | 60 | 0.016 | 70 | 0.014 | 60 |
| *Penstemon linarioides* | toadflax penstemon | Scrophulariaceae | 0.462 | 100 | 0.527 | 100 | 0.551 | 100 |
| *Peraphyllum ramosissimum* | squaw apple | Rosaceae | 0.002 | 10 | 0.002 | 10 | 0.007 | 10 |
| *Petradoria pumila* | rock goldenrod | Asteraceae | 0.158 | 50 | 0.165 | 50 | 0.108 | 50 |

Appendix A *continued*.

| Species | Common name | Family | 2007 Foliar cover (%) | 2007 Plot frequency (%) | 2008 Foliar cover (%) | 2008 Plot frequency (%) | 2009 Foliar cover (%) | 2009 Plot frequency (%) |
|---|---|---|---|---|---|---|---|---|
| *Phlox gracilis* | slender phlox | Polemoniaceae | 0.009 | 20 | 0 | 0 | 0.006 | 10 |
| *Phlox hoodii* | Hood's phlox | Polemoniaceae | 0.031 | 40 | 0.030 | 40 | 0.037 | 40 |
| *Phlox longifolia* | longleaf phlox | Polemoniaceae | 0.002 | 10 | 0.003 | 20 | 0.006 | 30 |
| *Phoradendron juniperinum* | juniper mistletoe | Viscaceae | 0 | 0 | 0.002 | 10 | 0 | 0 |
| *Poa fendleriana* | muttongrass | Poaceae | 4.596 | 100 | 4.042 | 100 | 4.202 | 100 |
| *Polygonum douglasii* | Douglas' knotweed | Polygonaceae | 0.013 | 100 | 0.019 | 100 | 0.015 | 100 |
| *Purshia tridentata* | antelope bitterbrush | Rosaceae | 1.297 | 90 | 1.398 | 90 | 1.412 | 90 |
| *Quercus gambelii* | Gambel oak | Fagaceae | 0.005 | 10 | 0.010 | 10 | 0.010 | 10 |
| *Sisymbrium altissimum* [a] | tumblemustard | Brassicaceae | 0.002 | 10 | 0.002 | 20 | 0.005 | 20 |
| *Sphaeralcea coccinea* | scarlet globemallow | Malvaceae | 0.001 | 10 | 0.003 | 10 | 0.005 | 10 |
| *Sporobolus cryptandrus* | sand dropseed | Poaceae | 0 | 0 | <0.001 | 10 | 0 | 0 |
| *Streptanthus cordatus* | heartleaf twistflower | Brassicaceae | <0.001 | 10 | <0.001 | 10 | 0 | 0 |
| *Taraxacum officinale* [a] | common dandelion | Asteraceae | 0.001 | 20 | 0 | 0 | 0 | 0 |
| *Tragopogon dubius* [a] | yellow salsify | Asteraceae | 0 | 0 | <0.001 | 10 | <0.001 | 10 |
| *Yucca baccata* | banana yucca | Agavaceae | 0.651 | 80 | 0.628 | 70 | 0.813 | 70 |
| Unknown MEVE08032007-1 | | | <0.001 | 10 | 0 | 0 | 0 | 0 |
| Unknown MEVE08032007-2 | | | <0.001 | 10 | 0 | 0 | 0 | 0 |

[a] Nonnative species

NPS 960/116999, September 2012